THE
CHINESE NATIONAL
CHARACTER

Studies on Modern China

Studies on Modern China

THE
CHINESE NATIONAL
CHARACTER

From Nationhood
to Individuality

LUNG-KEE SUN

AN EAST GATE BOOK

M.E.Sharpe
Armonk, New York
London, England

An East Gate Book

Library of Congress Cataloging-in-Publication Data

Sun, Lung-Kee.
  The Chinese national character : from nationhood to individuality / by Lung-kee Sun.
    p. cm.
  "An east gate book."
  Includes bibliographical references and index.
  ISBN 0-7656-0826-X (alk. paper); ISBN 0-7656-0827-8 (pbk)
  1. National characteristics, Chinese.

DS721.S857 2001
305.8951—dc21   2001034215

Printed in the United States of America

The paper used in this publication meets the minimum requirements of
American National Standard for Information Sciences
Permanence of Paper for Printed Library Materials,
ANSI Z 39.48-1984.

BM (c) 10 9 8 7 6 5 4 3 2 1
BM (p) 10 9 8 7 6 5 4 3 2 1

Contents

Acknowledgments

The author wishes to thank the staff of the Division of Special Collections of the Library of Congress and of the East Asian libraries at the following institutions: Cornell University, Hong Kong University, Stanford University, University of Alberta at Edmonton, University of Chicago, University of Illinois at Champaign-Urbana, University of Kansas at Lawrence, University of Michigan at Ann Arbor, Washington University in St. Louis, and my home institution. Their help was invaluable. Special thanks is due the University of Chicago's Center for East Asian Studies, which has provided travel funds for over a decade so the author could use the library on its campus. The author is also grateful to Ming K. Chan, Harold Kahn, Lyman van Slyke, Kristin Stapleton, and Peter Zarrow for their efforts in facilitating the publication of this book, and Laetitia Argenteri and Sarah Yeh for their moral support. People whom the author has consulted for a particular reference, a foreign term, or a source in another field are scattered in so many places on three continents that they cannot be listed here; nonetheless, their presence in this work deserves recognition.

Introduction

As indicated by a leading scholar in national-character study, the topic "requires a crossing or transcending of disciplinary boundaries and thereby presents a threat to established disciplinary viewpoints and identities" (Inkeles 1997, 3–4). As I am a historian by profession, I will approach the topic historically. This does not vitiate the multidisciplinary nature of the inquiry, as evident in almost every section of this book. My project also shows that the topic transcends national boundaries as well.

A historical study of the perennial Chinese national character controversy is long overdue. As the very first of its kind, this project proposes to confine the subject matter to the period from the 1890s to the present. It will begin with the dawn of "nationhood" among the Chinese, thus skipping the views of earlier Western missionaries, diplomats, and travelers, which only have an antiquarian interest for my purpose.[1] Unlike these earlier Western attempts to explore the Chinese "character," the Chinese concern at the turn of the twentieth century was how to become a nation. From this point of departure, a whole century of intellectual productions of "national character" have ensued.

The Project's Warp and Woof

The book contains eight parts—six chapters, an introduction, and an epilogue. The chapters are arranged historically, providing a chronological framework. Meanwhile the themes covered in them are streamlined into six categories: nationhood, the group mind, Orientalness, corporeality, regionality, and individuality.

Nationhood and Group Mind

The drama commences in chapter one with the finale of Confucian ecumenism. To replace this moribund worldview, late Qing opinion-leaders first tried yellow racialism, which failed to define nonbiological "nation." Thus the drama unfolds further in chapter two with the advent of "national psychology" in the last days of Imperial China. The occasion was not just a transition to "nation," but also the liquidation of a sacred worldview by modern social sciences. What the Chinese then called "national psychology" is an enigma, for it was a composite of several Western schools of thought through the mediation of the Japanese. In fact, it is the Chinese material showing this European intellectual trend in action in an East Asian context that helps me to retrace its contour, not available from European studies.

Orientalness and Corporeality

Chapter three shows that the "national character" discussion was transcending the issue of nationhood. In the May Fourth era (1917–1921), the New Culture movement subsumed the issue under the confrontation of Eastern and Western civilizations, arriving at a cosmopolitan solution. Its opponents, on the other hand, defined the Chinese character in terms of a spiritual principle having a common denominator with all Eastern peoples. Both employed the broader category of civilization.

In the same chapter, it is further demonstrated that the idea of the universal march of civilization cast a shadow called "degeneration." Under Darwinist influence, a people retarded in its progress was believed to be saddled with an accursed racial inheritance. In stark contrast to our own time which exalts narrative, text, and the symbolic, in the early twentieth century concepts such as heredity and instinct were dominant. Degeneration was understood as the weakening or perversion of instincts, and a people with a hoary yet unhealthy heredity like the Chinese was far gone toward racial doom. Chinese discussants evoked this theory to sound an alarm regarding their current national condition, yet the implications for the nation were rather pessimistic.

Lu Xun and the Problem of Chinese Individuality

This mood directly affected Lu Xun, the subject of chapter four. I adopt the unconventional approach of studying him together with his two brothers, Zhou Zuoren and Zhou Jianren, with unexpected results. Meanwhile, I question the conventional wisdom seeing his critique of national character as solely motivated by the nationhood project. Instead, I discern China's very first modernist statement pitting creative individuals against the crowd, a symptom of modern mass society. Lu Xun's contempt for the Herd did not square with nationalism, making his participation in the nationhood project problematic. Yet his writings were imbued with an obsession with the Chinese. I argue that, in his self-image, Lu Xun conflated the nineteenth-century romantic national icon inspiring his people toward national salvation with the twentieth-century modernist, an "outsider" of the mass society.

Early modernism, however, was still strongly informed by biologism. Its sentiment of decay was premised on the theory of degeneration, and its sense of alienation was expressed through the corporeal metaphor of "metamorphosis" instead of the high-modernist existentialism. Lu Xun's critique of the Chinese people is to be understood against the background of biological heredity. In fact, the "culturalist" picture of May Fourth iconoclasm as a whole, which is a post-World War II construction, needs to be revised under this new light.

Corporeality and Regionality

Chapter five proceeds to the 1930s and 1940s, when anthropogeography was in fashion. The discipline put a premium on "environment," the other pillar of the Darwinist discourse that complemented biological heredity. A discourse premised on the diversity of environments caused the nationhood project to unravel further, with one region blaming the "character" of another for the failure of the nation. Actually, it reflected the postimperial fragmentation of China. Although its strategy had shifted to the regional, the national character discourse remained biological in nature. Now it became fashionable to connect corporeal deficiency and mental feebleness to certain regions within China. Although biologism has fallen out of favor today, the link between character and region has assumed a new importance in the post–Mao Reform era, with the appearance of special economic zones in the South and its constant tension with the conservative North.

Orientalness and Individuality

Chapter six shifts the emphasis from the nationhood project to individuality, which is largely an American contribution. World War II provided the impetus for the United States to launch large-scale studies of the characters of foes and allies. The momentum persisted into the early Cold War years, and the Chinese were among those studied. Scholars who handled such projects, however, chose to examine how the "individual" was formed in different cultural milieux.

Formerly, Chinese iconoclasts had deplored the lack of individuality in their fellow-countrymen, but this concern was couched in terms of national salvation. As a scholar puts it, in China "the discourse of individualism found itself in complicity with nationalism" (Liu 1995, 91). In a totally different vein, the postwar American study focused mainly on the Chinese individual's sexual growth. Freudianism and the theory of gender role identities were ascendant at the time, but the academic trends also chimed in with a mid-century "crisis of masculinity." This climate could be sensed from coeval American popular culture that linked failed individuation with feminization. In stark contrast to the rest of the book, the sole concern of the American perceptions of Chinese national character is individual, not national, salvation.

National Character, Nationalism, and Orientalism

It is obvious that as a concept, national character is related to nationalism, yet not coterminous with it. If nationalism is defined as the yearning for nationhood, then only the national character discussions in the first two chapters directly addressed that issue. Although nation-building continued to be the central concern for subsequent controversies, their conclusions were often contrary to nationalism. If national character's affinity with nationalism is tenuous, is it, then, an Orientalist phenomenon in the sense of denigrating the Orient from the Western point of view? Again, I find Orientalism an over-used concept. For instance, in chapter three, those New Culture iconoclasts scornful of their own inheritance and the opposing "Eastern civilization" camp may both be guilty of self-Orientalizing.[2] Yet to use Westernism to combat conservative forces at home is not exactly the same as Edward Said's Western appropriation of the Other through an Orientalist gaze, and to defend one's "Oriental" heritage by affirming a self-perceived distinction from, and parity with, the West is even further from Said's original meaning of denigration.

The Vicissitudes of "National Character"

In this light, "national character" would appear to have a checkered career, zig-zagging between being a venue of self-denigration and a vehicle of self-aggrandizement. The 1980s saw a resurgence of "national character" discussions in both Japan and China. The former, called *Nihonjinron*, is an unmistakable sign of the country's new confidence as a superpower after decades of negative self review (Befu 1993, 124–125). The Chinese case appeared in the wake of the "triple crisis of faith, confidence, and credibility." With official Marxism no longer up to the task of the Reform era, the Chinese in the early 1980s turned to futurology, notably Alvin Toffler's theory of the Third Wave. This dalliance was brief as it soon made way for the revival of an old interest: national character. The controversy accentuated the sentiment of backwardness but also represented a groping toward modernity, and the fervor—or "cultural fever" as it was called then—peaked in 1988 with the television series, *River Elegy*.[3]

The 1989 Tian'anmen Square incident effected a sea change in the discourse. Piqued by China's new pariah status, a younger generation chimed in with official patriotism and defiantly reasserted their "Chineseness." They were able to tap the restored confidence of a nation with a double-digit growth rate and did so by appealing to a nascent public sphere. Unexpected allies were found among America's latest academic trends which privilege particularism, ranging from Edward Said's Orientalism, postcolonial critique of all shapes, to Samuel Huntington's prognostication of a clash between the West and the China-Islamic bloc (Xu 1998, 203–237). As of now, the Chineseness issue, like its Japanese counterpart, has converged with contemporary American identity politics, turning it into a truly global vogue.

Disturbing Implications of the Postcolonial Stance

This postcolonial fad privileges not the national character critique of the late 1980s and its May Fourth precursors, but the nativists of Republican China and their epigones in the 1990s. Such a reversal is highly disconcerting to those who still struggle to "modernize" China and use Westernism to defy an authoritarian regime legitimized by antiforeignism (Xu 1998; Chen 1995). Yet the dissidents are now seen as the liberal-humanist relics of the Reform era still enthralled with the universal validity of the European Enlightenment (Zhang 1998, 109–140). And those "relics" in turn vented their anger on American "postcolonial" scholars who, in all sincerity, attempted to deconstruct Eurocentric views of China.[4]

My contention is that postcolonial thinking has provided no clear criteria for distinguishing between alternative modernities and antimodern reactions. If no postcolonial critic in his or her right mind would bestow the title of "alternative modernity" on the Overcoming of Modernity in fascist Japan of the 1930s, it is a matter of political sympathies, not methodological rigor.[5] A formal criterion of "postcolonial" does exist, but it pertains more to discursive strategy than ideological intent: It is the "reassertion of space" to deconstruct any linear temporal scheme which has so far privileged the West. The advent of this "epoch of space," as Michel Foucault puts it, is a late twentieth-century phenomenon (Soja 1989, 11). I fail to discern, in the manner of Tang Xiaobing, a spatial strategy in earlier Chinese intellectual attempts to challenge the Western hegemony. In the May Fourth era, opponents of Westernism evoked an "Eastern civilization," but they resorted to an unchallenged linear temporality to predict a higher world-historical epoch for the East to stage a comeback. They did not invent heterogeneous space to accommodate "plural modernities" but looked forward to China's attaining global stature on a par with that of the West.

More Than Two Intentions

The complexity of the issue seems also to go beyond Lydia Liu's solution of treating the national character discussions as "translingual" adaptations of a Western missionary discourse by the Chinese to their own purposes. The following examples demonstrate that so-called translingual transactions cannot be simplified into two intentions. In 1793, Lord Macartney recorded with disgust the Chinese mandarins' behavior of spitting about the rooms and blowing their noses in their fingers. More than a century later, it was none other than Sun Zhongshan himself who told his countrymen that their behavior was disgusting to the foreigners (Fitzgerald 1996, 10–11). This simple disgust was not necessarily ideologically motivated. Bertrand Russell, who visited China in 1920–1921, opined that China had a lot to teach Westerners whose fetish of progress was really "a love of power." But when pressed by an eminent Chinese to say the "chief defects of the Chinese," he listed avarice, cowardice, and callousness. "Strange to say, my interlocutor, instead of getting angry, admitted the justice of my criticism, and proceeded to discuss possible remedies" (Russell 1966, 202, 209). Russell seemed sincere, but being no China expert he rehashed the views of the Christian missionaries whose aim was to proselytize.

For those Chinese who have their own reflective faculty, the "alien" origin of the criticism is no convenient excuse to evade self-improvement. A Chinese proverb avers that to polish a jade to perfection one needs "the rock from a distant hill," which I construe as being both hard and foreign. The idea of others being mirrors for one's moral cultivation is ultimately Confucian, as the master stated that in a group of three people he was bound to find a teacher. It is a far cry from the unalloyed power consideration that colors much of today's thinking.

To treat a century of controversy about Chinese national character as a regime of Orientalism and its resistance has the beauty of simplicity, but it does not do full justice to historical complexity. Instead of considering in a totalist manner all Western statements as essentially Orientalist and all Chinese ones as "translingual" acts of resistance by means of complicity, I propose the adoption of a non-binarist imagery: To view "Chinese national character" as a cluster of sites devoted to the same discussion on a world-wide web. This web indeed contains too many "sites," but I manage to consolidate them into a relatively few "links," namely, nationhood, group mind, Orientalness, corporeality, regionality, individuality, and so forth.

A Methodological Note

Today's postcolonial critique of Orientalism is part and parcel of a broader attack by postmodernism on the modernization theory. In order to desta-bilize well-established knowledge systems, it adopts a method called "post-structuralism," which questions all boundaries and immutable essences. It is in this spirit that I point out certain dogmatic applications of the otherwise insightful postcolonial stance. By the same token, I am not an adherent of the "modernization" paradigm, which has informed an early vintage of Chi-nese studies. Its crisis scenario of the "transition from tradition to modern-ity" invariably posited the intellectual hero at the center of a drama of tension-resolving, which he did by making rational and existential choices. Joseph Levenson (1964) even treats China as just such a personality re-sponding to the challenges of the West and attempting to integrate conflict-ing demands into a whole.[6] This act presupposes a free and integral agent of which poststructuralism is skeptical.

The Limitations of Binarist Thinking

I appreciate the poststructuralist insights into the artificial nature of "sub-jectivity" for opening up a new range of possibilities in analysis. It enables me to experiment with the idea of nationhood as a narrative woven from incongruous fragments. I will demonstrate in chapter one the hybrid nature of the new Han identity in the twilight years of the Manchu rule—it was fashioned from an anti-Manchu exigency, an imaginary descent from a Yel-low Emperor reinvented by Western pan-Babylonianist theory, and a hastily put-together pantheon of "national" heroes selected from history for their resistance against "foreign" invaders.

My questioning of the "Orientalist-postcolonial" binarism is also in the spirit of poststructuralism. Deconstruction stipulates that a term, which de-fines itself by suppressing its binary opposite, is never fully present. Un-derstandably, binary opposites are not natural—there is a degree of arbitrariness in the ways they are set up. Jacques Derrida questions Foucault's allegation that classical rationalism used "madness" to set up "reason"—for Derrida the two need not be binary opposites, they become so only in Foucault's version of them (Derrida 1978, 31–63).

The same may be said about Prasenjit Duara's pitting the centralizing "nation" against "provincial narratives." Duara, in the spirit of the postmodern politics of diversity and not having China's historical nation-building exigency in mind, charges that the modern Chinese nation is repressive of its fragments (Duara 1995, chapter 6). If history is to be "rescued" from the Chinese nation, the Chinese probably would have ended up not having a history (as an independent people) at all. His stress on the artificiality of nation as a narrative concoction makes one wonder whether the "fragments" which the modern nation is guilty of repressing are no less artificial.[7]

The Insertion of a Third Term

The binarist scheme is useful but the need to add a third term is always present. Derrida's binary opposites in fact function in a Saussurean "system of differences." Ferdinand Saussure sees a signifier acquiring its place in a system of signs because other slots have been taken; that signifier acquires a meaning not merely by defining itself against an opponent but in relation to a host of neighboring signifiers as well. In a "system of difference," a signifier has no single, fixed, or essential meaning and can be understood only as what it is not in a relational context. So even binary opposition can have an infinite number of permutations. Derrida shows that the opposition between nature and culture can assume the form of nature against law, art, education, technics, liberty, the arbitrary, history, society, mind, and so forth (Derrida 1978, 282–283). All these pairs are still oppositional, yet in a "system of differences" a signifier can assume a presence by being different from a kindred, not necessarily an antagonist.

Seen in this light, "nation" was indeed repressive of "provincial narratives" through the eyes of a republican warlord. A late Qing intellectual, on the other hand, would rather pit "nation" against "ecumene" in order to overcome the latter and usher China into the modern world. Meanwhile, while maintaining an animosity against "ecumene," "nation" was constantly confused with "race," which was not a binary opposite but a major constituent of it, and for that matter a difference needed to exist between the two for "nation" to come into presence. In this paragraph alone, we have at least three sets of binarism, which is better reformulated into a "system of difference."

Under the reign of poststructuralism, we have achieved the intellectual alertness not to treat any term as a monolithic totality or timeless essence, but this consciousness comes to naught if we hypostatize a single set of binarist opposition. Equipped with this understanding, I use the powerful concept of "system of differences" to throw light on the birth of the Chinese "nation" from the cocoon of Confucian ecumenism. This most cherished ideal of the 1890s had turned into a bane by 1900, calling for its own suppression by "nation." However, there is no such thing as "nation" itself, standing alone, unrelated to other signs in a transcendental manner. We can only speak of a Chinese "nation" at the turn of the twentieth century which, unlike the English, the French, or the Japanese nations, came into presence by suppressing an "ecumene." In other words, the ecumene-nation opposition was evoked by a specific historical circumstance.

Yet, with eyes only on the "ecumene-nation" opposition we will overlook the transitional phase of yellow racialism. "Race" was more kindred to "nation" than "ecumene," but nonetheless different. Race was biological and nation at the time was defined as a "psychological race." It is easy to collapse the two and conflate the discourse of nation with that of race, as in Frank Dikötter's book (1992) on the subject. By adding a third term I am able to untangle this historical skein by treating it as the free play of *difference* among ecumene, race, and nation in a circumscribed historical context.

In chapter six, the third term reappears as "Chinese as marginal text" amid the war of the sexes in America. Even masculinity and femininity, rooted in biology, are not inevitably binarist by nature. As cultural constructs we must refer to multiple masculinities and femininities, or even the protean "third sex." American femininity, in its battle against masculinity, finds a natural ally in Orientalness (or "Eastern-ness"). Both defy the "masculine" sense of dominance and ascendancy by valorizing boundary-blurring and interconnectedness. Yet American femininity accentuates its diametrical oppositeness to masculinity in order to delineate its own boundary and ultimately to allow both genders to individuate through the decoupling of heterosexual relationships. Thus, in order to be antagonistically *different* from masculinity, American femininity also has to *differ* from Orientalness, albeit in a kindred manner.

From the National to the Individual

The overarching theme of the book, "from nationhood to individuality," will become fully articulate in the epilogue. The book's discussion begins at the turn of the twentieth century, when nation-building was high on the agenda not only in China, and concludes with American perceptions of Chinese individuality (or the lack of it). In the advanced societies of our time, where postnational individuation is becoming the norm, the psychologized, sexualized, and gendered American individual has the potential to become the universal format of personality—and the freedom to concoct oneself from these ingredients has become contagious. The new problematic we shall be facing in the new century is the tension between this self-fashioned "postmodern" individuality and a host of national "identities" that are no less artificial.

Notes to Introduction

1. Nineteenth-century accounts have been adequately summarized by Otani Kotaro and need no repetition (Otani 1935). Western perceptions in the late Ming period are referred to in Lach and van Kley (1993, 1564–1571).

2. The concept of self-Orientalization is adapted from Dirlik (1996a, 96–118).

3. The same year also witnessed the publications of Wen Yuankai and Ni Duan's *The Reform of the Chinese National Character*, Wu Shenyuan's *The Heredity and Transformation of Traditional Chinese Culture*, Liu Zaifu and Lin Gang's *Tradition and the Chinese* and their *On Chinese Culture's Design of Man*. The latter is taken verbatim from a section title in *The Deep Structure of Chinese Culture* by Sun Longji (Lung-kee Sun), published in 1983 in Hong Kong. Sun's book also went through seven printings in 1987, although it was banned in Mainland China (as well as Taiwan) and written with a purpose other than promoting "reform and opening."

4. An example was the baffling controversy centered on James Hevia's *Cherishing Men From Afar: Qing Guest Ritual and the Macartney Embassy of 1793* (1995). In this exchange, we find American academics attempting to deconstruct a Eurocentric construction of Sinocentrism, while a Chinese critic charged them with distorting history and with dogmatism. He saw their "postcolonialism" as a new Western hegemony relegating China to a backward position not only in science and technology, but in "critical theory" as well. Worse still, it inadvertently reinforced China's official line and the new xenophobia of the 1990s (Zhang 1998, 56–63). Lately, Lydia Liu is under fire for a similar culpability.

5. Tessa Morris-Suzuki's recent work seems to be an exception. She questions the conventional wisdom of treating "Japanese prewar and wartime imperialism as essentially a reaction against modernity." Her intention, however, is not to rechristen it alternative modernity, but to alert us to the presence of universalist arguments justifying expansionism, which Japan shared with Western imperialism—in short, to avoid isolating the phenomenon as uniquely Japanese (Morris-Suzuki 1998, 102).

6. A study lists the tension-and-crisis rhetoric of East Asian studies of an earlier vintage as follows: "The tensions of intellectual choice," "conservative alternatives in Republican China," "modern (or ancient) China in transition," "between tradition and modernity," "the Chinese dilemma of modernity," "the dilemma of growth," "escape from predicament," "conflict and control in late Imperial China," "China in disintegration," "China in crisis," "the crisis of Chinese consciousness," "Chinese intellectuals in crisis," and so forth (Sun 1994, 356).

7. The term "the nation and its fragments" is borrowed from Chatterjee (1993).

THE
CHINESE NATIONAL
CHARACTER

— 1 —

The Birth of a "Nation"

In 1954, the Marxist historian Fan Wenlan argued that China had achieved nationhood at the Qin unification of 221 B.C.E. (Fan 1957, 2, 6–7). He applied Stalin's four criteria of nationhood derived from a discourse on nation popular in early twentieth century. According to the Stalinist canon, nationhood was a "bourgeois" phenomenon. Fan's misuse of this paradigm was therefore heretical, the sin of national vanity. It does not suit the author to settle this controversy here. What concerns me is how Chinese discussants of "nation" appropriated Western nationalism as a system of concepts, symbols, and organized sentiments at the turn of the nineteenth and the twentieth centuries.

Recent works on Chinese nationalism of a postmodernist bent show how China was in fact appropriated by the idea of Nation as the historical agent when she attempted to posit herself anew in a spatial-temporal order not of her own making. In other words, the nation-status is an entry permit to "modernity," a condition with a claim to universalism but in fact an order of things prescribed by the hegemonic West (Duara 1995; Tang 1996).

This chapter will pick up from where those works have left off: Even though "modern" nation-units need to meet certain uniform standards, one cannot ignore the unique context of the birth of the Chinese unit. At the turn of the twentieth century, it was the defunct Confucian worldview that yielded to modern nationalism via the intermediary of racialism. Therefore, the Chinese "nation" at its moment of birth needed to distinguish itself not only from Confucian ecumenism, but also from racialism. In short, Chinese nationalism, racialism, and ecumenism were caught in a "system of differences" custom-made for them.

At the time when the Chinese "nation" was born, the ideal of Nation was a mobilized citizenry confronting similar units in an international arena refereed by the jungle law of survival of the fittest. It was nationalism at its most naked, when the unapologetic "nation" was the favorite agent of the *Zeitgeist*. Since then nationalism has undergone a series of metamorphoses in the global scene. World War I and the Russian Revolution ushered in a new era, which camouflaged nationalism under supranational ideologies: communism, fascism, and democracy. World War II streamlined this schema into two camps, and this age of ideological confrontation lasted till our recent past. Now we are living in a new era, which started with the Iranian Revolution and the demise of the Soviet bloc, ending the dispensation of global ideologies and allowing the resurgence of more localized ethno-religious identities. Prophets like Samuel Huntington see a larger pattern of civilizational duel emerging from the melee, portending what is to come in the twenty-first century.[1] Attempts have already been made to reinvent post-ideological China into a Cultural China, to be on a par with Christendom and Islam (Tu 1991, 1–32).[2] A new rhetoric of postmodern, postcolonial multi-culturalism now claims to describe this new order. From this vantage point, it is refreshing to review the historical context of the birth of the Chinese "nation."

The End of an Autocosm

The "All-under-Heaven" Syndrome

An old way to account for the origin of nationalism in China is the culturalism-to-nationalism thesis.[3] My study pursues a different strategy: To trace nationalism's differentiation from both Confucian ecumenism and Darwinian racialism in a matrix common to them all. I also disagree with conventional wisdom that sees modern nationalism first appearing among the reformist generation of the 1890s (Chang 1980, 296). On closer scrutiny, the "nationalism" of the time was still overshadowed by Confucian ecumenism. This order, which placed China at the center of "all-under-Heaven," was to some extent theoretical and ritualistic, modifiable in practice. When the Qing Empire signed a treaty with the Russian empire in 1689 it was on equal terms, and the imperial court also displayed flexibility in accommodating the Macartney Embassy in 1793 (Mancall 1971; Hevia 1995). Alongside the ecumenist rhetoric, Chinese racial consciousness also had a long history, heightened at those moments when the Central Realm was threatened by barbarians (Dikötter 1992, chapters 1 and 2).

In the wake of the Second Opium War of 1857–1860, the coexistence of "ten thousand states" (*wanguo*) finally received official recognition with the creation by the Qing government of a quasimodern foreign ministry: The *zongli yamen*. Nonetheless, the Chinese continued to indulge in an ecumenist rhetoric. In 1894, Zheng Guanying published his proposal for modernization which began with a philosophical preamble on *dao* and *qi*, the Cosmic Way and its vessels. For Zheng, Western science and technology were the lost inventions of ancient China, and the very fact of Westerners converging on the Central Realm today was a sign that "ecumenical unification" (*dayitong*) was at hand; he thus congratulated his emperor for living up to the occasion (Zheng 1894, vol. 1, 242–243).[4] Zheng was no obscurantist; he started his sixty year–long career as a compradore in British firms in Shanghai and later served in China's textile, telegraph, steamship, and railroad enterprises. What strikes us is the late date: It was fifty-two years after the Treaty of Nanjing and in a decade when Japan already had a constitution and a parliament. Yet one of China's first technocrats still felt compelled to apply an ecumenist rhetoric for official consumption, at a time when the imperial court itself was being ruffled by the crisis of the Sino-Japanese War (1894–1895).

The intellectual "vanguard" credited with the birth of modern nationalism in China was even tardier in learning about a global reality that officials, treaty-port journalists, compradores, and overseas Chinese had already reckoned with on a pragmatic if not symbolic level. Kang Youwei discovered the existence of the world's continents and other countries in 1875, and Liang Qichao, in 1890, when both men happened to be seventeen years old, by having been exposed to the same work on world geography, *A Concise Treatise on the World Circumscribed by Oceanus* (*Yinghuan zhilüe*) (Kang 1975, 7; Liang 1902j, 16). It exposed the woeful inadequacy of China's educational system, as well as Kang and Liang's peripheralness to power and information. Nonetheless, it was Kang and Liang's generation that effected an epistemic revolution to end Sinocentric autism. As members of the scholar-official class they were singularly well positioned for such a task; they had the center-stage not accessible to the treaty-port or overseas Chinese, someone like Sun Zhongshan.

The Confucian-Evolutionist Synthesis

What remained of China's complacency evaporated by 1895, in a defeat by her eastern neighbor, the "dwarfish" Japan. This crushing blow precipitated a profound crisis that rocked the very foundation of Sinocentrism. It forced Kang's school to resituate China in a much expanded world picture, even as they continued to narrate the modern international arena in terms of Confucian ecumenism. This was the penchant for "ordering" the affairs of "all-under-Heaven" instead of a single country. Kang's school also reinterpreted Confucianism in order to accommodate Darwinism, but the former remained predominant. Late nineteenth-century "Darwinism" was manifest in linear evolutionist schemes. "Linear progress" in fact predated Darwinism and was wedded to the latter fortuitously—a product of the Victorian age (Stocking Jr. 1987, 128–129). Kang and Liang discovered social evolutionism after the mid-1890s through Yan Fu, the Chinese who introduced the work of philosopher-social theorist Herbert Spencer (Pusey 1983, 89; Huang 1972, 25). Yet earlier Kang had already derived the theory of Three Ages, also a "linear evolutionist" scheme, from New Text Confucianism (Hsiao 1975, 50). Onto this indigenous scheme a Spencerian terminology was now grafted, and New Text Confucianism came to resonate with Victorian social evolutionism.

New Text Confucianism, based on the Gongyang Commentaries of *The Spring and Autumn Annals*, had been dormant from late Han (i.e., the early years of the first millennium) to the mid-eighteenth century. Kang's marginality to official Confucianism was underscored by his sympathy for this heterodoxy, which he reenergized to convey the modern ethos of dynamism and progress. Before Kang's tampering, the Gongyang doctrine was a visionary agenda for peace and harmony under a universal state.[5] In this agenda, universal harmony for "all-under-Heaven" unfolds in three stages: Chaos, Approaching Peace, and Great Peace, with their own matching "institutions." The escalation of harmony in temporal sequence synchronizes with the spatial extension of peace and order, which ripple outward in concentric rings. The progression of harmony would finally erase distinctions between the "inner" (*nei*) and the "outer" (*wai*). Initially, the "inner" circle consists only of one's native state. In the second phase, the "inner" is expanded to encompass all the *xia* regions (synonymous with Chinese culture), leaving only the barbarians in the "outer" limbo. Great Peace is achieved when even the barbarians are finally harmonized by the all-encompassing Confucian world order. Great Peace is the state of entropy in terms of the distribution of benevolent affect, as "the far, the near, the great, the small are treated as the same, all-under-Heaven becomes one family, and China becomes one person" (Sun 1985; Hsiao 1975, 90).

Inner and outer realms are also characteristic of the Islamic world-picture of *Dar al-Islam* (the Abode of Islam) and *Dar al-Harb* (the Abode of War). Yet the Confucian version waged no jihad against the infidels and was to be implemented through the osmosis of harmony. The Gongyang doctrine, laid out as a temporal-spatial scheme, embodied the ideal of a universal state deemed coterminous with civilization. As an agenda for ecumenical rule, it also bore little resemblance to the preordained march towards salvation in the Judaeo-Christian fashion. In the Chinese "sacred history," the track from chaos to harmony is reversible, just as, spatially speaking, order may recede when the universal state disintegrates. Although Gongyang theorists differed, the cyclical interpretation was the norm. Not only were cycles of *luan* (chaos) and *zhi* (order) replicating in the cosmic forces' ebb and flow, they conformed with the historical dynastic pattern. Though traditional Gongyang thinkers saw the realization of Great Peace as renewal of an ideal rather than the revival of antiquity, they invariably set the exemplary Golden Age in a legendary past.

The "One World" Vision

In Kang's reinvented Gongyang doctrine, the "one world" vision was projected into a future when democracy, equality, and human liberation—notions of unmistakable Western origin—would be realized on a global scale. The march towards this goal was now evolutionary, though the Three Ages scheme remained Confucian and continued to define epochs by their "institutions." It did not distinguish between political process and social forces, thus allowing the Confucian sage-statesman to legislate new societal forms. Even Western democratic society was understood as such an "institution." Yet, the former barbarians, namely Europe and America, now occupied a higher place on the evolutionary scale than China.[6] Internally, democratic America had even arrived at Great Peace whereas autocratic China was in the early phase of Approaching Peace, but internationally Chaos still reigned (Liang 1897b, 7–11).

This mélange of Confucianism and social evolutionism might seem bizarre to us, but it was not at all out of step with coeval Western social thinking. In 1899, John W. Powell, founder of the American Bureau of Ethnology, published in the *American Anthropologist* an article, in which he assigned "specific social institutions" to each of the four grades of social evolution: savagery, barbarism, monarchy, and democracy (Harris 1968, 255). With a similar ladder of civilization in mind, Kang shifted the white man's burden onto the shoulder of Confucius. If Chaos still reigned in the international arena, then it was China's mission to work with other countries toward the global Great Peace. Meanwhile China, by being the birthplace of the "one world" program, retained her centrality. Liang put it succinctly in 1897: "Confucius authored *The Spring and Autumn Annals* for the sake of ordering all-under-heaven, not just one state; it was to ensure peace for ten thousand generations, not for one generation only. Therefore, he was the first to reveal the doctrine of the Three Ages" (Liang 1897a, 48).

Gestation of "Nation" in the Womb of Ecumenism

Shorn of its messianic hyperbole, the "nationalism" of the 1890s was largely an awareness that China now faced a world where many civilized countries coexisted and that the Qing state should outgrow time-honored institutions of a now localized universal empire and adopt new ones to cope with the demand of the times. Kang aired such views in his memorial to Emperor Guangxu in 1895 near the end of the disastrous Sino-Japanese War. His memorials during the 1898 Hundred Days Reform used Darwinian terms to describe a world in which "countries compete for supremacy," rendering China's "ecumenical rule" anachronistic. However, to avert the fate of partition by the powers, Kang also urged the emperor to join China with England, America, and Japan, to form a single state (Kong 1988, 77, 364, 414). Such naïveté was rooted in ecumenism, a vision to be realized by the "merging of countries, races, and religions" (Kang 1975, 14). It also revealed the tension between old and new epistemes[7] that would eventually tear apart the Confucian-Darwinist synthesis of the 1890s.

The ill-fated Hundred Days Reform ended in a palace coup by the faction of the Empress Dowager Cixi. She confined the young emperor for the rest of his life and forced Kang and Liang into exile abroad. Liang's direct exposure to the brave new world after his arrival in Japan sobered his "all-under-Heaven" fervor. In 1899, he wrote:

> We Chinese people do not lack patriotic qualities. If we are ignorant of patriotism, it is due to the unawareness of being a nation. China since antiquity has been an ecumenical entity. She has been surrounded by inferior barbarians lacking civilization, polity, and nationhood. We have not treated them as nations with equal status. Therefore, for millennia, we have stood alone, styling ourselves "the realm of Yu" (*yuyu*), or "all-under-Heaven" (*tianxia*), but not "nation" (*guo*) (Liang 1899a, 66).

Liang was less original than he sounded. Zhang Zhidong, a reformed-minded official, had in 1898 argued in his best-selling *Exhortation to Learning* that since Chinese civilization for millennia had had no strong rivals to whet its strength, it had "turned in upon itself" (Ayers 1971, 154).

The birth-pang of nationalism from universalism is not peculiar to the Confucian civilization. In Europe, the embryo of nationalism as known to the nineteenth century was gestated first within the womb of Christendom, then the secularized universalism of the Enlightenment. Of the latter, Immanuel Kant's notion of "perpetual peace" was a sample. If Kang Youwei premised universal peace on the spread of benevolence, the Kantian strategy was through the forging of a transcendental idea of right or law (Caponigri 1948, xi).[8] This kind of rational universalism still held sway over German intellectuals, even under Napoleonic domination, to the extent that many, Goethe and Hegel included, saw the conqueror as the "prince of peace," the "restorer of the unity of Western civilization on a new rational basis" (Kohn, 1967, 149; 1960, 36, 58, 72–73). Kant's disciple Johann Gottlieb Fichte was anti-Napoleon by 1806, but his notion of the "fatherland had no autonomous existence; it was only a place for the realization of the cosmopolitan idea" (Kohn 1967, 233). The "fatherland" of the Kang circle was equally abstract, for China was less a "nation" than the incubator of global Great Harmony (*datong*).

Racial Thinking as a New Episteme

As long as the Great Peace (*taiping*) was scheduled for the end of history, it left ample room for more mundane concerns such as survival in a hostile world. In April 1898, Kang founded the Society for the Preservation of Country in the capital, which listed "preservation of race" (*baozhong*), "preservation of country" (*baoguo*), and "preservation of teaching" (*baojiao*) as its principles (Kang 1898, 233). The slogans had been in the offing for some time. Liang in 1897 referred to the three preservations and especially emphasized the "racial" in the context of promoting education for women (Liang 1896–1899, 41). Combinations of any two of the trio often featured in the statements of the Hunan radicals on the eve of the Hundred Days Reform (Tang 1984a, 217–231).[9] Given the sectarian nature of the Gongyang doctrine, Kang's group realized that it would take a platform of general appeal to rally support for a broad-based modern political party.

As expected, the "preservation of teaching" aroused the strongest opposition, for it smacked of a ruse to set Kang himself up as a second Confucius. In June, Yan Fu dismissed "preservation of teaching" and gave top priority to race preservation (Yan 1898a, 78–83; 1898b, 83–85; 1898c, 85–87; in YFJ 1986, vol. 1). It was followed shortly by Zhang Zhidong, who asked pointedly: "Is there any other way to preserve teaching and race than the preservation of the country?" (Zhang 1898, 15). Known to posterity as a hidebound defender of Chinese Learning, Zhang was in fact less Sinocentric than the ecumenist-minded Kang circle. Lacking their messianic zeal—evident in his disapproval of Kang's transmogrifying of Confucius into Jesus—Zhang's Chinese Learning was largely defensive in the sense of preserving China's cultural identity. In contrast, neo-Gongyang messianism aimed at the global, even though it was a feeble narratological maneuver to reclaim the world from the hegemonic Eurocentric order that now stood for modernity.

From Racial Preservation to Racial Revolution

Of the three slogans, preservation of race is the focus of this section. Whether the Chinese also had home-grown racialism, its modern form was Western-inspired and defensive in nature. In 1895, Yan Fu, China's first Darwinist, sounded the alarm of "the fall of the country and the extinction of the race" (*wangguo miezhong*) (Yan 1895a, 4). In the same year, Kang warned that as Westerners most stringently observed racial discrimination, they had managed to reduce colonized peoples to lower castes in their own land; he exhorted Chinese people to fight for the preservation of their teaching and their own kind and for the defense of China as a country (Kang 1895a, 165–166; 1895b, 171–172; 1895c, 173–179; in Tang 1981). If the embryo of Kang's 1898 party program is to be found here, then "race" was already playing a central role in spite of Kang's ecumenist "teaching."

The activation of racialism by the Western stimulus had two opposite ramifications. It is senseless to talk about race except as a sign in a discursive "system of difference." If race was understood as Han-Manchu *difference*, the conclusion was perforce Han revanchism. In 1897, when Liang Qichao, Tan Sitong, Tang Caichang, and their cohort controlled the School of Current Affairs in Hunan, they promoted "popular rights" but agitated for "racial revolution." Tan was most harsh in his characterization of all the non-Han conquerors of China: "They came from unclean soil, their race carries a stench, they are bestial in heart, and their custom is to wear sheepskin" (Tan 1981, 180). To arouse racial consciousness, they illicitly reprinted and circulated the banned writings of late Ming loyalists and accounts of atrocities committed amid the Manchu conquest (Liang Ch'ich'ao, 1959, 101).[10]

Among late Ming loyalists, Wang Fuzhi was remarkable for his racialism. His *Huangshu* (Yellow treatise) (1656) was a critique of ecumenism by stressing the concepts of "boundary" (*zhen*) and "kind" (*zhonglei*). Following the tradition of Sima Qian, the father of imperial Chinese historiography, Wang saw the Yellow Emperor as the founder of the Central Realm. While he also lorded over other groups, he kept them sufficiently distinct. He "never boasted about Great Harmony," as he "maintained ecumenical unification in name but the multi-state system in fact." Seen in this light, the Qin-Han unification was a deviation from the "ancestral style." In dynasties to follow, the blurring of boundaries caused the Central Realm to be totally overrun by "other kinds." Wang lamented that his compatriots had lost the consciousness of kind, whereas even ants knew how to defend their territory against other insects (Wang 1992, 501, 504–505, 507, 534, 536). Wang's was a counter discourse to the Gongyang creed of "the far, the near, the great, the small are treated as the same, all-under-Heaven becomes one family, and China becomes one person." Confucius had no place in Wang's treatise. As we shall see below, Confucius as the icon of a civilization was to be displaced in the early twentieth century by the Yellow Emperor, the founder of a nation.

The Hunan radicals had not yet reached this conclusion. All they did was use the memories of late Ming resistance to reinvent the Ming-Qing transition as a site of racial war. Their version of Han racialism gave rise to the untenable position of supporting Emperor Guangxu but getting rid of the Manchus. From the debacle of the Hundred Days Reform to the Independent Army plot of 1900, the reformist party cast itself in the role of the Meiji "men of purpose." It was a mis-analogy, because the Chinese counterpart of the Tokugawa shogunate turned out to be "the Manchu tribe in its entirety" (Chen 1994, 101).[11] In 1899, Zhang Taiyan, then a reform sympathizer, proffered the bizarre proposal of retaining Guangxu as a "guest emperor"—a position he instantly regretted (Zhang 1899, in Tang 1977, 84–90; Zhang 1900, in Jiang and Zhu 1981, 118–120).

Asiatic Racial Solidarity

If "race" signified yellow-white *difference*, then the we-group perforce encompassed the Manchus and much more: all Asiatics. The Chinese concept of "yellow race" in the late 1890s was rather hazy. Zhang Taiyan thought that Asia was all yellow and that it was the sage kings of antiquity who fixed the racial boundary at the Caspian-Ural line to segregate the yellow from the white (Zhang 1897b, in Tang 1977, 5). Even the English-trained Yan Fu held the erroneous view of Asia being coterminous with the yellow race. He discerned four rounds of yellow-white confrontation before the present: the Persians against the Greeks, the Huns against the Romans, the Arabs against the Franks, the Mongols against the combined European forces. In his opinion, the "yellow race's lack of success" against the white in the past was ominous for the present (Yan 1898c, in YFJ 1986, vol. 1, 86–87). Zhang Zhidong, in his turn, mistook the five continents for the fivefold division of the human race. He saw all of Asia as yellow and was inevitably touched by the "radiance and teaching of the Three Sovereigns and the Five Emperors" (Zhang 1898, 38). In this collapsing of geographical division with the racial, and race with teaching (culture), the idea of a "Chinese nation" was left in the limbo.

Japan as the "Racial" Model

In the wake of the Sino-Japanese War, reform-minded Chinese had come to look favorably toward "The East Neighbor" (Japan) as a model. The Hunan radicals were avid readers of Huang Zunxian's *Treatises on Japan* (1895), which probed "the secret of Japan's success in building a strong nation in a short period of time" (Kamachi 1981, 215). They also created the cult of martyrdom out of Huang's narrative of the heroes of the Meiji Restoration (Ibid., 260).

Japan's Public Relations Stunts in China

In 1897, The East Neighbor, threatened by the renewed aggression of Germany, Russia, and Great Britain in East Asia, was anxious to extend overtures to China to heal the bad feelings of the Sino-Japanese War. As the Chinese were receptive, Japan's public relation campaigns in China from late 1897 on struck a sympathetic chord, notably with provincial officials like Zhang Zhidong and the Hunan radicals (Howard 1967, 281–287; Reynolds, 1993, 19–20).

Earlier in that year, Zhang Taiyan and Liang Qichao had aired pro-Japanese views. Zhang exclaimed that because Heaven took pity on the weak yellow race, It had arranged for Japan to rise a few decades earlier to save a tiny enclave for the survival of the yellow stock (Zhang 1897a, in Tang 1977, 49). Liang reasoned that India's fallen state was physically determined by the racial inferiority common to the black, red, and brown stocks; the yellow race, on the other hand, was closer to the white as evident in Japan's successful emulation of the West (Liang 1897c, 13).

Common Threat and Common Stock

In late 1897, Germany seized Jiaozhou Bay and Russia occupied Lüshun-Dalian. In response, England also forcibly leased Weihaiwai. The policy of Li Hongzhang, backed by Cixi, to ally with Russia to resist Japan was in shambles. The younger emperor's party countered with a pro-Japan policy, and it provided an opening badly needed by Japan to improve her chances on the Asian continent. In 1898, the Japanese premier Okuma Shigenobu announced the "preservation of China" doctrine that Japan, out of cultural indebtedness to China, should hold the West at bay to buy China time to stand on her feet (Jansen 1970, 136).

In this atmosphere, Kang Youwei presented *A Study of Institutional Changes in Japan* as a model for reform during the Hundred Days. He even advised the emperor to inaugurate the reforms with a public announcement that was taken almost verbatim from the Meiji Emperor's Charter Oath (Murata 1993, 30–32). "Follow Japan" became a craze in the summer of 1898, and one memorial urged the emperor to appoint Ito Hirobumi, who was visiting Beijing at the time, as prime minister (Howard 1967, 301). Japanese authorities assisted in Kang and Liang's escape after the Hundred Days Reform was aborted by Cixi.

Garden-variety supernationalism of the time included Anglo-American, pan–Germanic, pan–Slavic, pan–Turanian, and pan–Asian. In Japan, pan–Asianism as a political trend had been around for some time. By the mid-1890s academics also carved out a separate geo-historical space called *toyo* to revise the early Meiji "enlightenment history," or the linear concept of progress that privileged the West (Tanaka 1993, 47–49).

It was this heightened Asianist ambience that Liang stepped into, and his inchoate kindred-racialist feelings now became fully articulated.[12] The year before the arrival in Japan of the fugitive reformist party, Sun Zhongshan had already won the sympathy of the pan-Asianist circles (Schiffrin 1968, 140–143; Wilbur 1976, 56–57). In January 1898, it was none other than the head of the House of Peers, Prince Konoe Atsumaro, who envisaged the prospect of a global racial war: "We must ally with those of the same race, and we must study the China problem" in order to prepare for "a struggle between the white and yellow races" (Jansen 1980, 113).[13]

The Yellow-White Condominium

Like an echo to Prince Konoe, in December, when Liang launched the *Pure Opinion Journal* in Yokohama, he listed among its principles "the innovating of East Asian studies, for the sake of preserving the Asian essence (*yacui*)" (Liang 1898, 31). He anticipated a showdown between the yellow and white races on a global scale in the coming century and deemed it urgent to merge China, Japan, and Korea to be prepared for the final battle (Liang 1896–1899, 83). It was based on the assumption that a parity existed between the two races, in no small measures thanks to Japan's performance.

Parity with the White Race

At that time, Liang's comrade Tang Caichang also saw an "emerging confrontation between the European and the Asian races" as a dominant trend of the modern times (Tang 1968, 468). As the reformist party's ecumenism faded, yellow racialism began to loom large in their minds. Kang, in his founding statement of the Emperor Protection Society (July 1899), said:

"Our China (*zhongguo*) is not the name of a country, it is a racial branch of the Yellow Emperor's divine progeny, and all we yellow race belong to it." He spelled out its purpose as: "To rescue the emperor, to save China and the yellow race through reform" (Shanghai shi wenwu 1982, 245, 258). The fervor of Confucian messianism was now much subdued.

Tang Caichang, the hero and martyr of the 1900 Independent Army Incident, believed that the yellow and white were the master races: "Yellow and white are wise, red and black are stupid; yellow and white are rulers, red and black are slaves; yellow and white are united; red and black are scattered" (Dikötter 1992, 81). The traditional frame of the Central Realm was thus stretched to accommodate a new yellow-white co-center. In this spirit, Tang Caichang proposed the merging of the yellow and the white races (Dikötter 1992, 87). Kang Youwei, in his *The Book of Great Harmony* (allegedly completed in 1902) also envisioned the merging of the yellow race with the white and the extinction of the darker stocks in the global community of the future. Such parity implied the yellow and white races were equal matches.

The Coming Racial Armageddon

In the West, those who had a keen interest in the Pacific region also predicted a global war along the white-yellow racial divide. In 1895, Kaiser Wilhelm II visualized European nations as Valkyries defending their homeland against a Chinese dragon "bearing a seated Buddha upon its back" (Thompson 1978, 1). The fear of the "yellow peril" was heightened by the Boxer Uprising of 1900. In America, hostile feelings had long existed due to the issue of excluding East Asian immigrants. In 1904, Jack London published in San Francisco an article to conjure, for the consumption of an Anglo-American audience, the specter of the "organizing and ruling capacities of the Japanese" aligning with the "enormous working capacity of the great Chinese population" (Hofstadter 1945, 163).

The Japanese victory over Russia in 1905 prompted Wilhelm II to rehash the Yellow Peril. In 1907, the American president Theodore Roosevelt sent the "Great White Fleet" on a global tour but specially warned the commander to be on alert while in the Orient. In the same year, H.G. Wells published his futurist fantasy, *War in the Air*: Amid a war between the United States and Germany, "The Asiatic Confederation" of Japan and China, now equipped with superior aeronautical technology, launched a sneak attack on both sides (Thompson 1978, 422–426). In 1908, a science fiction novel called *Xin jiyuan* (New era) appeared in China, depicting her as the supreme superpower by the year 1999. The perennial yellow-white racial conflict in Hungary is now focused on the issue of whether to observe the Christian or the Chinese calendar. When the European powers back the white Hungarians, China intervenes militarily. In this global war, Chinese immigrants seize the Panama Canal and set up their own republics in Australia and Western America, prompting the United States to join the European alliance. Leading the yellow-race coalition, China confronts the combined Western fleet first in the South China Sea then in the Indian Ocean, then near the Suez Canal, and finally finishes off the Western powers in the Adriatic. "In its epic scale the novel is a maritime version of the Mongol conquest of Europe" (Wang 1997, 309).

Proud to Be a "Peril"

Meanwhile, the prospect of yellow race meeting the white as equals instilled pride in Liang's usage of the neologism *renzhong* (race) in 1899.[14] In the general euphoria about the yellow stock, Liang struck a confident note pondering on the future of the Chinese "race," who, he believed, would dominate in the new century. His list of the propitious Chinese racial qualities included: the flair for local autonomy, a venturesome and independent spirit exemplified in Chinese emigrations overseas, the premium placed on learning, a huge population, rich resources, mercantile prowess, and cheap labor. All that was required to develop these potentials were national cohesion and education (Liang 1899f; 1899c, 69–70). In vaunting China's population mass, rich resources, overseas diaspora, mercantile prowess, and cheap labor, Liang turned into an asset exactly those Chinese traits that were a nightmare to the Yellow Perilists (Iikura 1995, 257–292).[15]

Liang's positive appraisal of the Chinese was a far cry from his later denigration of their "national character." His thinking after 1902 was increasingly influenced by national psychology and by its criterion that China was poorly integrated as a "nation." It was a different matter to imagine the Chinese in terms of biological race, when the heartening example of Japan was close at hand and China also qualified as a "peril" in Western eyes. It was a typical case of a self-identity fashioned from an image in a hostile mirror.

A racialism based on common biological traits also allowed Liang to solve the thorny issue of anti–Manchuism, which was to inform much of the revolutionary thinking of the early 1900s. If China and Japan were to merge, what was the point of alienating the Han from the Manchus? The conclusion was only too facile: Unification of the yellow race had to start in China with the union of the Han and the Manchus, who amounted to 70 or 80 percent of the yellow race (Liang 1896–1899, 83). One may also discern a lingering Confucian penchant to merge countries and states in pan–Asianist thinking. In Liang's case, his pan–Asianism was "a way station" between his earlier Confucian ecumenism and his later "full-fledged nationalism" (Huang 1972, 49).

Liang Qichao's Transition to "Nationalism"

A century before Liang, the German intellectuals in the absence of nationalism also pondered the idea of merging their country with their neighbor's. They were still spellbound by the universalism of the Enlightenment, which, like Confucian ecumenism, was alien to "modern" nationalism. The early Romantic cult of the *Volk* was not incompatible with the Enlightenment to begin with—as evident in the works of Johann Gottfried Herder, who glorified the *Volk* yet frowned upon chauvinistic nationalism (Kohn 1960, 89). It was only after 1808 that the Germans realized that the Rhine Confederation under Napoleon's presidency was not the dawn of a new universalism. They began to launch a war of "national" liberation against the French, and their literary and philosophical awakening turned virulently political.

His Outgrowing of Pan-Asianism

It also took the Chinese some time to awaken to the brutal reality of modern nationalism. It was not long before Liang realized that pan–Asianism was a hoax to disguise Japan's continental policy. Liang thus relived the experience of the treaty-port journalist Wang Tao, who in the 1880s had also flirted with Japanese pan–Asianism but later backed away from it (Cohen 1987, 102–104). In Japan, the slogan *dobun doshu* (same language, same race) had "little credibility in a society where most citizens had embraced the state's quest for Westernization." In fact, the Japanese went to any lengths to scorn the Chinese "in order to win the approbation of the West" (Sato, in Dikötter 1997, 120).

In 1900, Liang welcomed the new century by declaring the birth of a new "nation" as he refuted Japanese denigration of China as a "senile empire." He stressed that China had not existed as "a nation" in the past—she was a nation to be actualized in the future and therefore a nation in her youthful vigor (Liang 1900c, 7, 9). The very imagery of Young China had an affinity with Mazzini's Young Italy and thus adjoined the genealogy of European nationalism since the French Revolution. The nationhood project dawned upon the Chinese intellectuals as an evocation of a European precedent as much as it was a reaction against pan–Asianism.

State, Country, Nation, and Guo—A Matter of Difference

In 1900, during the hectic preparation for the Independent Army uprising, Liang wrote his mentor Kang—in defense of "liberty"—that the French Revolution was the "mother" of the nineteenth century, whereas the Lutheran Reformation was at best its "grandmother" (Ding and Zhao 1983, 236). The reshuffled genealogy was a none too subtle upstaging of Kang's promotion of Confucianism as the state religion, a proposition to which Liang himself had committed as late as 1899.[16] Kang, the self-styled "Chinese Martin Luther," thought in terms not unlike Leopold von Ranke's. The German historian saw the "forces of order and disorder" finding their historical forms in the benevolent twin institutions of church and state on the one hand and the people on the other (White 1973, 169).[17] Attempting to neutralize the horrid effect of the French Revolution, Ranke saw the German national spirit embodied in official Lutheranism safeguarded by the state. Germany's nation-building experience differed from that of France in the central role played by Prussian statism. Liang would soon come around to the statist position, but in 1900 he was firmly in the French camp.

In 1902 Liang openly broke with Kang on the issue of "preservation of teaching," charging that the presence of any orthodoxy tended to shackle the minds of the citizens. Admitting that he was once a "foot solider" fighting under the old "tricolor flag" of the Three Preservations, he now even found the "preservation of race" meaningless and from now on would struggle exclusively for the "preservation of *guo*." The Japanese belonged to the same yellow race, he conceded, yet they needed no "preservation from us" (Liang 1902a, p. 50). Liang's *guo* in 1902 was a far cry from the "country" in the constitution of the 1898 Society for the Preservation of Country. The latter meant only "government and territory," as the document placed the populace into the separate category of "race and kind" (Kang 1898, in Tang, 1981, 233). In 1902, for Liang the same term *guo* definitely meant a "nation" of modern citizens—a goal yet to be realized.

Nation in the Age of Imperialism

Rereading Herbert Spencer

This intellectual evolution of Liang's almost immediately took a downturn. After his declaration of the *presence* of a new nation in 1900, the rosy prospect of a "young China" was soon offset by pessimism—due precisely to the *absence* of nationhood in China. This mood, ironically, deepened with the onset of Liang's full-fledged "nationalism." In the transition, he was swayed by Kato Hiroyuki's social Darwinism, which modified substantially the Spencerian version of Liang's pre-Japan days.

Herbert Spencer had consigned patriotism to the tribalistic "military" stage on his evolutionary scale, allowing it no place in "industrial" societies based on individual rights and laissez-faire (Huang 1972, 57). His evolutionism was also a semi-religious credo of humankind evolving towards perfection. In sharp contrast, Kato's social Darwinism spelled *Realpolitik*, as it glorified might, militarism, and collectivity. In his later life, the enlightener Kato went as far as glorifying despotism, war, imperialism, colonialism, and slavery as necessary factors of enlightenment and progress (Davis 1996, 104–105). Although criticizing Kato's theory as "extreme and prone to abuses," Liang by and large regarded it as valid (Liang 1902e, 92).

This shift reflected the crisis-laden 1890s, which witnessed the Sino-Japanese War, the Three Powers' Intervention, the scramble for concessions in China, leading to the Boxer Uprising of 1900 and the Russo-Japanese War of 1904–1905. Kato did not preach in isolation. The decade also saw the liberal Tokutomi Soho turning jingoist with his thesis of "the expansion of Greater Japan" or *Dai-Nihon bocho ron* (Vinh 1989, 48–61) and the appearance of Takayama Chogyu's Japanism or *Nihonshugi* (Pyle 1969, 193).

"Survival of the Fittest" in the International Arena

In a broader context, this current was symptomatic of the mounting global tension beginning in the 1890s and culminating in World War I. In 1901, the British eugenicist Karl Pearson averred that the national spirit would be "wholly good" if in the "struggle of race against race, and nation against nation," the nation was ready to "meet its fellows without hesitation in the field" (Pearson 1901, 34, 50–51). From 1900 to 1902, Brooks Adams, the prophet of American imperialism, advised arming America morally for a "war to the death" with the old continent (Hofstadter 1945,161–162). In 1902, John A. Hobson published his definitive work (*Imperialism*) on modern imperialism, a book that shaped Lenin's thesis of the Age of Imperialism. Liang also pondered the same subject in the years from 1899 to 1901 when international tension was increasingly engulfing East Asia.

Liang's nationhood project was therefore historically specific in carrying the mark of the Age of Imperialism. By 1899, he had achieved an understanding of the nature of global conflict as economic, rooted in the West's industrial overproduction, which by 1903 was fully developed into a treatise on "monopoly capitalism" and its connection with overproduction and imperialism (Liang 1903a, 33–61). He now stressed "national struggle" as different in nature from the rivalry among traditional imperial states. China, as such a state, had been the ruling family's patrimony for ages—a condition inhibiting her people from political participation. Devoid of national consciousness, the Chinese were not "fit to survive" in modern times, an era of struggle between entire national citizenries (Liang 1899b, 56–61).

From 1900 to 1901, Liang elaborated the "national struggle" notion into "national imperialism" and fitted it into a neatly tabulated historical schematic.[18] In this layout, residual Gongyang thinking habits are still evident in his trisection of social evolution into three major phases, the past, the present, and the future, subsuming six stages. The past includes the ages of familism, the rule of tribal chieftains, and imperialism. The present is nationalism and national imperialism. The future is Great Harmony among nations. This schematic reduced Chinese ecumenism to premodern "imperialism." Liang discerned that both China and the West were in a state of transition: "Today's Europe and America are in the age of transition from nationalism to national imperialism; today's Asia is in the age of transition from imperialism to nationalism" (Liang 1901b, 12–22). It is apparent that this scheme was inspired by Kato Hiroyuki, who, decrying the theory of the social contract, "believed that the earliest societies were formed when families came together to form tribes, and tribes, nations" (Davis 1996, 28). In treating "national imperialism" as the final throes on the eve of global harmony, Liang also echoed Lenin's thesis of imperialism as the highest stage of capitalism, yet unlike Lenin, Liang was concerned with his country's survival in the present.

Ancient Imperium and Modern Imperialism

Liang's emerging nationalism was not free of ambivalence regarding ecumenism from the Qin-Han to the present. As the "law of civilization" favored unification over warring states, he averred, China actually upstaged the West by two thousand years. Unfortunately, the advantage turned into a handicap, for perennial ecumenical rule had made the Chinese ignorant of people's rights. It hampered China in a brave new world of warring states (Liang 1899g, 61–67). This ambivalence betrayed that ecumenism, though sublated, was not fully suppressed by Liang's nationalism, for he envisioned a modern Chinese "nation" that would contain the Chinese imperium. As we will show later, the reincarnation of a multiracial ecumenical empire in the body of a modern nation-state would place both the Han and the non–Han nationalities in an untenable position.

But at the time when Liang wrote those lines, his ambivalence reflected more the vacillation between monarchism and republicanism.[19] While flirting with the idea of a revolution from below, he was also concerned with the integrity of the Chinese polity, a legacy bequeathed by the very same accursed imperial system. At one point, Liang stressed that even in the age of national imperialism, China still needed to achieve Rousseau's populist "nationalism" of an earlier stage, for to move directly onto the more advanced "national imperialism" would result in the disastrous transplant of the modern "omnipotent government" (Liang 1901b, 22). Lenin also shared this observation although he saw the enlarged role for the state under monopoly capitalism as a prelude to socialism.[20] Liang's ambivalence persisted in his futuristic novel, *The Future of New China* (1902s), where he split himself into two alter egos debating the virtues of the French Revolution and Prussian statism (Tang 1996, 121–137).

When Liang finally made up his mind, the theory of global imperialism helped him to resolve this dilemma to some degree. The need for national survival made it imperative to involve the entire people who, nonetheless, should not be tempted by revolution for it would invite partition by the Powers. In this balancing act, Liang fell back upon the role of the enlightener, or, a radical in words. In the eventful 1890s, the relatively inactive Yan Fu had advocated the development of people's strength, intelligence, virtue (Tang 1984b, 221)—concepts taken from Herbert Spencer (Chen 1992, 13). In 1902, expressing the urgent need for national cohesion, Liang recast the triplet into "group strength, intelligence, virtue" (Liang 1902L, 3). It was at this juncture that the Confucian concept of "renovating the people" (*xinmin*) took on a new meaning. In the 1890s, the reformists had used the same term to denote the development of people's intelligence, but now it increasingly assumed the meaning of reforming the people's moral character (Cui 1984).

Nationhood Defined As an Absence

Point of Departure: People's Moral Character

Liang the enlightener came to emulate his Meiji counterparts, not only the Meirokusha gentlemen but their opponents the Minyusha and Seikyosha thinkers as well (Bao 1992, 40–43).[21] In the 1870s, Fukuzawa Yukichi had put a premium on the "spirit of independence, initiative, and responsibility" (Pittau 1967, 62). Another Meirokusha member, Nakamura Masanao, translated Samuel Smiles' sermons on "self-help" and imbued Liang with those Victorian values (Liang 1899e, 16–22).

Sharing their conviction that a nation's strength or weakness hinges on her citizens' quality, Liang in 1901 began a more systematic discussion of the Chinese character. It was discouraging, for the comparison of the Chinese "nation" with the West and Japan simply disqualified the Chinese as modern citizens. Lacking the spirit of independence and gregariousness, they are dependent and selfish. In their thinking they are dependent on antiquity; in politics, on foreigners. The people depend on officials and the monarch, who are parasites in their turn. Dependency breeds slavishness, a herd-like quality not conducive to group cohesion. In China, each province had innumerable small units unrelated to each other. Retracting his positive view of the Chinese flair for local autonomy, he now blamed the same trait for turning the nation into "a plate of loose sand." In Western-style civic society the citizens enjoy liberty but are law-abiding, for liberty is based on respect for the liberty of others. Both virtues are alien to the Chinese. Whereas a broad-minded modern citizen is self-confident but also modest, the Chinese are self-denigrating yet at the same time perpetuate an arrogance rooted in obscurantism. Unlike a modern citizen who cultivates self-interest but also manages to be beneficent to others, the Chinese forsake both rights and responsibility. This self-depreciating egotism, harmful to self and society, renders the Chinese "unfit" to survive as a group in the modern world (Liang 1901c, 42–49).

The Discourse on the Slave Character

Echoing Fukuzawa Yukichi's critique of Confucianism for producing the slave character, Liang charged that China was a nation of slaves, hierarchically enforcing servility and transferring beatings from superiors to subordinates—making the Chinese singularly amenable to foreign conquerors. This bred cowardice, and their "spinelessness, bloodlessness, and lack of energy" reinforced each other, leading to inaction (Liang 1901d; 1900b; 1901a; 1902h).[22]

Liang's "slave character" discourse had a broad impact. Two articles titled "On Slave" appeared in Liang's *Pure Opinion Journal* in 1900 and 1901 (Shangxin Ren 1900; Gong Nuli Lishan 1901), and Qin Lishan, a field leader of the abortive Independent Army uprising, signed one of them with the name "Gong Nuli Lishan," which literally means "The Public Slave, Powerful Mountain." This awkward name was probably Qin's attempt to simulate his pen-name to a Japanese name (which, unfortunately, made him sound like a sumo wrestler).

The anti-Manchu camp, notably Zou Rong in his *Revolutionary Army* (1903), soon adopted the "slave character" discourse, to the extent of seeing the "histories of twenty-four dynasties" as nothing but "a monumental chronicle of slavery" (Zou 1958, 31). Chen Duxiu's *The National Daily Gazette* in Shanghai also serialized an unsigned article, "On Slave," in 1903 (Anonymous 1903i). In the republican era, the Nietzschean writer Lu Xun would elaborate the "slave character" into a national stereotype. Lu Xun's literary portrayal of the Underman also echoed Liang's lamentation of the universalization of envy among Chinese: "Among the Chinese, the inept resent the able; those with tardy careers resent those who are advancing; the non-achievers resent those who achieve." Liang regarded such "malicious qualities" as part of the racial "heredity," formed through millennia of "social habit," thus "impossible to eradicate" (Liang 1903f, 5).

A Nation Scorned

In early 1903 Liang wrote "Zhongguo guomin zhi pinge" (Chinese people's quality and character). The whole title, with the exception of "Chinese," seemed to have been lifted from a Japanese editorial, "Nihon kokumin no hinkaku" (Japanese people's quality and character) (1893), of the influential Minyusha journal, *Kokumin no tomo*. It classified nations into three categories, those revered for their civilization and might, those respected for their barbarous strength, and lastly, those that were scorned, and it lamented that Japan, the most advanced Asian nation, was still scorned by the white nations. The editorial in particular referred to the large number of Japanese prostitutes in foreign countries and the low social status of Japanese emigrant workers in North America (Pyle 1969, 167–168). Liang also classified nations in terms of *pinge* (the translation of the Japanese *hinkaku*) into three categories, the respected, the feared, and the scorned, and he placed the Chinese in the last category. In spite of the great number of overseas Chinese, Liang lamented, their lack of dignity and grace had turned them into chattel-slaves for the host countries. Their behavior, such as gambling, armed affrays, opium-smoking, and tolerating unhygienic conditions readily played into the hands of host countries predisposed to exclude Chinese immigrants (Liang 1903d, 1–5).

Apparently, on the immigration issue, Liang was no longer proud of his fellow-countrymen for being a "peril" in Western eyes. Liang spent the greater part of 1903 touring North America. He was thoroughly disgusted by San Francisco's Chinatown, the "disorderliness" of which was "unsurpassed by any community on the globe" (Liang 1904b, 188).[23] The orderliness of North American audiences attending a speech or an opera performance greatly impressed him. In contrast, a Chinese audience, "even if it manages to keep quiet, can never refrain from producing four kinds of noises: coughing, yawning, sneezing, and blowing out snivel" (Liang 1904b,

193). When Liang wrote those passages, he had reached the conclusion that what the Chinese needed was not democracy, but more discipline. Beginning in 1903, the pendulum of Liang's political thinking began to swing to the pole of Prussian statism.

Decentering Confucius

Liang's influential essay, "On the New People," serialized in his *New People's Magazine* from 1902 intermittently till 1906, registered his transition from a wavering democrat to an advocate of "enlightened despotism." The earlier portion of the essay, reflecting his radical phase, also pointed an accusing finger at Confucianism.[24]

Homey Virtues in a Darwinian World

In his reformist days, Liang had blamed Daoism for Chinese apathy and inertia and charged the heterodox Confucian Xunzi for corrupting the true Confucian spirit through the ages (Chang 1971, 74–76). Now, Liang simply pitted "new Western ethics" against the "old Chinese ethics." The former governs a person's conduct toward community, the latter is only concerned with the obligation of one private person to another, thus irrelevant to the cultivation of modern civic virtues (Liang 1902r, 2). This dichotomy between public and private virtues was adapted from Fukuzawa (Gao 1992, 168).

If Liang had faulted the "all-under-Heaven" syndrome for China's lack of national consciousness, he now traced its origin to the teachings of ancient sages, notably Confucius, who preached ecumenism long before the advent of the universal state (Liang 1902n, 8–9). Ancient Chinese sages taught magnanimity and nonaggression, and advised against getting even when one's rights were trampled on. Such teachings, in their corrupted versions, became synonyms of passivity, cowardice, and spineless servility. The Chinese badly needed to develop the concept of "defending one's own rights." To show that his break with Gongyang Confucianism was complete, Liang stated that the Chinese virtue of benevolence might make sense in the Great Harmony, "tens of thousands years from now." Liang regarded the Western virtue of justice as apropos to the present (Liang 1902m, 7–8).

Although Liang at times exonerated Confucius himself, he laid the blame squarely on the doorstep of Confucian teaching: The Doctrine of the Mean and filial obsession with preserving one's body weaken the character. While the Christians are warlike and the Buddhists take the matter of life and death lightly, Confucians are singularly gutless—they have bred a nation of cowards and weaklings (Liang 1903e, 7–8). Liang also criticized the Chinese family system for eroding the nation's political capabilities. Again, the "ancient sages" were held responsible for channelling the individual's loyalty to the family, at the expense of any larger community (Liang 1904e, 6–7).

The Orientalist Trap

In 1897, Liang had debated with Yan Fu over the preservation of Confucian teaching (Liang 1897d, 106–111). Yan compared the Chinese spirit unfavorably to the dynamic Western ethos, saying that the sages' teachings were intrinsically wrong (Schwartz 1964, 48–49, 64–65). Now, by coming around to Yan's position, Liang also adopted his approach of comparing civilizations, which contradicted his earlier critique of the Chinese character with an eye on history. Then, he used the evolutionary notion of "epoch" (*shidai*) to build a historical argument: China's "unfitness" in the modern era of national struggle was the fault of an unduly protracted ecumenical rule. The latter he likened to the "dark ages" of medieval Europe (Liang 1902p, 8). Now he turned ahistorical as he started blasting not the wrong "epoch" but Chinese heritage *per se*. The long duration of Chinese despotism has already made it look like an aberration from the global evolutionary norm. Now, to blame Confucianism is to blame something uniquely Chinese, not a product of a certain evolutionary stage. From a postcolonial viewpoint, Liang seems to have fallen into an Orientalist trap of identifying an essence that is both "historical, since it goes back to the dawn of history, and fundamentally a-historical, since it transfixes . . . the object of study within its inalienable and non-evolutive specificity."[25]

Toward the end, Liang's political sympathies discouraged him from seeking a cure for the Chinese character through a popular revolution; instead, the Chinese lack of "political capabilities" served as an excuse for enlightened despotism. Yet the critique of Confucianism paved the way for the New Culture iconoclasm of the early republican period and beyond. Subsequent critiques of Chinese national character along Liang's line also inherited his *aporia* of seeing China's problems as a matter of modernization and as a malaise lodged in the national ethos from its origin.

This aporia was created by positing Western modernity as the *telos* and China's tardiness as something inherent. This monolithic ethos, needless to say, was cast in the mold of modern nationhood. "Nation" as a new totalizing principle ascribed a uniform "character" to the heterogenous subjects of the Chinese empire, which had once been coterminous with *tianxia* (all-under-Heaven). This totalization was meanwhile destabilized by Liang himself, who maintained that at least three different cultures, those of the Yellow River, Yangzi River, and Pearl River regions, existed within the boundaries of China (see chapter 5). Nonetheless, a unitary China was called for to serve as a vessel to hold the national shame.

Retrieving the Han Identity

When Liang used the yardstick of "national imperialism" to gauge the Chinese and found them woefully inadequate, his China became the inverted mirror-image of an imperialist power. Such self-denigration might serve as an impetus, but it also undermined self-confidence. Even in his most negative moments, Liang took as a point of departure for "renovating the people" the assumptions that a nation able to establish itself in the world must have a unique "spirit" that permeated its morals, laws, custom, habits, literature, and art. As something "handed down from ancestors to descendants," this spirit was the fountainhead of nationalism (Liang 1902o, 8).

Inventing the Nation via Public Memory

The Romantic cult of national spirit was more prominent with the National Essence school on the side of revolution. The two camps, reform and revolution, were finally polarized when the Chinese Revolutionary Alliance coalesced in Tokyo under Sun Zhongshan's leadership in 1905. If Liang after 1903 increasingly used the unregenerate Chinese character to argue for strong authority, the revolutionaries attacked the problem differently: They saw China's sorrowful state as a result of alien Manchu domination. Zou Rong in his *Revolutionary Army* (1903) blamed the Chinese slave character not on ecumenism or Confucianism like Liang, but on the lack of racial consciousness. Zhang Taiyan, who wrote the preface to Zou's immensely popular tract, was a founder of the National Essence school and its journal launched in Shanghai in 1905.

Zhang, a Confucian scholar and an early sympathizer of reformism, had made a public anti-Manchu stand in 1902 by convening a "Gathering to Commemorate the 242nd Anniversary of China's Loss of Nationhood" in Yokohama. Zhang adopted a strategy different from Liang's in the invention of nationhood. By reimagining the dynastic change from Ming to Qing as a "foreign" conquest, he conjured a moral community of the Han by means of public memory. Zhang unwittingly revealed nationhood to be a foreign import by adopting the Japanese term for China, *shina*—read in Chinese as *zhina*—in the formal title of his public gathering. Apparently, at that time an official name for the nation other than the ruling dynasty's was wanting.

In 1898, when Empress Cixi crushed the Hundred Days Reform, the imperial edict for Kang Youwei's arrest accused him of setting up the Society for the Preservation of Country to "only preserve *zhongguo* to the exclusion of the Great Qing" (Zhongguo shixue hui 1957, vol. 2, 103). In 1900, amid the Independent Army uprising, the reformists and the revolutionaries joined forces to launch a "Parliament of China" in Shanghai, using the term *zhongguo*, but the chairman of the meeting also used the term *zhina* in his speech (Ding and Zhao 1983, 243).

National Essence and Local Identities

To dissociate China from the ruling dynasty, both camps tended increasingly to adopt the Japanese appellation for China. They also borrowed the term for national essence, *guocui*, from *kokusui*, which "first came into common use in Japan in 1887" (Bernal, in Furth 1976, 101). In 1902, Liang contemplated launching a journal for promoting "national essence" but was talked out of it by Huang Zunxian (Ding and Zhao 1983, 292; Kamachi 1981, 246–247). This thought did not conflict with Liang's critique of Confucianism, for Liang's national heritage meant the hundred schools of the pre-Qing era. Liang was perhaps also apprehensive that "national essence" might lead to Han revanchist conclusions, which were precisely drawn by the anti-Manchu camp. Launched in 1905, the National Essence group echoed Liang in arguing that the Chinese nation had declined since the founding of ecumenical rule under despotism in the third century B.C.E, and in her present state she was "no more than a slave nation with a slave culture" (Schneider 1971, 37). Drawing upon the slave discourse, the school aimed at a cultural renaissance, an idea Liang also had pioneered. In 1899, Liang, long before Hu Shi, had raised the idea of a future "renaissance" in China after a long "dark age" (Liang 1899f, 52).

Yet the school joined the revolutionary camp as it linked cultural renaissance with Han revivalism. National Essence thinkers, who opposed their Old Text Confucianism to Kang Youwei's New Text version, were also the earliest Chinese sociologists and anthropologists (Chen 1990; Zheng Shiqu 1992). Though speaking in evolutionist terms, they stressed origin and cultural identity. Like the German Romantics' apotheosis of the *Volksgeist*, they exalted "a most abstract idea of the identity of the culture as essence," defined as "the accumulated spiritual legacy of a particular people," the Han Chinese (Furth 1983, 337).

In 1906, at a reception for his arrival in Tokyo after finishing a jail sentence due to the *Jiangsu Daily* case (Wong 1989, 39–43), Zhang Taiyan lashed out against those "Europeanizers" who denigrated the Chinese and undermined "patriotic and racial feelings" (Zhang 1906, in Tang 1977, 276). A logical step along this line was to look for heroic models in Chinese (read "Han") history, since the dominant social-psychological theory at the time explained group formation through "sympathy-suggestion-imitation," the social equivalents of the affective, cognitive, and conative faculties of individual psychology (Allport 1968, 8, 23). It was in this spirit that Zhang, in his 1902 commemorative gathering, named the late Ming loyalists who resisted the Manchus and exhorted their fellow provincials to emulate them, (Zhang 1902b, 189).[26]

Back in his reformist days in 1897, Zhang had already experimented with the founding of a Reviving Zhejiang Society, which barely disguised its anti-Manchu intents with its hallowing of late Ming patriots from that region (Zhang 1897c, in Jiang and Zhu, 1981, 10). In the same period the Cantonese Liang Qichao, who happened to work in Hunan, also fanned the flame of a Hunanese autonomous movement (Duara 1995, 154–156, 180). After 1902 local patriotism definitely took on a more articulated revolutionary flavor. Following Zhang's agitation at the "loss of nationhood" commemoration, a number of Chinese student journals, mostly organized along provincial lines, all with anti-Manchu intent, appeared in Japan by 1903.

Reimagining the Manchu–Han Animus

The boundary of "Han race" was highly negotiable. As a term, it never appeared under Mongol domination—the conquerors named the former Liao-Jin subjects, including the Khitans and Jurchids, "Han people," and Song subjects, "Hua people" (Li Zefen 1978, 552). Wang Fuzhi, Ming loyalist at the Ming-Qing transition, made no reference to the Manchus, which is understandable. He used allusions such as "the barbarian kind" (*yilei*) or "not our kind" (*feizu*), but the term "Han race" did not appear in his writings. For him, China was *huaxia*, *zhongguo*, or the "realm of the Three Sovereigns, Five Emperors, Han and Tang." Toward the end, the Manchus had become thoroughly Sinified; their dynasty was in fact the most Confucian in Chinese history. The Manchu–Han distinction was artificially magnified by both parties for their political agendas.

In 1904, a political commentator thought that all the recent troubles had their origins in the power struggle between northern and southern court factions in the 1880s. He saw the rift ramifying into the rivalry between Manchus and Han, the Empress Dowager and the Emperor Guangxu factions, the pro-Russian and pro-Japanese parties, and, eventually, the conservatives and the reformists (Anonymous 1904a). The revolutionaries ushered this binarist momentum a bit further, by transforming Qing official usages such as "Manchu people" (*Manren*) and "Han people" (*Hanren*) into modern ethnic nomenclature.

The Yellow Empire as the Font of "National" History

The Old Text Confucians, now turning into romantic architects of the *Volk*, had little use for Confucius, who would remain the obsession of Kang Youwei, the crusader to salvage the Teaching. They actually had the iconoclasts Yan Fu and Liang Qichao to thank for the dethroning of Confucius to clear the center. Celebrating their common roots in the Han "race," the Han nationalists now launched the cult of the Yellow Emperor, "the first great man of nationalism in the world."[27] To push the origin of the "nation" farther than the Ming, back four millennia in time, they adopted a system of dating from the "founding" of China by the Yellow Emperor in lieu of the reign of Guangxu or the Christian era.

From Dynastic to National Genealogy

The idea was first proposed in 1903 by Liu Shipei on the basis that a "nation must trace its origin" (Shen 1997, 40). When it was widely adopted, it led to discrepancies in the computation: *The Soul of the Yellow Emperor* (1904) equated 1904 with the year 4614; *The Chinese National Magazine* equated the same year with 4395; *The People's Journal* (1905), *Twentieth-century Zhina* (1905), *Dongting Tide* (1906), and *The Han Banner* (1907) agreed on the same system, and used 4603, 4604, 4605, respectively. The Manchus' two-hundred-sixty years' "alien" rule was thus imaginatively displaced by a recovered Yellow Genealogy of five millennia.

Huang Jie of the National Essence school credited Wang Fuzhi for establishing this genealogy (Huang 1905, 9). At the time, the idea of the Yellow Emperor setting the "boundary" for the Chinese race (whatever that meant) seemed to be commonly accepted, even by Liang Qichao (Liang 1903b, 1). Wang Fuzhi's *Yellow Treatise*, oblivious of modern racialism, used the color "yellow" to signify centrality, as in the theory of the Five Elements (Wang 1992, 538).[28] The Han nationalists, baptized by Western racial thinking, inevitably linked yellow to race. Jiang Guanyun said: "Having migrated to China, our race of necessity drew its boundary as a race, but in terms of the broader race, we belong to the yellow race of the East" (Guanyun 1904, 11). This argument placed China within the pan–Asianist orbit, while setting her apart from other Asian nations.

The Creation of a "National" Pantheon

The Han nationalist high tide put Liang in the defensive as he had sought after an almost exclusively foreign genealogy: Columbus, Cromwell, Washington, Madame Roland, Lord Nelson, Bismarck, Kossuth, Cavour, Mazzini, Garibaldi, Gladstone, Yoshida Shoin, and the Meiji "men of purpose." But his difference with the revolutionaries was more apparent than real. Liang had a Han revivalist streak that dated back to his radical days in Hunan, but it was suppressed. In 1904, after reaffirming his commitment to defend the Qing Dynasty, Liang rather surprisingly wrote an article on General Yuan Chonghuan, the late Ming hero who kept the Manchus at bay for a decade. This blatant anti-Manchuism on Liang's part is perplexing— unless we see him also badly in need of an "indigenous" model for the resistance of any "foreign" encroachment. Indeed, he exalted General Yuan as the "role model for the military man" (Liang 1904a, 24).

It is clear that as the self-professed founder of the new "national" historiography, Liang would be self-defeating if he continued to resort to foreign models. Earlier, to avoid mentioning the Manchus, the Jurchids, or even the Mongols, Liang had largely evaded the last thousand years of history in his search for models of "patriotic" heroism, turning his eyes instead to heroes who battled the Huns in antiquity. Thus, in 1902 Liang published articles on King Wuling of Zhao, Zhang Qian, and Ban Chao.[29] At around the same time, Liang wrote a short history of Sparta. He even found his way across Eurasia to eulogize Lajos Kossuth, the Hungarian patriot who defied Austrian domination, as the "pride of the yellow race" (Liang 1902t, 1). The Hungarian connection was a residue from Liang's pan–Asianism.

The racial background of Kossuth was trivial because the concept of biological or "natural" race was not viable for nation-building, as "nation" was now increasingly understood as a historic-psychological unit. In 1904, Liang's comrade Jiang Guanyun serialized a lengthy treatise in *The New People's Magazine* on "common feelings," the social-psychological concept of sympathy. He expected this sympathy to be the "right source" to generate modern nationalism (Guanyun 1904–1905). In 1906, the same journal carried another article by Jiang on the Chinese deification of Yue Fei, a hero of the Southern Song dynasty who resisted the Jin barbarians. Jiang attributed the Yue Fei cult to a demand from the "national psychology" of the Chinese people. "Today's theorists of national psychology invariably state that a nation's existence is predicated on its particular ethos acquired through history." He saw China's salvation in the persistence of this "psychology" of hero worship, even if China might vanish as a territorial entity

(Guanyun 1906, 83, 93, 95). The "Jin barbarians," also of the Jurchid ethnicity, was a transparent allusion to the Manchus. This association between the Jin and the Qing, which in fact made its historical debut as the "Later Jin," had caused Chen Duxiu in 1903 to name his anti-Qing group in Anhui the Prince Yue Society (Yue wang hui). Yue Fei was also among the national heroes promoted by the National Essence school (Schneider 1976, 75–76).

The presence of similar Han nationalist sentiments in the reformist camp revealed its yearning to share with the revolutionaries a common, albeit invented, national genealogy which excluded the non-Han peoples. This was inevitable when these Han nationalists compressed China into the straitjacket of the Western nation-state and tied the nationhood project inextricably to the anti-Manchu cause. On the other hand, they also wished to keep the Chinese ecumene together (unlike Kemal Ataturk, who aimed only at preserving the Turkish heartland after World War I). In the wake of the 1911 Revolution, the situation turned grievous when Mongolia and Tibet showed signs of wishing to secede. Attempts were made to reincorporate the non-Han peoples through the formula of "a republic of five nationalities" (*wuzu gonghe*). Inevitably, a degree of ambivalence lingered when Han "national" heroes continued to serve as role models of resistance against "foreign" encroachments in the modern world. It was in this spirit that the Yuan Shikai regime combined the cults of Yue Fei and the war god Guandi in a state-sponsored "martial temple," *à la* Japan's Yasukuni Shrine (Yuan 1914b). This ambivalence has persisted under the People's Republic of today.[30]

The Making of an Estranged Genealogy

The "Conqueror" Fixation

While the historical heroes, who affirmed Han-ness by their model resistance against non-Han peoples, were now enshrined in a newly constructed "national" pantheon, the origin of the Chinese nation was, paradoxically, attributed by the Han nationalists to a foreign conquest. Their revival of the Yellow Emperor "was relatively sudden and was almost certainly connected with the appearance of [Terrien de] Lacouperie's theories in Japanese." The French scholar identified the Yellow Emperor as Nakhunti, who led a "blue eyed people" from Mesopotamia to China and founded the nation by vanquishing the "black natives" (Bernal 1976, 96–99).

Jiang Guanyun, who subscribed to the theory, preferred to believe that the Yellow Emperor's tribe was purely Turanian (i.e., Asiatic) (Guanyun 1903, 7). Nonetheless, the common origins of China and the West bolstered the sentiments of a yellow-white condominium. Besides Jiang Guanyun, others who warmly received Lacouperie's theory were Zhang Taiyan, Huang Jie, and Song Jiaoren, whereas Liang Qichao and Liu Shipei upheld a modified "western origin" version that the Chinese race came from the Pamir. In 1915, this motif was incorporated into the national anthem of the Yuan regime (Tang and Luo 1986, 53–56). Sun Zhongshan referred to the same theory as late as 1924, that the Chinese, as conquerors from the West, had driven the aborigines to the southwestern periphery (Sun 1924, 652).[31]

The Social Darwinist canon of the time dictated that at the very inception of its biography, the Chinese nation must be conquerors like the Aryans in India or the Normans in England, not aborigines like the native Americans. This sentiment was most apparent in Kang Youwei's manifesto of the Emperor Protection Society to the effect that if the Chinese should lose out to the white race, they would suffer the same fate the Yellow Emperor's progeny had inflicted on the southwestern aborigines such as the Miao, Yao, Dong, and Tong (Shanghai shi wenwu 1982, 251). Liu Shipei, writing from Japan, projected the contemporary fervor of "racial war" into the legendary antiquity, alleging that the Yellow Emperor conquered a China occupied by the Turkish Xianyun in the north and the negroid Miao tribes in the south: "In short, when the Han race first arrived in China, it was like the Spaniards entering the American continent" (Shen 1997, 38). In 1905, the revolutionary Song Jiaoren was planning to write a "History of the Invasion by the Han Race" (Hanzu qinlüe shi) (Chow, in Dikötter 1997, 48).

The Contemporaneity of Origins, the Hybridity of Identity

Benedict Anderson perceives a paradox in "nation": "The objective modernity of nations to the historian's eye vs. their subjective antiquity in the eyes of nationalists" (Anderson 1991, 5). China as a historical subject certainly had existed since antiquity. Yet this subject had never before been represented as a Western-style nation. The Andersonian position is that of a poststructuralist historian who would see the Chinese nation "invented" at the turn of the twentieth century against the claim of the first-generation Chinese nationalists that their nation dated back millennia to the Yellow Emperor. Those nationalists themselves were products of modernity and their invention a contemporaneous one.

Their new yellow identity was in fact a hybrid fashioned out of Wang Fuzhi's and Lacouperie's retellings of Sima Qian's imperial chronicles, as it also mirrored the white race's fear of this color in the form of a "peril."

In this new genealogy of the nation, if the origin of the Chinese nation was Babylonian, its modern destination was no less estranged. The appellation *zhina*, which the first-generation Chinese nationalists adopted for their modern identity, was derogatory in Japanese. Before the Meiji Restoration, the Japanese had used the name *chugoku*, the equivalent of *zhongguo*, which they would revert to after World War II. During the interval, "*shina* emerged as a word that signified China as a troubled place mired in its past, in contrast to Japan, a modern Asian nation" (Tanaka 1993, 3–4). More precisely, the term's contemptuous undertone can be traced back to the Sino-Japanese War of the 1890s, but the Chinese people became more aware of its insulting ring only after the incident of the 21 Demands in 1915. By 1930, the term *shina* had become so insulting that the Nationalist Government officially protested to Tokyo to insist on the use of the correct title, but the gesture had very little impact on the Japanese (Saneto 1983, 184–199). Thus, between its *archia* and *telos*, the genealogy of the Chinese nation was an epitome of decenteredness.

Notes

1. According to Huntington, post–Cold War humankind "identify with cultural groups: tribes, ethnic groups, religious communities, nations, and, at the broadest level, civilizations" (Huntington 1997, 21).

2. Tu Wei-ming's "Sinic world" is comparable to Samuel Huntington's "Sinic civilization" with the exception of the emphasis on the Chinese diaspora. Tu addresses the problem of diversity under an overarching civilization in his vision of "a Chinese civilization-state with a variety of autonomous regions or even a loosely structured Chinese federation of different political entities" in the core area (p. 15).

3. For example, Joseph Levenson and his cothinkers. James Townsend advises caution in the application of the thesis for "both nationalism and culturalism carry multiple meanings and refer to complex phenomena" (Townsend 1996, 3–4, 11).

4. Part of this book might have been published as early as 1862 under a different title and the work bearing the current title was largely written in the 1870s and 1880s (Xia 1979).

5. A genealogy of New Text Confucianism can be found in Liang Ch'i-ch'ao (1959, 85–91) and Elman (1984, 22–26, 234–242).

6. Kang compared George Washington to the ancient sages of China (Hsiao 1975, 90). A lecturer at the School of Current Affairs in Hunan, Han Wenju, praised America as having the best government and expected that the unification of the world would be achieved through that country (Ding and Zhao 1983, 89).

7. "Episteme" is a term coined by Michel Foucault meaning a "knowledge system" that includes the implication of domination.

8. Kant's *Zum ewigen Frieden* (On perpetual peace) was published in 1795.

9. For the Hunan radical reforms that began in 1897 and suffered the same fate as the Hundred Days Reform in the capital, see Esherick (1976, 13–19).

10. According to Ding Wenjiang and Zhao Fengtian (1983, 88), this radical line had Kang's approval. Wong Young-tsu, on the other hand, dismisses the "revolutionary

intention" of the Kang circle (Wong 1992, 513–544). A distinction needs to be made between the reformist party's loyalty to emperor Guangxu and the party's anti-Manchu sentiments, which still showed even when the reformists faced the rivalry of the revolutionary camp after 1903 (see below).

11. Perhaps one should distinguish between the moderate and the radical elements in the reformist party. If the radicals shared the same anti-Manchu sentiment with Sun Zhongshan's revolutionaries, then their main difference was whether the transformation of China should be effected through the centralized authority of the monarchy. In this respect, Tang Caichang's role in the Independent Army plot of 1900 is especially controversial. (Tang 1984a) and (Kuang 1982) held the view that Tang was actually leaning toward Sun Zhongshan while posing as a Kang supporter. (Chen 1994), on the other hand, argues that Tang manipulated the Sun party to serve the purpose of loyalism.

12. Liang's pan–Asianism is evident in an instalment of "Bianfa tongyi" published in December 1898. The article was serialized from 1896 to 1899, from *Shiwu bao* to *Qingyi bao*, and Philip Huang is misled by the initial date into believing that Liang harbored pan–Asianist sentiments "as early as 1896" (Huang 1972, 48).

13. Konoe Atsumaro was the founder of Toa Dobunkai, a Japanese cultural front in China, and the father of the future wartime premier Fumimaro.

14. It appears that what was novel for Liang was already old in Japan. Tessa Morris-Suzuki points out that after 1890 a growing number of Japanese writers showed a preference for *minzoku* (nation) over *jinshu* (race)—the Japanese equivalent of the Chinese *renzhong*. She thinks that the Japanese were less comfortable with the latter because its usage evoked the sentiment of superiority of the white races. My judgment is that national psychology, no less racist in its implications, was on the rise in the 1890s to redress the shortcomings of biological racial theories. However, as Morris-Suzuki points out, even in the 1930s and 1940s, theorists like Shinmei Masamichi and Tada Tetsuji were still rejecting *jinshu* by devising nonbiological definitions of "nation" (Morris-Suzuki 1998, 87, 98).

15. R.A. Thompson (1978) also discusses these threats under the headings of "the population peril," "the economic peril of oriental immigration," and "economic competition from the Orient."

16. Liang promoted Kang's "religion of the Great Harmony" in a speech to the Japanese Philosophical Society in 1899. He compared Kang's teaching to the European Reformation, which restored the true meaning of Christianity buried under centuries of false teaching. Although Liang saw the Chinese Reformation as liberation rather than the birth of a new official cult, it was to be the one correct path to advance the Chinese people's intelligence and ability (Liang 1899d, 54–61).

17. In Japan, Ranke's exaltation of Lutheranism as the unique spirit of Germany was imitated by Inoue Tetsujiro and Shiratori Kurakichi who privileged Shinto and the divine imperial institution (Tanaka 1993, 56, 65).

18. Liang referred to "national imperialism" in his "Song of the Twentieth century and the Pacific Ocean," written in the few minutes between the last day of the nineteenth century and the first day of the twentieth century, when Liang was crossing the international date-line in the Pacific Ocean, on a ship to Hawaii (Liang 1900a, 19). The "Song" was published in 1902.

19. To the chagrin of Kang, after launching the *Pure Opinion Journal*, Liang had refused to carry a single article by the Emperor Protection Society, under the excuse of maintaining secrecy. At the time of plotting the Independent Army uprising, Liang wrote Kang from Hawaii on April 12, 1900 suggesting the republican alternative in case Emperor Guangxu should die. Yet in his April 28 letter to Sun Zhongshan pro-

posing cooperation, Liang floated the idea of both parties supporting Guangxu as the first president (Ding and Zhao 1983, 238, 221, 258). Liang actually put this idea into his futuristic novel, *The Future of New China* (1902s), in which a Chinese republic has become a reality through reformist means, with a fictional version of Guangxu serving as the first president, who is succeeded by a fictionalized alter ego of Liang himself.

20. After seizing power, Lenin was especially fascinated by Germany's wartime "state capitalism" and thought of transplanting it to Russia as a jumping board to socialism (Pipes 1991, 677–678).

21. The Meirokusha, Minyusha and Seikyosha were intellectual societies with the aim of spreading enlightenment in Meiji Japan.

22. The most sustained discussion is, of course, "On the new people." An early reference to the Chinese people's "slave character" (*nulixing*) was in an April 1900 letter to Kang Youwei (Ding and Zhao 1983, 235).

23. Philip Huang believes that San Francisco's Chinatown greatly distressed Liang, contributing to his conclusion that the Chinese were simply not ready for democracy (Huang 1972, 79). Liang's negative view of the Chinese in general, including the overseas inhabitants, seems to predate his 1903 trip to North America. The alleged "shock" he received from the Chinese community there might have served as an excuse for changing his political position.

24. In a 1902 letter to Kang Youwei, Liang confessed that he had planned with four of Kang's former disciples to write "a huge volume, exposing the shortcomings of Confucianism" (Ding and Zhao 1983, 278).

25. Observations by Anwar Abdel Malek, quoted in Edward Said (1979, 97).

26. This article from Zhang's collected essays published in the Republican era has changed the name of China from *shina* to *zhongxia* in the title, but not in the contents.

27. The caption of the Yellow Emperor's portrait in the volume *The Soul of the Yellow Emperor* (1903) and *The People's Journal* (1905), the organ of the Revolutionary Alliance. In the latter, the Yellow Emperor's portrait was followed by those of Rousseau, Washington, and the ancient Chinese philosopher Mo Di, as icons of nationalism, democracy, and socialism.

28. Marcel Granet believes that Sima Tan and Sima Qian (father and son who, in succession, served as imperial chronicler at the Han court) placed the Yellow Emperor at the beginning of history because their emperor Han Wudi picked yellow as the dynastic color and proclaimed a new calendar in 104 B.C.E. The old cycle had been completed and, with the reign of Wudi, history had begun again (Granet 1950, 46–47). In the ancient cosmic diagram, yellow also occupied the central position.

29. There is an exception, however. In the same year Liang also published a poem after reading the works of Lu You, a "patriotic" poet of the Southern Song Dynasty. The emphasis is again on the cultivation of martial spirit, for he said that Lu, unlike most people, celebrated the joy of joining the army (Liang 1902c). Perhaps Liang was making excuses for himself for moving closer and closer to the last millennium of Chinese history.

30. Official historiography has managed to use Marxist "class analysis" to shore up Han chauvinism, invariably characterizing any centrifugal tendencies of the other nationalities as plots carried out by their "upper-stratum aristocracy" (*shangceng guizu*) in the interest of "separatism." It implies that the interest of the Han majority's own "upper-stratum aristocracy" somehow coincided with that of the nation as a whole. Yet it does not serve the interest of national unity to deny the non-Han peoples an occasional voice at the center. A recent Sichuan TV series inspired by the Southern Song's resistance to the Mongol invasion glorifies the Song heroes and condemns the

Song traitors, but at the end also allows the dying Mongke Khan to say that "all-under-Heaven" should belong to the virtuous.

31. Sun argued that, for the lack of nationalism, the Chinese would suffer the same fate as their former victims—an argument already made by Kang Youwei in 1900 (see the following paragraph in the text).

— 2 —

National Psychology

The displacement of *Da Qing* (the Great Qing—the official name of the Qing Dynasty) by *zhina* or *zhongguo* accompanied a gathering of forces for the radical transformation of China. If elements peripheral to Confucian scholar-officialdom were the vanguard of the 1890s, center stage was now yielded to new intellectuals trained in modern educational institutions. And we find the outlook of the former elements adapting increasingly to that of the latter. Even the plebeian Sun Zhongshan, who had so far worked with overseas Chinese and the Chinese Triads, felt it necessary to tap the new intellectual community, notably its diaspora in Japan.

The new intellectuals were equipped with symbolic capital different from the kind invested in imperial scholar-officialdom. Their utmost concern was how to situate themselves in a modern "nation," a subject increasingly circumscribed by the French Revolution, German nationalist philosophy, and the newly emerging social psychology. These texts were adopted as they went through a Japanese filter. Westernism was now privileged over the indigenous, but Confucian ecumenism faded also because it left little room for the imagination of nation. After a false start in pan–Asianism, the Chinese discussants very quickly appropriated a narrative of nation which, though originally European, was no longer Europe's exclusive intellectual property.

Europe's Seminal Experience

At the very inception of "nation" were the French Revolution and German Romanticism, and they proved to be inescapable for the Chinese. In early modern Europe, rudimentary national sentiment had expressed itself through religious and dynastic struggles. The second half of the eighteenth century saw Frenchmen, disenchanted with absolutism, increasingly switching their allegiance to *la patrie* (Shafer 1955, 108–109; Schama 1989, 37). The French Revolution saw the emergence of a citizenry that enabled popular participation in national affairs. The revolutionary regime attempted to impose the French language on all its citizens—a radical conversion of dynastic subjects into communicative members of a modern nation (Shafer 1955, 123–124).

In neighboring Germany, in the absence of statehood, Romantic thinkers posited "nation" as the subject of history. If the Great Revolution amplified French nationalism, its German counterpart was a reaction against Napoleonic domination. Not in a position to create "citizens" by administrative fiat, German Romantics evoked the "nation" imaginatively. They invented the nation as a community with common descent, language, customs, and national characteristics. In a nutshell, they presumed the preexistence of nationhood as something organic and natural long before state formation. This act prescribed things to come rather than describing the past, therefore producing an inverted image of historical nations.[1]

One may call the French Revolution the *mise-en-scène* of seminal nationalism, and it was neighboring Germany that provided its dramatic theory. German Romantics, in their reaction against French nationalism under the guise of civilization, emphasized the uniqueness of *Kultur*. As poets, they applied the trope of individuality to their "nation," imagined to be in possession of a soul, spirit, or character, just like a person (Kohn 1960, 52–57). National character perceived in this manner was a mystical quality shared by every member of the nation. In the Romantic mode, to sing paeans to the unique character of a nation was also to celebrate its "genius."

The notion of national character underwent a sea change in the later part of the century. It its heyday, Darwinism spawned a host of racial-degeneration theories, and such *fin-de-siècle* pessimism deflated the lofty notion of national character. Its study now became racial psychology, a science for the diagnosis of a nation's *malaise*. As if with a vengeance, racial psychology developed in France after her humiliating defeat by the Germans in the war of 1870–1871, and went on to become a central concern of the emerging modern discipline of social psychology.

Germany and France were part of a West that had achieved world domination by the late nineteenth century, yet their rich contributions to the theory of nation were motivated by national humiliation. Prior to France's discomfiture, Germany was near total subjugation by Napoleon, who reorganized the country into the Confederation of Rhine and assumed the presidency himself. Thus, in nationalist thinking, it seems that the "subaltern" is more vociferous than the power that dominates. Countries fully secure in their strength like England and the United States might be admired by

the Chinese but had little to offer in terms of ideology. The Chinese nationalists also empathized with the Italian *Risorgimento*, the Japanese Meiji
Restoration, and the martyred Poland, but it was the German and French
nationalist experiences that were rich in the realm of theory. Furthermore,
they came from the "center" yet also carried a "subaltern" relevance. Thus,
the national character discourse, with both its Romantic and Darwinian
shades, profoundly affected China of the late Qing period and beyond. As
the earlier Romantic nationalism was sublated by the *fin-de-siècle* psychology of nation, we shall begin with the introduction of social psychology in
China.

The Advent of Social Psychology

Even before the abolition of the imperial examinations (the civil service
examinations centrally controlled by the imperial government and held pe-
riodically), Western social sciences had made inroads into the Chinese educational system. Beginning in 1902, the Qing regime hired Japanese
instructors to teach social sciences in teachers' colleges (Reynolds 1993,
103). They introduced psychology as part of pedagogy, and, dating from
1902, nearly all early Chinese textbooks on the subject were translated from
the Japanese (Ma 1984, 39–43; Wan 1987). In the aftermath of the Boxer
Uprising (1900), the number of Chinese students in Japan gushed from a
trickle to a torrent (Wang 1966, 59, 64), exposing a whole generation to
modern learning and the equally subversive idea of revolution.

Outgrowing Herbert Spencer

According to Kawamura Nozomu, in turn-of-the century Japan psychological interpretation of society, represented by Gabriel Tarde and Franklin
Giddings, began to challenge the dominant organismic school of Auguste
Comte and Herbert Spencer. It not only signaled a revolt of human volition
against official collectivism, but also the outgrowing of synthetic sociology
by specialized social sciences (Kawamura 1973, 280–283). In fact, the psychological school laid at the very threshold of sociology's transition from
grandiose speculative systems to a rigorous modern profession. The Frenchman Tarde laid the foundation of the new sociology by using the mechanism
of "imitation" to explain how society worked. He saw innovations originating in great individuals and society as formed through interactions between creative and imitative minds, which accounted for progress as well
as uniformities. The American Giddings used "imitation," "sympathy,"
"consciousness of kind," and "concerted volition" to explain the formation

of the group mind (Davis Jr. 1968, 89, 47–48). It remained to be seen whether this new trend also affected those Chinese who were schooling in Japan.

The Japanese development coincided with Chinese intellectuals' outgrowing of the mystico-evolutionary cosmology of the 1890s, which was an amalgam of New Text Confucianism and Spencer's synthetic philosophy. New Text Confucianism, albeit couched in evolutionist terms, was largely religious in sentiment, as it attempted to reconcile Confucianism, Buddhism, and Christianity. The Spencerian creed of the human species evolving towards perfection also had a semireligious ring to it (Bury 1932, 337–340). At the turn of the century, with Confucian ecumenism yielding to the *Realpolitik* of "nation" under the shadow of imperialism, a more naturalistic concept of man also emerged among Chinese thinkers. The human spirit was no longer seen as an ether contiguous with a moral universe, now it became "psychology" governed by its own amoral, naturalistic laws (Furth 1983, 351). In short, secularization and specialization, the unmistakable symptoms of modernity, had set in.

One Alternative: The State as Organism

Amid this epistemic change, Spencer's philosophy was also ripe for rupture, torn as it was between his defense of individual rights and his organismic view of society. This tension was exploited by both liberals and conservatives in early Meiji Japan. In the later Meiji period, due to Spencer's own conservative advice to the Japanese government and the abandonment of liberalism by the upper classes, who looked toward strong government leadership, the conservative version of Spencerism became dominant (Nagai 1954; Liang 1903c, 99–101). It was at this juncture that the radicals presented social psychology as an alternative. Meanwhile, ultra-conservatives like Kato Hiroyuki had also outgrown Spencerism by 1900 and come to rely increasingly on Prussian concepts of statism to defend their position. A major influence on Kato was the naturalized German, Johann Kaspar Bluntschli (Abosch 1964, 357, 362, 389–90, 405–6). The latter's teaching, though known as the "organismic theory of the state," in fact also had a psychological dimension missing in Spencer's organicism.

Kato, in his turn, influenced Liang Qichao after the latter's arrival in Japan. In 1903, as Liang's antirevolutionary position hardened, he was drawn directly to the statism of Johann Bluntschli and Gustav Bornhak. The about-face had been in the offing for a while, for the year before Liang had produced a translation of Bluntschli's work under the title, *An Outline of the Theory of the State*.[2] The Swiss thinker saw in the state the highest form of organism, far above nation and people. He stipulated the thesis of "no State, no Nation," for "the Nation comes into being with the creation of the State" (Bluntschli 1885, 86).[3] If the radical Liang had championed people's sovereignty from below, he now opted for "state rights" aloof from the general will of its citizens and sanctioned by its own reason. In Bluntschli's terms, it is pitting *Statssouveränität* against *Volkssouveränität* (Bluntschli 1885, 500), yet Liang went further than his master, who insisted that the state should protect individual rights. For Liang, the Chinese nation was to be forged by the state, for the Chinese at present had only "the qualification of tribesmen, not that of nationals." The supremacy of state over nation and society allowed him to refute the divisive racialist-republican revolution directed at the Manchu Dynasty: "What is most wanting and urgent in today's China is organic unity and strong order; liberty and equality are secondary concerns" (Zhongguo zhi xinmin 1903, 4).

The Other Alternative: Nation as Group Mind

The Chinese revolutionary camp in Japan took a different turn in the revolt against Spencerism. In 1902 Zhang Taiyan translated *Sociology* by the Japanese socialist Kishimoto Nobuta, and in the preface he hailed the American sociologist Giddings' concepts of "the consciousness of kind" and "imitation" as superior to Spencer's "misleading physiological jargon" (Zhang 1902a, in Jiang and Zhu 1981, 145–146). Wang Jingwei and Zhu Zhixin, spokesmen of the Chinese Revolutionary Alliance, later challenged Liang Qichao's statism by resorting to social-psychological reasoning. Wang, in refuting Bornhak's monarchism, saw "nation" as the concerted wills of individuals and "social psychology," as equal to the aggregate of "individual psychologies" (Jingwei, 1906, 8, 16). For Zhu, the Qing state was based on legal right but not on psychological cohesion. Legal statism can be used to justify monarchism and even slavery, but patriotism is generated only by "psychological statism," a willing and conscious identity of nationals based on a common historical heritage—a statism that would survive even the loss of statehood (Xuanjie 1908, 1–23). The anti-Manchu camp went beyond the *Rechtsstaat* to opt for the *Volksstaat*, which was not only forged from below but based on racial feelings.

However, it is simplistic to see the two camps, reform and revolution, neatly divided along the battleline between organicism and social psychology. Both camps strived for change in China, and their competition was not a replica of the rivalry between Japanese conservatives and radicals. At the end of chapter 1, I showed Jiang Guanyun resorting to social-psychological reasoning in the pages of the *New People's Magazine*. Liang

Qichao, on various occasions, also referred to Gustave Le Bon, the spokes-man of the French school of collective mind. The school was antirevolu-tionary in its ideology and on friendly terms with the organicists (Nye 1975, 62–63). For Liang, the distinction between organicism and social psychol-ogy was probably not very pronounced, because in his perception Le Bon and Bluntschli complemented each other. Even Japanese academics at the time discerned a difference between the old and the new organicism and saw the latter as leaning toward social psychology. In fact, Liang translated an essay by a certain Onozuka Kiheiji, who, seeing the two trends as over-lapping, discerned two kinds of organismic theory of the state: The age-old "natural organicism" descended from Plato, and the new "psychological organicism" of Bluntschli (Yinbing 1906b, 10–12). As we shall show below, Bluntschli's theory, though not ostensibly psychological, was readily an-nexed by the emerging discourse on national psychology.

Spencer Dies Hard

Certain Spencerian concepts still persisted among the Chinese discussants, adding more confusion to their imperfect grasp of the nascent discipline of social psychology. Spencer, neglecting the whole problematic of the psy-chological cementing of human groups, "remained essentially individual-istic in his discussion of human relations." To account for how society existed above individuals, he fell back upon the biological metaphor of "organic interdependence." As individual psychology was the only one at his disposal, he had to resort to a mechanical analogy to explain group character to the effect that "the properties of the units [i.e., individuals] determine the properties of the aggregate [i.e., society]" (Karpf 1932, 29, 35, 37).

This view continued to affect Chinese intellectuals' understanding of so-ciety at the time. Both Liang Qichao and Deng Shi of the National Essence school referred to "the group as *tuodu* [total], and the individual as *yaoni* [units]," and saw "*tuodu*'s character and shape as being determined by the *yaoni*" (Liang 1903g, 1; Zheng Shiqu 1992, 50). When the *People's Journal*, in refuting Liang's legal statism, defined the nation as the concerted wills of individuals and social psychology as the aggregate of individual psy-chologies, it was confusing Rousseau's general will and Spencer's reduc-tionism with "social psychology." Social psychology was quite the opposite. As a reaction against nineteenth-century introspective psychology, social psychology saw society as the manifestation of a group mind supra-summative to the aggregate of individual minds, or went further, eliminating individual psychology altogether by treating it as purely a social artifact.

The Historical Backdrop

Social psychology, a product of its time, cannot help bearing on the issue of nation. With the spread of urbanism and universal male suffrage, the West in the *fin de siècle* experienced the onset of mass society. Globally speaking, the second half of the nineteenth century was also punctuated by efforts of modern nation-building, which inevitably mobilized mass consciousness. Both Germany and Italy had completed their national unification by 1871, after having weathered the stormy 1860s. It happened that in the same decade China and Japan also launched their modernization programs. Russia ended serfdom in 1861, and the United States emerged in 1865 from the Civil War a new union, prompting Canada to confederate in 1867. The same year also saw Mexico regaining her independence from a French puppet. In 1901 Australia became a commonwealth, and New Zealand achieved dominion status in 1907. Meanwhile, the Indian National Congress, launched in 1885, was fighting for nationhood. By the turn of the century, pan–Germanism and pan–Slavism had turned virulent; the disintegration of Austria-Hungary and the Ottoman Empire also began in earnest, releasing an inordinate amount of ethnic hatred. The same forces that had underlain the breakup of multiracial empires were also at work in national integration. For countries that had already achieved political unification, the same period witnessed intense efforts to transform peasants and immigrants into citizens with a "national" consciousness.[4]

Small wonder that nation occupied a central place in the intellectual life of the time, comparable to the preeminence of gender in ours (on which we shall focus in the last chapter). By the end of the nineteenth century, theories about nation had become a booming industry. Two Chinese works in the 1930s, which summed up the state of the art, may serve as an overview of the discourse. In 1937 Luo Jialun listed the key factors of "nation" as race, geographical environment, population, the economy, politics, religion, language and writing, education and culture, but above all, history. As for "national character," he reasoned that it began with rudimentary "sympathy," which facilitated "imitation," paving the way to a "collective psychology" and a "national consciousness" but eventually the fruition of a "national style" (Luo 1937, 97–111). Wang Shaolun in his *Outline of the Philosophy of Nation* (1938) summarizes the scholarly tradition on nation with schools emphasizing native soil, blood, race, culture, language, common interest, and psychology (Wang 1946, 12–16). The last-mentioned, by the early twentieth century, not only thrived on the prestige of social psychology, its concept of a relatively stable psychological formation on a collective scale was able to include culture and coordinate factors of both heredity and environment in a dynamic scheme of historical evolution. It is also the most relevant to the notion of "national character."

Historical Race versus Natural Race

Introducing a New Racial Concept

A nation, as a psychological or historical race, is not to be confused with biological race, which is only one of its ingredients. In this light, I reex-amine the controversy about Zhang Taiyan being a "racialist revolutionary" (Rankin 1970, 55–56; Wong 1989, 61–64; Laitinen 1990, 94). Intriguingly, in 1902 Zhang used the notion of "historical race" to undermine Kang Youwei's attempt to lump the Han and the Manchus in the same "natural race." For Zhang, pure races no longer existed, the long history of the Chinese was a chronicle of racial amalgamation, and the crime of the Man-chus was their refusal to assimilate (Tang and Luo 1986, 48–49). As for Kang's natural-race reasoning, it had been shared earlier by Zhang himself. It harked back to a brief phase when Chinese reformers were caught be-tween ecumenism and racialism, giving rise to schemes such as a yellow-white condominium over the darker races or the forming of a pan–Asian union against the whites. As indicated earlier, between the two poles of ecumenism and biological racialism, "nation" was left in limbo.

Zou Rong's treatise in 1903 did no better, as he tried to stir up hatred of the Manchus by placing them among the "Siberian races" (Zou 1958, 25–26). The more sensible argument of Zhang Taiyan was later picked up by Wang Jingwei who wrote in 1905: "Sociologists used to say that a nation must put up a racial barrier to maintain purity, but this measure would weaken the race and make it unfit for survival; only by extensively absorb-ing different races can it become stronger and stronger socially" (Jingwei 1905, 4). For Wang, the crimes of the Manchus were not only refusal to assimilate but their discrimination against the Han.

Thus Zhang initiated a line of argument radically different from Kang Youwei's biological racialism, which led the latter astray from national-ism—to indulge, in his *The Book of Great Harmony*, in an ecumenist dreamland where yellow and white races will meld and the darker ones become extinct. Zhang was more conversant with the latest Western thinking on the subject of nation. Notions of "natural race" and "historical race" undoubtedly had been around for some time. In Japan, Kato Hiroyuki re-ferred to *Naturvölker* as early as 1893, when he argued that "unevolved, natural peoples" no longer existed in historical times and if they did they were closer to the higher animals than to the advanced human races (Davis

1996, 40). Yet definitive works such as Alfred Vierkandt's *Naturvölker und Kulturvölker* (1896) appeared only recently. In 1903, an article in a Chinese student journal in Japan referred to this binarism in exactly those German terms (Liu 1903, 4).

Yet as a propagandist, Zhang Taiyan was not always consistent. The latest Western theory appealed only to a sophisticated audience who felt it imperative to be intellectually up-to-date. On the other hand, the indigenous craze of genealogical studies was also evident in Zhang's usage of the term "surname-race" (*zhongxing*). This line of reasoning grounded ethnicity in the genealogy of a kinship group—in the Chinese case, it was common descent from the Yellow Emperor. When a nation was defined by blood ties, in the manner of the common Jewish descent from Abraham, the Manchus simply cannot become Han people by accepting Chinese culture (Chow 1997). The Manchus had to go under one reasoning or another, meanwhile this theoretical high-handedness allowed Han nationalists to claim both purity and hybridity among their race's superior qualities. A study of Japan in the same period shows that both images of racial purity and racial hybridity were used to prove Japan's superiority among nations. "The first depicted the Japanese as a racially homogeneous group literally descended from a common blood line whose senior branch was the imperial family," in much the same way as the Chinese were all related to the legendary Yellow Emperor. The second stressed the hybridity of the Japanese racial origins as a proof of Japan's ability to absorb other Asian nations to form a greater Asian community (Morris-Suzuki 1998, 88–95). A similar belief also attained cliché status in Republican China, to the effect that the "Chinese nation" always absorbed her conquerors, including the hated Manchus. In having their cake and eating it, few Han nationalists realized that, in the binarism of historical versus natural race, each was present because of the other.

The "Racial Science"

An up-to-date inventory of racial theories can be found in Yan Fu's 1906 lecture series. The popular determinants were: Blumenbach's using color, Retzius' using cranium, the more recent approach of using hair, but for Yan the "most reliable" was language. This factor removed race from the realm of nature, enabling him to speculate on a common origin of the yellow and white races. Yan Fu put his finger on the crux of the matter when he said that none of these factors was adequate in explaining nation-formation or why America and England were separate countries (Yan 1906, 1246).

Apparently, Chinese and Japanese thinkers at that time were enthralled with the racial science of the West—a "science" perfected in the span of over a century. In the first academic human racial classification, made in the 1770s at Hanover's Göttingen University, J.F. Blumenbach placed whites—whom he named "Caucasian" for the first time in 1795—at the top of the hierarchy (Bernal 1987, 27, 219). Between 1770 and 1810, other Göttingen scholars transformed history-writing from the chronicles of kings and wars to the "biographies" of peoples and developed an academic theory of *Zeitgeist* to the effect that each age and place had a special mentality (Ibid., 217). The Romantic movement also injected a linguistic awareness, which gave birth to categories such as the "Indo-European" or "Indo-Germanic" in 1816 and 1823, respectively (Ibid., 227). Meanwhile, Barthold Niebuhr, who was hailed by Jules Michelet for having discovered the "ethnical principle of history," reinstated biological racialism at the expense of the linguistic (Ibid., 305).

These European developments were faithfully summarized in Liang Qichao's "New History" (1902L). First he grounded history in geography, which in Romantic thinking was inextricably linked to *Volk*. Liang then criticized traditional Chinese historiography for privileging only individuals at the expense of the group. It erred in "not treating great individuals as representatives of Epoch (*shidai*), but instead treating Epoch as the appendage of great individuals." The subject of history should be the study of "interaction between groups and connection between epochs." Liang paid special attention to the "relationship between history and race" (Liang 1902L, 3–4, 11). For the racial division of mankind he referred to, among others, Blumenbach's fivefold taxonomy, which he simplified into the yellow, the white, and the black. But the eclectic Liang soon complicated this biological table by introducing linguistic categories, namely, in his subdivision of the white race into Hamitic, Semitic, and Aryan, and had the latter further broken down into the Greco-Romans, the Celts, the Teutons, and the Slavs. Liang displayed the confusion of an eager student who tried to absorb all that was labelled as "new" and "scientific."

The Racial Hierarchy

Liang's "New History" also classified the races of mankind into the "historical races" and the "nonhistorical races." Only the yellow and white races were "historical," a category he further divided into "world-historical races" and "non–world-historical races." So far, only "the Aryans among the whites" had entered the world-historical class. Among the Aryans, the Teutons, especially the Anglo-Saxons, had become the "undisputed masters of the world history of today" (Liang 1902L, 12, 20). In Liang's eclectic picture, there was still a space with no account for the psychological cohesion of individual nations. This lacuna was filled by the so-called psychology of nation, which Liang would increasingly turn to after 1902.

As a late nineteenth-century development, this new development was the final crowning of Western racial science. We find Le Bon, the doyen of the new "psychology of peoples," having already incorporated in his theory the same kind of racial hierarchy as Liang's. Le Bon's "science" was largely about artificial or historical races. For him, racial purity might be found among savages, but "historical races" were "created by the chances of conquest, immigration, politics, etc." Le Bon's racial scale ran as following: (1) the primitive races, (2) the inferior races, namely, the Negroes, (2) the average races, such as "the Chinese, the Japanese, the Mongolians, and the Semitic peoples," (4) the superior races, which include only "the Indo-European peoples." And, within the latter, the Anglo-Americans have eclipsed the Latins in modern times. Although this is unalloyed racism, Le Bon did not use biological traits but historical achievements, notably nationhood and national-imperialist capacity, as criteria for setting up his "psychological hierarchy of races" (Le Bon 1974, 15–16, 25–30, 50). Le Bon's order of things was a taxonomy that, like Liang's, privileged those races capable of forming historical "nations," especially favoring those currently in the rank of global domination.

How did this racial hierarchy help the Chinese—or Le Bon's fellow Frenchmen, for that matter? Contrary to Edward Said, Le Bon's psychology of nation was largely for domestic consumption: To blame the nation's problems on the Left, which he regarded as the worst manifestation of the anarchic Latin character.[5] As for the Chinese, they were above all overawed by the racial "science" from the West. They became complicit with its racial hierarchy because it had reserved for China a place among the "historical races," simply by not being very far below the white vanguard. The awareness of being one notch below could be a very powerful impetus to join the race, as it at the same time placed oneself above the other colored peoples.

The Enigma of "National Psychology"

Nation as a historical race implied a psychological dimension, and the social psychology of the time complied with the notion of the "group mind." This concept was to be discredited after 1920 by behaviorism, but at the turn of the century it was in its heyday. "Group mind" was central to the Chinese imagination of nation as it began in earnest at exactly this time.

In 1903, an article in a Chinese student journal in Japan, *The Voice of*

Han, stated that historical study should take into consideration a society's physical, cultural, and psychological conditions. The last it subdivided into individual psychology, social psychology, and national psychology. The author defined "social psychology" as the "psychology of the epoch," which is the mean psychology of the people in a certain period and would change over time. "National psychology," on the other hand, is the permanent psychology of a people, equivalent to its national character (Anonymous 1903h, 1–9). It was around 1903 that "national psychology" (*guomin xinli*) became a chic term in Chinese discussions on nation. What was its original in a Western language?

German Völkerpsychologie?

The first candidate that comes to mind is *Völkerpsychologie*, a product of German Romanticism. In the struggle for liberation against Napoleon, the German patriot Father Jahn urged the founding of a new discipline to study the *Volk* (Kohn 1960, 88). By mid-nineteenth century, this call was answered in *Völkerpsychologie*. An early application of the term was made by Wilhelm von Humboldt, as a descriptive approach to the cultural characterization of nations (Karpf 1932, 48). The psychologist Wilhelm Wundt also named the obscure Karl Hillebrand as a representative of this approach, which he regarded as radically different from that of the second school bearing the same name launched by Moritz Lazarus and Heymann Steinthal in 1860, and inherited by Wundt (Wundt 1916, 1–3). It was to culminate in Wundt's ten-volume magnum opus on the subject concluded in 1920. Lazarus and Steinthal defined the discipline as the study of the historical development of the *Volksgeist* in general and the *Volksgeists* of particular peoples; in both cases, the aim was to discover the underlying psychological principles. Their project was to study language, religion, mythology, customs, literature, and art as elements of collective mental life. Wundt preferred to focus on the general, relegating the study of particular peoples to ethnology and philology, but his own attempt at formulating four psychological eras of mankind was "essentially a matter of anthropological concern." This school fell short of social psychology as it simply extended the principles of individual psychology to the collective, even though, as an antidote to biologism, it helped to boost the psychological study of culture (Karpf 1932, 47–48, 58–59, 61, 64).

If *Völkerpsychologie* had an affinity with philology, ethnology, and anthropology, it was an unlikely candidate for our "psychology of nation." In German historiography of the 1890s, we find Karl Lamprecht attempting to convert the discipline into a study of the collective psychology of nation, as he saw Germany history in terms of "the manifestation of the changes in the German *Volksseele*" (Breisach 1994, 279). Lamprecht's belief that "history is primarily a socio-psychological science" was shared by the American school of New History as represented by James Harvey Robinson (Lamprecht 1905, 3; Iggers 1997, 32). It testified to the rising popularity of social psychology in the historical profession, but the advocates did not found a school called national psychology.

French Psychologie des Peuples?

That leaves the French school of *psychologie des peuples*, the English renditions of which are "psychology of peoples" or "racial psychology." Le Bon was a founder of this school, which failed to find a niche in the academic system (Nye 1975, 4). This peripheral status was compensated for by the immense popularity of his writings, which, compared to the works of the academics, always had a more direct bearing on current political issues. As a conservative liberal of the French Third Republic, he used his ideas to combat the baneful effects of the French Revolution and socialism. Less rationalist in outlook than Tarde and Giddings, Le Bon was better known for his psychology of the crowd, which sought to explain mob phenomena by means of suggestion, imitation, credulity, and mental contagion. This theory had more impact in China in the Republican period (Sun 1991). Although he is largely presented as a mob psychologist in the histories of Western thought, his psychology of nations in *Lois Psychologiques de l'Évolution des Peuples* (1894) was more relevant to the history of late Qing China.

If Romantic nationalism was the response of German intellectuals to Napoleonic domination, then as if with a vengeance, racial psychology developed in France after her humiliating defeat by the Germans in the Franco-Prussian war. To excoriate the French nation, Le Bon exalted the Teutonic character (though opting for the Anglo-Americans rather than his German neighbors) over that of the Latins (Nye 1975, 19–36). It was a *fin-de-siècle* pathologization of the Romantic "nation." Late Qing patriots readily resonated with this pathology because they found their country in similar straits.

An excerpt from Liang Qichao's North American *Travels*, written in 1903 (published in 1904), described the deplorable behavior of overseas Chinese communities as a logical manifestation of an all-pervasive "national psychology, according to Le Bon's theory" (Liang 1904b, 189–190). A section of "On the New People" written in 1904 cited an interesting observation by Le Bon.[6] In 1903, Liang Qichao's brother Liang Qixun commented on Le Bon's "psychology of nation" (*guomin xinlixue*), as opposed to the "physiology of the state" (*guojia shenglixue*) of Comte and Bluntschli (Liang Qixun 1903, no. 25, 2). This distinction reflected the animus between social psychology and organicism in Japan at the time.

As indicated above, this division was not as sharp as it appeared, and both rivals thrived under an overarching Darwinian framework. In spite of his psychological jargon, Le Bon extended the biological metaphor to the "historical race," which possessed "a mental constitution" as unvarying as "its anatomical constitution." A nation, "a psychological species," is shaped by its unique historical inheritance just as "an anatomical species" is determined by its biological heredity. A nation has inherited certain shared "moral and intellectual characteristics," which not only form the foundation of all its institutions, arts, and beliefs, but also determine its course of evolution. The sum total of these characteristics forms "the soul of a race," which is also its character. A racial soul is "the synthesis" of a nation's "entire past," or "the inheritance of all its ancestors." He put a premium on stable hereditary traits: "the first and certainly the most important [influence on the individual] is the influence of ancestors," and "the weakest, is the influence of environment" (Le Bon 1974, 5–6, 9, 15–16, 18). This dreadful stranglehold of the dead on the living directly contributed to Lu Xun's "gate of darkness" imagery in the Republican era (see chapter 4).

In 1904, Liang Qichao formulated his view of a nation's historical inheritance by combining Darwinian "heredity" with Buddhist "karma." Buddhism definitely twisted biological heredity in a mentalistic direction as Liang expounded his Buddhist evolutionism unabashedly in psychological terms: "The world is produced by the psychologies of all of mankind in the world, a society is produced by the psychologies of all its members, just as an individual is produced by his individual psychology." Even though he unwittingly retained the mechanistic Spencerian view of "units" adding up to the "total" and mistook it for social psychology, he was in a mentalistic mood. Liang used the term "heredity" interchangeably with character (*xingge*), which was "the sum total of experience, conduct, habits, and traits one transmits to the progeny." His comparison of mental constitution—the moral character of a nation—to biological heredity is akin to Le Bon's. Tilted more toward mentalism by Buddhism, his psychologized "heredity" is a cultural bequest to one's descendants that can be purposively produced. His Buddho-Darwinism is less pessimistic than Le Bon's version—for one emphasizes "descendants," the other, "ancestors"—but there are hints of the influence of the French thinker. In the same essay Liang says: "Today the science of 'national psychology' and 'social psychology' is steadily developing. What is national psychology? What is social psychology? It is that deathless something [i.e., heredity] that the dead of an entire nation or society bequeath to their descendants" (Liang 1904d, 2–4; Pusey 1983, 303).

In Le Bon's opinion, it is "character" and "intelligence" that distinguish superior races from inferior ones. Of the two, character is by far the more important factor, for high intelligence unaccompanied by character is a sign of "decadence." Le Bon defined character as "perseverance, energy, and the power of self-control, faculties more or less dependent on the will" (Le Bon 1974, 31–33). Liang could not have agreed more, for, in "On the New People" and elsewhere, he never tired of stressing the Chinese need for character-building, i.e., to inculcate in the national character "Western" qualities such as perseverance (*yili*), the adventurous and enterprising spirit (*maoxian jinqu zhi jingshen*), and self-mastery (*zizhi*) (Chang 1971, 205).

The Bluntschli Factor

At this point, a caveat is necessary to the effect that Le Bon's *psychologie des peuples* was not the totality of "national psychology" as the Chinese understood it. His school, as a rather late phenomenon, was able to cash in on the *fin-de-siècle* psychological craze, but a greater part of its content was not new and was traceable to German sources. As shown earlier, *Völkerpsychologie* came in two versions: The earlier one (Humboldt, Hillebrand) applied the descriptive approach to national character, thus lacking the theoretical finesse of social-psychological reasoning; the later version (summed up by Wundt) was both theoretical and "psychological," yet more the precursor of anthropology than of national psychology. It seems that the Germans had thus yielded the field of "national psychology" to the French school. However, much of what Le Bon said could be found in Bluntschli as well—under the rubric not of psychology but of the theory of the state.

The distinction between "natural races" and "historical races" can be found in Bluntschli, who also had a grasp of the supra-summative nature of the group mind that eluded Spencer: "We are justified, then, in speaking of a national spirit (*Volksgeist*) and a national will (*Volkswille*) which is something more than the mere sum of the spirit and will of the individuals composing the Nation" (Bluntschli 1885, 85, 91). In his view, "if a whole Nation or the main part of it belongs to one people, it is naturally pervaded by the common spirit, character, language and custom of that people. If, on the other hand, it is composed of parts of different peoples, it has less community of feelings and institutions than a People" (Bluntschli 1885, 87). This thesis, anticipating the social-psychological concept of sympathy, was echoed by Le Bon in his belief that a nation's racial soul is ill-formed if it is composed of heterogeneous peoples, a problem afflicting France, in comparison to the more integrated English people (Le Bon 1974, 57–58).

Bluntschli's theory of the state was first published in 1852 and brought to a conclusion in 1876, not only anterior to the social-psychological fad, but it closely predated Darwinism (1859). Its closer affinity with the German Romantic cult of nation was evident in his concepts of *Volksgeist* and *Volkswille*. His ascribing a personality and a masculine gender to the state had nothing in common with Darwinian thinking, but the organismic metaphor was in tune with an age when biologism was hegemonic. I have shown how Le Bon also resorted to organismic analogies in his "psychology." Coming from the other end, Bluntschli's personality simile inevitably took on a psychological hue. As a student of the "group mind" school points out, to liken the spirit of a nation to the individual mind is to see it as "an organised system of mental and psychical forces" (McDougall 1920, 142).

Bluntschli did not develop the psychological implications because in the 1850s social psychology was hardly in place, whereas Le Bon's theory, taking shape in the 1890s, carried the weight of Gabriel Tarde's and Emile Durkheim's authority (Karpf 1932, 134–135). In attacking the problem of nation formation, Bluntschli's theory was less elaborate than Le Bon's. In terms of state-building, Le Bon's psychology was less adequate and had a more pathological import, evident in its fuelling of Liang Qichao's denigration of the Chinese national character. Bluntschli linked nation-building directly with state-building and this, as a more robust version of national psychology (albeit without the jargon), was also used by the revolutionary camp, notably Wang Jingwei and possibly Sun Zhongshan. What appealed to the revolutionary camp was Bluntschli's view of state right as embodied in law, in contrast to Liang Qichao's peculiar reading of him as a defender of constitutional monarchy (Xia 1991, 88–89).

National Spirit and National Soul

At the turn of the century, together with "national psychology," new phrases like "national soul" (*guohun* or *minzu hun*) and "national spirit" (*minzu jingshen*) also entered the Chinese language. In a 1899 essay, Liang Qichao called out for the "soul" of China, modelling such a soul on the "soul of Japan"—the way of the samurai (Liang 1899h, 37–39). His rival, the National Essence school, never tired of reiterating that national learning was the national soul (Ding 1995, 2). In a manifesto, the anti-Manchu Southern Society also exclaimed: "The nation exists if the nation has a soul; the nation perishes if the nation loses its soul" (Zhang 1990, 132). They appeared to be adaptations from terms of French and German origins.

From Montesquieu to the German Romantics

In the West, the earliest traceable usage of "national spirit" was Montes-quieu's *"l'esprit général d'une nation"* in his *De L'esprit des Lois* (1748), which Yan Fu translated into Chinese in 1909 and rendered the term as *guomin jingshen*. In 1754, Voltaire covered, in his *Essai sur les moeurs et l'esprit des nations*, the Chinese, Indian, Persian, and Islamic civilizations. The German adaptation of the term first appeared in Friedrich von Moser's 1765 pamphlet, *Von dem deutschen Nationalgeist* (Kohn 1944, 350, 371, 374). Later it was better known in the form of *Volksgeist*, which was pop-ularized by Herder and Hegel.

"National soul" was a distinctly Romantic concept as it first appeared in 1814 as *Nationalsseele* during the war of liberation against Napoleon (Schulz 1942, 182). Later, when Wundt was confronted with the problem of the group mind, he preferred "to call it the *Volksseele*, a less objective term than the more commonly used *Volk[s]geist*" (Boring 1968, 584). Wundt's usage, shying away from the objective spirit of Johann Gottfried von Herder and G.W.F. Hegel, is more akin to Le Bon's psychologized *l'âme des races*. Predictably, Chinese users inherited the confusion. When those terms were used in the Romantic mode, they were cultic in import and uplifting in effect. At other times, when the Chinese users equated "national soul" to the *fin-de-siècle* "racial mind," it was psychologized and pathologized, with a depressing effect. Those terms, with their tangled meanings, came to inform the national-psychology discourse shared by the reformists and the radicals.

Spirit and Soul: Which Is the Evil Double?

This tangled way of thinking is evident in Liang Qichao. Even in his most devastating view of the Chinese national character, he affirmed "national spirit" as the fountainhead of nationalism. In 1903, a radical student journal, *Jiangsu*, carried a fuller exposition on the national spirit. It stated that history and land were the vessels of national spirit. A Chinese person might admire the West, but he is bound to love his own country, due to uniquely Chinese "ancestral blood, social habits, and personal feelings." National spirit originated in history and the author was proud of China's long history and her achievements. Up to this point in the essay, "national spirit" serves the same exaltational function as that used by the German Romantics. The purpose of the essay, however, turns out to be condemning as much as it exalts. To the author, "history" carried some ambivalent baggage. In the second half of China's history, she was often conquered by alien races from the north—alluding to the Manchus' share of the blame for the decline of China's national spirit. But the author also attributed this degeneration to the Oriental denigration of the individual and China's seclusion from the world, resulting in the effeminacy of the modern Chinese (Anonymous 1903d, no. 7, 6–8). Because national spirit had failed him, so "national soul," another rhetorical device, came to the author's rescue. He thought that China's soul was still intact, despite her conquest by the northern barbarians. Yet "national soul" turned out to be an equally treacherous concept. A product of the Romantic imagination, it had been mediated by the racial psychology of the late nineteenth century. The author, in using this concept, was confronted with the low level of psychological integration of the Chinese due to undeveloped communication, resulting in regional differences. The northern Chinese were martial in spirit, but lacked "political capabilities." The customs of Fujian and Guangdong were most different from the rest of the country. He saw his own Jiangsu natives as the most "effeminate" and disappointing (Anonymous 1903d, no. 8, 3–5). In short, Chinese people lacked "sympathy," the cement of a collective racial consciousness. Thus, it appeared that Chinese "land," the other vessel of Chinese national spirit, also offered little consolation, for it was the disjointed body of an equally malformed national soul.

The distinction between national spirit and national soul was not at all clear. One Chinese author defined national spirit as "national characteristics," which constituted the soul of a national organism. "In terms of content, it is called the national spirit; in formal terms, it is called the national soul" (Anonymous 1903e, 17). One way or another, Chinese discussants attempting to imagine a nationhood for their country by means of an assumed national spirit or national soul were often let down by those concepts. "National spirit," a precursor and an objectivist version of our modern notion of national identity, was an indispensable impetus to nationalism, but China's national spirit left a lot to be desired. The notion of national soul, defined as a racial mind cemented by the psychological mechanism of sympathy, tended to highlight its absence in China. Thus the Chinese intellectuals' semiotic exercise to invent their "nation" was subverted by the very conceptual tools employed. The subversion was then exploited to serve exhortatory purposes—to arouse their compatriots in the face of "national" emergency.

Innate or Implanted?

The Chinese discussants were also faced with the dilemma of having to import a foreign soul but at the same time keeping the old one as a matter of identity. In 1903, the *Zhejiang Tide* carried an essay on the national soul, asserting that a modern nation was formed from the "common will" of the people, unlike the premodern state based on "the power of one man"—the despot. This Rousseauist argument also echoed Giddings' social-psychological notion of concerted volition. The author urged the transformation of China's national soul in order for her to survive in the modern world. In this sense, national soul was something that needed to be created and it would be stillborn if "vile old habits" fostered by despotism were not eradicated. An aporia ensued: China was able to establish herself as a "historical race" in the world precisely due to her deeply rooted characteristics, hence they must be taken into consideration in the forging of a national soul (Feisheng 1903, 2–3, 16, 12).

For another radical student, a nation as an "organism" must also have a "soul." He admitted that this soul was a Western concept, for the Chinese traditionally regarded soul as a haunting apparition. The very alien nature of both "organism" and "soul" opened the gate to foreign influence. The author lamented that the Chinese soul, once great, had degenerated into the soul of the slave, the concubine, the prisoner, the entertainer. The "calling of the soul," in the manner of ancient sorcery, was inadequate. China's old soul, in order to regenerate, needed to absorb the "essences" of foreign countries and they were five in number. The first, "the venturesome soul," was exemplified by Columbus, Magellan, Captain Cook, and Livingstone. The second, "the martial soul," was embodied in the spirit of Sparta, the ancient Romans, and the modern Bismarckian principle of "iron and blood." The third, "the knight-errant soul," lost in China due to Confucian dominance, can be retrieved by imitating Franklin, Jefferson, Danton, Robespierre, Garibaldi, Bakunin, Saigo Takamori and Miyazaki Torazo. The fourth, "the social soul," was to be based on "the economic revolution [i.e., socialism] which had yet to occur in Europe," but nonetheless useful as a "gunpowder fuse" for the political revolution in China. The fifth, "the demonic soul," was desirable for conducting clandestine activities of subversion and assassination against the Manchus (Zhuang 1903, 1–9).

In 1904, Liang Qichao collected the stories of the assassins of ancient China in his "China's bushido" for the purpose of inculcating martial spirit in his countrymen. The same assassins were eulogized by Liu Shipei and his associates in the National Essence school who saw assassination both as a means to overthrow the Manchus and to "revive national spirit" (Bernal 1976, 100).

Souls Multiply

The multiplicity of souls seemed to be a Japanese elaboration on a German Romantic idea—its heroic overtone bears little resemblance to the pathologized "racial soul" of late nineteenth-century thinking. One Matsumura Kaiseki discerned four great souls among European races, the secret of their strength. They were: the venturesome soul, the religious soul, the knight's soul, and the democratic soul (Feisheng 1903, 7–10). In the same period, Chen Duxiu's journal in Shanghai, the *National Daily Gazette*, also featured an article, "The Chinese soul," in which Matsumura's influence is unmistakable. The author averred that China lacked the four "national souls" of the Europeans and Americans: The ocean-faring "commercial soul"; the altruistic and martyrdom-seeking "religious soul"; the defiant and aggressive "knightly soul"; the freedom-loving and antidespotic "democratic soul" (Anonymous 1904b, 69).

In 1903, Chinese students in Japan were aroused by the news of Russia's refusal to terminate the occupation of Manchuria since the Boxers Uprising of 1900. The students formed an Anti-Russian Volunteer Corps and engaged in military drill, with the aim of going to Manchuria to fight the enemy (Price 1974, 119). The Corps emulated the 300 Spartans who defied the mighty host of king Xerxes of Persia. Lu Xun wrote an article for the occasion, "The Soul of Sparta," which appeared in the *Zhejiang Tide* (Lu 1903a). The Chinese cult of Sparta seemed to be inspired by a Japanese cult linking bushido with the Spartan martial spirit.[7] The Spartan connection was already in the offing when Liang Qichao in 1899 equated the Yamato soul with the samurai spirit, hoping to instil a similar martial ethos among his countrymen. He then published in 1902 a short history of Sparta, glorifying its "martial spirit," and attributing it to the "Spartan national education" (Liang 1902k).

The "soul" rhetoric was the rage of the time. A Chinese student journal published in Tokyo in 1904 was called *The Women's Soul*. In Shanghai, volumes by the names *The Soul of the Yellow Emperor* and *The Racial Soul* appeared in 1903 and 1904, respectively, and a novel, *The Soul of Rousseau*, in 1905 (Zhang 1954, 285, 289, 292–293).[8] In 1903, the American W.E.B. Du Bois also published his *The Souls of Black Folk*.

National Psychology and National Education

National psychology also left its imprint on the national education controversy of the time. The overhauling of the school system was on the agenda of the Hundred Days Reform. After the Boxer Uprising of 1900, educational reforms were urged on the Qing court by governor-generals like Zhang Zhidong, who in 1902 referred to free lower elementary schooling in foreign countries as a feature of "national education" (*guomin jiaoyu*) (Ayers 1971, 218). It was prelude to the abolition of the imperial examinations system in 1905.

Pestalozzi and Fichte

In the West, experiments with a national system of elementary education began with Frederick the Great of Prussia and Maria Theresa of Austria, but it was left for the French Revolution and Napoleon to achieve a system of state education (Barker 1948, 212). It was in the revolutionary Helvetian Republic that a Swiss pedagogue, Johann Heinrich Pestalozzi (also an honorary citizen of Revolutionary France) distilled this trend into a philosophy. Liberal in spirit, he advocated every man's right to an education and believed it was society's duty to implement that right. These ideas paved the way for universal national education, especially the modern *Volksschule* (obligatory primary education). Yet his vision was the development of the moral self in society rather than nationalism (Osterwalder 1994, 4415–4419).

The Chinese debate on national education was more ideologically charged. Transcending partisan lines, the consensus was to use national education to serve the cause of national salvation. In this respect the Chinese came to resonate with the ideas of the Prussian patriot Johann Gottlieb Fichte. The Chinese ferment prior to the abolition of the imperial examinations was not unlike that in Prussia around 1805–1806 when the reorganization of universities was hotly debated. It was at this juncture that Fichte argued for the state control of universities and an all-German orientation so that "a national German character" could be forged to overcome narrow provincialism (Engelbrecht 1968, 91–92). Later, when Germany was under French domination, Fichte raised national education to a "systematic cult." He looked upon it as "the first and most important preliminary measure for the liberation of the country from the yoke of the foreign ruler," by creating "a new generation familiar with the sacred mission of the nation" (Rocker 1937, 190).

The Prussian educational reform after Prussia's defeat by Napoleon was heavily influenced by the Pestalozzi doctrine, resulting in the emergence of a modern school administration and a reform of teacher education. Like the Qing court's educational reforms, these were modernization measures along the line of secularization and statism. The Pestalozzi project loosened church control through the cultivation of a pietistic inner self and replaced the ontological concept of truth with empiricism, and the project was to be implemented by the state. Its Chinese counterpart was for the Qing court to initiate actions to shelve Confucianism to make room for modern subjects.

The Chinese nationalists, however, tended to see "national education" through Fichtean eyes, as they embraced his vision of using national education to inculcate national spirit. In 1906, the Commercial Press in Shanghai published a biography of Pestalozzi combined with a biography of Fichte by Zhu Yuanshan (Bauer and Hwang 1982, 314, entry 07149). It was a reading of Pestalozzi, the father of the modern pedagogical theory, through Fichte, the nationalist agitator who has no place in the history of Western pedagogy.

The Bastardization of the Pestalozzi Vision

This tunnel vision of "national education" was apparent in a student-journal article summarizing its developments in the West. It tended to use national conflict as landmarks. For example, the national education system, greatly expanded by Prussia in 1854, was credited for her victory over France and her unification of Germany; the Prussian example was followed by Austria where a compulsory eight-year education was instituted after 1866, the year of her defeat by Prussia; France repeatedly expanded her national schools between 1870 and 1883, also due to the impact of the Franco-Prussian war, (Wan 1903, 11–13). Evidently, the Chinese national education fervor seethed under a similar sense of national crisis.

The popularity of Fichte's ideas had something to do with recent Japanese developments. Education in early Meiji Japan, in terms of content, had tilted toward Anglo-American individualism, even though its French-style administrative setup was based on strong central control. Beginning in 1885, Mori Arinori restructured the whole system along Prussian lines, viewing the strongly centralized system of schools primarily as an instrument of the state and serving the interest of the state (Hall 1973, 331–333, 352). Mori's "statist education" was only a formal structure until the Imperial Rescript on Education injected the *kokutai* (national form) ideology into it. This notorious form lasted until 1945; it is responsible in part for the rise of militarism in Japan.

The Chinese national-psychological view of national education was not quite the same as Japanese "statist education," which was rendered in Chinese as *guojia jiaoyu*. China's national education system was hardly in place at the time and few radical intellectuals welcomed the idea of centralized control by a strong Manchu state. As indicated above, the social-psychology discourse had leftist affinities, emphasizing people rather than the state, even though it was equally attractive to the radical right. As it turned out, the Chinese debate on national education was yet another site of the national character contestation.

National Education as a Site of the National Character Discourse

Back in the 1890s, Liang had written copiously on educational reform, but the tone was hardly distinguishable from "self-strengthening" thinking as he aimed at the modest figure of 400,000 elementary school students, 11,840 high school students, and 1,850 college students (Liang 1896–1899, 20). In 1902, with the new understanding of the nation as a psychological milieu, Liang's argument changed substantially: "The public education of a country has the purpose of cultivating nationals with distinct characteristics, so that they may form a community able to hold its own in the arena of survival of the fittest" (Liang 1902g, 53). Liang now not only aimed at universal education but was also endorsing the Fichtean vision.

Fichte, in his "Addresses to the German Nation" (1807–1808), elevated the Germans to the status of the *Urvolk* ("original" or "ancestral" people), but their deplorable current state led him to a diatribe against "the lack of cohesion among the individuals who composed the states, the passion for money-getting and individual success." It also led to his exhortation "to substitute for the principle of self-seeking, the principle of self-devotion" (Reisner 1922, 127). We find the Chinese polemicists writing on the same national issue lifting their wordings almost verbatim from Fichte. Yang Du, who would soon become an influential member of the Chinese community in Japan, admitted the German origin of the national education concept and that it was badly needed in an age of national struggle. It would provide a remedy for the Chinese lack of the "public virtue of the group." Although the Chinese "instinct" of profit-seeking was the envy of other nations, it was unfortunately directed against compatriots instead of outward to benefit the nation as a group. Yang looked forward to the awakening of China's national spirit (Yang 1902).

Wan Shengyang echoed Yang's opinions on the Chinese people's profit-seeking inclination. In a rather anti-monarchical mood, he lamented that China's imperial examinations system was based on the profit-seeking motive, which worked in the despot's interest but corrupted the character of the students. This motive was so deeply ingrained in the Chinese mind that the modern three-tiered system—the elementary and secondary schools, the university—was reduced to "newly created profit-seeking fields." Wan also attacked the old educational system's authoritarianism, which inculcated subservience in students and enfeebled their critical ability. Again, this was in the interest of the despot. Wan regarded the two malaises as the major obstacles to China's effort to institute national education (Wan 1903, 13–16).

In the Fichtean spirit, national education was seen as in tune with the trend of the time, nationalism; it was an instrument for cultivating a citizenry with a unique character (Zhang 1903, 6). An essay advocated national education as a key to nation-building by the following reasoning: "A nation is born in a psychological sense, as a moral and emotional aggregate" (Anonymous 1903f, 2). Another underlined the importance of inculcating "ethical thought" in the citizens. Chinese ethics, so far, had put a premium on self-cultivation and the family; it had failed to develop a national psychology. The author argued, in terms of the psychological concepts of the time, that the Chinese must focus their cognition, feelings, and volition to actualize a national psychology that would be the foundation of nation and state (Anonymous 1903g, 7–8).

Liang Qixun's 1903 essay on Le Bon also sought to uplift Chinese national psychology through education. For that purpose, he criticized Le Bon's inflexible and pessimistic view of national psychology. Yet he agreed with Le Bon's appraisal of the Latin peoples, in comparison with the British, that their "common sentiments, common interests, and common beliefs" were relatively undeveloped. He followed with the rather defeatist statement that the Chinese, devoted only to their family and village, had an even less developed racial soul than the Latins. Thus, Qixun's program of national salvation through education remained an optimistic wish. His article's main thrust appeared to be largely an exhortation to his countrymen based on the Le Bon thesis: "The notion of a native country is not possible until the national soul is formed" (Liang Qixun 1903, no. 25, 9; Le Bon 1974, 14).

In 1904, another treatise on the education issue delved into "national characteristics," the product of history, geography, language, and political and religious habits. The author believed that the majority of Chinese had the positive characteristics of being hardworking, thrifty, and deeply conservative. The negative ones included laxity in emotions and will and the absence of unity, for "each individual does what is profitable and convenient to himself alone, lacking patriotic passions." The author reiterated the antimonarchical sentiment that "two thousand years of despotism" had stifled the positive qualities and perpetuated the negative ones. He assigned to national education the dual role of developing the positive qualities of the Chinese people and preparing for constitutional government. National education must be designed to fit national characteristics in much the same way that children's education must conform to child psychology (Shulou 1904).

In the same year, a Shanghai journalist also deplored the Chinese "lack of nationhood," for a nation should share "common character and sentiments, common customs, common language." In China, each province had its own character and sentiments, customs, and language. He saw education as a panacea for all the ills in China including the lack of nationhood (Kexuan 1904, 225, 226–27). The three "commons" were typical of national-psychological thinking—for example, Le Bon defined the "three fundamental bases" of the national soul as "common sentiments, common interests, and common beliefs" (Le Bon 1974, 13).

National Psychology and National Revolution

If reformists and radicals concurred on national education, they parted ways on the political solution to China's future. Unlike their consensus on fostering a unitary psychology through national education, with regard to politics they gave the theory of national psychology either a revolutionary or an antirevolutionary reading. According to Le Bon, the "racial souls" of Latin peoples are not as well-formed as those of the Anglo-Saxons. The Latin nations are so lacking in psychological cohesion that they are often caught in vicious cycles of Jacobinism and Bonapartism and never actually solve any problem. A radical reading of national psychology, however, could also lay the blame for the lack of national consciousness of a people on the doorstep of the Old Regime. It remained to be seen whether revolution could serve as a catalyst for the birth of a nation in China.

The Volatile Latin Character

In his 1903 article on Le Bon, Liang Qixun criticized the latter's pessimism concerning the immutability of a people's psychology, for such a conclusion would extinguish all hopes for betterment of an inferior nation like China. Qixun's interpretation of Le Bon, however, expressed the wish for transforming China's racial soul through education instead of revolution. His arguments were tightly circumscribed by Le Bon's negative view of the French Revolution. Qixun cited the contrast between the French people's cruelty in the National Convention era and their docility under Napoleon as an example of the volatility of national character (Liang Qixun 1903, no. 30, 1). This example was drawn from Le Bon, who treated both Jacobinism and Bonapartism as alternate and equally deplorable expressions of the perennial Latin character (Le Bon 1974, 18, 20–21).

As for Qixun's brother, Liang Qichao, his negative view of the French Revolution and his Anglophilism predated his acquaintance with Le Bon's ideas. Even during his "radical" phase in 1901, Liang asserted that France had been unstable since the revolution of 1789, meanwhile still falling short of the level of people's rights attained by the Anglo-Americans. It was a clear sign that the French had less ability to practice self-restraint. From this negative example he derived the lesson of gradualism (Liang 1901c, 46–47). In his "On the New People," Liang also compared the Latin character unfavorably to the Teutonic and illustrated his point with the French Revolution: "In the entire century [after their revolution], the French have changed their polities six times and their constitutions, fourteen times; yet in spite of their theoretical democracy, they have made very little progress in local self-government and individual rights" (Liang 1902q, 6).

Liang never tired of using the French Revolution, as a manifestation of the "inferior" Latin character, to allude to the futility of revolution in China. In this respect, Le Bon's view was reinforced by Bluntschli's that "the French national character is most unsuitable for republicanism," for the French lack the capabilities for self-government and their polity is highly centralized, centered on Paris (Zhongguo zhi xinmin 1903, 19).

A Contested Site: The French Revolution

In 1903, a radical Chinese student journal in Tokyo defined a nation psychologically as an expression of the common will of the people directed at a common goal, which led to public acts. A common feeling (sympathy) would be absent in a state that is a mere collection of heterogeneous peoples, not sharing thoughts, language, customs, and habits. This theory threw a new light on Chinese despotism, which emerged early because the flatness of the Yellow River basin enabled a geographical unification of peoples with "contrary feelings." This despotism by necessity resorted to compulsion, which not only sapped the people's political capabilities but "lowered their intelligence, enfeebled their spirit, and silenced their voices." In such a nation, "monarch and people do not communicate, the latter do not know the existence of nation, and each individual pursues his or her selfish ends." The author instilled the urgency of nation-building with an unambiguous antimonarchical message. He credited both the French Revolution and Napoleon for giving birth to nationalism (Yuyi, 1903, 11–13, 17–19).

The anti–Manchu partisans, in their turn, perceived their goals and programs as rooted in the demands of Chinese national psychology. They appeared to have turned back to an idea of Montesquieu and Rousseau that the laws of a country, in order to work, should be tailored to its people's morals, customs, and belief. Writing in the language of the *fin de siècle*, they understandably presented this earlier thesis in a psychologized rhetoric. To harness racial psychology to their own purposes, they excluded the Manchus from the Chinese race.

According to Wang Jingwei, a nation or a historical race is defined by six criteria: common blood descent, common spoken and written language, common habitat, common habits, common religion, common spirit and physical type (Jingwei 1905, 1–2). Wang's list appears to be an adaptation from Bluntschli: common habitat, common blood descent, common physical form, common spoken language, common written language, common religion, common customs, common economy (Zhongguo zhi xinmin 1903, 8). Sun Zhongshan was to streamline this list to four items in his "First Lecture on Nationalism" (Sun 1924, 621). Wang argued that the Manchus were very different from the Han people; they were conquerors who, unlike those before them, refused to be assimilated but instead attempted to destroy Chinese culture and obliterate Chinese history, "the vessel of the national spirit." Wang looked forward to the "consolidation of [China's] national spirit" with the aim of overthrowing the Manchus. As Wang put it: "Social psychology is oftentimes the mother of reality" (Jingwei 1905, 22, 19).

Wang's "mind over matter" thesis was badly needed. Even he had to admit that the traditional concept of rebellion rooted in China's national psychology was ill-suited to the purpose of a modern revolution. But, "certain [undesirable] aspects of the national psychology can be changed," while certain latent positive elements, such as the ideas of "citizenry" and "nationalism," can be revived. Those (alluding to Liang and his ilk) who calumniated the Chinese people for their deficient political capabilities for practicing democracy were "ignorant of human psychological functioning." Human beings differ from animals in having the faculty of "imitation," which would come into operation now that China has emerged from seclusion and begun contact with the outside world (Jingwei 1906, 15, 29).

Wang was defensive on the issue of the French Revolution, betraying the fact that national psychology, with its Le Bonian background, was initially linked to mob psychology. "In the opinions of some people, in a revolutionary condition, as the national psychology is given free rein and turns wild, the revolution might fail and degenerate into a reign of terror; even if it succeeds, the outcome might not be what we expect; whereas what we seek is a republic, the outcome might be a return to despotism." Wang tried to convince his readers that his camp had a preventive: the revolutionary party's conscious intervention to impose a revolutionary compact delineating the purviews of military and civil authorities (Jingwei 1905, 20–22).

Liang Qichao retorted with the Burkean argument that national psychology was grounded in history and took time to evolve toward the republican goal. He exposed Wang's version of national psychology as a corruption of the "social psychology" of the Japanese jurist Kakehi Katsuhiko. Giving Kakehi's ideas a voluntarist twist, Wang assumed that he, a prophet, could forge such a "psychology" and foist it on the nation (Yinbing 1906a, 23, 26, 28–29).

Will There Be a Nation After the Revolution?

In 1907, in response to the Qing government's promise of a constitution, Liang launched the Political Information Society. Yang Du advised him to agitate for the opening of parliament and to use the issue as a rallying point for party-building. Liang, deeply impressed by Yang's idea, agreed that it was the best way to "funnel the national psychology into one channel" (Ding and Zhao 1983, 395).

The Qing authorities banned Liang's Political Information Society in 1908 for its agitation to open parliament. His resulting depression was compounded by the shadow of impending doom. His constitutionalist cause failed as the Qing court's delay in convening parliament led to the outbreak of revolution in 1911. During the transition from imperial rule to republic, Liang wrote another group of essays on national character to allay his worst fears, first in *National Mores* and later in *Justice* after his return to the mainland. (*National Mores* and *Justice* were journals started by Liang in 1910 and 1912, respectively.) These essays expressed his ambivalence in those anxiety-laden days. With imperial China at an end, Liang again looked to the Chinese national character as a key to the nation's future. Thus, "national character" became at once the reservoir of hope and a whipping boy for the failed nationhood project.

The Optimist

Liang launched the journal *National Mores* [Guofeng] in 1910 in Shanghai but edited it from Japan. He chose the term "mores," for the Chinese equivalent, *feng*, had multiple meanings such as customs, virtues, trends, fads, and wind. According to Liang, every "distinguished nation" in the modern world had her unique national mores but, of the six leading nations—England, France, Germany, Russia, the United States, and Japan—only England, France, and Germany had mature national mores. The implication was that it was not too late for China to catch up. Liang was in a meta-phorical mood: "The most volatile element in the world is wind." England in the fifteenth and sixteenth centuries was not a seafaring country and was even "contemptuous of commerce, like traditional China." The Confucian metaphor of wind (superior men) bending grasses (the people) allowed Liang to entertain the hope that the "mental power of one or two persons" would set a new trend and lay the foundation of new mores (Liang 1910b). This was the social-psychological mechanism of "suggestion–imitation" but might as well be a leaf taken from Zeng Guofan, the scholar-general who saved the dynasty from the Taiping Rebellion. The same source would later inspire Generalissimo Jiang Jieshi (Chiang Kaishek) to launch the New Life Movement in the 1930s.

Liang took upon himself to combat the "social psychology" of doom prevalent among his countrymen. It was also his debate with a similar voice within himself. If the whole nation is convinced of China's immediate doom, Liang averred, then China would die, not a natural death, but of suicide. However, his own position was not much of a consolation for he claimed that China's present condition was the outcome of historical "bad karma." Karma is different from fate—the latter is predetermined while the former could be altered by self-effort. As Liang compared karma to the Darwinian theory of "cellular heredity," it became doubtful that doom could be averted in a single generation. Indeed, he resorted to the parable of the "foolish old man moving the mountains"* (Liang 1910a)—a favorite leit-motif of the future chairman Mao Zedong (Mao was an avid reader of Liang).

A Balance Sheet

Liang's tension between hope and despair was played out in a dialogue between two opposing voices in an essay, Mingshui (MS) and Changjiang (CJ). CJ was Liang's pen-name in *National Mores* and MS was that of his assistant editor Tang Juedun (Fang 1981, 576). But, as the latter aired views that Liang had held earlier, MS can be treated as his alter ego. The style of Liang's essay is strikingly similar to that of Fichte's *Patriotic Dialogues* (1806–1807) between two voices, A and B, with the latter representing Fichte's own (Engelbrecht 1968, 95).

---

*In a fable, an old man and his family attempt by manual labor to level two mountains blocking their exit to the outside world, and expected it to be achieved in 10,000 generations. The gods are moved by this single-mindedness and relocated the two mountains elsewhere.

In Liang's dialogues, MS was the prophet of doom predicting China's pending partition by the powers and CJ allayed these fears by placing hope in the international balance of power. The debate introduced today's standard Chinese term for "national character," *guomin xing*, presumably adapted from the Japanese *kokuminsei*. CJ saw national character, like individual character, unavoidably containing both strength and weaknesses, and in China's case the strength was remarkable: she had the largest population on earth who had formed a state that lasted for thousands of years, a feat unsurpassed in world history. China's national character might be unfit for the modern world, but its very solidity vitiated any prospect of doom or partition. CJ quoted a certain "He-te" (Fichte?) to the effect that to destroy a nation, her character must first be erased (Liang 1911, 1–12).*

MS saw government as "the product of national psychology," thus poor government in China was symptomatic of a sick national psychology. CJ countered with three positive characteristics: China has the ideal of equality of all classes, which the Europeans only began to implement in the previous century. Her people have thrived on self-sufficiency and local autonomy under her government's laissez-faire attitude. Lastly, China is known for her ability to absorb conquerors and immigrants. CJ again relied on He-te's authority to argue that China's national character was stronger than those of her conquerors. It was strong enough to assimilate even those Jews, Persians, and Arabs who had settled in China (Liang 1911, 12–14).

MS came up with a list of Chinese shortcomings such as hidebound resistance to outside influence and the lack of scientific spirit, martial spirit, and patriotism. For CJ, these negative aspects were secondary and remediable. In medieval times China not only embraced Buddhism but developed it to a new height. As for scientific spirit, it is not innate to any race and is thus adoptable: "Even the Japanese of thirty years ago did not know what was science." CJ admitted that China's ecumenism had put her martial spirit to sleep, but it only awaited re-activation. The charge that the Chinese lacked patriotism had been made by Liang himself earlier. Now Liang's persona CJ continued to blame it on China's ecumenism and cited Edward Gibbons' similar diagnosis of the Romans. But, this time, CJ also credited ecumenism for integrating a large area of territory and bequeathing it to

---

*"He-te" is my Mandarin pinyin of a name that Liang might have pronounced in his Xinhui (Guangdong) dialect, which in its turn might have resulted from his reading of a Japanese transliteration of the German name Fichte. Lacking "f" phonemes, Japanese as a rule substitutes "h" for "f" in the transliteration of foreign terms, e.g., "coffee" becomes "kohee." Liang did publish an *Introduction to Fichte's "Über die Bestimmung des Menschen"* in 1915 (n.p.), and this time he rendered "Fichte" as "Feixide" (Bauer and Hwang 1982, 41, entry 01416).

the modern-day Chinese. Instead he now blamed China's vast geography for the Chinese lack of political capability for democracy, and for fostering despotism (perhaps an idea inspired by Montesquieu).[9] Nonetheless, Chinese culture had an inherent democratic ideal embodied in popular uprisings, and her people only needed a constitutional channel to actualize this ideal (Liang 1911, 14–27).

In the face of revolution, Liang used geographical necessity to exonerate despotism and warned that, without such a centralizing agency, China's vast territories might simply fall part. Admitting that the Manchu regime was totally hopeless, CJ at this eleventh hour still wished that the people would refrain from revolution. In his opinion, for citizens to resort to such a solution was to abdicate their own responsibility. He preferred to place hope on a few outstanding individuals (like himself) who could transform the nation's "social psychology" and customs through their "mental force." Detecting MS's skepticism about the emergence of such individuals, CJ cited Le Bon: Extraordinary historical situations have often evoked the latent potentiality in ordinary men, enabling them to live up to the requirements of the situation (Liang 1911 27–40).[10]

Is the Republic Lacking in Character?

At the end Liang found himself involved, at a distance, in palace intrigues and a *coup d'état* plot in the last days of the dynasty. He aimed at putting one court faction in power with himself playing a central role in the new ruling circle (Yang 1998, 80–83). But Liang the prolific polemicist turned out to be an ineffectual politician like his rival Sun Zhongshan. Power eluded both men in the transition from monarchy to republic, as it fell into the hands of the military strong man of the *ci-devant* Qing regime, Yuan Shikai.

The Elusive Character of the Republic

In late 1912—the year of the founding of the Chinese Republic—an article, "The Republican Polity and the National Psychology," appeared in *Dongfang Zazhi* (Eastern Miscellany). The author was Du Yaquan, the editor of that influential magazine and a future defender of "Eastern civilization" against May Fourth iconoclasm (see chapter 3). He attributed the origins of the Chinese republic to the practicality of the Chinese people, a trait so strong that their new polity had little to do with such abstract principles as the inalienable rights of man. Instead, it was born of the need for national salvation. The same practical trait also accounted for the preponderance of military power over legal power and executive over legislative, in the nascent republic. As the polity could conform only to the national psychology, the author saw no need to deplore these predilections and instead looked forward to their gradual melding with the Western emphasis on "principles"(Chuangfu 1912, 1–4).

Du Yaquan was perhaps the first to mention Chinese practical-mindedness as a national characteristic, and it was picked up in less than a year by another discussant who pointed out certain negative aspects of this mentality, such as conservatism, myopic egotism, and a deficiency in rational thinking (Yu 1913, 38–46). In post-Mao China of the 1980s, the same thesis was reincarnated in the philosopher Li Zehou's exposition of Chinese "practical rationality." In the context of 1912, Du's thesis served as a justification of the post-revolutionary reality in which the shadow of the military loomed large.

Du's premises were actually Le Bon's, to the effect that the political form of a nation could not go against the national ethos. The same arguments also surfaced in an article published in January 1913 in *Minli Bao* (People's stand), the organ of the Revolutionary Alliance. The unknown author warned that, due to the difference in national psychology, the Chinese republic was bound to be different from the American and the French. China was the most ancient nation in the world and, in order to avoid the disasters of the copycat "South American republics," her insuperably solid national psychology should not be ignored. In short, the Chinese republic needed to carry its own unique characteristics (Anonymous 1913, 8–9). They, however, remained elusive.

Quest for a Moral Foundation for the New Republic

It was Liang Qichao who took it upon himself to search for a moral foundation for the new polity in conformance with the national psychology. Liang had returned to the Mainland in October 1912. Two months later, he wrote two essays on national character for *Yongyan* (Justice), a journal he launched in Tianjin with the aim of salvaging China's national identity amid political disintegration. His anxiety was most evident in statements like: "With an immature national character, a nation may still be founded but it will not be stable. After the founding of the nation, if its national character is lost then the nation is doomed." Although China had a foundation of five thousand years, it was shaken in modern times by outside forces. Liang was unnerved by the centrifugal forces unleashed by the disintegration of imperial China (Liang 1912a).

These anxieties compelled Liang to assess China's national inheritance most positively. He reiterated that China was the sole survivor of ancient nations, testifying to the presence of a unique and not easily destructible national character. A human community, he averred, is based on shared moral beliefs and it would disintegrate if they are lost. In this case, it would be futile for a few outstanding individuals to attempt to transplant the morals of another society (e.g., the West) they admire, for they are not rooted in the people's psychology. Having lost faith in the voluntarism of the superior few (including his former self), Liang now placed his faith in the "psychology of the majority in our country." In this moral majority he discerned three basic ideas, results of heredity and acculturation through the ages (Liang 1912b, 12–14).

The first idea is "moral indebtedness" (*bao'en*), a unique feature of the Chinese belief system. It forges an "interlinking chain" uniting man and the gods, ancestors and posterity, parents and children, clan and clansmen, and society at large. It is this collectivism grounded in religious duty that contributes to the cohesiveness and continuity of China as a nation. "We Chinese have never comprehended such a thing as absolute individualism." Liang was unsettled by the fact that this ideal had been shaken by modernity, and he hinged the nation's survival on the ideal's revival. The second idea is "to know one's station and status" (*mingfen*). This trait was not in conflict with equality before the law but a realistic recognition of society's division of labor for the sake of social stability. At this point, Liang cited a study of national character by "*Ba-er-xun*" (probably the Anglo-Australian historian Charles Pearson's *National Life and Character* [1893]), to show that the French character, constantly dissatisfied with the status quo, was counterproductive in contrast to the German character. The third positive Chinese trait is "concern for posterity" (*lühou*). The Chinese are the "most realistic" people, for, unlike believers in many religions, they equate "afterlife" with "posterity." Here Liang was backed by Darwin's authority to the effect that those species that have numbers on their side are the fittest to survive. He looked askance at the individualism and "instant hedonism" of the West, especially the French, which contributed to declining population and the increase of illegitimate births. Liang exhorted Chinese moralists not to look toward "dazzling novelties" from the West, but to return to the fundamentals of Chinese culture, namely, the three basic moral ideas: *bao'en* connects the present with the past, *lühou*, the present with the future, and *mingfen* preserves the stability of the present (Liang 1912b, 14–20).

Making a Virtue Out of Immaturity

The republic was the very antithesis of the stability Liang yearned for. With the fall of Qing, the outlying regions of Mongolia and Tibet began to break away in late 1911 and early 1912 (Young 1983, 210). In the first year of the republic, President Yuan Shikai and the Nationalists (the former revolutionaries) who controlled the majority in the parliament maintained an uneasy truce—a situation also reflecting the rift between northern and southern China. In March 1913, the delicate balance was upset when Yuan had Song Jiaoren, a Nationalist leader and a would-be premier, assassinated. This act resulted in civil war and dictatorship. The republic's turbulence caused one of the discussants on national character in *Justice* to comment that "chaos" (*luan*) was deeply rooted in the "national psychology" of the Chinese (Hu 1914, 1).

At the incipience of the republic, Liang attempted to use the ex-constitutionalists to build a third force, the Progressive Party, between Yuan and the Nationalists and was willing to go along with Yuan. For a while, he even saw in Yuan the potential "enlightened despot" he envisaged. To justify enlightened despotism, Liang published an essay on Chinese "infantilism" in early 1913, four days before Song's murder. This article is a discussion on child psychology to which Liang likens the mind of the Chinese people. The child's mind is emotional, easily excitable, devoid of judgment and analytic power, destructive, disorderly, fickle, imitative, vainglorious, full of fantasies, forgetful, credulous, impatient, oblivious to sorrow, and selfish. The child is also wholly dependent and without the sense of responsibility. Reversing his former verdict on Western individualism, Liang now condemned the "childlike" Chinese psychology as "extreme individualism." According to evolutionary theory, childhood in the individual is the equivalent of a semi-civilized stage in the development of the human race. However, the child is also malleable and easy to control. Toward a child, Liang argued, the best policy is protective nurturing or "enlightened despotism." The state should enforce it; otherwise, outsiders would do it on behalf of the state in the manner of the British tutelage of India and Japan's rule of Korea (Liang 1913b).

The infantilism thesis could also lead to different conclusions. Tang Erhe, a spokesman for China's modern medical profession, wrote in Liang's journal, *Justice*, that an infant was malleable and easy to control but also quick to grow. Given the right protective nurturing, an "infantile people" would grow "with a much quicker pace than nations in their adulthood" (Tang 1913, 2–3).

It appeared that Liang's Progressive Party was treading a narrow middle path. While committed to republicanism, it also came out strongly on the side of a strong political center. It pitted its centralist platform to the federalism of the Nationalist Party, thus playing into Yuan's hands. Liang's enlightened despotism was echoed by Yuan Skikai's American advisor, Frank Goodnow, who "agreed that autocracy represented the only form of government suitable for the unruly Chinese" (Fogel 1984, 166).

China's Senility as Her Best Defense

Ironically, in this period it was Naito Konan who wholeheartedly defended the Chinese republic. In Japan, the Chinese Revolution also fuelled a debate on the compatibility of the republic and the Chinese character. In 1912 and 1913, Nakajima Hajime and Sakamaki Teiichiro had commented on China's lack of national character and her unfitness for republicanism and predicted a destiny of dismemberment. These popular views in Japan compelled Naito to publish, in 1914, a more positive assessment of China's past, the *Shinaron (On China)* (Fogel 1984, 163–165). He saw China as having reached the maturity of "old age," manifest in the rise of "populism." This concept was akin to Liang Qichao's earlier acclaim of the Chinese "ideal of equality" and "local autonomy." Naito saw populism as steadily developing since the end of the Tang Dynasty, culminating in the republic. Its roots were the local self-governing bodies, the bastions of Chinese familism, which Liang also valued as a source of national strength. Naito expected these local bodies to be the building blocks of a Chinese federation. The Chinese masses, headed by village elders, would seek peace at any price. He regretted that the Chinese revolutionaries "did not understand the national character of the Chinese people," while the villain Yuan Shikai understood it well enough to pervert it to serve his ambition. He saw Yuan as a reactionary going against the long-term trends of Chinese history (Fogel 1984, 174–90).

Naito's populist stance was an ambivalent solution to his own intellectual tension between admiration of Chinese culture and promotion of Japan's continental expansionism. His "populism" was a symptom of senility, for China, unlike Japan, had already passed the youthful stage of state-building and should be content to exist only as a high culture (under the political aegis of Japan, like Greece under Rome). Chinese "political capabilities" had declined long before (an opinion with which Liang would agree). To Naito, "the Chinese aspiration to build a powerful, centralized government was the cause of both internal troubles and external dangers" (Okamoto 1976, 164).

Naito's senility thesis and Liang's infantilism thesis expose the metaphorical nature of their national character discussions. Naito's defense of republicanism (read: decentralized populism) was convoluted and served Japan's interest. Liang's enlightened despotism, on the other hand, aimed at state-building. Naito condemned Yuan Shikai outright, whereas Liang initially hinged his hope on the dictator.

Yuan Shikai's Corruption
of the Chinese Psychology

Blame It on the French Virus

Yuan Shikai did not live up to Liang's expectation of an enlightened despot. In the aftermath of Song's assassination, Liang condemned the crime even though he disapproved of the Nationalists' Second Revolution. His disillusionment with the nation was evident when, in April 1913, he charged that if a "nation's thought and character" had not been flawed, "they would not have produced despotism." Paradoxically, the faulty aspects, while under control in the despotic age, were given free play in a republic. Now they took the form of self-serving graft, regionalism, and improvidence. Liang lamented that the political situation of the past year had encouraged pessimists to glorify despotism and pray for the advent of a Cromwell and a Napoleon (he himself had done so a month before!). Despotism might provide a partial cure for the "national vices," but it is sad that the people themselves have failed to eradicate those vices through their own effort (Liang 1913c, 16–18). Liang's whole argument here is still tightly circumscribed by Le Bon's thesis of the anarchic Latin character that invariably invites dictatorship.[11] It also sounded like an apology for his continual collaboration with Yuan. After all, Liang in the past had used the Chinese character to share the blame with Manchu despotism for China's problems.

The Progressives were habitually opposed to the Nationalists. In the face of the latter's Second Revolution, Liang published in the June 1913 issue of *Justice* a social-psychological diagnosis of the phenomenon of "successive revolutions" and its "baneful effects." Rarely sympathetic toward revolution, Liang understandably saw it as a French malaise that had affected Central and South America and, most recently, Mexico. In those countries, as in China, revolution gave free rein to society's most unstable elements, destabilized the mass psychology, and thus locked itself into a repetitive pattern (Liang 1913a). In the July issue of *Justice*, Liang's follower, the philosopher Zhang Dongsun, cited Le Bon to the effect that revolution tended to bastardize the national character by promoting "criminal mentalities" (Zhang Dongsun 1913, 3–4, 10–11).

During 1913 and 1914, the French Revolution simile turned into a cryptic code under the pen of Li Dazhao, the future "father of Chinese Marxism," but then an associate of the Progressives. He took the group mind to task for producing a Yuan Shikai in China: "It was the French as a group who produced Napoleon, and because of Napoleon, the French have become Machiavellian even to this day. It was the Americans as a group who produced Washington, and thanks to Washington, the Americans have persisted in righteousness and justice to this day." While using "Napoleon" as his code for Yuan Shikai, Li at the same time alluded to the Nationalists as the equally negative "Jacobins" (Sun 1991, 5).

The Nationalists and the Progressives at Crossroads

Thus the Progressives played into Yuan's hands in the events of 1913. Following their debacle, the fugitive Nationalists resumed the contestation for the claim to interpret national character in their magazine, *Minguo* (The republic), launched in May 1914 in Tokyo. In "On the National Character," Shao Yuanchong bemoaned the corruption of the traditional Chinese character by power and the profit motive, which he held accountable for the modern Chinese proneness to sycophancy and subservience (Xuanzhong 1914, 2–3, 6). In "Revolution and Psychology," Zhu Zhixin observed that a backward nation might have progressive policies, but if the majority failed to grasp the true meaning of republicanism, then their support of the system was blind; by the same token, their support of despotism was also blind (Qianjin 1914b, 9, 11). Zhu believed that Yuan and his cohort, finding it impertinent to promote monarchism openly, spread alarm over "mob rule" to paint the nation as too immature for republicanism (Qianjin 1914a, 1–15).

However, the Second Revolution did fail for lack of popular support. In many quarters, the Nationalists were viewed as wreckers of national unity. Once again a fugitive in Japan, Sun Zhongshan confided to his followers that since it sided with Yuan against the revolution, the nation was indeed immature; hence the urgency of raising the "level of the people" (Shao 1933, in Xuanpu 1954, 362).

In suppressing the Nationalist uprising, Yuan had co-opted the Progressives by inviting them to form a new cabinet. Yuan then moved against the Parliament by the turn of 1913 and 1914, and the Progressives broke with Yuan. Liang Qichao became involved in plotting the Yunnan Uprising, which eventually defeated Yuan's monarchical designs. From late 1913 to early 1914, *Justice* carried a series of discussions on Chinese national character by Wu Guanyin, Wang Tongling, Chen Shen, and Hu Yilu. They were allusions to the political life under Yuan.

National Character Discussions as Anti-Yuan Innuendos

Wu Guanyin, quoting Thomas Carlyle, elevated great "personages" to the center stage of human history and saw the types of great men worshipped in various countries as symptomatic of their respective national characters. In the West, great men are praised for their achievements but not for their moral characters; in China, the opposite is often the case. He cited the example of Cao Cao, the archetypal usurper in the Three Kingdoms period: "His literary talents surpassed those of his contemporaries, and his exploits cannot be overemphasized, yet throughout the ages, even when a kid heard Cao Cao's name he would call him evil." This criterion for viewing greatness "has become the national psychology for thousands of years." Wu named those great men in each dynasty who were venerated not simply for their exploits but for their ability to rectify the mores of their age. He lamented that crafty bureaucrats and machiavellian politicians had become the norm of the "new epoch" of today (Wu 1913).

Wang Tongling listed six Chinese characteristics: reverence for Heaven's command, reverence for ancestors, wealth and profit-seeking, love of peace and disdain for the martial spirit, emphasis on rituals and rhetoric, a strange mixture of extreme self-respect and self-denigration. Wang regarded the Confucian "reverence for Heaven's command" as mainly positive for the Chinese people's moral cultivation. It enabled them to maintain peace of mind in the face of adversity. The same belief in the mandate of Heaven, however, was also bent to serve the ambition of "political usurpers." In other words, Wang saw Liang Qichao's *mingfen* as effective in instilling contentment in the majority of Chinese but not in restraining the power of political usurpers. Wang's "reverence for ancestors," though akin to Liang's *bao'en*, saw Chinese as captives of an antiquity cult to the detriment of the future. Chinese "wealth and profit-seeking" was most negative, for "they would acquire money even by abandoning their rights." Chinese "psychology" also dampened the martial spirit, so unlike the ancient Spartans and the modern Japanese. Chinese people were overcivilized, as evident in their emphasis on rituals and rhetoric, which had unfortunately degenerated into hypocrisy and sycophancy. The Chinese, though often succumbing to military conquests by foreigners, were condescending to their conquerors. So far, they had been able, with their superior culture, to absorb all conquerors. Wang expected the outcome of China's encounter with the "culturally superior Westerners" to be quite the opposite (Wang 1913).[12]

Chen Shen, on the other hand, attempted to "evoke" China's national soul, which had been lost to Western ways. This evocation was another condemnation of the deplorable political reality under Yuan. Whereas Wang regarded the Chinese as inherently greedy to the extent of selling their birthrights, Chen bemoaned the loss of traditional virtues to the extent of serving Mammon as the master. Money facilitated the abdication of the Qing monarchy, the payoff of the republican "founding fathers"; it underlay the formation of political parties (an allusion to Yuan's phony Citizen Party?); it had the power to "buy" members of parliament and to purchase publicity in newspapers; it engineered *coups d'état*. Chen also denounced the fad of Darwin and Spencer for corrupting the simple and noncompetitive character of the Chinese. Even in the West, Chen averred, an "idealist" trend had recently emerged to remedy the baneful effect of materialism (Chen 1913). Western "idealism," as Chen understood it, was probably the vitalism of Henri Bergson and Rudolf Eucken, soon to become the icons of the Eastern Civilization camp, the rival of the May Fourth iconoclasts.

While Chen lamented the spiritual pollution caused by Mammon and Darwin under the Yuan regime, Hu Yilu blamed the failed republic on traditional traits. He saw the lust for power and machiavellianism as deeply rooted in China's "national psychology," accountable for the "chaos" that prevailed in the greater part of her history. Hu displayed a modicum of knowledge about the psychology of the inferiority complex, just emerging then in the West as a research subject.[13] He attributed the lust for power to "the sense of inferiority and the instinct of aggrandizement" as well as "sentiments of fear and conceit." Arguing in a social-psychological vein, Hu saw these syndromes as foundations of collective life. A strong man is able to dominate large groups by playing with these syndromes, but his manipulations inevitably result in vicious cycles and backfire. He manages to instil fear and slavishness among the people, but at the same time whetting their appetite for aggrandizement and magnifying their conceit through identification with his power. By resorting to machiavellianism, a strong man may succeed in maintaining power, but only temporarily. His example would soon be copied by those who harbor the same syndrome, and the outcome is lamentable: cycles of chaos and the corruption of the national psychology in general (Hu 1914, 1–5).

The discourse of the vile character of the Chinese nation as the psychological underpinning of despotism directly contributed to Chen Duxiu's and

Gao Yihan's iconoclastic blasts in the New Culture movement that was to follow (see chapter 3).

The Heyday of National Psychology, and Its Decline

The Yuan Regime's Official Parlance

"National psychology" was to become the shibboleth of early republican politics, as it was the theoretical site contested by both the anti-Yuan forces and the Yuan regime. When the last emperor abdicated on February 12, 1912, the edict, which was Yuan's handiwork, dabbled in the rhetoric of modern social science: "The psychology of the entire nation is now prone toward a republic" (*Neige guanbao* 1912, 1–2). On April 8, Yuan inaugurated the Chinese Parliament with a speech, legitimating it as the crystallization of "the psychology of four hundred million people" (Yuan 1913a, 13). In 1913, when the anti-Yuan forces in the south began to stir, Yuan charged them with destroying the unity of the nation, an act going against the "national psychology," thus placing themselves in the ranks of public enemy (Yuan 1913b, 5).

The defeat of the Nationalists' Second Revolution encouraged pro-Qing elements to attempt a restoration, compelling Yuan to chide them for their ignorance of global trends as well as the "national psychology" (Yuan 1914c).Yuan then proceeded to disband the parliament, a move hailed by Vice-President Li Yuanhong, who telegraphed from Wuhan claiming to be in touch with "people's psychology" in the provinces, where people utterly detested the wanton behavior of the members of parliament (Li 1913).

As an aftershock of the unsuccessful "Second Revolution" of the Nationalists, a "bandit," Bai Lang, rose up in north China to challenge Yuan's authority. After the suppression of Bai Lang's uprising in 1914, Yuan felt sufficiently secure to assume the imperial title himself. Promonarchical "citizens' groups" began to proliferate, questioning the compatibility of the republican polity with the Chinese national psychology (Anonymous 1915). A presidential order in October 1915 cited the perennial anarchy of Mexico and South America as testimony to the mismatching of polity with national conditions, and it diagnosed China's problem likewise: The republican form did violence to the Chinese "people's psychology" which had been monarchical for millennia (Yuan 1915).

Yuan's monarchical designs provoked the Yunnan Uprising and, in a late December decree announcing a punitive expedition, Yuan reiterated his belief that the constitutional monarchy was the "genuine expression of the national psychology" and that it was his duty to flush out the residual republican poison so as to restore the ancient nation's spirit (Li 1980, 351). Yuan eventually failed, as even his right-hand man, Feng Guozhang, declared neutrality in Nanjing. General Feng paid Yuan with the same coin in a telegram, urging his boss to abdicate so as not to defy the "national psychology" (Liu 1965, 229). Yuan died soon afterward.

From Mexico to Russia

China was no exception to an era in which the fad of psychology of nation was global, appearing in places as far apart as Mexico and Russia. In Mariano Azuela's 1916 novel about the Mexican Revolution, *The Under Dogs* (Los de abajo), one passage reads: "We must wait a while, until there are no men left to fight on either side, until no sound of shot rings through the air save from the mob as carrion-like it falls upon the booty; we must wait until the psychology of our race (*la psicologia de nuestra raza*), condensed into two words, shines clear and luminous as a drop of water: *Robbery! Murder!* What a colossal failure we would make of it, friend, if we, who offer our enthusiasm and lives to crush a wretched tyrant, became the builders of a monstrous edifice holding one hundred or two hundred thousand monsters of exactly the same sort. People without ideals! A tyrant folk! Vain bloodshed!" (Azuela 1967, 72–73; Munguia 1929, 114–115). In this passage, the influence of Le Bon's low opinion of the Latin character is unmistakable.[14]

Joseph Stalin's *Marxism and the National Question*, written in 1912 and 1913, also dabbled in national psychology: *"A nation is a historically constituted, stable community of people, formed on the basis of a common language, territory, economic life, and psychological make-up manifested in a common culture"* [italics in original]. He went on to elaborate: "It might appear that 'national character' is not one of the characteristics but the *sole* essential characteristic of a nation, and that all the other characteristics are, properly speaking, only *conditions* for the development of a nation, rather than its characteristics" (Stalin 1954, 16–17). Thus the Marxist Stalin conceded that a nation, unlike an economic class, was psychological.

National Psychology as New History

National psychology loomed large in Liang Qichao's *Research Methods for Chinese History* (1922) and his historical writings of the same period. Liang bolstered national-psychological thinking with the mentalistic trend popular since the Great War, namely Henri Bergson's creative evolutionism and

William James' theory of personality. The former reinforced Liang's own notion of "mental force" (*xinli*) in history (Liang 1922, 111, 116).[15] He regarded the distinctive personalities of great men as the "foci" of historical-temporal units called "historical-event aggregates" (*shiji jituan*). These are psychological units, for he used the term interchangeably with "national psychology" and "social psychology" and saw them as the "enlarged and compounded products of individual psychologies." Notably, he exhorted historians to study the "basic mental component of a historical event" (Liang 1922, 114, 118, 120).[16] As history operated in a mental milieu, great men who were epitomes of national or social psychology also managed to impose, through the mechanism of suggestion-sympathy, their personalities on the collective and the epoch (Liang 1922, 115).

A contemporary of Liang, Bertrand Russell in his *The Problem of China* (1922) also equates "national character" with a "homogeneous mental life" and believes that "a great deal [of it] depends upon the character of dominant individuals who happen to emerge at a formative period, such as Moses, Mahomet, and Confucius" (Russell 1966, 186–187). The "group mind" theory seemed to affect historical methodology on several continents, from Germany's Karl Lamprecht to the American historian James Harvey Robinson. The latter's *The New History* (1912) regarded it "part of the historian's business . . . to follow out the actual historical workings" of Gabriel Tarde's law of imitation (Robinson 1958, 97–98).

When these thoughts were committed to paper by Robinson, the behaviorist critique of the "group mind" was in the offing; by the time of its promotion by Liang the school was already under heavy fire and its decline became irreversible after 1920. The idea of suggestion–imitation lingered on in isolated cases such as Arnold Toynbee's *A Study of History*—in his thesis of the interplay between the "creative minority" and the "mimetic majority." In China, national psychology was on its way out as it was being promoted by Liang, and China's New History, in the sense of a "comprehensive theory of history," was soon to be Marxist in orientation.[17]

Although the "group mind" theory has lost its appeal today, the idea of a homogeneous culture as the backdrop of a nation is still very much alive. In fact, in postmodernist theories of nationalism, a shared symbolic milieu has taken over the function of an objective national psychology as a precondition for nation-formation. In the "cultural war" in the United States of the 1980s, national education's role in the making of a common cultural literacy and its significance for cohering a homogeneous national population was noted (Hirsch 1988).

Notes

1. Even in Europe, birthplace of the national state, the most homogeneous nations are formed of several nationalities. The so-called national language was, more often than not, spoken by only a fraction of the population at the state's inception; sometimes, it needed to be created artificially. In either case, its general usage is, as a rule, enforced by the government after statehood is achieved. A modern state, once formed, is also in a position to instill a national consciousness or a common way of life among its heterogeneous subjects, through national education (Hobsbawn 1990, chapter 2).

2. *Guojia xue gangling* (An outline of the theory of the state), published by Guangzhi shuju. A copy is extant at Guangzhou's Zhongshan University (Li 1986, 70).

3. The organismic view of state could be traced back to Plato. Its modern variations thrived largely in the German intellectual tradition, predating Darwin, but certainly received a boost from the biologism of Spencer and the like (Coker 1967).

4. Carol Gluck sees this process occurring in Meiji Japan, a period coeval to that of the conversion of peasants into Frenchmen studied by Eugen Weber (Gluck 1985, 37–38).

5. Edward Said says: "Since the Oriental was a member of a subject race, he had to be subjected: it was that simple. The *locus classicus* for such judgment and action is to be found in Gustave Le Bon's *Les Lois psychologiques de l'évolution des peuples* (1894)" (Said 1979, 207). This is a simplistic statement to suit Said's single-minded diatribe against Orientalism.

6. Liang said: "The intelligence of the Romans in the medieval times was not inferior to that of the Goths. Even the intelligence of the Indians, according to psychologists, is on a par with that of the English, or even surpassing the English (a theory of the French scholar, Le Bon). Then, how do we explain the fact that the former [the more intelligent ones] were vanquished by the latter [the less intelligent ones]?" (Liang 1904c, 2). This passage is inspired by Le Bon: "The influence of character is sovereign in the life of peoples, whereas that of intelligence is in truth very feeble. The Romans of the decadence possessed an intelligence far more refined than that of their rude ancestors, but they had lost the qualities of character of the latter. . . . It is due to their character that sixty thousand English are able to maintain beneath their yoke two hundred and fifty millions of Hindoos, many of whom are at least their equals in intelligence, while a few surpass them immensely as regards their artistic taste and the depth of their philosophic views" (Le Bon 1974, 33–34).

7. "When hearing stories about Sparta from their teachers, schoolchildren in our country are astounded at the extraordinary traditions of the Spartans. The Japan of our ancestors was in fact a militant society like Sparta, or one with an even more elaborate and thoroughgoing military organization than Sparta's" (Tokutomi 1986, 133). An editorial of *Kokumin no tomo* (The citizens' friend) in 1893 also referred to Japan as "Sparta of the Orient" (Pyle 1969, 168).

8. The novel *The Soul of Rousseau* used Rousseau as an introduction to expose the corrupted officialdom in China, as advertised in the first issue of *Min Bao* (People's journal).

9. Montesquieu argues that despotism is more likely in a large country, and the Republic is more likely to occur in a small country.

10. Liang referred to the following passage in Le Bon: "Take, for example, the 'giants of the Convention' who held Europe in check, and sent their adversaries to the guillotine for a mere contradiction. At bottom they were respectable, pacific citizens like ourselves, who in ordinary times would probably have led the most tranquil and

retired existence in their studies or behind their counters. Extraordinary events caused the vibration of certain of their brain cells which under usual conditions would not have been called into activity, and they developed into those colossal figures, whom posterity is at a loss to understand. . . . To remove all doubt as to the accuracy of these provisions it is sufficient to note that [under Napoleon, the remnant Terrorists] became staid officials, tax collectors, magistrates or prefects" (Le Bon 1974, 20–21).

11. "Was there much difference in reality between the centralised, dictatorial and despotic *regime* of our strict Jacobins and the centralised, dictatorial and despotic *regime* to which fifteen centuries of monarchy had accustomed the French nation? All the revolutions of the Latin peoples result in this obstinately recurring *regime*, in this incurable need of being governed, because it represents a sort of synthesis of the instincts of the race" (Le Bon 1974, 21–22).

12. Wang later incorporated these views in his *Zhongguo shi* (A history of China), published in 1926 (Otani 1935, 650).

13. The study of "psychopathic inferiority" began with I.L.A. Koch in the late nineteenth century and by the early twentieth century became the main focus of the theory of the Freudian Alfred Adler (Kahn 1931, 1, 9–12).

14. Referring to the Latin American republics, Le Bon says: "[A]ll these republics, without a single exception, are perpetually a prey to the most sanguinary anarchy, and in spite of the astonishing richness of their soil they are victims one after the other of every sort of political and economic disaster, of bankruptcy and despotism" (Le Bon 1974, 149).

15. While the name of Bergson is not spelled out in these passages, Bergson's influence, together with Rudolf Eucken's, are referred to in his *Excerpts of Mental Impressions of the European Trip* (Liang 1919, 18).

16. William James' influence is also implicit in this text but referred to in another (Liang 1919, 17–18). For Liang's notion of *shiji jituan*, also cf. (Tang 1996, 213–214). In a different analytical framework, Tang prefers to see Liang's new history as a postmodernist "spatial" deconstruction of Eurocentric temporality.

17. This observation revises Arif Dirlik's view of Marxist historiography as directly substituting "for the Confucian view a comprehensive theory of history that could account for the interrelationship of historical phenomena or the dynamics of historical change" (Dirlik 1978, 10).

— 3 —

Orientalness and Degeneration

After the mid-teens, the national character issue merged with New Culture iconoclasm—the hallmark of the May Fourth era (1917–1921). New Culture was born in the battle against Confucianism, seen by the conservatives as the mainstay of the national psychology. The skirmish was an episode of a much broader *Kulturkampf*, as China at that point was suffering a most cataclysmic disjunction. The revolution, though disappointing to many, did end an imperial system of two millennia and ushered in the very first republic of Asia.[1] Its very existence was an eloquent indictment of the old on behalf of the new in every facet of national life.

Yet, in terms of the nationhood project the republic was a fiasco, precipitating an intellectual crisis of far greater magnitude than ever. Now it became the vogue to curse China's very "Oriental" identity, the synonym of stagnancy. Still under the shadow of Darwin, the national character discussants were haunted by the prospect that the Chinese people might be a degenerate race. The demise of the imperial system and the total collapse of the traditional worldview left behind an intellectual vacuum that made China fully vulnerable to a whole range of Western intellectual fads. In the problematization of national character, the discussants could now go beyond a few Darwinian alternatives such as organicism or national psychology and tap into biological reasoning of every hue, from theories on heredity and eugenics to the Instinct School.

The May Fourth era is known for its all-out onslaught on tradition. It is tempting to interpret self-denigration in the face of a "progressive" West as succumbing to Orientalism, and this seemed to be the case in New Culture critique of Eastern civilization. Yet, while the Chinese saw themselves as decadent and degenerate, the same epithets were being applied by Western observers to their own society. If a Western hegemony is discernible here, it is only in the sense that the Chinese borrowed the vocabulary of the Western crisis of modern civilization to describe their own problems.

Confucianism and the National Psychology

The Kulturkampf in the Nascent Republic

The republican revolution was not simply a change of polity, it also ushered in a cultural revolution. The provisional government in Nanjing, though short-lived (January–April 1912), abolished the study of Confucian classics in the schools. The conservative forces saw the act as a signal for a general assault on the cherished teaching of the Sage. By 1913, Confucian societies all over China protested the destruction of Confucian temples, the confiscation of land allocated for their support, and the conversion of their buildings into modern schools or shelters for the homeless. The offenders were as a rule the local assembly, the provincial education bureau and financial office, or the local educational society controlled by those who believed that there was no place for Confucius in a republic (Beijing shifan 1977, 296–302). It was a replay of the anti-clericalism of the French Revolution. As an anecdote shows, the republican revolution had such corrosive effects on old values that in the very year 1911 Wu Yu, who was to make a name as an anti-Confucian crusader in the May Fourth era, had a physical scuffle with his father and the two continued the battle in court (Tang Zhengchang 1981, 88–89).

The conservative forces wasted no time in mounting a counterattack. Kang Youwei, elected president of the All-China Confucian Society in 1913, saw the teaching of the Sage as the quintessence of the "Chinese soul," and the preservation of the national soul as prerequisite to China's survival (Feng 1994, 63; Hsiao 1975, 545). In July 1913, the Nationalists in the parliament barely thwarted the Progressive Party's attempt to insert an article in the draft constitution to establish Confucianism as the state religion. The issue turned into a nationwide controversy, and a compromise was reached in an article stipulating Confucian principles as "the basis for the cultivation of character in national education" (Chow 1960, 291–292). This was a replay of Meiji Japan's conservative turn, where traditionalists failed to install Shintoism as state church but managed to proclaim the Imperial Rescript of Education to be the guidelines for national education, at the same time (1890) as the inception of parliament.

Yuan Shikai's "Psychology of Venerating Confucius"

When Yuan Shikai formally assumed the presidency in October, his inauguration speech dabbled in progressive rhetoric such as "adapting to the times" so as to follow the path of "evolution." In the same speech he warned against the destruction of "the teaching of our predecessors of four millennia" (Beijing shifan 1977, 270). By late 1914, Yuan had crushed the Second Revolution and Bai Lang's uprising. In a presidential order reinstating the sacrificial rites of Confucius, he complained that China's recent change of the "national form" (*guoti*) had caused the negligence of the age-old "psychology of venerating Confucius," hence the decline of morality (Beijing shifan 1977, 273).Yuan's docile senate complied with a proposal to base the "national character" on a moral foundation, to cultivate those virtues inherent in the Chinese "national spirit" such as loyalty, filial piety, integrity, righteousness (Yuan 1914a).

Yuan camouflaged his attempt to subvert the republican political form (*zhengti*) with the rhetoric of restoring the age-old national form (*guoti*). It was a quest for permanence and the model was the Japanese emperor system. Meiji ideologues had distinguished the ephemeral political system or *seitai* from the eternal and immutable national form or *kokutai* which was "the concept of national morality grounded in the rational consciousness and religious psychology of the people" (Irokawa 1985, 247). Joseph Levenson discerns an irony in Yuan's attempt at "restoring" a foreign import. It was also futile, for unlike the *bansei ikkei* ("a single line throughout ten thousand generations") of the Japanese Shintoist prototype, the Chinese Mandate of Heaven was slippery (Levenson 1964, 136–138).

In early 1915, when Yuan's monarchical restoration was in the offing, Wu Guanyin wrote that the national character argument was a pretext used by "old people" to exclude "new people" from power. Wu traced this fad to Liang Qichao and his journal *Justice* (to which Wu was a contributor) but discerned that the need to combat centrifugal tendencies existed then. By 1915, the same discourse had come to serve reactionary purposes, which flew in the face of reality: "Let us pose the question: Did titles like president, secretary of state, minister, deputy minister, secretary, section head, ever exist in antiquity?" For those who defended China's national character as an immortal spirit that transcended matter, Wu retorted that even spirit changed with the epoch (*shidai*): "National character is based on national psychology, subjected to change caused by external stimuli, and when national psychology changes, national character also follows" (Wu 1915, 1, 11).

Chen Duxiu's "The Psychology of the Confucian Nation"

Indeed, Yuan's regime and the ensuing Beiyang regime were staffed by "old people"—high officials and military personnel from the Qing dynasty—and this makeup of the "republican" government ended only with the successful conclusion of the Guomindang's Northern Expedition in 1927. While the situation lasted, the "new people" remained outsiders. On the other hand, the champions of Confucianism did not always fare well with those "old people" in power. Kang Youwei's candidate for the restoration was the Holy Duke, a descendant of Confucius, and when Yuan claimed the throne himself, Kang joined the National Protection cause. After Yuan's demise, Kang continued to petition President Li Yuanhong to promote Confucianism as the state religion. In July 1917, Kang was part of General Zhang Xun's coup to restore the former Qing emperor Puyi, but the farce ended after twelve days when the perpetuators were driven from the capital by General Duan Qirui, then the hegemon of the Beiyang forces.

The "new people" therefore did not limit their attacks on the Confucian movement but aimed them at the backward "psychology" of the Chinese people. A critic proposed in 1916 to "probe deeper into the national psychology and to scrap superficial explanations," for under a republic his countrymen could no longer blame the nation's malaise on the Manchus or even despotism (Qian 1916, 1). In the aftermath of the failed Second Revolution, Sun Zhongshan's fugitive party in Japan had already reached the same conclusion. All-out iconoclasm, however, was not waged by Sun's party but by other ex-revolutionaries such as Chen Duxiu and his associates (Chen Wanxiong 1992).

To look for a deeper cause of the national malaise, Chen's colleague Gao Yihan resorted to the generally accepted group-mind theory: "Changes in political reality depend not on political forms, but on where the majority of the nation's psychology leads" (Gao 1915a, 1), for "the state is a psychological coagulation rather than a physical form" (Gao 1915b, 1). And, it is "mass psychology" that manifests itself in a "thought current." In China, this mass psychology has been poisoned by "despotic thought," requiring a revolution in the realm of spirit conducted by the enlighteners (Gao 1917, 1).

Between Yuan Shikai's attempt and Zhang Xun's second restoration, Chen Duxiu wrote that Yuan was able to undermine the republic with his monarchical designs precisely by "exploiting the weakness of the people, and catering to the psychology of the old society." Yuan was dead, but Chen was more concerned with the possible advent of a Yuan the Second, for, as the French precedent showed, after the demise of Napoleon, there was a Napoleon III to repeat the same feat of burying the republic (Chen 1916d, 1–2). Less than two months after the farce of the second restoration, Chen warned that judging by "the minds and hearts of the majority of the people," the Zhang–Kang clique's failure was inconsequential. They were indeed guilty of treason against the republic, but *not* of "going against the psychology of the Confucian nation" (Chen 1917a, 161, 167).

The Problem of "Eastern Civilization"

In the iconoclasts' cultural war against the moral majority, it was no longer sufficient to dwell on national psychology.[2] The earlier applications of national psychology had placed China on a universalist ladder of nation-building and found her lagging. But now the reactionary confirmation of the Confucian "national psychology" as the cohesion of the new Chinese republic had induced such a profound sense of cultural malaise among the iconoclasts that, to them, China had gone astray from the universal march of human civilization. They resumed Liang's earlier attack on Chinese civilization in general and Confucianism in particular, a position, as I have pointed out in chapter 1, of blaming something inherently Chinese, not simply her low level of national cohesion.

The nationhood project and iconoclasm were different tasks, calling for different strategies. Now it became imperative to force an awareness of China's "Oriental" stagnancy. For that purpose, the iconoclasts consigned China and the East *in toto* to the unitary category of the "old," opposing it with an equally monolithic category of the "new." This "temporal" demarcation accompanied a "major spatial and cultural reorientation," in the equating of the new with the West (Liu 1995, 81).

The Shidai Rhetoric

Pertaining to the temporal axis, the iconoclasts' conceptual linchpin was *shidai* or "epoch," which spoke for itself: The present epoch is superior to the past, and the future is superior to the present. When the iconoclasts gauged Chinese tradition by the relentless footsteps of unilinear progress, they logically proclaimed it a thing of the past, no longer "fit" to survive in the modern epoch.[3] In the May Fourth era, "to adapt to the times" (*shiying shidai*) was synonymous with being modern. The era's New/Old polarization thrived in the absence of "the traditional versus the modern" binarism symptomatic of the modernization theory of our time, which, we must be aware, was certainly not the first to air the "modern" sentiment. In late seventeenth-century Europe, the erosion of traditional authority had provoked the "Quarrel between the Ancients and the Moderns" (Calinescu 1987, 23). Our modernization theory was a postwar product which came with its own grid of meaning, shaped by Talcott Parsons upon his reading of Max Weber. Unlike its Parsonian approach, which lays down the formal conditions of the traditional and the modern, the Old/New binarism in the May Fourth era was evolutionist. Deep down, it was Comtean in origin and ultimately rooted in the Enlightenment but was deceptively couched in Darwinian terms. In other words, it was a blind faith in linear progress bearing the misnomer of "evolutionism."

The New Culture Mode of Discourse

Chow Tse-tsung pinpoints the onset of the controversy over Eastern and Western civilizations "toward the end of, and in the years following, the May Fourth period, especially after 1921" (Chow 1960, 327). In fact, the debate commenced at the beginning of the period, as it intertwined with the debate on the new and the old.[4] It was the New Culture camp who fired the first salvo. In 1915, Chen Duxiu put nations into polarized civilization clusters: "Western nations are based on war, Eastern nations, on peace and tranquillity"; "Western nations are based on the individual, Eastern nations, on the family"; "Western nations are based on the rule of law and utilitarianism, Eastern nations, on feelings and empty forms." Chen's binarism affirmed the artificial divide between East and West, and lumped all Asiatic peoples into one category. For example, on the Eastern penchant for peace and tranquillity, Chen said: "[T]he Chinese nation finds peace and tranquillity on earth, the Jewish nation, in the kingdom of heaven, the Indian nation, in nirvana" (Chen 1915b, 1–4).

There was nothing original about matching Chinese characteristics in a one-to-one correspondence manner with antipodal Western ones—this style was already present in Yan Fu's writings. Nonetheless, this rhetoric was popularized in the May Fourth era, becoming its dominant mode of discourse. In a typical Orientalist manner, Chen held Western civilization as universally valid and the judge of the East. In 1916, Chen criticized Chinese slackness and tendency to waste precious time: "When Westerners make an appointment with another person, they always specify the time, down to the minutes; the Chinese, on the other hand, only specify the day. When Westerners walk, they walk straight ahead; the Chinese, on the other hand, always loiter on their way, as if they have no business to take care of." Chen criticized unclean Oriental habits through Western eyes: The three most filthy peoples in the world were Indians, Koreans, and Chinese (Chen 1916a, 2–3).

Chen's hierarchy of an inferior East and a superior West was challenged by Du Yaquan, the editor-in-chief of the *Dongfang Zazhi* (Eastern Miscellany). Du affirmed a dualistic view of cultural differences based on their intrinsic value, refusing to see them as backward or advanced levels of a universal civilization. Nonetheless, in the final analysis his view was equally bipolar. Chinese civilization sought unity, tranquillity, and harmony with nature, whereas the Western ways did the opposite: It glorified strife, was charged with dynamism, and was in conflict with nature. The two were equally valid, each with its own shortcomings. To jettison Chinese tradition with its prowess for synthesis in exchange for a Western civilization fraught with internal conflicts was to lose one's moorage in the modern world. Du believed that wealth and power should not be the criteria for judging the value of spiritual civilization. The spiritual crisis of the West was disclosed in the Great War, and its remedy seemed to be socialism. In a complementary spirit, Du opted for an emerging global synthesis of Eastern and Western civilizations (Chuangfu 1917; 1919).

Chen and Du set the keynotes for the two rival camps, since the other views were variations on theirs. Following both, Li Dazhao pressed their antipodal rhetoric to the extreme: "Eastern civilization emphasizes stillness, Western civilization emphasizes dynamism. . . . Eastern civilization is the civilization of the southern zone, Western civilization is the civilization of the northern zone [perhaps an idea inspired by Montesquieu]. . . . The former is natural, the latter is man-made; the former is peaceful and tranquil, the latter is warlike; the former is passive, the latter is active; the former is dependent, the latter is independent; the former is satiable, the latter is venturesome; the former is conventional, the latter creative; the former is conservative, the latter is progressive; the former is intuitive, the latter is rational; the former is speculative, the latter is empirical; the former is artistic, the latter scientific; the former is spiritual, the latter is material; the former pertains to the soul, the latter, the flesh; the former looks up to heaven, the latter stands firmly on the ground; the former is dominated by nature, the latter conquers nature" (Li 1918, 557–558).

On the surface, Li endorsed the iconoclasts' Orientalism. He singled out eight negative aspects of Eastern civilization: (1) a world-denying lifeview, which goes against the law of cosmic evolution; (2) inertia; (3) disrespect for individuality and its rights and its power; (4) hierarchical thinking, which reduces the individual to a part of the whole, a part treated as incomplete in itself, which has no right to life of its own and is completely devoured by the whole; (5) contempt for women; (6) the absence of sympathy; (7) the emphasis on theocracy; (8) wanton despotism. In spite of all these, Li, like Du Yaquan, believed that Westerners had a lot to learn from the Eastern way of life, in order for them to restore stillness and tranquillity of mind "amid a materialistic and mechanistic life" (Li 1918, 560).

Postcolonial Critique?

Du Yaquan had been a teacher of mathematics and natural science and the director of translation of the natural science section at the Commercial Press, before he became the editor-in-chief of the *Eastern Miscellany* in 1912. In the late Qing period, he had published in Shanghai a journal promoting science, one of the earliest. Du's credentials as an enlightener were therefore more impressive than Chen Duxiu's. Nonetheless, he objected to the latter's nihilistic attitude toward the native cultural heritage. Because of his "politically incorrect" anti-New Culture stance, Du had been forgotten since the May Fourth era—to the extent of being entirely left out of Chow Tse-tsung's authoritative account of that era—only to be rescued from oblivion in the "postmodern" 1990s (Gao 1994; 1996). Today, it has become fashionable to see Chen Duxiu and company as guilty of "self-Orientalizing" and Du and his cothinkers in Asia as "postcolonial" critics of Western hegemony.

As the old/new, East/West controversies were retold in the postwar narrative of the crisis of "modern transformation," they are presumably also amenable to postmodernist readings of the 1990s. While offering new interpretive possibilities, the more recent theories fail to do justice to these events in early twentieth-century China. Du Yaquan, for example, was not "postcolonial" and barely qualified as a "multiculturalist." He simply borrowed the epochal rhetoric of the Eurocentrist and the global evolutionary scheme it predicated. He coined the phrase "epochal relation" (*shidai guanxi*) to argue that total westernization had been "new" since the Hundred Days Reform but was rendered "old" by the European War, which ushered in the "new epoch" (*xin shidai*) of the convergence of Eastern and Western civilizations in a forthcoming global synthesis (Chuangfu 1919, in Chen 1985, 161–163). Du saw the bankruptcy of materialism and the rise of "Hebraic" socialism in the West as moving in the Chinese direction (Chuangfu 1917, in Chen 1985, 30–31).

Going a step further than Du's vague socialist vision for the era after the Great War, Li Dazhao looked forward to the "rise of a third, new, civilization" in the Russian Revolution of 1917 to remedy the global crisis, brought on by the malaise of both East and West (Li 1918, 560). Varying on the old/new binarism, Li consigned both East and West to the category of the old, and projected his vision of the new onto the nascent Soviet Union. This vision of global convergence is not the same as advocating "plural modernities" in our postcolonial sense. Instead, it was the quest for a new monolith.

This point is further demonstrated by the case of Liang Qichao, who joined Du Yaquan in defending Eastern civilization after returning from the Paris Peace Conference, having witnessed Europe lying in ruins. Liang told his readers that Western savants entreated China to be the redeemer of a West in a state of moral bankruptcy (Liang 1919, 15). This latest position of his was the culmination of a long departure from his early Eurocentric disdain for nativism. His new awareness can doubtlessly be rephrased in postcolonial terms as resistance against Western hegemony. Yet, Liang did not set China apart in an "anthropological space, which affirms a global imaginary of difference" (Tang 1996, 216). Instead, he saw China as having the potential to save the whole world—by contributing to a new universalism based on a synthesis of the East and the West. As he put it: "To use Western Civilization to expand our civilization, and to use our civilization to supplement Western Civilization, so that they would meld into a new civilization" (Liang 1919, 35). It is this penchant for patching up differences, not the postcolonial, multicultural celebration of *difference*, that strikes us here.

Furthermore, the Eastern civilization camp also upheld the credo of linear progress, by amending its sole yardstick of scientism with that of spiritual values. This universal temporality was inescapable for the discussants of both camps, as it set the legitimate parameters of their discourse. The only "space" recognized by the evolutionist thinking of the time was "environment" (*huanjing*) which in tandem with "epoch" constituted the composite *shidai huanjing*, with the temporal coordinate as the dominant one.

The "Eastern Civilization" champions had profound intellectual and emotional investments in the Chinese classical tradition, which distinguishes them from today's Chinese parrots of postcolonialism. However, both take the hint from, and lean on, the prestige of the Western intellectual center. The Chinese in the New Culture era were told by Western savants that the Great War had bankrupted the West spiritually, and that they were calling for the East to come to the rescue, which led to Liang Qichao's European anecdote. Meanwhile, the home audience were treated to the lecture tours of Bertrand Russell and John Dewey, who went out of their way to avoid Eurocentrism by promoting the reconciliation of East and West. This position chimed in with new intellectual trends in Europe, from the "philosophy of life" of Bergson and Eucken to the anti-Western Bolshevism. Today, a no less eager Chinese audience remains mesmerized by Western postcolonialist savants who says it is no longer "cool" to think in terms of universal modernization, now the new fashion is to assert one's identity. The difference is that, the early twentieth century intellectuals did not think in terms of symbolic resistance and imagined identity, they were still under the sway of universal evolution and believed that the only viable way to upstage your oppressor was by literally positing one's group on a higher evolutionary "stage" in global history. Spatial and multiculturalist politics were not options then.

Evolutionary Stages? or Ideotypes?

At that time, linear temporality was so ubiquitous that Chang Naide, even in questioning the validity of the spatial East/West binarism, felt compelled to reinstate it as "the distinction between ancient and modern civilizations." Using the Comtean three stages, Chang placed Chinese civilization in the second stage, the metaphysical *shidai*, and Western civilization in the third, the scientific *shidai*. The Great War has exposed the shortcomings of the third-stage civilization, portending the advent of a fourth one. But China's solution still lies in evolving from the second to the third (Chang 1920, in Chen 1985, 269–270, 273–274, 277). Chang, in a roundabout manner, advocated Westernization. His universalism also concealed a particularist, national-characteristic subtext. To dismiss the platitude of materialistic West versus spiritual East, Chang portrayed the Chinese as a very mundane people. Their religions are related to practical, not spiritual, life. Their philosophy is this-worldly. Their passion for truth and their aesthetic sense are undeveloped. Chinese culture is lopsided, not only in comparison with modern Western civilization, but with the civilization of ancient Greece as well. Chinese practicality has produced "a national character of resigning oneself to circumstances, following old custom, improvidence, and dispiritedness" (Chang 1920, in Chen 1985, 275–277). Thus, Chang's critique of the Chinese particularism was couched in terms of universal civilization and linear temporality.

The East/West binarism was also modified by Liang Shuming to accommodate his trio, China, India, and the West. Liang inevitably subscribed to the Comtean three-stages scheme, but inverted it by relegating the positivist West to the lowest stage of gratifying basic human needs, to be followed by the Chinese "art of living" phase, and capped by a denouement in nirvana, the Indian way. His scheme's pseudo-progressive nature is belied by his treating the three principles as three different yet equally valid, and therefore relativized, "roads"—quite unlike Auguste Comte's idea of man's ascent from obscurantism. Liang conceded that the present cultural defeat of China and India was due to their incompatibility with *shidai*, but their time would come. Tactically, he endorsed total Westernization to the extent that at the present stage of Western ascendancy China had no choice but to adopt Western culture in toto. Having thus co-opted all of the rival camp's positions, Liang declared that in the aftermath of the Great War the Western way was about to play itself out and the West was going the Chinese way. Like Westernism, this coming Sinification was also to be global in scope.

Set in an inverted Comtean scheme, Liang's characterization of the Chinese inevitably assumes two dimensions, the ideal and the actual. Ideally, the Chinese attitude is to seek harmony with, not opposition to, nature. Unlike the Western way, which promotes individual self-interest and dominance by developing the faculty of rational calculation at the expense of emotion, the penchant for harmony enables the Chinese to swim in the flux and fullness of life in Bergsonian terms. (The Bergsonian tradition in opposition to instrumental rationality is still very much alive today, in Martin Heiddeger's notion of human existence as the "thrown-ness".) Liang equates this true spirit of Chinese culture with Confucian benevolence. In reality, since China never had the material foundation to actualize this ideal, "benevolence" has ossified into rituals and codes of behavior. The Chinese, as individuals, chafe under their oppressive demands, and the concept of self is stifled. Their ideal of harmony has also been corrupted, having degenerated into a mere easy-going slackness (Liang 1985; Alitto 1979, 82–125).

Ah Q's "Spiritual" Victory

Liang presents his "ideal" dimension of the Chinese cultural spirit in the language of *Geistwissenschaft*, an approach later adopted by Otani Kotaro and Tang Junyi (Otani 1935; Metzger 1977, 29–47). As for the "actual" Chinese national character, Liang's portrayal is not very different from the picture painted by the iconoclasts. He preempted them by confirming their unflattering view of China, only to have her reinstated in an inverted Platonic mirror image. Hu Shi was not taken in, and he refuted Liang with a much less convoluted linear schedule. He saw only one "race-course" and on the same track, even though the West had already won the championship, the other contestants still needed to touch the goal (Hu 1923, 176).

While the East/West controversy was raging, Lu Xun demolished the *spirituality* of the "Eastern Civilization" with his satire, *The True Story of Ah Q* (1922), in which the pathetic hero resorts to the "spiritual victory" tactics after having been physically worsted by his molesters whom he calls "junior." Much less harsh were the distinguished foreign guests in China at the time. Rabindranath Tagore, an Indian poet and Nobel laureate, was a champion of Eastern civilization and his sympathy toward its defenders was predictable. Yet even Bertrand Russell held a view not much different from Du Yaquan, Liang Qichao, and Liang Shuming's: "The distinctive merit of our civilization, I should say, is the scientific method; the distinctive merit of the Chinese is a just conception of the ends of life. It is these two that one must hope to see gradually uniting" (Russell 1966, 194). Among the New Culture stalwarts, after Chen Duxiu and Li Dazhao turned to Marxism, the East/West controversy was kept alive by people like Hu Shi. It was restated in 1930s by Chen Xujing and revived by Li Ao in Taiwan in the 1960s.

Evolution's Shadow: Degeneration

Undoubtedly, the New Culture champions sided with progress and, like their Meiji counterparts, also promoted civilization. Yet the May Fourth euphoria about progress was often marred by pessimism. If progress was universal and inevitable, why had China remained outside the mainstream? When it came to civilization, the Chinese version was even hoarier than its Western junior, but this overly mature state reeked of senectitude. Civilization, like progress, thus also cast its long shadow, conjuring its doppelganger: Decadence.

Darwin and Lamarck

As New Culture sought to reenact the French Enlightenment, it was oblivious to the fact that Darwin and Decadence, both symptomatic of the late nineteenth century—the so-called *fin de siècle*—had intervened between the seminal Enlightenment and its Chinese emulation. The Enlightenment (with the exception of Rousseau) glorified civilization, the *fin de siècle* pathologized it. We will introduce further below the Decadent temper in Western literature and philosophy of history. In this section we begin with its corollary in *fin-de-siècle* science: The biological notion of degenerescence, a topic hitherto neglected by students of Darwinism in China.[5] Because of this lacuna, scholars of the May Fourth movement tend to simplify the era's evolutionism into a simple faith in linear progress, though May Fourth "evolutionism" subsumed both progress and degeneration.

When Yan Fu first introduced evolutionism in the late Qing, he called it *tianyan*, meaning Nature's permutations. By the May Fourth era, its standard translation had become *jinghua*, or progressive transformation, and it readily fortified the fallacy that "evolution" was the synonym of "progress" (*jingbu*). The May Fourth concept of linear progress was descended from the European Enlightenment, through its nineteenth-century scion, Comtean positivism or the cult of scientism. The bridge between Comtean linear progress and Darwinian evolutionism was Herbert Spencer. His unilinear view was similar to that of his fellow-Victorians, namely, social theorists Henry T. Buckle and Henry S. Maine. They theorised in the Comtean vein but did not make the transition to Darwinism (Stocking Jr. 1987, 128–129). Spencer, on the other hand, took part in the formulation of Darwinism by contributing the phrase, "survival of the fittest." His evolutionary scheme, from military society to industrial society, did not fit Chinese historical reality, nonetheless his authority sanctioned their faith in linear progress.

By the *fin de siècle*, the "Spencerian equation of evolution and progress" was increasingly "called into question" (Pick 1993, 217). Darwin's intellectual precursor was certainly not Comte but another Frenchman, Jean-Baptiste Lamarck. In the greater part of the nineteenth century, Lamarck's evolutionism was the dominant one and had an impact on Darwin himself. Lamarckian evolutionism was highly conducive to speculation about degenerescence. In its view, genetic material was highly malleable through adaptation to environment and traits acquired in this manner were transmittable as inheritance. This idea gave rise to a whole spectrum of alarmist projections of racial degeneration caused by the conditions of modern society, for example, industrialism, urbanism, and the revolt of the masses.

The Degeneration Scare in Europe

Degenerescence fed the discourse on national decline in France, where the sense of crisis was more acute than in England due to the traumatic defeat in the Franco-Prussian War and a legacy of internal upheavals bequeathed by the French Revolution (Pick 1993, 177). In England, a sense of racial crisis was accompanied by the advent of eugenics, which had different theoretical premises.

Against Lamarck's, Darwin had proposed a rival interpretation of the nature and cause of heredity, namely, the survival of the fittest in the winnowing process of "natural selection." Its emphasis was on a recalcitrant yet undefined heredity, with the environment only performing selection from the pool. Lamarck's assumption of the malleability of heredity was also challenged, from the 1880s onward, by the German naturalist August Weismann. He developed the theory of a hereditary material, the "germ plasm," passed on from generation to generation, unaffected by the environment. Weismannism lent support to the eugenics movement launched by Darwin's cousin, Francis Galton. It was based on the belief that disease, pauperism, immorality, and criminality, as well as genius were largely a matter of inheritance. The movement aimed at a social engineering directed, not at the social environment, but the hereditary material. It fed on an apprehension of the peril to human evolution posed by the high birth rate of the lower classes. This fear of racial deterioration precipitated the eugenic scare over national efficiency in the aftermath of the Boer War (1899–1902), when the poor physical quality of army recruits was fully exposed (Jones 1980, 84, 115). The Victorian Age's complacency based on the linear-progress credo was on the wane.

A French Eugenics Society came into existence only in 1912, in the wake of the first International Conference on Race Betterment held in that year in London. In spite of the rising influence of Weismann and Mendel among English eugenicists, most of their French colleagues remained faithful to Lamarck (Pick 1993, 101). In biology, Gregor Mendel's genetics, together with Hugo de Vries' theory of mutation, began to question Lamarck's environmentalism by the early twentieth century. It appears that the Mendelian laws of heredity were generally accepted by the second decade of the twentieth century (Mayer 1982, 687–688).

The New Culture Dilemma

These Western developments provided the backdrop of the coeval Chinese intellectual scene. By the May Fourth era, most enthusiasts of progress had come to understand evolution in a rather facile manner, as keeping abreast with "epoch" and being adaptable to the new "environment." This double faith inspired hope in the melioration of the Chinese people through enlightened critique and education. This sentiment was bolstered by American Progressivism, epitomized in John Dewey and introduced by Hu Shi.

Unwittingly, this popular version of evolutionism had a Lamarckian flavor. In 1919, Fu Sinian ascribed the failed republican revolution to the "historical heredity" of its players, including such notables as Sun Zhongshan, Zhang Taiyan, and Liang Qichao, and sought the remedy in the "intellectual revolution" of his own generation. He regarded the present epoch as similar to the Hundred Days Reform epoch, as both saw the beginning of a revolution, the political and the intellectual, respectively: "It is vital to identify our *shidai* and, once identified, know how to use our *shidai*" (Fu 1919, 124–125). From the anti-Lamarckian point of view, heredity cannot be so easily tampered with by "epoch," and certainly not by an "intellectual revolution."

What conclusion can one draw if the Chinese continue to be out of tune with *shidai* and ill-adapted to the modern milieu? If the urge to catch up made it imperative for the Chinese to think in progressive terms, the enormity of China's national crisis, which eclipsed those of England and France, also made degenerescence a staple for their thoughts. Inevitably, eugenic thinking of all hues found a receptive audience in China. Before we turn to this subject, it is necessary to clarify early Chinese perceptions of heredity and to trace the life of the concept of degeneration from its inception in the late Qing to the May Fourth era.

Early Chinese Understanding of Heredity

Yan Fu's Darwin

In 1895, Yan Fu introduced Darwin's concept of heredity: "[According to Darwin's *The Origin of Species*,] various species were descended from a single origin. They eventually became diversified, due to differences of environment, and also by virtue of small graduated variations in physiology" (Yan 1895b, 5).

The early Darwin had flirted with the Lamarckian concept of genetical malleability, but his lifelong concern was "natural selection" as the mechanism of evolution. Nature selects among a high degree of random and fortuitous variations in any species, allowing certain inherent traits to be transmitted and others to perish. Although Darwinian "environment" also causes variations, his environment-induced variation has very little in common with the Lamarckian "environment" that instructs hereditary material to metamorphose in order to serve a certain adaptive purpose. His *The Origin of Species* (1859) was published during his least Lamarckian phase. It reduced the role of environment, reaffirmed natural selection, and left the nature of heredity open. Darwin in his later years rekindled the Lamarckian thesis of environment molding heredity through "use and disuse," but "it never became a major component of his interpretation" (Mayer 1982, 689–693). Yan Fu seemed to collapse all phases of Darwin and made no mention of the rival position of Lamarck.

Liang Qichao, the Lamarckian

In 1903, Liang Qichao referred to heredity in the context of the organismic theory of the state, to the effect that a state "is an organism formed by nature, due to hereditary habits accumulated through the generations" (Liang 1903g, 2). He likened the Chinese people's political capability to the eyesight of the "blind fishes in the [underseas] Italian caves," a disused, hence degenerated capability—an example probably taken from Le Bon.[6]

Liang regretted that China's perennial economic backwardness had weakened her people's political "instinct." According to the "principle of heredity," it has resulted in a poor "inheritance" in political capability, which even periods of temporary prosperity could not redress. To air his antirevolutionary sentiments, Liang cited Western authorities to the effect that babies with a high rate of insanity were born during the French Revolution, attesting to the "horrible effect" of social upheavals "inherited by the collective psychology" (Liang 1904d, 5, 9–10). He echoed French medical opinion in the wake of the Paris Commune Uprising (1871) that the legacy of the Great Revolution had resulted in "potentially fatal hereditary modifications in future generations" (Pick 1993, 70).

Liang's fatalism was more than offset by his voluntarism, for he defined moral cultivation as the will to fight "society's cumulative influence through the centuries, the fixed habit lodged in my brain" (Liang 1904c, 6). Such mentalism cannot be attributed exclusively to Buddhist influence, for Lamarckianism itself contains a similar ambiguity. We find English Lamarckians such as Henry Maudsley and Walter Bagehot sharing the same optimism and using similar arguments. Bagehot regarded the nervous system as a decisive factor in evolution and believed that "conscious effort produced habit which in its turn became fixed as a reflex of the nervous system." For Maudsley, "environment worked upon mental forms and was subsumed through reproduction as a given physiological and neurological condition" (Pick 1993, 205, 207).

A Protean Notion

In most of his statements Liang seemed to understand heredity according to Lamarck—as acquired, transmittable, and malleable habits. There is no evidence of late Qing intellectuals having been exposed to Weisman's thesis of the immutability of the hereditary material, which became better known in the republican period. Anyway, finesse in theory was not necessary in polemical writings. In polemics, it sufficed to evoke a rather general rhetoric of heredity. When pessimism prevailed, entailing an emphasis on the dead weight of racial heredity, the polemicists as a rule conjured up an unregenerate national character. A voluntarist solution was invariably sought, and the rhetoric of human will triumphant over environment, thereby altering the course of national destiny, would then rush to their rescue.

As "heredity" was used in an elastic manner, its mechanism was left unclarified. More often than not, heredity was simply a term for stable, long-lasting traits. In 1904, a Shanghai journalist identified two kinds of custom, those handed down from antiquity and those that emerged through the ages. He compared the former to hereditary disease, the latter to sickness by contagion (Kequan 1904, 135).

There are indications that Weismann and Galton became known in the early Republican era. An essay in *Tiger* magazine in 1915 attempted to combine their theories with that of Le Bon in explaining the formation of national character (Lao 1915). In a 1919 exchange between the philosopher Zhang Dongsun and Chen Jiayi on the merit of synthesizing the new and the old, both referred to Mendel's genetic law and Hugo de Vries' theory of mutation (Chen Jiayi 1919).

But in polemical writings, generalized and ill-defined rhetoric of "heredity" persisted in the May Fourth era, as the term was turning into a cliché in New Culture parlance. In 1916, Chen Duxiu lamented that even today's "new youth" were captives of a "heredity transmitted from distant ancestors through the generations," namely, the thought of "entering officialdom to make a fortune," which had "permeated their nerves and filled their marrow" (Chen 1916b, 2). Here Chen was employing a Lamarckian metaphor, even though its validity was being questioned at the time. Yi Baisha, an editor of *New Youth*, saw Confucius-worship and the eight-legged essay (a style of writing used in the imperial examination) as entrenched "habits" in the Chinese psychology (Yi 1916, 2). Fu Sinian lamented that new ideas were transmogrified in China due to the "problematic heredity" of the Chinese. Just look at students who learn English today, they harbor the "same psychology" as those who studied eight-legged essays in the past, all motivated by fashion and profit (Fu 1919, 120–121)! In the same year, Li Dazhao penned an essay, "The Heredity of Attending Civil Service Examinations." This inherited trait, Li quipped, implanted by a historical institution, affected all their modern enterprises to the point of even treating *shidai* as a chief examiner—by catering to its demands (Li 1919). The centuries-old "civil service examinations" syndrome also informed Lu Xun's "Kong Yiji" (1919a) and "Bai guang" (The white light) (1922), stories of its human residues.

Nature versus Nurture

Trained in medicine, and once a biology teacher, Lu Xun was better equipped than fellow polemicists to deal with scientific subjects. In his diagnosis of the moral disease of the Chinese, Lu Xun found himself torn between nature and nurture. In his short story, "The Misanthrope" (1925), the protagonist tells the narrator: "On my way here I met a small child with a reed in his hand, which he pointed at me, shouting 'Kill!' He was just a toddler" (Lu 1925g, 92; Yang and Yang 1981, 238). The episode surfaces in an argument between the two men. One holds "environment," the other, "bad heredity," responsible for such behavior, leaving the reader undecided. The very fact that Lu Xun entertained a plausible "bad seed" explanation revealed his doubt about "saving the children," the future Chinese, which he had advocated in 1918.

Among coeval Western scholarship on the subject, a popular solution was opting for a middle ground. A Chinese commentary on a statistical study in *The Scientific American* on the racial factor and crimes pointed out that the rate and the type of crime hinged on both inborn and environmental factors (Luo 1919, 71–72). Chinese polemics at the time were concerned with other issues, and the uncertain nature of heredity continued to fan the dispute between determinism and voluntarism. In Mao Dun's *Rainbow* (1929), a novel about the May Fourth era, a female of the new epoch blames women's weaknesses on centuries-old heredity. She is countered by another female who declares that they can be overcome if one makes an effort (Mao 1984, 85).

It is clear that in their attack on Chinese tradition, May Fourth iconoclasts accused it of perverting the biology of the Chinese race. Their stress on the corporeal calls for a revision of the culturalist interpretation of May Fourth iconoclasm. In fact, even in America, a liberal, cultural-anthropological concept of society began only in the late 1920s, and its triumph over relentless biologism was not complete until the postwar era (see chapter 6). It is certainly misleading to see the May Fourth era through postwar lenses, which obscure the ascendancy of biologism in that period.

Heredity Against Instinct

Another contrast between early twentieth century thinking and ours is that the former's obsession was with "instinct," whereas the artificial and the symbolic has become our fetish. Virtually every school of early-century thought capitalized on the protean notion of instinct. It assumed guises such as the "will to power" (Nietzsche), "residues" (Vilfredo Pareto), "*élan vital*" (Henri Bergson), "will to believe" (William James), and "libido" (Sigmund Freud). Even Carl G. Jung, who delved into symbolism, called the archetype or primordial symbol in the human psyche "the self-portrait of the instinct" (Jung 1919, 136). "Instinct" was the dominant cliché of the previous *fin de siècle*, akin to the sway held by "discourse" in our own.

If in the late twentieth century we theorize in terms of *la langue* and *le parole*, early-century thinkers problematized "instinct" and "heredity" instead. Heredity is the historical heritage unique to a particular race, whereas instincts are a small number of innate tendencies common to the species.

Heredity inevitably modifies instincts, and from the writings of the late Qing reformists onward the term became a negative synonym of Chinese tradition. The derogatory ring of "heredity" (*yichuan*) was amplified in the May Fourth era. The above-mentioned condemnation of the "heredity of civil service examinations" from almost all quarters was an indictment of Chinese civilization's ossified formalism, which had stifled the vital forces of her people.

Is the Human World Unnatural?

Again, no self-Orientalizing is detected here. The Chinese discussants simply dwelled on the same problematic that was troubling their coeval Western thinkers. Science, especially the new biology, had compelled an urgent search for new life-values compatible with its findings. The picture of the natural world as an arena of struggle for survival made the life-denying Christian morality look like an aberration—a pathological outgrowth that smacked of decadence. Among those who upheld such a verdict were Friedrich Nietzsche, Ernst Haeckel, and D.H. Lawrence (Milton 1987, 3–5).

Others who were unsettled by this crisis of values preferred to question the validity of treating the evolution of human society as an extension of the natural world, as typified in Herbert Spencer's synthetic philosophy. To refute Spencer, Thomas Huxley discerned a higher "ethical process" that transcended the Darwinian laws. He saw in the "history of civilization" humankind's triumph in "building up an artificial world within the cosmos" (Schwartz 1964, 103–104). Thus, Huxley the scientist argued in a most pious manner about "the grandeur of the place Man occupies" in nature (Pusey 1998, 5).

A third position was offered by Prince Kropotkin, Edward Westermarck, Benjamin Kidd, and William McDougall. Together they were known as the sociological Instinct School, which saw self-denial and altruism as a "social instinct." This school was an alternative to both Lamarckianism and Galtonian eugenics in evolutionist social theory. Unlike both, it was interested less in the environment/heredity issue than in the ratio of intelligence and irrationality in the evolutionary process. This school deemed social institutions "structured instincts," and saw society as also modifying instincts by education and moral teaching (Jones 1980, 119–120, 127). In 1902, Liang Qichao spoke highly of Benjamin Kidd for his theory that the individual died in order to accelerate the evolution of the progeny, which explained why higher species had shorter longevity in contrast to the "immortality" of lower life forms such as the amoeba (Liang 1902f, 81). McDougall, whose *An Introduction to Social Psychology* (1908) was translated into Chinese in 1920, attributed nearly all human social behavior to some instinctual basis. Another classic of the school was the Finnish anthropologist Westermarck's *The History of Human Marriage* (1891), the Chinese translation of which was serialized in the literary supplement of Beijing's *Morning Post* in the early 1920s, but a translation of an article on marriage by him appeared earlier in *New Youth* (Yang 1918).

In facing the crisis of instincts, the Nietzscheans and the Instinct School reached opposite conclusions—one leading to egotism, the other, to mutual aid. The Nietzschean position as a rule bolstered iconoclasm, whereas the Instinct School, with the exception of the socialist Kropotkin, was conservative. Both, however, agreed that instincts are dynamic forces in human evolution and that a certain cultural "heredity" might work against instincts by weakening them. This line of reasoning gave rise to the degeneration-regeneration thesis, the program of saving civilization through the recovery of instincts.

Lu Xun Collapsed the Altruistic and Selfish Instincts

The degeneration-regeneration thesis underlay Lu Xun's attempt to marshal the forces of common instinct against the baneful Chinese heredity. "For life to continue," Lu Xun averred, "another instinct" needs to be revived, "that is sexual desire." In the animal kingdom, sexual instinct is related to "parental instinct," equally vital for racial preservation. He exhorted his generation to reassert their instincts of survival, racial continuity, and parental love: Let them hold up the descending "gate of darkness"—symbolizing China's antievolutionary, life-denying cultural inheritance—to allow future generations to make the passage to a better world (Lu 1919d, 130–133)!

This call to sacrifice the present for the sake of the future is basically Kidd's idea, and Lu Xun's "parental instinct" argument also echoes Westermarck and McDougall. The pro-Christian Westermarck especially regarded the pairing family, crucial for the survival of human society, as rooted in the instinct to protect the young. If it amazes us to see Lu Xun the Nietzschean agree with Westermarckian "family values," his position is to be understood in the context of the New Culture crusade against concubinage. In the same article Lu Xun supported monogamy for eugenic reasons. He believed that polygamy, practised by the Chinese, was moral degeneration, which had led to racial deterioration (Lu 1919d, 130–140).

The "gate of darkness" article, which preached self-sacrifice, was perhaps one of Lu Xun's least Nietzschean moments. Kidd's death wish for the sake of posterity differs substantially from Freud's death instinct (*Thanatos*), which, as the ultimate resolution of all tensions, has an affinity with sexual gratification. The sexual instinct of the Instinct School, which Lu Xun applied in that article, also has a ring similar to today's pro-life movement, unlike the Freudian notion of Eros as the individual libido. In 1922, Lu Xun fortified his Nietzschean stance with Freudianism and wrote "Bu tian" (Repairing the heavens) to apotheosize sexual instinct as the fountainhead of creativity. A story based on the ancient myth of the Goddess Nüwa, it allegorically restated the thesis of civilization's regeneration through the sexual instinct—but this time to celebrate the creative individual (Lu 1922c). Six years later another thinker who combined Nietzschean philosophy with instinct theory, D.H. Lawrence, in his *Lady Chatterley's Lover* (1928) used a fictional Sir Clifford's sexual impotence to allude to the decline of genteel society, seeing regeneration in the virility of the rustic gardener, symbolizing nature.

Civilization Against Nature

In the West, the concept of the decline of civilization can be traced back to antiquity. Though eclipsed by the idea of progress in early modern Europe, it surfaced as a countercurrent even in the Enlightenment, when Montesquieu and Edward Gibbon wrote about the decline and fall of the Roman Empire, whereas Rousseau blamed civilization for corrupting nature. In the nineteenth century, even at the height of the Victorian age, voices skeptical of "progress" were audible. They described modern life as the morbid outcome of industrialism, urbanization, toxic wastes, air pollution, alcoholism, narcotics and stimulants, and diseases (such as syphilis), among other banes (Hurley 1990). In 1881, the introduction of the term "neurasthenia" (nervous exhaustion) into clinical terminology "set the tone for literature on the increasing tempo of [modern] life and its nefarious consequences" (Kern 1983, 125).

The **Fin-de-Siècle** *Mood*

This crisis of modernity made the *fin de siècle* the fount of pessimistic philosophies of history. In 1895 an American, Brook Adams, published *Law of Civilization and Decay*. Oswald Spengler's *The Decline of the West* came out in Germany in 1918, and H.G. Wells' *The Salvaging of Civilization* was published in England in 1921. Meanwhile, Arnold Toynbee pondered the fate of Western Civilization, wondering if it had travelled down the same road as Hellenic (Greco-Roman) Civilization.[7] The cyclical view of history was shared by a Russian cothinker, Pitirim Sorokin. Not all of these "crisis philosophers" were Darwinians, but they unanimously sang the same tune of civilizational decline.[8] At the time, the idea of decline was so prevalent in social theory that even leading Marxists like Lenin and Trotsky talked about the "degenerate" worker state.

From our vantage point, we may see this school as a symptom of the crisis of modernity, which questioned blind faith in modernization as progress. The problematization of modern civilization persisted in Freud's *Civilization and Its Discontents* (1930), Toynbee's *Civilization on Trial* (1948), and Foucault's *Madness and Civilization* (1961), although by the time of the last-mentioned publication, biological reasoning was no longer in fashion. Nonetheless, Foucault continued to treat the "body" as the locus of resistance against an all-encompassing symbolic domination.[9] Anyway, decadence as a leitmotif looms large in the postwar American critique of the shallow theories of modernization and economic growth. In the place of progress, these observations deplore the family's decline, the softening of the urban middle class, the rise of the Mass Man, or modernity as a form of neurosis.[10] Civilization against nature is a theme kept very much alive by today's environmentalists.[11]

From the late nineteenth century, alongside the crisis philosophies, the "decay of civilization" and "civilization as malaise" were popular motifs in literary works, namely, those of Norway's Knut Hamsun, Germany's Thomas Mann, Austria's Franz Kafka, and England's D.H. Lawrence. These developments were contemporaneous with the May Fourth era. In 1919, Liang Qichao returned from Paris to paint a West in profound crisis: "In their own words, it is called the 'fin de siècle' (*shijimo*); in a narrow sense the concept is analogous to the approaching of the year's end when all fiscal accounts need to be settled but one is at a loss about how to go about it; in a broader sense, it is tantamount to the pending end of the world and the extinction of civilization" (Liang 1919, 15).

In China, those who were less sanguine than Liang about the redeeming role of China were afflicted with their own version of the modernity crisis. In China's case, the erosion of traditional values was occasioned less by rapid industrial development (as in the West and Japan) than by a gnawing sense of national weakness. The pessimistic mood was not confined to the quandary of nation-building, though. On a deeper metaphysical level, homespun antiprogressive thinking, emerging amid the decay of Confucian civilization, had already questioned the very concept of progress. On the eve of the republican era, Wang Guowei and Zhang Taiyan had wedded Buddhism to Western pessimistic philosophy. Zhang especially rendered "progress" as an illusion with his theory of the "simultaneous evolutions" of both good and evil (Sun 1996,197).

The Chinese Civilization Is Life-denying

The home-made tranquilizer to the euphoria of progress was fortified by the Western decadent discourse and its corollary, the degeneration theory. Thus we also find that May Fourth thinkers bemoaned the decline of instincts. Chen Duxiu talked "progress" when he quoted Auguste Comte, Herbert Spencer, and Jeremy Bentham. But for him, Chinese civilization's decline began early: "Ever since the Zhou and Han Dynasties," the Chinese had departed from "reality" and "exalted empty formalities" (Chen 1915d, 5). To put it in the idiom of the time: Chinese people had gone against Nature and been bogged down in artifice. Lu Xun was more explicit in 1919: "We Chinese since antiquity have been going against nature, hence the withering of human capabilities, and the standstill of progress" (Lu 1919d, 132). Popular in the European *fin de siècle* was the belief that humankind had declined since the Greeks. Francis Galton argued so by way of eugenics, and Nietzsche reduced two millennia of Christianity to a chronicle of decadence.

Lu Xun, a disciple of Nietzsche, commented on a Japanese critic Hasegawa Nyozekan's physiognomic observation: "human + beastliness = Westerners." He wondered whether the Chinese had become more "human" by simply living up to another formula: "human + domesticated animal nature = certain type of people" (Lu 1927b, 413–414). In line with his program for the revival of instincts, Lu Xun advocated aggression most emphatically: "If in this world there are still people who have the will to live, first they must dare to speak out, dare to laugh, dare to cry, dare to rage, dare to curse, dare to strike, so that in this damnable place, this damnable *shidai* can be beaten back" (Lu 1925d, 43).

Lin Yutang, who in the 1920s was an associate of Lu Xun and his brother Zhou Zuoren, wrote a sequel to *Thus Spake Zarathustra*, imagining Zarathustra as a guru visiting China. Zarathustra is amazed at how "extremely quick it was for the Chinese to evolve from wolves to domesticated canines in just four thousand years." He exclaims: "I have seen people that are civilized (departing from Nature), but not that civilized" (Lin 1925b, 158, 18–19). In 1903, Jack London had moralized in a reverse manner in his *The Call of the Wild*, the story of a dog turning into a wolf through the recovery of instincts by going back to nature. The idea of averting degeneration through the revival of instincts was continued in the recent past by Konrad Lorenz, the author of *On Aggression* (1966). For him "there is nothing left in civilized society which could prevent retrograde evolution except our *non rational sense of values*" (Jones 1980, 137).

In Lu Xun's eyes, the Chinese are capable of aggression only when they hide themselves in a cowardly way amid the anonymous "Herd," and their sexual instincts are likewise perverted. They derive sado-cannibalistic pleasure from watching public executions and torture. Great men who sacrifice themselves for the masses often end up as entertaining spectacles to gratify the Herd's depraved curiosity. While exalting aggression, Lu Xun took pains to distinguish between two types of destructiveness: "lackey-style destruction" aiming at "intact and monumental objects" and the destruction unleashed by "the creator" (Lu 1925L, 194).

In Europe, degenerescence theorists also saw in the bestiality of the crowd not the healthy revival of instincts but atavism, which "inverted the law of evolution and moved from present to past," from individuation back to nondifferentiation. Mob psychologists of the time as a rule employed the "image of castration, cannibalism, mutilation, homogeneity" to depict the crowd (Pick 1993, 92, 96). That the corruption of healthy instincts is conducive to extreme cruelty was an insight that Nietzsche and D.H. Lawrence elevated to a quasi-law.[12]

Lu Xun also discerned instinctual decline in the Chinese Herd, meaning its perversion in the direction of deadly destruction. Lu Xun was no articulate theorist, but his dialectic of nature and civilization must read like Thomas Mann's: "Nature corrupts Spirit; Spirit corrupts Nature; Nature heightens Spirit; Spirit heightens Nature" (Heller 1966, 211). The Chinese case, unfortunately, is one of mutual corruption.

The Specter of Racial Degeneration

In 1897 Liang Qichao wrote Yan Fu to challenge his thesis that the monarchical institution was at the root of the "decline of the yellow race" (Liang 1897d, 108). This specter loomed even larger in Yan Fu's 1898 essay on racial preservation in which he introduced the term *tuihua*, or "degeneration" (Yan 1898c, 87). In 1903, Lu Xun in one of his earliest articles applied the term to the Chinese, warning that their degeneration was leading them towards extinction and that eventually they would leave their own fossils behind to incite the pathos of future occupants of China (Lu 1903b, 3). In 1904, Liang Qichao likened the Chinese people's political capabilities to the blindness of those fishes in underseas caves. The concept soon became popular as it entered the middle-brow language of journalism (Guyin 1904; Editorial 1905; Wu 1914; Jianmeng 1921; Zhou Jianren 1922c; Hua Lu 1922; Xusheng 1925). In the May Fourth era, Sun Zhongshan asserted that only the written Chinese language had made historical progress, while the spoken Chinese had degenerated. This thesis confounded the vernacular champions' decadent view of the literary Chinese, and Hu Shi was piqued by Sun's amateurism (Hu 1920, 1–2). More in line with the vernacular revolution was the view of Chang Hui, a leader of the folk literature movement: "[T]he further civilization progresses, the more degenerate folksong becomes" (Chang 1922, 3).

The Senility Metaphor

Understandably, degenerescence became the standard idiom in May Fourth discussions of national character. Chen Duxiu, who generally subscribed to the Comtean scheme of linear progress, at the same time called the Chinese "a degenerate and enfeebled people" (Chen 1915e, 6). Using a cytological metaphor, he compared youth to "fresh, lively cells" beside "old, decaying" ones in the metabolism of the body. Unfortunately, in China, the new cells had been affected by the "virus" of the old. "When I look at our youth, five out of ten are young in age but senile in body, nay, nine out of ten are young in age and body, but senile in their brain nerves" (Chen 1915d, 1). Chen's senility thesis was corroborated by Lu Xun, who observed: "Chinese men and women tend to age ahead of their time; before they reach twenty, they are already senescent" (Lu 1919d, 138). Lu Xun saw the Chinese way as antinatural: It suppresses the youthful stage in human development, allowing old people to "block all the roads" and "breathe all the fresh air" meant for the young (Lu 1918b, 338).

The literary critic Hu Yuzhi also saw the condition of the nation as "senile." He chose not to use the eugenicists' concept of "racial deterioration" and preferred the view of the "national psychologists" who saw nations passing through youth, adolescence, and senility, like individual organisms. This fine distinction, being academic, did not offer much consolation, as the symptoms of "senility" he discerned among the Chinese included greediness, baseness, cowardice, cruelty, and callousness (Hua 1922).

The Similes of Feminization and Infantilism

In the Western *fin de siècle*, degenerescence theorists often viewed "abnormal" sexualities as degenerate. From the premise that sexual differentiation stood for a higher stage of evolution, it followed that sexually aggressive women who took on "male" traits were atavistic. By the same token, men should resist feminization to avert degeneration, thus homosexuals were considered "degenerates" in the literal sense (Dijkstra 1986, 158–159, 219). As the war of the sexes was not a major concern of most May Fourth polemicists, they adapted the argument to the purpose of national salvation. In their writings, feminization simply became a synonym for being weak. Their remedy, namely, to reassert one's aggressive instinct, was meant for the entire nation.

Chen Duxiu lamented as he switched from the metaphor of senility to that of feminization: "Let us look at our educated youth: their weak hands lack the energy to tie up a chicken, their hearts do not harbor the virility of a real man; with pallid faces and slim waists, they have the seductiveness of a woman; they recoil from cold and are apprehensive of heat like an emaciated sick man" (Chen 1915e, 6). Chen quipped that "pale-faced scholar" was an expression of admiration in China, and it betrayed a sure symptom of "racial decline" (Chen 1916b, 1). Lu Xun also remarked sardonically: "In our China, the greatest, most enduring, and most popular art is man cross-dressing as woman" (Lu 1924e, 187).

In the spirit of those "evolutionists" who warned against "degeneration and enfeeblement" (and echoing Lu Xun's position on aggression), Chen Duxiu advocated "beastliness" as a remedy (Chen 1915e, 6). He also called it "the power of resistance." Lacking this power, the Chinese people "have formed a national character of baseness, shamelessness, cowardice, contentment with temporary ease, slyness, and glibness" (Chen 1915a, 4). Within the human race, man and the white race were conquerors, woman and the nonwhite races were the conquered; among the Far Eastern peoples, the Mongols, Manchus, and Japanese were conquerors, the Chinese were the conquered; and among the Chinese, the inhabitants of the Yangzi Valley were the most easy to enslave, due to their "cowardice and contentment with temporary ease" (Chen 1916c, 2–3). "Resistance" happened to be a favorite word of Nietzsche's. Another writer for the *Xin Qingnian* (New youth), who glorified war, quoted Nietzsche to the effect that the ultimate immorality was being weak (Liu 1916, 4–5).

The *fin-de-siècle* discourse on women also compared them to children: Women and children were devoid of moral self and thus harbored more evil tendencies than men (Dijkstra 1986, 196). Chinese polemicists who used infantilism as a metaphor tended to emphasize childishness and lack of ability. In 1913, Liang Qichao had employed infantilism as an analogy for Chinese political immaturity (see chapter 2). Chen Duxiu, in his turn, used it to refer to poor racial qualities: "[As for Chinese youth,] although their age has reached youth, their physique is that of a child with teeth fully grown. Among a million of them, it is well-nigh impossible to find one with sanguine face and robust physique, who has the dominance and aggressiveness of European and American youth" (Chen 1916b, 1).

Degenerescence in Political Polemics

The May Fourth era's national character discussion was also tapped by partisan politics. Beginning in 1920, Chen Duxiu was busy building the Chinese Communist Party and combating the anarchist influence among youth. He blamed anarchism and nihilism on indigenous origins, "the corrupted and degenerate national character" of the Chinese. What China needed was not more anarchism, but "enlightened despotism" (Duxiu 1920; 1921b). Chen backed his Leninism with the Le Bonian thesis that crowd psychology was blind (Duxiu 1921a, 3; Chen and Ou 1921). It betrayed the lingering elitism of a May Fourth enlightener.

The Chinese Youth Party, another offshoot of the May Fourth Movement that championed statism, was also keen on French sociology. The statists did not have a theory comparable to Marxism, so they relied heavily on the national character discourse. To refute the class concept of the Communists, they upheld *la nationalité*, a "national personality" defined in its static mode by race and environment, with its dynamics manifest in culture and beliefs (Li 1924, 3–4). This theoretical formulation was probably adapted from the work of Alfred Fouillée, a French social psychologist.[13] The statists believed that each nation had its own "racial genius," which should be allowed to blossom; the Chinese genius lay in its ability to effect reconciliation (Qiu 1926, 4)—a leaf taken from the Eastern civilization camp. Not all statists were positive about this reconciliatory genius, though. One wrote that China's "national spirit" had degenerated from a "masculine" into a "feminine" one since the Eastern Han dynasty (Jieshi 1925).

A Voguish Discourse

In the late 1920s, China's "Dr. Sex," Zhang Jingsheng, spotted degeneration in his examination of Chinese private parts. Zhang, who had a reputation as a crackpot, deplored the underdevelopment of Chinese male genitals, but in his opinion the female counterparts were in a more sorrowful state. Fully developed vaginal labia, which should resemble "the shape of overlapping flower-petals," are rare in China. Not only the clitoris is inconspicuous among most Chinese women, their vaginal labia are also pathetic, for they resemble "flimsy and wizened leaves" (Zhang 1927, 6).

In early twentieth century, degenerescence was blown to cosmic proportions in the West, as the faith in progress took a downturn from the *fin de siècle* to the holocaust of the Great War. A post-World War I book by A. Linckewicz, a professor at the University of Vienna, averred that once there had existed a telepathetic human species, higher than today's human beings. The former, due to their decadent life-style, had degenerated into apes, and from those apes our species were descended (Ma 1921; You 1921). In 1917, the Chinese iconoclast Tao Menghe, who had studied under Edward Westermarck in London, referred to the theory of apes as "degenerated human species" (Tao 1917, 1–2). Chinese readers in the May Fourth era were also acquainted with the theory of a Kang-ke-lin (E.G. Conklin?), a professor at Princeton University, that today's humankind had not surpassed the ancient Greeks, the evolution of our species had reached its organic limits, and no further progress was possible (Lu Guancun 1920). The ambiguity of eugenics lay in the fact that it lent scientific support to such gloomy views but at the same time, by its very existence, held out the hope for race betterment.

The Beginning of Chinese Eugenic Thinking

Race Advancement as a Reformist Program

Liang Qichao's 1897 correspondence with Yan Fu referred to the latter's theory of race betterment and in particular his "thesis of selecting and preserving the good stock" (Liang 1897d, 109, 110). In 1898 Yan Fu, in his exhortation about "racial preservation," warned against the "propagation of the wrong stock," i.e., people weak in physique and feeble in mind, at the expense of "superior" ones. He deplored the Chinese penchant for procreation regardless of their poverty, weakening the race as a result, and sounded the alarm: "Europeans have recently advanced the theory of selecting and preserving only good stock, beginning with marriage restrictions. Even white people find it pertinent to implement this theory, what should we say about China?" (Yan 1898c, 87–88). Around the same time, the martyr of the Hundred Days Reform, Tan Sitong, advocated the "science of race advancement" for the creation of a superior humanity (Dikötter 1992, 168).

While Tan had his eyes on cosmic evolution, Yan's "racial preservation" became a national concern of Chinese intellectuals in the early twentieth century. As early as 1903, a radical Chinese student journal in Tokyo promoted the "study of national hygiene" to avert racial degeneration and for racial preservation (Anonymous 1903c, 1–6). It was a Chinese rendition of "racial hygiene," another name for eugenics.

Meanwhile, Tan's cosmic vision was perpetuated by Kang Youwei in his utopian treatise, *The Book of Great Harmony*, which took shape at around

1902. Kang's "race reform" (*renzhong gailiang*) was not for the sake of preserving the Chinese or even the yellow race, but to realize his ecumenical vision. He envisioned a future in which racial boundaries would be eradicated when "all would approach the physiognomy of the Caucasians" (Kang 1956, 197). He wished that geography and climate, together with interracial marriage, would attenuate and eventually transform the brown and black races. "For those browns and blacks who are unregenerate in character, too reprehensive in appearance, or harboring diseases, doctors should apply to them drugs of sterilization, to put a stop to their propagation," thus preventing them from "undermining the good stock and causing racial degeneration" (Kang 1956, 122).[14] As indicated in chapter 2, while Kang was indulging in utopian hyperbole, Liang Qichao addressed himself to the more mundane nationhood project by urging the improvement of Chinese heredity.

Eugenics and the Chinese Enlightenment

In 1916, an editor of *New Youth*, Li Yimin, wrote an article introducing the eugenics movements in Europe and America. It reported the first International Conference on Race Betterment held, in 1912, in London. The article also lauded the castration laws adopted by the states of Indiana in 1907 and California in 1909 (Li 1916).[15] Li Yimin probably also wrote under the pen-name Li Ping, who was alarmed by the proliferation of "inferior stock" in China, due to the Chinese practice of polygamy and the wide spread of syphilis (Li 1916, 7). A contributor to the journal's special issue on population (April 1920) proposed "putting an end to" the "inferior stock" in the spirit of "eugenics and the study of race betterment" (Yan 1920, 5). At that time, the editor-in-chief Chen Duxiu saw eugenics as conflicting with the ideals of individual freedom and the equality of man; nonetheless, the eugenic program of weeding out inferior elements regardless of their social background carried more sense than the anti-pauper position of Malthus (Chen 1920, 7).

Eugenic thinking was not compatible with the enlighteners' Lamarckian faith in amelioration through education. In 1919, a Chinese eugenic treatise dampened this faith by asserting that "acquired character," such as the education one has received, was not inheritable, while "inborn or inherent character," such as insanity, feeble-mindedness, and syphilis, could be transmitted to progeny (Chen Changheng 1919, 12).

Varieties of Eugenics in the May Fourth Era

A Chinese pioneer of eugenics was a younger brother of Lu Xun, Zhou Jianren, biologist, and translator of Darwin's *The Origin of Species.*[16] Jianren moved to Beijing in late 1919 to join Lu Xun. He audited classes at the National Peking University and, beginning in 1920, went to work for the Commercial Press in Shanghai. Later he taught biology at the Communist-run Shanghai University (Zhou Jianren 1979, 11–12; Xu 1991, 523). From 1920, Jianren had written profusely on eugenics, introducing August Weismann, Francis Galton, Karl Pearson, Gregor Mendel, and Hugo de Vries to Chinese readers (Zhou Jianren 1921a; 1920b; 1921d; 1921c; 1922b). Jianren informed his readers of the difference between Mendel's "experimental method" and Galton's "statistical method," that the former was suitable for studying the heredity of single traits, the latter was more appropriate for observing patterns in large groups (Gao 1922).

When Mendel's law was rediscovered in 1900, Galton refused to accept it. Unlike the adherents of the Galton-Pearson school, who used statistical method to trace the distribution of complex traits, the Mendelians were concerned only with the study of the transmission of single traits. The Galtonians ignored the Mendelian distinction between hereditary (genotypical) and nonhereditary (phenotypical) qualities and insisted, instead, upon the all-pervasiveness of heredity (Sutton 1988, 5; Jones 1980, 117). In England, William Bateson championed the Mendelian cause against the eugenics establishment represented by Karl Pearson, leading to a split in the movement. The Mendelian idea of heredity had better reception among American eugenicists, who nonetheless adhered to Galton's social philosophy (Pickens 1968, 48–50). Charles Davenport was the spokesman for this American synthesis, which was also known in China by 1920 (Dikötter 1992, 171).

In 1911, when Galton died, Karl Pearson succeeded him as the leader of the British eugenics movement; he found an admirer in Ding Wenjiang when the latter was studying in England. Ding, a geologist who dabbled in eugenics, listed in 1919 the basic principles of Galtonian eugenics in an introductory article (Furth 1970, 69–74). Other May Fourth eugenicists were largely nonpartisan. Zhou Jianren even attempted to incorporate neo-Lamarckianism, undoubtedly a minority voice by the 1920s, in his view of heredity. He was particularly attracted to the theory of M.C. Coulter, a professor at the University of Chicago. Jianren charged that Weismann's view of heredity, the transmission of "germ plasm"—an immortal material independent of environmental influence—left "deterioration" unaccounted for. Coulter, on the other hand, attributed it to the poisonous by-products resulting from the consumption of materials absorbed by the protoplasm from its milieu—these alterations by the environment were deemed inheritable (Zhou Jianren 1921a, 47–49; 1922c, 43–48).

Coulter's notion of transmittable poisonous residues in the cells enabled Jianren to apply it as a metaphor to the body social. Racial deterioration does not happen only physiologically but is also due to social causes. Old customs and habits that have not passed rational critique are akin to poisonous residues. On the other hand, modern social institutions that allow insane, mentally deficient, and sick people to procreate also deposit poisonous by-products in the social tissues. In short, "custom which is useful in one *shidai* might fall into disuse, or even become harmful, in another" (Jianmeng 1921). Thus Jianren attempted to combine Lamarck's environmentalism with Weismann-Galtonian racial engineering aiming at the undesirable stock.

Most May Fourth eugenicists, being nonpartisan, also resorted to Lamarckianism to improve the Chinese racial stock. One observer regarded this task as the concern of eugenics as much as "enthetics [euthenics?]," the science of environment-improvement" (Yuan 1921, 42). Chen Changheng, following the English eugenicist C.W. Saleeby, saw human-controlled evolution as consisting of two procedures, "the betterment of our environment," and "race betterment" (Chen Changheng 1919, 9). Zhou Jianren, though eclectic, was a sympathizer with the maverick neo-Lamarckian position in eugenics.[17] When Lu Xun, in his preface to Jianren's *Evolution and Degeneration* (1930), alleged that "De Vries' theory of mutation was once ascendant and has declined by now, while Lamarck's environmental thesis, once discredited, has risen again" (Lu 1930, 250), it was probably Jianren speaking through him.

Eugenics in the May Fourth era, like its Western counterpart, had radical implications. A Chinese writer blamed the institution of private property for effecting "negative selection" in society (Yuan 1921, 40). Eugenics also opened up an area where sex could be discussed. For eugenic reasons, Chen Changheng argued, concubinage should be abolished, men and women should be allowed "free choice" in selecting their mates (Chen Changheng 1919, 16). Eugenics also lent support to the birth control movement of Margaret Sanger, whose visit to China in 1922 was the occasion for Zhou Jianren to write an article advancing the same cause (Zhou Jianren 1922a, 7–18). Eugenic reasoning was behind the enlightened attitude toward sex promoted by the English eugenicist Havelock Ellis, whose leading Chinese fan was none other than Zhou Zuoren, the second-born of the three Zhou brothers.

Eugenics and the Cult of Genius

Refuting the Altruistic Instinct

In the May Fourth era, Liang Shuming was a lone voice speaking out against eugenics. He faulted Galton's eugenics for putting a premium on health, energy, intelligence, and courage of the individual organism, at the expense of virtue. To counter this sort of competition-oriented Darwinism, Liang fell back upon the ideas of the sociological Instinct School, notably those of Benjamin Kidd. This Darwinian alternative, which saw emotion and the ethical instinct as more decisive in human evolution than individual intelligence, placed "social instinct" at the biological foundation of the behavior of mutual aid (Liang 1985, 202–205; Alitto 1979, 113).

The "mutual aid" theory of another member of the school, Prince Kropotkin, also prepared Li Dazhao intellectually for his acceptance of Marxism (Dirlik 1989, 45–48). Zhou Jianren, who was professionally better equipped, thought that the Chinese had abused "struggle" and "mutual aid" as metaphors. Kropotkin's mutual aid, Jianren said, in fact refers to a specific way of "struggle for survival" under certain circumstances. Kropotkin is nonetheless guilty of observing biological phenomena through the lenses of human society. His Chinese followers are worse, for they "misunderstand the struggle for survival as mutual killings among one's own kind, and mutual aid as the recipience of benevolence" (Zhou Jianren 1920a). In 1921, Jianren translated for New Youth a chapter from a book by Francis Galton, "Gregariousness and Slavish Instincts" (Zhou Jianren 1921b).[18] Jiaren's introduction to Galton gave "scientific" credence to his brother Lu Xun's portrayal of the Nietzschean Underman.

Evolution of the Few

Lu Xun, as indicated above, managed to combine the altruism of the Instinct School with Nietzschean egotism. In the next chapter I will show that this synthesis was central to the non-resolvable dilemma between his self-sacrifice for the masses and his program to save outstanding individuals. Lu Xun never tired of promoting the cult of genius, as much as he deplored the fact that China was not its "right soil" (Lu 1924f; 1976). In 1919, he composed the following parable for the pages of New Youth: Some monkeys had evolved into human, while others had failed; among the latter, perhaps a few did try to stand erect and speak like humans but they were bitten to death by the rest for "daring to be different" (Lu 1919c, 325).

In 1925 he quoted Ernst Haeckel, a German evolutionist, to the effect that the differences among men often out-distanced those between apes and primordial men (Lu 1925f, 239). Back in the 1880s, Haeckel, in combating socialism, asserted that natural selection was "aristocratic" in the strictest sense of the word (Kelly 1981, 59). It is worth mentioning that the very first article in the official *Complete Works of Lu Xun* is Lu's translation of Haeckel's "Man's History" (Lu 1907).

Lu Xun wedded Nietzschean philosophy to eugenics in a way that is no longer familiar to us today. Underneath layers of the existentialist Nietzsche of high modernism and the postmodernist Nietzsche who pioneered in deconstructing universal truth was a *fin-de-siècle* (or protomodernist) Nietzsche who thought in corporeal terms. It was this one who exclaimed: "Is our morality—our modern sensitive European morality, which may be compared with the morality of the Chinese—the expression of a physiological regression?" (Nietzsche 1968b, 212). It was this Nietzsche who adopted the Lamarckian metaphor of "genealogy" in his critique of morals.[19] The editor of the English version of Nietzsche's complete works (1909–1911) suggested that his philosophy should guide "the knife" of the eugenicists, so that they would not "sterilize in the dark" (Levy 1964, xxxii-xxxiii).

The Nietzsche of Lu Xun's time was certainly not the denazified and existentialized Nietzsche of the postwar era. Yet it is also true that Nietzsche had not yet been Nazified, and eugenics then was well received in many quarters. Notably, it thrived among the intellectual elite who judged the majority of the human race to be a hindrance to the further advancement of the species, as they condemned modern mass society as a disease.

Civilization as Syphilisation

Europe's Maladie fin de siècle

Although eugenics offered a remedy through racial engineering, the movement in fact thrived on the alarmism of a doomsday of the species. Thus, eugenic thinking converged with the decadent view of civilization to contribute to the panic over syphilis, the *maladie fin de siècle*. Syphilis aroused a greater scare in the last *fin de siècle* than AIDS has in ours, due to a misguided Lamarckian hereditarianism, which saw syphilis-induced deformity and mental derangement as leading to racial degeneration and eventual doom. In the 1890s, medical authorities blamed syphilis, with its proclivity to attack the nervous system, for causing general paralysis (popularly known as GPI) and thus hereditary insanity. Lu Xun's icon, Nietzsche, became insane twelve years before his death in 1900 due to an unusual GPI indicative of tertiary syphilis.

In France, the period from 1890 to 1914, bestriding the *fin de siècle* and the *belle époque*, was the "golden age of venereal peril" (Nye 1984, 137), and the mood was indicative of Europe as a whole. To be expected, syphilis as a potent image was capitalized on by thinkers of various tendencies. While anti-Semites saw in syphilis a perfect allegory of Jewry, Victorian and Edwardian feminists used the disease to symbolize men's depravity. For the Decadents it became a trope of modern civilization as they, in league with the eugenicists, saw in the "revolt of the masses" a distinctly modern disease. In their turn, Chinese iconoclasts turned the powerful trope against the accursed tradition, as sickness had become the standard trope of the Chinese national character.

A Weapon of Chinese Iconoclasm

In 1918, Lu Xun compared Chinese tradition to syphilis, hoping that "those fellows whose noses have rotted away in the spiritual sense will not resist medication for the sake of preserving our 'time-honored ancestral malaise.' " Based on an analogy to 606, a newly discovered cure for syphilis, he wished that there was a 707 to cure the spiritual malaise of the Chinese. But Lu Xun despaired, as he quoted Le Bon's *Lois Psychologiques de l'Evolution des Peuples* (1894) to the effect that dead members of a race were more numerous and powerful than the living ones, who can hardly escape the ancestral stranglehold (Lu 1918a, 313).

In his "gate of darkness" article (1919), Lu Xun likened Chinese culture to a syphilitic heredity. He warned that offspring of syphilitic ancestry might survive by a fluke now, but one day, with "the advancement of learning and social reconstruction," they would be "inevitably disposed of by the experts of Eugenics [the term originally in English]" (Lu 1919d, 134). In that article, Lu Xun quoted from Henrik Ibsen's *Ghosts* (1881), the tragedy of a son inheriting syphilis from his father. Ibsen's play was translated by Pan Jiaxun for the May 1919 issue of *New Tide* and exerted considerable influence. Hu Shi likewise quoted from it in his diatribe against filial piety: "If I contract syphilis, and give birth to a son both deaf and blind, or deformed for life, should I earn his respect?" (Hu 1985b, 692). Lu Xun's "gate of darkness" article also adopted from the same source a syphilitic imagery to condemn the "sin of the father," by implication filial piety, which in his view "goes against nature."

Syphilophobia haunted the *fin-de-siècle* literary imagination of Europe. According to a student of the period, the monster-hero in Bram Stoker's *Dracula* (1897) has the peculiar physiognomy and unnatural habits of a syphilitic patient; Mr. Hyde in Robert Louis Stevenson's *Dr. Jekyll and Mr.*

Hyde (1886) has a similarly repulsive look betraying a disease of the soul; Oscar Wilde's *The Picture of Dorian Gray* (1891) uses the "physical imagery of syphilis" to symbolize the hero's putrefying soul; in his *The Time Machine* (1895), H.G. Wells' depiction of the Morlocks, a future human race, suggests a heredity of syphilitic deformity (Showalter 1986, 99, 101–104). Although syphilis is not explicit in every one of them, these works attest to the *fin-de-siècle* penchant for making metaphors out of disease-induced physical defects, especially hereditary ones. Lu Xun also creates in "The True Story of Ah Q" (1921–1922) a composite figure epitomizing all the pathetic Chinese characteristics. He depicts Ah Q, a half-witted village ne'er-do-well, as carrying "a few unfortunate physical blemishes," notably certain "shiny ringworm scars" on his scalp (Yang and Yang 1972, 71). In a fashion typical of degeneration literature, the visible physical defects symbolize disease of the soul.

Lu Xun's awareness of syphilis might have been heightened by Zhou Jianren, who sounded the eugenic alarm that hereditary syphilis, even more than hereditary insanity, was responsible for racial deterioration (Jianmeng 1922, 85–86).[20] In 1925 Zhou Zuoren reopened the discussion on civilization as syphilisation. He reiterated Le Bon's thesis of the power of "ghosts" over the living and defined Chinese culture in four terms: paralysis, gonorrhea, ulcer, insanity (Zhou Zuoren 1925d, 309–310). Since Zuoren proposed figurative "castration" as a solution to the Chinese malaise, the GPI allusion and the eugenic message are unmistakable. This trope met with approval from Qian Xuantong, a professor at the National Peking University, Wang Duqing, a poet of the Creation Society, and Lin Yutang. Lin's response also had an eugenic ring to it, for he stressed that "castration" (figuratively speaking) was indeed the most thorough "final solution" to the malaise of the Chinese people, a "degenerate race" (Lin 1925a, 4). It was in precisely the same period that Adolf Hitler penned his *Mein Kampf*, comparing Jewry to a bacillus.

In the 1930s, Lao She was to incorporate the syphilis motif into his *Camel Xiangzi* (1937), the story of a rustic and robust youth who tries to make a living in the city but contracts syphilis toward the end (Wang 1994, 120–122). It was a problematization of civilization that, by the 1930s, had spawned a host of back-to-the-native-soil movements in many countries.

Notes

1. Not counting the abortive republics of Taiwan (1895) and the Philippines (1898).

2. Even though the old discourse on "national character," which listed the strength

and the weaknesses of China as a "nation," persisted on the pages of *New Youth* (Guangsheng 1917).

3. There is a full-fledged study of the "epoch" rhetoric and its corollary, the new/ old binarism, in my unpublished manuscript, *The Apotheosis of Shidai*.

4. This revision is facilitated by the publication of Chen Song (1985).

5. The two works by J.R. Pusey (1983 and 1998) do not mention "degeneration" once. Dikötter's works, which are not exclusive studies on Darwinian theory, have begun touching on the subject.

6. "Every organ that does not fulfil its function soon ceases to be able to fulfil it. The eyes of fish that live in the lakes of caverns lose the power of sight after a time, and this infirmity ends by becoming heredity" (Le Bon 1974, 212).

7. Toynbee published twelve volumes of *A Study of History* between 1934 and 1961. His sense of civilization in crisis dated back to the time of the Great War, coeval with the May Fourth era.

8. Adams, for example, employed the metaphor of entropy. Wells held the general assumption that entropy would prevail over evolution eventually. Spengler, inspired by the "biology" of Goethe, saw civilization as the denatured finale of an organism called Culture whose sole destiny was to allow its innate form to blossom fully before its ultimate ossification. Sorokin applied to civilization a then-popular art theory, that all art styles have a life cycle of "the archaic," "the classical," and "the decadent." Toynbee, the most Darwinian of them all, saw civilization's breakdown as the failure of Bergsonian *élan* in its responses to new challenges posed by the environment.

9. Is this "body" in the same class as Roland Barthes' "nature"—a semiotic invention? If that is the case, where do the vital impulses required for the act of resistance come from?

10. American literature on the family's decline and the urban middle class' effeminacy (e.g., the malaise of Momism dealt with in chapter 6) is legion. A postwar masterpiece on the Mass Man is David Riesman's *The Lonely Crowd* (1950), which sees the rise of the "other-directed type" as coinciding with a decline in sexual energy. Max Lerner, in his *America as a Civilization* (1957) offers a "neurotic" view of American civilization. A work that combines all of the above is Christopher Lasch's *The Culture of Narcissism* (1979).

11. Crisis philosophy of history also has attitudes in common with the ecologists. True to the decadent definition of civilization, Toynbee condemns the modern world founded on the Industrial Revolution in a posthumously published work: "Man, the child of Mother Earth, would not be able to survive the crime of matricide if he were to commit it. The penalty for this would be self-annihilation" (Toynbee 1976, 588).

12. "Lawrence invoked the psychological mechanism which Nietzsche calls 'introversion' in which powerful impulses which have been repressed or frustrated re-emerge in extreme, corrupt and destructive form. It is not the freeing of instinct which is dangerous, but its suppression, which distorts it, turning something naturally healthy and creative, like sexuality, into something cruel and destructive" (Milton 1987, 194).

13. For a similar theory of Fouilleé's, see Zhuang and Chen (1949, p. 33).

14. An American historian has compared *The Book of Great Harmony* to Karl Marx's *The Communist Manifesto* (Thompson 1967). Yet in many ways it is more akin to Adolf Hitler's *Mein Kampf*.

15. Following the example of Indiana, by 1915 twelve states had passed similar legislations (Hofstadter 1945, 139).

16. Date of publication unclear. This piece of information is in Lu (1926b, 339, note 38). According to Lu Xun's widow Xu Guangping, Lu Xun had three younger

brothers—the youngest had died young (Xu 1961, 49). In that case, Jianren was the youngest surviving brother of Lu Xun.

17. Unfortunately, Zhou Jianren's *Evolution and Degeneration* is not available to affirm this allegation. There are, however, clues in his articles, and some of them might have been collected in that work, such as (Zhou Jianren 1923; 1924).

18. The chapter is in Galton's *Inquiries into Human Faculty and Its Development* (1883).

19. This biological sense of genealogy is now entirely obscured by the Foucauldian twist of the term, which means that in the life history of a discourse, certain narratives are selected (privileged) and others excluded (suppressed).

20. He referred frequently to the issue—see also under the pen name of Qiaofeng (1923) and Jianmeng (1923).

— 4 —

Superman and Underman

Lu Xun has been the most overresearched subject in the People's Republic, and now he is as solidly enshrined in the narrative of national liberation as a beetle buried in amber. Fresh readings are badly needed to pry the subject loose from this compact contextual entombment. Western Lu Xun research, coming from a different tradition, has largely consisted of literary studies. In America, historians writing in the previous decades in the mold of the "transitional crisis" between tradition and modernity eagerly fitted him into that ready-made pattern (Lin 1979).

Lu Xun's lifelong effort, with the exception of the last six years on the left, constituted a most relentless condemnation of the Chinese people. A recent literary study that touches on national character singles out the Chinese obsession with "face" to illustrate how a missionary discourse was "translated" by Lu Xun into a critique in the service of the Chinese Enlightenment (Liu 1995, chapter 2). While this study is a skilful exercise in demonstrating the contestatory nature of any discourse, the issue of "face" happened not to be Lu Xun's major concern.[1] In studying Lu Xun's Western sources of inspiration, it is more fruitful to discern a whole episteme, such as the Decadent Movement of the late nineteenth century, the literary corollary of degeneration. It is also a moot question whether Lu Xun's motive was national salvation by means of enlightenment. There are strong indications that he was more concerned with rescuing the "individual," and his thinking was more in line with the irrationalist "anarcho-psychological" tradition which is antithetical to the Enlightenment (Carroll 1974). The epitome of this tradition is the German philosopher Friedrich Nietzsche.

China's First Proto-Modernist

The official *Complete Works of Lu Xun*, in attempting to eradicate the traces of Nietzsche in Lu Xun's writings, has been too successful in concealing the very cornerstone of his thought, albeit overresearched in China. The official commentary liquidates Nietzsche in a footnote the very instance he first appears in Lu Xun's earliest writings: "His theory reflected the wishes and demands of the monopoly capitalists in the second half of the nineteenth century and later became the theoretical foundation of German fascism." Fortunately, Lu Xun corrected his "misunderstanding" and in 1935 finally called Nietzsche a *"fin de siècle"(shijimo de)* thinker (Lu 1908c, 59)—as if the epithet itself spells guilt. Since Lu Xun died in 1936, the official foot-noter unwittingly gives the impression that our national icon was heavily influenced by a German "fascist"!

Identifying the Fin de Siècle

In 1907 and 1908, at the threshold of his literary career, Lu Xun wrote a series of essays, which constituted the seminal statements of his lifelong philosophy. The first, "The Lopsided Development of Culture," saw nineteenth-century European civilization as amiss, to the detriment of spirit and individuality. It diagnosed the malaises of "the civilization at the end of nineteenth-century" as materialism and the rule of the majority: "The ideas of equality, liberty, social democracy . . . all wish to close gaps be-tween high and low, superior and inferior, reducing everything to a state of no differences. . . . Such tyranny of majority over individual uniqueness was a major current of nineteenth century. . . . The other major current was the so-called material progress." Such unevenness had already provoked a re-action: "nineteenth-century European civilization . . . toward the end, re-vealed its own shortcomings. Reacting against it, a new school of thought has arisen." "In this sense, the intellectual change at the end-of-the-nineteenth-century . . . occurred to correct the nineteenth-century civiliza-tion." Lu Xun traced the new school's genealogy through Max Stirner, Arthur Schopenhauer, Søren Kierkegaard, Henrik Ibsen, and Friedrich Nietzsche; the latter's "Superman doctrine" he regarded as "the foundation of twentieth-century culture." In China, he yearned for "the appearance of a few geniuses, to move society." For national salvation, Lu Xun argued, China should "discard the material and elevate the spirit, rely on the indi-vidual and exclude the masses" (Lu 1908c, 46, 48, 49, 53–55).

    Lu Xun's intellectual genealogy, beginning with Max Stirner and cul-minating in the *fin de siècle*, places him squarely within the anarcho-psychological or anarcho-individualist tradition. The latter differs from both liberalism and socialism by not believing in progress but instead dwells on the irrational constant in humans (Carroll 1974; Lin 1992). Nietzsche, the apogee of this tradition, in fact saw the "nineteenth century" as a "problem" (Nietzsche 1968b, 69). In this respect, both Nietzsche and his Chinese disciple were partisans of the *fin de siècle* and ushers of modernity.

Conflating the Romantic "National Icon" and the Modernist "Outsider"

Lu's second essay, "The Power of Satanic Poetry," saw the Satanic poets of every country, whose prototype was Byron, as saviors of their respective nations (Lu 1908a). Lu Xun's Byronic worship seems to land him in the romantic camp. This essay, if read intertextually with the first, actually uses Byron to embody Nietzschean Supermanhood, which has other exemplars, namely Dr. Stockmann in Henrik Ibsen's *An Enemy of the People* (1882). The doctor declares war on his own community, which, for the sake of profit, refuses to close down its disease-infested spas to tourism. The disease metaphor of the philistine public is unmistakably *fin-de-siècle*. Here, Lu Xun seems to conflate the lone warrior fighting against modern mass society with the romantic genius. To elevate the poet to the rank of savior was indeed a romantic stance in the early nineteenth century, and this connection is evident in Lu Xun's reference in his "Satanic" essay to Thomas Carlyle's hero worship. But, by the *fin de siècle*, the same stance had turned into the Decadent secession from a soulless society of crass materialism and mass democracy. As Decadence was the bridge between romanticism and modernism, the latter has inherited the same penchant to enshrine the marginalized artist-rebel.[2]

For Lu Xun, patriotic poets in Eastern European countries were especially heroic in arousing their respective peoples to the task of national salvation. It is understandable that Lu Xun valorized the stirring of people's spirit above economic development and political reforms—the recipes proffered by most of his contemporaries. But the evils of modern society listed in the "Lopsided Development" essay were apparently not applicable to those backward countries. They were equally irrelevant to late Qing China, where industrialism was at its most rudimentary and democracy in any form was well-nigh nonexistent. Furthermore, how can Lu Xun conflate national icons such as Alexander Pushkin, Adam Mickiewicz, and Sandor Petofi with Ibsen's "enemy of the people" or ultimately the Madman—the total outsider? Lu Xun's Byronic ideal turned out to be a centaur: The upper half the haloed standard-bearer of a struggling nation and the lower half the alienated misfit of modern mass society.

In short, Lu Xun, as early as 1907 and 1908, was giving his Chinese readers a foretaste of the modern writer who would assume the persona of the "outsider" in the twentieth century—yet Lu Xun did this under the guise of setting up the Byronic poet as the national prophet. If Lu Xun's diatribe against industrialism and mass democracy seemed premature and had all the signs of parroting European modernism, he could have been its first scout in China provided that his country would subsequently travel down the same track. Although China's socialist revolution derailed artistic modernism, Lu Xun did achieve his goal of becoming the national icon—ironically, by cursing the nation that venerates him.

Critique of Mass Society as "National Salvation"

Lu's third seminal essay, "A Refutation of Vile Voices," lashed out against various national-salvation panaceas proffered by the opinion leaders. Lu Xun singled out nationalism and cosmopolitanism, both guilty of "the elimination of all individuality in man, so that none dare differ from the next, and all dissolve into one great mass." He saw the "appearance of tyrants *among* the common people" as being "dated from the present era." Whereas "in olden days, autocrats ruled over the masses, but the masses sometimes had opportunities to rebel against them or flee," he bemoaned that "today, those who stand alone are made to suffer at the hands of the crowd and are denied the option of resistance." Typically, both nationalists and cosmopolitans "have seized upon science, utilitarianism, evolution and civilization as shields to defend themselves." Couched in such terms, "progress" was soul-destroying. He went against the grain by censuring the enlightened gentry's campaign to eradicate rural superstition. The crusaders themselves "are spiritually dead," therefore ignorant of the mysteries of life, "from which came poetry and song." Their recipe for national salvation was to destroy "others' sources of inner strength." Curiously, the essay juxtaposes the romantic idealization of the *Volk* with the abhorrence of modern mass culture, yet to be born in China. Lu Xun had a jaundiced view of the "newspaper articles" and "publications" sponsored by the inland gentry as "effective tools for the introduction of modern civilization to China," with "their listeners all nodding in approval." In spite of (or because of) this broad approval, silence continued to reign in China. When everybody "sings the same tune, this singing cannot come from the heart, it is mere chiming in with others," and "such a chorus is more disturbing to the ear than the rustling of leaves in a forest or the pathetic cry of birds because it emphasizes the profound silence in the background" (Kowallis 1986, 109, 110, 111, 112, 113). It was a precocious critique of the uniformity fostered by modern mass culture that was yet to be born in China.

When newspapers of mass circulation first appeared in late nineteenth century, in the wake of universal male suffrage and legislation enforcing universal elementary education, they roused widespread hostility among European intellectuals. The nascent mass medium not only "created an alternative culture" based on profit, but worse, it empowered the faceless masses who were spiritually as good as dead. This cultural crisis was an impetus to the birth of artistic modernism, a penchant to write in a deliberately arcane manner so as "to exclude the masses from culture" (Carey 1992, 6–7, 16–17).

In America, the motif of newspaper as a venue for the mob persisted in Ayn Rand's *The Fountainhead* (1943). By that time, the newspaper had yielded its position as the bugbear of the high-modernist intellectuals to the radio. Typical was Theodor Adorno's critique of the radio for its desecration of music and his derision of jazz for promoting "standardization and pseudo-individuality" (Jay 1973, 191–192). With the exception of Walter Benjamin, the Frankfurt school, in the guise of anticapitalism, blamed the mass media for degrading modern civilization. By mid-century the intellectual scorn of the radio would make way for the critique of the more advanced forms of modern mass media such as television.

Proto-Modernism, Modernism, and Postmodernism

From our postmodern vantage point, this sharp cleavage between elitist and popular culture is symptomatic of modernism. Can Lu Xun then be called the first modernist in China? The answer depends on whether one sees Decadence as a prelude to modernism or its first swallow.[3]

Decadence conveyed a sense of entrapment within civilization, but the closure was not complete for nature was still at large in the guise of instinct. This gap enabled the setting up of the "madman" as the locus of resistance. Modernism continued to derive this secessionist impetus against society from the libidinal unconscious, and the rebel would mutate into the sexual, the criminal, and the existential "outsider." In high-modernist existentialism, modernism eventually shed the decadent rhetoric and opted for that of "alienation" to carve out a space for self-determined subjectivity amidst the faceless masses. This space, unfortunately, is now pronounced an illusion by postmodernism which reduces nature, self, and unconscious alike to semiotic. In celebrating the total triumph of artifice—the best dream and worst nightmare of Decadence come true—postmodernism also announces the blurring of the boundary between mass and elite cultures, with the former winning the battle.

Postmodernism, in defining itself as the binarist opposite to modernity, tends to collapse the critique of modernization and its positivist pretensions with postmodernism's abandonment of the elitism of artistic modernism. In fact, decadence, artistic modernism, and postmodernism concur in their refusal to equate modernity with progress. Modernity is not a monolith; it subsumes the gospel of "modernization = progress" and its nemesis, artistic modernism with its secessionist spirit. The "modernity" that postmodernism claims to have overcome is the former, whereas it has in fact inherited the latter.[4]

Yet, postmodernism does differ from its radical precursor in not treating the rebellious subject as an "outsider." Today, it is not only fashionable to talk about the "death of the author" but to question subjectivity itself. In eliminating the "outsider," postmodernism has relocated it as a marginal "voice" at the periphery of the dominant discourse. Understandably, with the new awareness that culture is a matter of plural coding and one can target only a customized audience, the elitism of literary-artistic modernism is much subdued now. It was not so in Lu Xun's time, when pitting the lone genius against the life-denying Herd was central to discourse.

The Madman as Visionary

In his *Degeneration* (1893), the Austrian critic Max Nordau saw the *fin-de-siècle* writers and artists as symptoms of the feeble and the degenerate. Holding a clinical notion of decadence, Nordau completely misjudged the birth symptom of modernism. His biased view of "degenerate art" was shared by Marxist theorists Antonio Gramsci and Georg Lukacs and later adopted by Nazi Germany and Stalinist Russia.

Lu Xun, in "Random Thoughts 38" (1918), relied on Nordau's authority to claim that insanity was the mark of genius, meanwhile inverting the argument for his own purpose. Nordau condemned the "egomania" of the *fin-de-siècle* writers and artists as a symptom of the degenerate. He devoted a whole chapter in his *Degeneration* to "The Psychology of Ego-mania" (Nordau 1968, book 3, chapter 1). Lu Xun, on the other hand, deemed it necessary to promote egomania in his own country to counter the "collective mania" and "patriotic mania" of the Chinese Herd. Egomania is "to declare war on the philistine masses," he averred. Collective mania and patriotic mania, on the other hand, coerce exceptional individuals to conform to the mob, and therefore to "declare war on a handful of geniuses."

The essay refers to the "psychology" of the mob and Gustave Le Bon's national psychology (Lu 1918a, 311–316).

Lu Xun, the Hesitant Decadent

Nordau's humorless application of medical diagnosis to the *fin-de-siècle* secession had scientific pretensions but actually reflected Victorian biases. He was the typical antidecadent who held a lopsided view of modernity— i.e., defined by scientific progress alone. On the other hand, let us not hastily conclude that Lu Xun was a decadent. He was also committed to progress based on a faith in science. He condemned the fad of psychic research (Si 1918) in much the same way that Nordau attacked the decadents' "mysticism" and "occultism." Lu Xun's position might not be very different from Cesare Lombroso's. The latter saw genius as a freak of nature representing "both the highest evolutionary development and the most atavistic throwback," and, in a later edition of his *Genio e Degenerazione*, chided his overzealous disciple Nordau for one-sided application of his science (Spackman 1989, 8, 21).

Lu Xun's attitude toward literary Decadence was ambivalent. In 1928, advising against a friend's intention to stay single, he warned him of the risk of contracting venereal disease: "The men-of-letters of the late nineteenth century used to glorify alcoholic intoxication and death by [disreputable] diseases. To glorify them is one thing, but it is painful to have them visited upon you" (Lu 1928b, 619). Yet, Lu Xun himself often appeared "decadent" in the eyes of contemporaries. In 1927, the leftist critic Cheng Fangwu saw Lu Xun as a pathetic aesthete indulging in "leisure, leisure, leisure" (Lu 1932b, 6, 9). In 1930, an official request by Guomindang's Zhejiang Party Branch for his arrest called him "the degenerate man-of-letter (*duoluo wenren*), Lu Xun" (Lu 1932a, 3).

Madness as a Modern Condition

In his major writings Lu Xun's sympathy lies not with normal society but with the aberrant. His "A Madman's Diary" (1918), written in the same year as the "dialogue" with Nordau, uses the eyes of a paranoid schizophrenic to see "normal" society as filled with cannibals. "Madness," in the European *fin de siècle*, "serves as a great weapon of discourse" (Karl 1988, 169). A locus classicus is the Madman in Nietzsche's *The Gay Science* (1882) who "lit a lantern in the bright morning" in the marketplace seeking God.

Lu Xun's narrative of a madman's journals had European predecessors beside Nikolay Gogol and Guy de Maupassant. A text akin to its eerie confessional format is Daniel Paul Schreber's *Memoirs of My Nervous Illness* (1903). Freud made this important text the "subject of the most extensive paper he ever wrote on psychosis," regarding it "a classic case of both paranoid and schizophrenic illness." Although it was written by a rehabilitated patient and not meant to be a manifesto of avant-gardist secession, many of its themes are now seen as matching the "central and defining features of the modern self" (Sass 1992, 143).

Was Lu Xun, then, unmistakably modernist? Unarguably, he created the first specimens of the modern Chinese story, but he was no Western-style avant-gardist committed to the "tradition of the new" whose "only constant is change itself" (Sass 1992, 30). The language he experimented with was the vernacular, which reached a wider readership than the dethroned classical canon, as it was also more communicative than the arcane lingo of the modernists. The cult of the "new" in the May Fourth era (see chapter 3) had a modernist flavor to it, but it bespoke a cultural revolution of a far greater magnitude than artistic avant-gardism. The penchant for a permanent revolution in literary styles reached China only in the 1930s as an ephemeral trend among a few writers before it was overwhelmed by socialist realism (Lee 1999, chapters 5–8). Unlike Western modernists, who felt entrapped in "iron cage"-like modern conditions that were soul-destroying, members of the May Fourth generation were haunted by a modernity that was stillborn.

The Doppelganger's Monodrama

The "modernization" paradigm in older-vintage Chinese studies has cast Lu Xun's agony into a transitional crisis between tradition and modernity. A postmodern reading of the same subject would discern a narrative attempt to fashion a self out of incongruous fragments. It is not surprising that Lu Xun was unaware of the hybridity of some of his personae, as in his conflation of the twentieth-century avant-garde and the nineteenth-century national icons like Byron and Hugo. In the aftermath of the anticlimactic 1911 Revolution, the disillusioned Lu Xun sank into passivity and took refuge in Buddhist studies. Thus he also assumed the eremitic persona of Ji Kang, one of the Seven Sages of the Bamboo Groves.[5]

The Shadow Persona

A most conflicted self emerged in the ensuing phase of engagement with the New Culture and its aftermath, when the New Culture camp broke up.

In "Farewell of the Shadow" (1924), Lu Xun consciously invented a split persona, a Shadow who, despairing of wandering between light and darkness—because "darkness will engulf me; yet I shall cease to exist in the light"—seeks to lose itself in darkness (Lu 1924g; Hsia 1968, 150). Lu Xun's Shadow echoes Nietzsche's *The Wanderer and His Shadow* (1880).[6] As a powerful literary imagery, the Nietzschean motif of "the wanderer-seeker in search of self" was also appropriated by Franz Kafka, for the two took "a very similar view of the degenerate 'civilization' of their time" (Bridgwater 1974, 10, 14–15).

An understanding of the rich intertextuality of the Shadow requires us to look into a few more texts. On the same day he penned "Farewell of the Shadow" (September 24, 1924), Lu Xun also wrote Li Bingzhong:[7] "I always feel that inside my soul there is a poisonous and diabolic spirit which I extremely abhor but fail to get rid of" (Lu 1924c, 431). He lifted this sentence directly from the mouth of Mrs. Alving, the heroine in *Ghosts* (1881) by Henrik Ibsen, one of Nordau's "degenerates." Ibsen let Mrs. Alving exclaim: "There is in me something of that Ghost-like, inherited tendency, I can never quite get rid of," because "we are all of us Ghosts. . . . It is not only what we have inherited from father and mother, that walks again in us. It is all kinds of dead opinions and all manner of dead old beliefs and things of that sort. . . . If I do but take up a newspaper to read, it is as though I saw Ghosts come sneaking in between the lines. There must be Ghosts all the country over. . . . And that is why we are, one and all, so dreadfully afraid of Light" (Ibsen 1890, 54–55).

Mrs. Alving's bias against newspapers of mass circulation was, of course, the author Ibsen's. This sentiment of European highbrow intellectualism would persist into the twentieth century, fuelled by the belief that the masses were "not fully alive" for they lacked "souls" (Carey 1992, 10–11). Ibsen's motif of "seeing ghosts between the lines" was borrowed by Lu Xun in his "A Madman's Diary," in which the Madman discerns the phrase "man-eating" creeping between the lines of Chinese historical chronicles. The stale social values and the unregenerate masses are mutually reinforcing themes. The Norwegian play uses the plot of a son with syphilis inherited from his diseased father to condemn the "dead old beliefs." Yet it is the benighted—genetically flawed—masses who allow "what we have inherited from father and mother" to "walk again in us."

The Doppelganger *Persona*

The penumbra world in which the Shadow is trapped can conjure a different persona, one of resistance and hope. Nietzsche exclaims: "Apart from the fact that I am a decadent, I am also the opposite . . . I am a *Doppelganger*, I have a 'second' face in addition to the first" (Nietzsche 1968a, 680, 681). Lu Xun likewise saw himself as a borderline case, fighting the dead weight of the "gate of darkness" and perishing in the act so as to give future generation safe passage to the light. Nietzsche would die, ironically, of insanity due to a syphilitic attack, thus living the role of the *fin-de-siècle* "mad genius" who perished in his battle against a syphilitic society.

Lu Xun's Doppelganger seemed not to convey the Nietzschean message of "that which fails to kill you makes you stronger," but rather an exhortation to self-sacrifice for a future China. In the last chapter we have indicated that, in his instinct theory, Lu Xun subscribed to both Nietzschean egotism and the altruism of the conservative Instinct School, which amounts to mixing oil and water. This incongruity is compounded by his hybridization of Nietzschean Supermanhood with Thomas Carlyle's hero worship as a social function.

Epitomizing the Decadent motto of *l'art pour l'art*, the Nietzschean Superman—or self as an artistic ideal—is supposed to be an end in itself; not only that it must not serve as a national icon, its selfhood is a secession from the rest of a society toward which it is nonchalant. In Nietzsche's own words, contrary to the *ressentiment* typical of the Herd's slave morality, "the reverse is the case" with master morality because "there is indeed too much carelessness, too much looking away and impatience involved in contempt, even too much joyfulness, for it to be able to transform its object into a real caricature and monster" (Nietzsche 1967, 37). In this light, Lu Xun's impassioned diatribe against the Chinese Herd seems to stand Nietzsche on his head by a misapplication of the latter's Superman philosophy to the task of national salvation.

The Pathetic Superman versus the Apathetic Masses

This verdict is sensible only if we presume that Nietzsche's own philosophy is innately coherent, not a narrative quilt made up of incongruous patches. The above-quoted passage is from *On the Genealogy of Morals*, which Lu Xun had not read.[8] In *Thus Spake Zarathustra*, which he read, the Superman feels lonely and decides to descend from his ice-clad mountain abode to preach in the marketplace down below. Nietzsche philosophized at the heyday of social psychology, which, although it disdained the group mind, also saw civilization being advanced through "suggestion-imitation," by innovative individuals pointing the way for the masses. Nietzsche, however, gave this popular thesis of his time a twist that was at once poetic and pessimistic: if the Superman had a function in the regeneration of civilization, it was by discarding the masses. So, what is the Nietzschean stance if it is not a "caricature" or demonization of the Herd?

In the postmodernist way of thinking, the Superman comes into narrative existence only by defining itself against a binary opposite. It is the mono-drama of the Superman that evokes its alterity, the Underman. That the Superman is not fully "present" is evident in its emotional dependency on its binary opposite. One may pin the Underman label on an individual who, failing in self-development, nurses an impotent rage against those who do better. But a herd is a reification configured only in the spiteful imagination of its opposite number: the individual who craves to stand out.

To apply postmodernist insights to demolish modernist elitism is to compound yesterday's bias with today's. Critics who feel unsettled by post-modernism's capitulation to mass society have the right to be nostalgic for the lonely stance of the "outsider." Some might even admire Nietzsche for having forecast the loss of value, beauty, and individuality in today's society, where only power matters and the mass-person gratifies his or her "will to power" by riding on the bandwagon of identity-group politics. While this controversy cannot be resolved, one thing is certain: Lu Xun's attitude toward the Chinese Herd was not typified by "too much careless-ness, too much looking away" or "even too much joyfulness." In fact, it looks more like an unwholesome drama of the pathetic Superman and the apathetic masses.

The Empathetic Misanthrope

Although our deconstructionist exercise helps to unravel a picture of Lu Xun overdetermined by the national-salvation narrative, it is nonetheless ahistorical to read only a power motive behind Lu Xun's degrading of the Other—in this case, his countrymen. He lived at a time when the cosmo-politan elite urgently felt that the Chinese were sick, hence the untiring condemnation of the national character. It was a major reason why Lu Xun's Nietzschean stance did not evolve into the exclusive esotericism of Western modernists but is well-received by his own people even to this day, because they take it as a diagnosis of the "national" malaise.

An Antinational Project

Nietzsche saw nationalism as reflective of a herd mentality, a view reflected in Lu Xun's "Vile Voices" article (Lu 1908b). This essay, which denigrated newspapers of mass circulation, was inimical to the nationhood project if we adopt Benedict Anderson's view of the print medium, especially the newspaper, as a key factor in the making of a nation as an imagined community (Anderson 1990, 34–35, 67–68). As for Lu Xun's antiprogram, it was in fact a membership badge of the transnational community of high-brow modernists. Still immersed in the intellectual concerns of late Qing China, Lu Xun's message was presented as a national-salvation recipe: "Rely on the individual and exclude the masses."

This was in fact Nietzsche's program for a higher humankind when he summed up the whole human agenda in the parable of walking a tight-rope from subhumanity to Supermanhood. It can be read as a faith for a better humanity if we use his philosophy, as many of his contemporaries did, to serve the regeneration of civilization. Yet Nietzsche also promulgated the doctrine of "eternal recurrence," which was scornful of evolutionism defined as progress. He held that modern humankind had not surpassed the Greeks (the average modern is certainly no higher than an Aristotle or an Alexander). "The *goal of humanity* cannot lie in the end [*Ende*] but only *in its highest specimens*" (Kaufmann 1974, 319). The one and the same drama of the Superman versus the Underman is therefore reenacted in every age throughout eternity.

Seen in this light, Lu Xun's national salvation program can only be the preservation of exceptional individuals. The only lesson he derived from the 1911 Revolution was the wasting of the flower of the nation. In his "Yao" (Medicine) (1919), a revolutionary martyr dies in vain; those he intends to save understand only how to bribe the executioner to obtain his fresh blood to cure the consumption suffered by a sick child. The child dies anyway and is buried outside the same city wall as the executed revolutionary, but their burial sites are on opposite sides of a graveyard segregated by a zigzag path. This ending was unacceptable to the editors of *New Youth*, so Lu Xun changed it by allowing a mysterious wreath to be placed on the martyr's grave (Lu 1919e).

How Lu Xun Was Pressganged into "National Salvation"

It is a typical case of the "death of the author"—regardless of Lu Xun's original message, it was pressganged into the service of "national salvation," which is the only way it is taken in today's China. When his friend Qian Xuantong, an editor of *New Youth*, first approached him to write for the journal in order to awaken the Chinese, Lu Xun retorted with his famous "iron house" parable, that it is better to leave its slumbering inhabitants to perish in their sleep than to arouse them to die in horror (Lu 1922b, 419).

The new light my study can shed on this episode is that Lu Xun was applying the early modernists' standard idiom to the masses. D.H. Lawrence had this to say about them: "The mass of mankind is soulless. . . . Most people are dead, and scurrying and talking in the sleep of death." From the mouth of one of H.G. Wells' fictional characters in *The Island of Dr. Moreau* (1896): "[People in trains and omnibuses] seemed no more my fellow creatures than dead bodies would be, so that I did not dare to travel unless I was assured of being alone" (Carey 1992, 11, 139).

In Europe, the advent of modern nationalism was accompanied by the Romantic cult of the individual genius. This balancing act was necessary as European society was entering the modern mass society, and Lu Xun was performing the same act for China. The "modernist" guise of the Romantic cult of the individual, however, was a bit premature for China's condition. In the name of the individual, he inveighed against "materialism and the rule of the majority" when these things were quite absent in China. His application of modernist consciousness to the China of his time is not unlike the Chinese mimicry of postmodernism in our time. Whether today's China is ripe for postmodernity is another interesting issue. Yet, as long as the West remains the intellectual center and the non-West the periphery, even though the latter is in a less developed condition, it is out of the question for the periphery to pick up only those ideas that are no longer considered fashionable in the center. Perhaps an analogy can be found in Leon Trotsky's thesis of "uneven and combined development," that is, the very presence of global imperialism has warped the natural course of social development, making the conventional bourgeois revolution impossible for the rest of the world, which has yet to go through it. In the understanding of today's cultural studies, ideas do not have to correspond to a designated reality, they produce a reality of their own. Thus Lu Xun's modernism was transformed by the task of national salvation into a most insightful critique of the Chinese national character.

Yet, tension between Lu Xun's Superman philosophy and national salvation cannot be easily resolved. Bitter memories of the senseless martyrdom of exceptional individuals like Qiu Jin for the disappointing republican revolution also informed Lu Xun's "Misanthrope" (Lu 1925g). Yet what was the point of dwelling on old memories two decades after the fact, or even writing about them at all? We have shown above that Lu Xun subscribed to the instinct theory in both its egotist and altruistic shapes. A study on his imagery of cannibalism also indicates that the imagery was both an abomination of the masses and a wish to sacrifice for them (Sun 1986).

Retrieving the Personal Dimension

This "to be or not to be eaten" dilemma pertaining to the masses might have begun with Lu Xun's family situation. We have shown (in chapter 3) in the case of Wu Yu that his anti-Confucian zeal was rooted in his hatred of his father. Such examples immunize us against readings that are over-determined by impersonal factors such as the task of national salvation or enlightenment. Recently, affected by the American "child abuse" epidemic, Lu Xun scholarship in China has begun to take note of his exploitation by his mother and brother Zhou Zuoren; his arranged marriage, which was also unhappy; and the underlying motif of "revenge" in some of his writings (Wang 1995, 10–13). This feeble attempt to "denationalize" Lu Xun does not venture as far as rereading those writings that have been canonized into "antifeudal" texts. It is more a Freudian slip than an anti-feudal ploy in "A Madman's Diary" for the Madman to accuse his mother and brother of conspiring to have him eaten. Another text that has been neglected because it ill suits the antifeudal paradigm is "Brothers" (1925), in which the hero feels guilty about harboring thoughts of denying support to his brother's children should his brother die prematurely.

This new light shows "A Madman's Diary" to be in tandem with Franz Kafka's "The Metamorphosis" (1915). Two years Lu Xun's junior, Kafka was, like him, also a petty bureaucrat. In Kafka's story a clerk who is exploited by his ungrateful father, mother, and sister, wakes up one morning to find himself transformed into a huge insect. The story, though defying a single reading, was inspired by Kafka's family situation (Karl 1991, 462–473). Early modernism used biological metamorphosis to represent what stood for *alienation* in high modernism. Lu Xun's writings also use this metaphor, notably his metamorphosis into a poisonous snake "with venomous fangs" that gnaws not others but itself (Sun 1986, 469).

Some of Lu Xun's self-images, such as Atlas—as in holding up the "gate of darkness"—or "an ox in the service of the younger generation," allude to exhaustion or being sucked dry.[9] The other side, equally necessary to sustain his drama of Superman versus the Herd, was the persona of the misanthrope. A symbolist essay of his written around the time of "The Misanthrope" is about an old woman driven to bitter vengefulness by un-grateful family members who have sucked her dry (Lu 1925k, 204–206).

The Vengeful Misanthrope Posed as Jesus

The revenge motif was central to Lu Xun's misanthropic persona. He wrote both "Revenge" and "Revenge 2" in 1924. The second essay imagines Jesus hanging from the cross feeling compassion for his persecutors but also deriving "consolation" from their damnation (Lu 1924b). The first essay urges that a symbolic "carnage" be meted out by outstanding individuals to the spectacle-hungry masses (Lu 1924a). This "carnage" language seemed to be inspired by the final action of Mikhail Artsybashev's *Shevyrev,* which Lu Xun had translated earlier. Written in the wake of the failed 1905 revolution, the novella depicts a Russian terrorist shooting randomly into the audience at an opera house.

It is rather chilling that Lu Xun harbored such misanthropic thoughts the year when Chicago's Leopold and Loeb committed murder, inspired by the same Nietzschean source. In the 1920s, inspired by Nietzsche's parable of the "flies of the marketplace," Lu Xun on more than one occasion likened the Chinese masses to insects and vermin (Sun 1986, 468).[10] The word "vermin" (*Ungeziefer*) was most unfortunate as it was later used by the Nazis to designate the gassed. In the interwar years, ideas we commonly associate with the Nazis were not confined to that quarter. D.H. Lawrence once entertained the thought of building "a lethal chamber as big as the Crystal Palace" and using a musical band and a cinematograph to lure there "all the sick, the halt, and the maimed" from back alleys and main streets to deal to them the final solution (Carey 1992, 12). If high modernism showed its contempt of the masses in its war against mass culture, this elitism in its early modernist guise tended to dwell on their defective corporeality.

The Chinese Herd

Lu Xun's dark view of the Chinese was premised on the theory of biological heredity, yet official hagiography has managed to transform him into an "antifeudal" warrior in the manner of the Russian "revolutionary democrats" of the 1860s. This *tour de force* has succeeded so well that Lu Xun is now an undisputed national icon. It is hard to imagine an Alexander Pushkin or a Sandor Petofi heaping so many abuses on their own peoples. Many of Lu Xun's observations concerning the stunting of individuality in Chinese society are truly insightful, and it is supremely ironic that he was the only literary icon remaining on the pedestal during the Cultural Revolution—the worst case of the kind of mob politics he had abhorred. A major reason for his acceptance by the Chinese, even as they misunderstand him, must be found in their penchant for self-denigration since the dawn of the national character discourse.

Enslavement of the Spirit

In the early 1900s, opinion leaders like Liang Qichao, Zou Rong, and Chen Duxiu had launched the "slave character" discussion—as a critique of despotism. During his days in Japan, Lu Xun must have been exposed to this discussion. He, however, tilted the political discourse on the slave character in the direction of Nietzschean "slave morality." Under the republic, despotism had gone, but the slave character remained the soul-substance of the Chinese.

In Lu Xun's view, Chinese people throughout their history have never fought for the right to be human. Making a mockery of the grandiose labels used by patriotic historiography to periodize Chinese history, and adding a sardonic twist to the cult of epoch, he quipped that Chinese history alternated between only two kinds of epoch: (1) the *shidai* of wanting but failing to become slaves and (2) the *shidai* of achieving slavehood on a temporary basis (Lu 1925b, 212–213). With this kind of heredity, the Chinese as a people never dare to look life straight in the face; instead of redressing wrongs, they indulge in self-delusions of a "happy ending" in a fantasy world. Offering no resistance to domination, they are contented with the canonization of the loyal ministers and chaste women who were martyred in the new masters' wars of conquest. "It proves that the [our] national character is one of cowardice, lethargy, and glibness" (Lu 1925f, 239–40).

The Sado-Masochistic Wimp

The subjects of tyrants, however, are crueller than their masters. "The procurator wanted to release Jesus, but the mob wanted to crucify him." The victims of tyrants wish to see tyranny also visited upon others so that they may enjoy watching cruelty-in-action as an entertainment and use the suffering of others as pastime and compensation (Lu 1919b, 366). The Chinese have accumulated pent-up resentments resulting from their molestations by the strong. As they never dare to fight back against the strong, they take it out on the weak (Lu 1925m, 225).

Lu Xun used these insights to bear on the issue of women's chastity, a popular topic of May Fourth iconoclasm. Chinese people condone polygyny in men, but resort to a double standard when it comes to women and require them to be chaste. If men fail to defend their women who are raped by outsiders, the men expect their property to self-destruct. In China, when a woman is violated, their male relatives as a rule "are not ashamed of their own cowardice and impotence, nor do they seek to punish the rapist; instead, they twaddle about why she has not committed suicide" (Lu 1918d, 120).

Throughout Chinese history, when the nation was defeated by the barbarians on the battlefield, dynastic rulers often used women, through so-called alliance marriages, to "pacify" the enemies. Today, Lu Xun quipped, the practice has assumed a novel but equally self-deluding euphemism, "cultural assimilation [of foreigners]" (Lu 1925b, 215). The same pusillanimous logic is behind the Chinese "national form of cursing" (*guoma*), a term meant as a mockery of the "national essence" (*guocui*) cherished by the traditionalists. This nation-class cursing invariably aims at the "mother" of one's opponent. Lu Xun saw it as a kind of "genealogical warfare" waged by the impotent, the vanquished, and the subjugated. The person who first invented this cursing, Lu Xun mused, must be a "genius," but he hurriedly added: "a base one" (Lu 1925e).

The Victim-Victimizer Cycle

Lu Xun saw in his fictional Ah Q, betraying symptoms of feeble-mindedness and moral degeneration, the epitome of every kind of Chinese malaise. Ah Q preys on the weak and cowers before the strong. He sexually harasses a young nun, who is female and socially marginal, but becomes as meek as a lamb in the face of abuses by the landlord of the village. Physically worsted by other village ne'er-do-wells, Ah Q consoles himself with the self-delusion that he is the "father" of those who have molested him. Lu Xun renamed this genealogical warfare tactic "the method of spiritual victory." It was a transparent snipe at the Eastern-Civilization camp in the ongoing East/West controversy, which held China's senior "spiritual civilization" to be superior to the younger but victorious "material civilization" of the West.

The Chinese are exemplars of *moren*, the Nietzschean Undermen whose evolution is arrested yet who attempt to impose their limitations on others, meanwhile holding an impotent grudge toward those who are superior. In such a manner, the Chinese allow themselves to become victims, which also licences them to victimize others. They prey on the misfortune of others, deriving amusement and "fulfilment" from their sufferings. Lu Xun developed these themes in other works besides the story of Ah Q: "Kong Yiji" (1919a), "Tomorrow" (1920), and "The New-Year Sacrifice" (1924). In the last, a woman who has been twice widowed and has lost her only child to the wolves is stigmatized, through her fellow villagers' insinuations, as an accursed person. In this sense, the callous fellow villagers are the real "wolves." Before the miserable widow is hounded to death, she has internalized the social ostracism. She is talked into donating a doorsill to the local temple to be her substitute, "so that thousands of people can walk over and trample on it," to atone for her sins "in this life and avoid torment after death" (Lee 1987, 74).

The Devouring Masses

Lu believed that in seeking perverse gratification, Chinese people always act as anonymous, conformist members of a crowd. They especially delight in watching the public parade and execution of the victims of society, who, by virtue of their misfortune, *stand out* from the faceless masses. In the final scene of Ah Q's parade to the execution ground, the victim meets the eyes of the spectacle-hungry crowd, which are reminiscent of a wolf's.[11]

Lu Xun never tired of rehashing the theme of the benighted masses wasting the exceptional few, including their would-be saviors. The Chinese, who are enslaved in their spirit, behave like the Lackey, a character in an essay by Lu Xun, who wallows in his victimhood yet brings grief to anyone foolhardy enough to rush to his rescue (Lu 1926a, 216–218). Those who attempt to save the benighted masses end up either like the state criminal in "The Public Display" (1925), an entertaining spectacle for the crowd, or, worse still, eaten by the people he wanted to save, as in the story "Medicine" (1919).

Lu Xun excelled in depicting scenes of sadistic masses relishing the spectacle of public torture and execution. "The masses—especially those in China—are always spectators at a drama. . . . Before the mutton shops of Beijing a few people often gather to gape, with obvious enjoyment, at the skinning of the sheep. And this is all they get out of it if a man lays down his life. . . . For masses of this kind there is no cure, except by depriving them of spectacles" (Lu 1923, 163). This *auto-da-fé* imagery of the masses is a far cry from Mikhail Bakhtin's *carnivalèsque* celebrating the postmodernist inversion of elite culture by popular culture.

A Chinese Demonology

Cannibals

Lu Xun reduced the "spiritual civilization" of the traditionalists to a subhuman milieu of sadomasochism, a colossal chain-reaction field of victim/ victimization. "China's past has been a cannibalistic feast; there are those who have eaten others and those who have been eaten by others; those who are being eaten have eaten people before; those who are now eating people will also be eaten one day" (Lu 1927a, 454).

Readers and students alike have treated this famous trope in isolation, so it appears idiosyncratic. Actually, in *fin-de-siècle* culture, cannibalism was often associated with atavism, madness, and flawed heredity. Jean Rodes, in his *Les Chinois, Essai de Psychologie Ethnographique* (1923), unfailingly couched his study in the fashionable terms of his time. Besides detecting "erotomania" among the Chinese, he also saw them as neurotic (*névrose*) and hysterical. During social upheavals such as the 1911 Revolution, they behaved "as if their brains had been affected by alcoholic intoxication," and this Chinese mania manifest itself in cannibalistic incidents (Otani 1935, 409, 411–413). Rodes' work foreshadows that of Zheng Yi, who has recently written about cannibalistic incidents during the Cultural Revolution (Zheng 1996).

Claustrophobia

A sentiment related to devouring, in the Nobel laureate Elias Canetti's observations, is claustrophobia: "Teeth are the armed guardians of the mouth and the mouth is indeed a strait place, the prototype of all prisons. Whatever goes in there is lost, and much goes in whilst still alive. The readiness with which the mouth opens in anticipation of prey, the ease with which, once shut, it remains shut, recall the most feared attributes of a prison. It can scarcely be wrong to assume that the mouth did in fact exert a hidden influence on prisons. . . . In times when these used to be torture chambers they resembled a hostile mouth in many respects. Hell still presents the same appearance today" (Canetti 1962, 209).

Lu Xun's claustrophobia was evident in his famous "gate of darkness" metaphor and "iron house" parable. As the iron house's slumbering inhabitants would slowly die of suffocation, the simile of sleep is also evoked here. A variation on themes of sleep and claustrophobia is being buried alive, or, in his words, "hemmed in from six sides" (Lu 1925j, 211). This remark concludes his scenario of a dream in which he lies dead on a thoroughfare but this "death" is only the cessation of the motor function of his nerves while his mind retains full consciousness; to his horror he finds himself powerless in the irritating presence of insects but worse still, his dead body becomes a spectacle for a gathering crowd. Here "live burial" is the metaphor of being threatened by the crowd. The obsession with premature burial is reminiscent of Edgar Allan Poe, a cult figure in the French Decadence, thanks to promotion by Baudelaire and Mallarmé (Pierrot 1981, 27–33). Lu Xun's brother Zhou Zuoren did refer to Poe's "life-long phobia of being buried alive" in his *Memoirs*, adding that: "I have a similar phobia of being eaten" (Zhou Zuoren 1970, 580). The Zhou brothers' claustrophobic tropes expressed in unambiguous terms the fear of the devouring masses.

The Living Dead

A related theme was the masses as the living dead, which had been the standard representation used by the European elite since Ibsen's *Ghosts*. We have shown how Lu Xun directly lifted a passage from this play, that is, "there is in me something of that Ghost-like, inherited tendency, I can never quite get rid of," because "we are all of us Ghosts." The fear of being devoured was therefore synonymous with anxiety about contamination. In England, thanks to Nietzsche and T.S. Eliot, "the assumption that most people are dead became, by the 1930s, a standard item in the repertoire of any self-respecting intellectual." George Orwell allows one of his fictional figures to exclaim: "We're all dead. Dead people in a dead world" (Carey 1992, 10).

Compared with the watered-down mortal imagery of the 1930s, the "living dead" in Decadence and early modernism was by far more macabre. In 1923, Zhou Zouren expounded on *Ghosts*' Norwegian title, *Gengangere* or "revenants," which means "corpses returning from the dead, not ghosts separated from their bodies." Zouren equated them with vampires, werewolves, and the undead, the favorite subjects of "Allan Poe and Maupassant" (Zhou Zuoren 1923b, 25–28). In the West, besides Poe, Maupassant, Ibsen, Charles Baudelaire had also written a poem, "Le Revenant." The undead figure entered the modern popular culture in Bram Stoker's *Dracula* (1897) (Tracy 1990). Borrowing this modernist demonology, Zouren depicted China as a nation of revenants who walked the streets in broad daylight (Zhou Zuoren 1923a; Kaiming 1924b).

Twentieth-century popular culture, especially Hollywood, has perpetuated the Decadent repertoire of the *fin-de-siècle* imagination, thus the "living dead" has become a staple in the realm of modern entertainment. Hardly anybody realizes that the Zhou brothers also applied this repertoire to the portrayal of their countrymen.

Fiends

This understanding places Lu xun's trope of Chinese civilization as "a banquet of human flesh" in a new light. An occurrence of this simile in Lu Xun's writings was in April 1925 (Lu 1925b, 216–217). From January to

March, Zuoren, as coeditor of *Word Threads*, had arranged a series of articles and correspondences on the inhuman tortures meted out to political enemies by the Ming emperor Yongle. After usurping the throne of the legitimate ruler, his nephew, Yongle took revenge on the families of his forty-eight loyal ministers. They were condemned to death by slicing and their bodies were fed to dogs. He specifically ordered that their womenfolk be raped on a multiple, daily, and long-term basis, their future male children fed to the dogs, and their female offspring sold into houses of prostitution (Kaiming 1925d).

Zouren did not confine his accusation of inhumanity to despots, but levelled it at the Chinese as a whole, from Confucian pundits to street hawkers. In this spirit, Zuoren composed a doggerel, "The Goblin Hawker," modelled on the English Pre-Raphaelite Christina Rossetti's "The Goblin Market." He attempted to instill the latter's "fiendish aura" into his own piece about a demon hawking severed parts of human bodies on a bridge in Beijing (Kaiming 1925b; 1925a; Chuandao and Kaiming 1925, 7–8). This condemnation *in toto* did not spare even Chinese patriotic sacrifices. After the May Thirtieth massacre of the same year, Zuoren, in the same cynical vein as his older brother, quipped that the martyrs had been "eaten" (Zhou Zuoren 1925a).

Somnipathy

The *fin de siècle* was the heyday of irrationalism, as evident in the popularity of the instinct theory, mob psychology, and depth psychology. In its wake, the early twentieth century witnessed a general fascination with the unconscious, hypnotism, somnolence, somnambulism, amnesia, and necrophilia—in short, the dark side of the human psyche. Coeval with the writings of the Zhou brothers was the German cinematic production of *Das Kabinett des Doktor Caligari* (1920), a story about a somnambulist being used as a killing machine. The sleepwalker, the living dead, the deranged cannibal, and the depraved sadist all pertain to the irrational.

This irrationalist trend had a brief impact in China in the early twentieth century. Lu Xun and Zhou Zuoren both developed an interest in hypnotism. The former, inspired by Kuriyagawa Hakuson, referred to literary creativity as a dreamy state rooted in the psychic depth of the writer and to its effects on the reader as hypnotizing (Sun 1993, 80–81). Zuoren relied on the American Freudian critic Albert Mordell, author of *The Erotic Motive in Literature* (1919), to assert that literary works were the unconscious expressions of repressed sexuality (Zhongmi 1923).

The Chinese as Sexual Degenerates

Influenced by Freud and Havelock Ellis, the Zhou brothers at the time were also promoting sexual modernism. If modernist European thinkers demolished Victorian social values to lay the foundation of the sexual attitudes of the twentieth century, the Zhou brothers tried to do the same to conventional Chinese morality. In the attempt, the Chinese masses inevitably became their demon.

The Zhou Brothers' "Sexual Modernism"

In line with the Nietzschean view of the Underman who stifled his own and others' vital forces, Lu Xun applied Freudian insights to his critique of hypocrisy, false prudery, and sexual perversion in Chinese society. In his story "Tomorrow," a man who offers help to a widow in fact harbors lewd feelings toward her. Lu Xun's awareness of the mechanism known in Freudian jargon as reaction formation is evident in his "Soap" (1924), in which the hero objects to schools for girls and is especially enraged by the girl students' bobbed hair on moral grounds—he turns out to be a lecher in his subconscious mind.

Zuoren echoed Lu Xun's critique through reading the works of Havelock Ellis, Edward Carpenter, and the anthropologist James Frazer. He charged that the old society's view of sexuality was unhealthy, "like the perverted sexuality of old men" (Zhou Zuoren 1923c, 49). Old sexual morality was sustained by barbaric taboo, so a cultivation of new sexual morality was needed for the new epoch (Zhongmi 1921, 2; Kaiming 1924a). The human body had upper and lower sections, but conventional thinking absurdly attached moral judgments to them and denigrated the lower (Kaiming 1925c). Commenting on a provincial educational association's proposal to impose long trousers as a uniform for girl students, he exclaimed that an object in itself was never inherently indecent, therefore society should ban, not a certain type of clothes, but those people who projected indecent thoughts onto trousers (Zuoren 1924, 8). Zuoren believed that all sanctimonious reactions to sex were motivated by prurience (Qiming 1928, 41).

Zuoren saw the origins of society's sexual taboos in the magical rites of barbaric times and in jealousy. Commenting on the famous White Snake legend, Lu Xun also saw a jealous motive in the monk Fahai, who broke up the romance between the White Snake and her lover and had her incarcerated under a pagoda (Lu 1924d). Chinese society was full of busybodies like Fahai, intending to imprison libido. Lu Xun and Zuoren's sexual modernism was supported by the eugenicist Zhou Jianren, who advocated multiple love partners based on the consent of all parties (Zhou Jianren 1925a, 5–8; 1925b, 12–15).

Below the Belt and on Top of the Scalp

In 1925, Lu Xun sided with the students of Beijing Women's Normal College in their rebellion against the educational authorities. He charged the female principal, Yang Yinyu, of displaying the psychology of an old maid who, deprived of erotic love, managed to project her own repression onto girl students (Lu 1925c). Principal Yang, who tried to restrict student activities, was in fact living her own suppressed erotic "dream contents" vicariously through her students (Lu 1925h, 291). In the politics of upper and lower sections of the body, Lu Xun's attack on Yang was hitting below the belt.[12]

Zuoren, in 1923, had translated a section of Havelock Ellis' *Affirmations* (1898) referring to the "hysteria" of old maids, due to unfulfilled erotic impulses (Zhou Zuoren 1923d, 80). Lu Xun's own source was Freud, whose "psychoanalysis" had "ripped off the facade of many a self-righteous prig" (Lu 1925i, 116). Having penned "The Story of Hair" (1920) and "On Moustache" (1924), Lu Xun was charged by a famous professor at the Peking University with having a "downward"-moving imagination that would eventually reach the private parts of the body. Lu Xun used this incident as a point of departure to expose the perverted Chinese mind. He referred to a bald school principal who, out of "moral" indignation, objected to girl students' bobbing their hair. Another example was a Chinese medical theory that attributes toothache to "weak kidneys," implying sexual deficiency. Lu Xun, who had had tooth problems since childhood, was once chided by an elder for having "performed acts harmful to the body." The mortifying innuendo still rankled in his adult memory (Lu 1925a, 243–55).

The world of Beijing in which Lu Xun lived was under the thumb of the northern warlords. At that time, a rival regime existed in the southern city of Guangzhou; the regime was founded by Sun Zhongshan, father of the Chinese republic, with Communist backing. Lu Xun left the academic world of Beijing and went south in 1926 and proceeded to "progressive" Guangzhou in 1927, only to be flabbergasted by the violence of revolution and counterrevolution shown in the North Expedition. The perverted minds of academics paled beside the bestial depravity of rampaging solders and sadistic torturers.

Lu Xun noted that, in one incident when forces that opposed bobbed hair occupied a city once held by forces promoting it, they seized women who bobbed their hair, plucked them out one by one, and, in addition, amputated those women's breasts (Lu 1927c). The bob was the fashion of the New Woman in America's "roaring twenties." This trend had also spread worldwide. In 1928, Zhou Zuoren wrote from Beijing on the phenomenon, that the bob had scandalized societies from Manila to Harbin, from Bombay to Tokyo. In Japan, long-haired men were looked upon as communists while women with bobbed hair were treated as degenerates; the latter incurred legal penalties equivalent to those for public nudity. But in China women with bobbed hair were arrested and executed (Qiming 1928, 37–41). The Zhou brothers intended to stress the extreme barbarity of the Chinese.

The Fin-de-siècle *Sadistic Imagination*

Lu Xun lamented that, in his capacity as an enlightener, he had contributed a course to the "cannibalist feast," by turning educated youth into "marinated raw shrimps." Raw shrimp is a Chinese delicacy based on the belief that "the friskier the shrimp the greater the eater's delight and relish." Lu Xun felt that, having raised the consciousness and sharpened the feelings of youth, he only succeeded in providing torturers with "more lively sufferers to savor," so much so that these "eaters' pleasure was greatly enhanced." He imagined that the counterrevolutionary torturers would "arrive at extraordinary pleasure, by observing a keener and finer expression of suffering pain" on the part of students and intellectuals who had fallen into their hands (Lu 1927a, 454). His concern was still with the waste of the better elements of Chinese society.

The source of this particular passage by Lu Xun is Mikhail Artsybashev, a vulgar Nietzschean of the Russian *fin de siècle* (Sun 1986, 482).[13] A cult figure in the European Decadence was actually Marquis de Sade, who contributed to the era's fascination with torture. He is actually seen as a "cultural progenitor of Decadence" by an academic authority on that epithet (Gilman 1979, 80–81). According to another authority, descriptions of sadistic behavior, namely torture, proliferated in works of the Decadent period (Pierrot 1981, 141). The most ingenious methods of torture were symptomatic of an "overcivilized" state. In a similar vein, Haisei (or Miyatake) Gaikotsu also wrote about the art of torture in Japan's historical past. His and other similar works were introduced by Zhou Zuoren to the Chinese readers (Zhou Zuoren 1925b; 1925c). Although the literary fad of sadism was "primarily a manifestation of an elitist disdain" for social conventions, the real offenders, labelled by the medical profession as sadists, were mostly "crude and violent members of the very lower classes, whom the decadent novelists most feared." Far from being a sign of the revival of instincts, this anomaly sprouted from "the soil of psychical degeneration" (McLaren 1997,

170, 175). To phrase it in an alternative theory, it is a sign of atavism that the masses are retarded at a lower stage of evolution—that of the savages or even the beasts. It was within this *fin-de-siècle* discourse on torture that the Zhou brothers made their observations.

Lu Xun's accusation of depravity and cruelty was not limited to the ruling class or the counterrevolution. He condemned the whole Chinese nation, and his favorite target was invariably the Chinese masses. As late as 1928, when he was leaning toward Marxism, in order to chill fellow leftists' naiveté about the masses, he imagined a recent incident in Changsha: After the execution of some Communists, the mob must have flocked to see the severed heads and the half-naked female bodies of the victims (Lu 1928a). In the same period and in the same journal, *Yusi* (Word threads), the eugenicist Zhou Jianren also published an article accusing the unspeakable cruelty of the Chinese as "cannibalistic." Considering shooting and garrotting as too easy on the victims, in modern times they had revived decapitation. Bookstores in Shanghai sold photos of these public executions, mostly to foreigners because Chinese "had gotten used to it." Jianren even obtained a photo of a crowd watching two young females—one had bobbed hair, the other, indiscernible—who, tied to crucifixes stark naked, had had their breasts amputated and the rest of the body mutilated in public. He claimed that the picture was withheld by the editors. These victims were probably revolutionary activists who had fallen into the hands of a warlord (Jianren 1928).[14]

The Perversion-Heredity-Degenerescenece Cycle

For the Zhou brothers, the Chinese collectively betrayed the syndrome of Jack the Ripper, the *fin-de-siècle* pervert and serial killer (1888). The understanding of sexual perversion at the time was set in the general paradigm of degenerescence. The concept was the underpinning of a variety of theories, ranging from Francis Galton's eugenics movement to the idea of the "natural-born criminal" of Cesare Lombroso. Max Nordau applied Lombroso's notion of atavism to modern artists and classified them as degenerates, meanwhile the misogynist Otto Weininger saw women as degenerate males.[15] Richard von Krafft-Ebing, in his turn, applied degenerescence to sexual perversity in his *Psychopathia Sexualis* (1886).

Michel Foucault concludes that in the second half of the nineteenth century a new discourse on sex based on the "perversion-heredity-degenerescence system" became a strategy of state control. This discourse used a heredity fraught with maladies to explain the origin of a sexual pervert and used sexual perversion to account for the depletion of one's line of descent. This biological way of thinking was challenged by the new psychology that was emerging in the *fin de siècle* (Foucault 1990, 118–119).

Foucault's insights alert us to the possibility that the Zhou brothers' attention to sexual perversion, Chinese polygamy's baneful effects, defective heredity, and racial and moral degeneration might not be fortuitous. It seemed that they turned a strategy of state control in the West into a critique of the Chinese people, a critique they also peppered with Decadent imagination. However, in Lu Xun and Zhou Zuoren, if not in Zhou Jianren, "perversion-heredity-degenerescence" reasoning was already overlapping the new psychology of Freud and Ellis.

Lu Xun's fascination with perversity and pathology survived his conversion to Marxism. In 1931, as figurehead of the League of Chinese Left-wing Writers sponsored by the communists, he stated that no literature in China, revolutionary or otherwise, honestly reflected reality. More genuine than both were the social news, namely, the story of a woman suing her husband for forced sodomy and beating, which was dismissed by the judge, allowing the husband to countersue the wife for false charges (Lu 1931, 303). In 1933, Lu Xun likened Shanghai society to a gold-capped jar for marinating human flesh (Lu 1933, 194).

The Epigones

In post-World War II Taiwan, the "marinating jar" imagery was inherited by Bo Yang as his master trope of the Ugly Chinamen, while Lu Xun's "syphilitic" trope of Chinese culture was appropriated by another epigone, Li Ao. The "banquet of human flesh" became the leitmotif in the Mainland Chinese author Mo Yan's *Jiuguo* (Wine Country) (1992). This magical-realist novel depicts a city in the Reform era providing culinary delights such as cooked babies as tourist attractions.

In 1993, the writer Zheng Yi revealed horror stories of cannibalism in the Guangxi Zhuang Autonomous Region during the Cultural Revolution. Predictably, he quotes Lu Xun to bolster his own verdict on the "entire totalitarian Han culture" as "one of cannibalism" (Zheng 1996, 149). Cannibalism in fact erupted among the Zhuang minority of Guangxi in the turbulent 1960s, but Zheng attributes it to a deadly combination of Zhuang and Han cultures. In the latter, tales of cannibalism are legion; in Zhuang mythology he finds the story of father sun eating his star children whom mother moon attempts to protect (Zheng 1996, 144).

Zheng Yi's reasoning is a bit tenuous—the Greeks are not called cannibals for their myth of Chronos devouring his own children. In the United

States, the 1990s was the decade that witnessed the phenomenon of Jeffrey Dahmer and the fascination with the fictional Hannibal Lecter as a cultural symptom, and yet it has not occurred to anybody to muse that cannibalistic yearnings are on the rise among the Americans. On the other hand, Lu Xun's cannibalistic motif will remain a powerful trope of the "Chinese people" although originally it was a Nietzschean simile of the atavistic masses.

Notes

1. "The True Story of Ah Q" (1922), the alleged site of the contestation depicts a malaise much graver than the foible of face-loving as Lydia Liu assumes, and the story had appeared four years before Lu Xun took note of Arthur Smith's "missionary" text. The Chinese love of face, though it appeared early in missionary writings such as Arthur Smith's, became a topic of scholarly attention only in the postwar era following the seminal work by Hu Xianjin (Hu Hsien-chin). It has come to be connected with another popular topic, *guanxi*, as in Bond (1991).

2. Lu Xun did not collapse the romantic poets with the late nineteenth-century Decadents out of ignorance. In *fin-de-siècle* Europe, after the hiatus of realism and positivism, there was a trend to win back for the artist "the right to follow his inspirations, to be revered for his gifts and forgiven his extremes, and if necessary to be a little bit mad." The revival of this earlier romantic ideal was conducted in the Decadent context, which paved the way for modernism (Grossman 1973).

3. The second view is upheld in Karl (1988).

4. Today's postmodernists, in believing that they have overcome modernity, still subscribe to a linear temporality that turns the multiplex "modernity" into a monolith. To avoid confusion, we should pinpoint the "modernity" overcome by postmodernism as largely modernization and rationalization. Unfortunately, it is not possible to avoid using the term "modernism" in lieu of modernization in all situations.

5. The Seven Sages of the Bamboo Grove were seven intellectuals with mystic inclinations and were anti-Establishment in the transition between the Wei and Jin dynasties, late third century C.E.

6. There is, however, no evidence that Lu Xun had read that book. What I am referring to here is the general mood of the time. Not to give all the credit to foreign models, Lu Xun's "wanderer" was more directly traced to the ancient poet Qu Yuan who, in his *Lisao*, speaks of a mythological odyssey through the heavens and Earth. Chinese scholarship, not keen on the issue of identity fashioning, tends to interpret Lu Xun's quote from Qu Yuan as a "quest for ways to save China."

7. The same person whom he would warn later on about the hazard of unmarried life by using the syphilis scare.

8. David Kelly is of the opinion that "the only work [by Nietzsche] Lu Xun is known to have studied in any depth was *Thus Spake Zarathustra*" (Kelly 1991, 154).

9. A Freudian Rorschach-testing manual places images pertaining to "Burdens" under its "Demand; oral-aggressive orientation" category. It states that "if 'oral' themes are emphasized, these images may relate to feelings of being 'drained' or 'sucked dry'," and they include "ox, yoke, camel, mule, man weighted down by a pack, Atlas" (Schafer 1954, 132).

10. Lu Xun admitted that the vermin metaphor in "A Madman's Diary" was adapted from Nietzsche's *Zarathustra* (Tang Dahui 1981, 173). "Nietzsche's most

common image of the mass is as a herd of animals. But he also figures it as a swarm of poisonous flies, or as raindrops and weeds, ruining proud structures" (Carey 1992, 24).

11. An English article in 1886 also used the wolf-pack imagery to describe the "collective inhumanity" and the "shameless cowardice of the crowd" (Pick 1993, 222).

12. Yang was a protégé of Lu Xun's personal enemy, the minister of education Zhang Shizhao. She died a patriot at the hands of the Japanese during World War II.

13. For Artsybashev, see Clowes (1986).

14. The former Red general Gong Chu recalls in his memoirs an incident in the Red-White civil war, of two female military cadres, Peng Juan and Yang Peilan, falling into the hands of the enemy in late July 1928—they were brought back to their home county, paraded naked in public, and executed by slicing (Gong 1978, 194–195). For similar incidents, see (Croll 1978, 150–151). Mao Dun's novel *Vacillation* (1928) also contains fictional scenes of the kind. One episode is about three women with bobbed hair, members of a women's association, who have fallen into the hands of counter-revolutionary thugs; they are stripped stark naked in public, dragged on the road with iron wires piercing their breasts, and eventually killed with sticks thrust into their vaginas. To show that rampaging soldiers merely use their hatred of the bob as an excuse to cover up their more extensive rape and molestation of women, Mao Dun also depicts a long-haired naked female corpse by the roadside who has had one breast amputated (Mao 1928, 245, 255–256).

15. Weininger believes that "homo-sexuality in a woman is the outcome of her masculinity and presupposes a higher degree of development." He avers: "However degraded a man may be, he is immeasurably above the most superior woman . . ." (Weininger 1975, 66, 252).

— 5 —

North and South

Is it imperative that the nationhood project require imagination to homogenize incongruous parts into a seamless whole, to impose common characteristics on peoples assumed to be a "nation"? Not necessarily. The same undertaking could chop the nation into two halves so that one part would assume the leadership of the project or take the blame for its failure. A classic case was postunification Italy, where the north regarded the south, which was forcibly attached, as an incubus. Other historical occasions show that a favored region was believed to harbor a certain positive ethos—for example, the "Prussian spirit" with its crucial role in the unification of Germany. Chinese discussants of national character also regionalized the nation for similar reasons. The trouble was that there was hardly any consensus, indeed, the accursed region for one often turned out to be the source of hope for another.

"Think regional" is an important theme in today's postmodernist discussion of nationalism. Instead of nationalism and national identity, theorists see "nationalisms," or national identity mediated by numerous local contexts (Jackson and Penrose 1993). Local patriotism and regional rivalry did exist in Republican China—in fact they were the norm in this period of disunity. Thus, regions also took on their own characters, which did not contradict the notion of a unitary national character. Mutual disdain between Beijing's and Shanghai's residents still exists today, but that does not prevent them from being the same nation.

Heredity and Environment

To "think regional" in this way is similar to today's fad of theorizing about the "body," which tells more about our intellectual dispositions than the historical age we study. In order to avoid indulging in "presentism" and to think historically, we need to set both corporeality and regionality in the context of the first half of the twentieth century. Heredity was a main pillar of the Darwinist discourse then, the other being environment. A discussant of "national character" in 1925 defined the subject as composed of "prenatal" and "postnatal" factors; the former he subdivided into physique (anthropological) and temperament–instinct (psychological) and the latter were further broken down into nature (geographical) and society (sociological) (Li 1925, 2). Pan Guangdan in 1927 reduced the components of culture into the natural environment, the human environment, and race, but since he emphasized race at the expense of the "cultural," his scheme can be simplified into *heredity* and *environment*: "Sometimes, environment is more important than heredity; at other times, heredity is more important than environment" (Pan 1927b, 1, 5).

The corporeal and the instinctual factors of national character have been amply covered in the previous chapters, so now let us turn to the geographical (the sociological and the cultural will have to await their turn in the postwar era, in the next chapter). Like the pundits of heredity and the Instinct School who applied their privileged concept in an overdetermined way, natural environmentalism also had its counterpart in the school of geographical determinism. On the other hand, the less dogmatic application of anthropogeography did bear fruit in other quarters, namely, the historical *Annales* School—the title of its journal was virtually adapted from the geographer Paul Vidal de la Blache's *Annales de Géographie* (Burke 1990, 21). In 1938, critical of geographical determinism, Luo Jialun quotes Lucien Febvre's *Le Terre et L'Évolution Humaine* (1922) to the effect that geographical environment bears on human affairs in the sense of providing many "regional possibilities" (Luo 1938, 142). To trace the vicissitudes of geographical thinking in modern China, we must again hark back to late Qing politics.

The Regional Strategy of Anti-Manchuism

Forging a Southern Identity

In 1897, the Hunan reformists launched the Southern Study Society which "began as an officially sanctioned gentry debating society," but to Liang Qichao it was the embryo of a "provincial legislature" (Esherick 1976, 15). It was a localist assertion against the center, as the reformists also saw in the project a revival of the ancient *fengjian* (feudal) ideal in the face of the centralized state. One may even detect the burgeoning of "civil society" in this effort (Duara 1995, 154–156). The very title of the society also underscored the sentiment that reformist initiative did not come from the conservative north.

After his escape to Japan, Liang Qichao saw the north-south rift as perennial. The east-and-west direction of China's river systems, notably the Yellow and Yangzi waterways, had given rise to north-and-south cultural differences. Therefore throughout her history there had been northern and southern schools of philosophy, classical scholarship, Buddhism, literature, art, and music. The Yellow River region (north) had declined, allowing the ascendancy of the Yangzi region (south) today. Liang, a native of Guangdong, saw the rise of yet a third center, the southernmost West (Pearl) River Valley, as a recent (and future) trend in Chinese history (Liang 1902u). To dwell on the strategical relationship between the north and south was traditional statecraft thinking, but Liang was also inspired by the regional pluralism of Western civilization. At the same time as he regionalized China, Liang also trisected Europe into the Latins who dominated in the past, the Teutons who are ascendant in the present, and the Slavs who will rise in the future (Liang 1902i). Later the philosopher Tang Junyi, who insisted on the monistic origin of Chinese civilization, would hold Liang Qichao culpable for initiating the blunder of making a geographical misanalogy between China and the West (Tang 1982, 2). This accusation alerts us that Liang, who was instrumental in the birth of Chinese nationalism, was likening a nation to a continent in his geographical discourse.

Contestation over the Site of Pristine China

A little bit earlier, the Japanese art critic Okakura Tenshin had written on the difference in ethos between north and south China (Okakura 1894). There is a possibility that expositions of this kind in Japan inspired a similar discourse among the Chinese. In 1905, *Guocui xuebao* (the National essence journal), while hostile to Liang Qichao's reformism, also serialized a long article by Liu Guanghan with a similar thrust. For Liu, there has been a north-south division since the most ancient times, spawning schools of thought governed by very different ethoi. He discerned them in the "hundred schools" of ancient China, in the Han dynasty's scholium of the classics, in Song and Ming neo-Confucianism, in the Qing school of evidential investigation, in literature, and even in occult studies. Like Liang, Liu saw the north as more advanced in the past but surpassed by the south in modern times. He pinpointed the barbarian invasions that ended the Western Jin dynasty (265–316 C.E.) as the beginning of the gradual rise of the south. The abundance of the water supply in that region also contributed to its development (Liu 1905).

In the same year as the appearance of Liu's treatise, *Guocui xuebao* began serializing Huang Jie's *Yellow History*, an important text of the Yellow Emperor cult. Curiously, this new Han identity was now a southern monopoly, for the text also devoted ample space to "scholar patriots, southerners for the most part, who resisted northern barbarians" (Schneider 1976, 66). The promotion of the memories of the late Ming loyalists had already begun with Zhang Taiyan as early as 1897 during his reformist days. In 1907, the practice crystallized in the poetic Southern Society, whose purpose was "to use our southern accent to keep alive the memory of our ancestors," and the society even referred to a *dao* of the south. The National Essence poets and essayists saw the sub-Yangzi region not so much in geographical but "in timeless aesthetic or moral terms." The Yangzi became a moat, "an outer perimeter between barbarism and the pure traditions of Chinese civilization" (Schneider 1976, 62, 68, 86).

The North and the South as Belligerents

In 1904, a more detached political analyst traced the "unprecedented calamity" of regional antagonism to conflicts between northern and southern court factions in the 1880s. Omitting the Taiping Rebellion, and focusing only on court politics, he saw the rift ramifying into the rivalry between Manchus and the Han, the Empress Dowager and the Emperor Guangxu factions, the pro-Russian and pro-Japanese parties, and, eventually, the conservatives and the reformists. The author saw the latest mutation of this perennial antagonism in Beijing's attempt at centralization, notably the building of a new army, with southern revenues (Anonymous 1904a). In the name of enforcing the "new measures" (*xinzheng*), the Qing regime's attempt at centralization was interpreted by southerners as Beijing's build-up at the expense of the provinces, and perceived as a "Manchu reaction" by Han people in general. These sentiments presaged the dynasty's downfall.

The First Round: The South's "Independence" from Beijing

It was the southerners who started the revolution to overthrow the Manchus. For that purpose, Anhui's Chen Duxiu in 1903 planned to establish a "citizen's alliance" to fight for the "independence" of the southeastern provinces (Chen 1982, 29). When Sun Zhongshan founded his revolutionary alliance in 1905, its alleged nationwide scope was belied by the inclusion of only the contingents from Guangdong, Hunan, and Jiang-Zhe. It came as no surprise that the revolution of 1911 assumed the form of secession, or "declaration of independence," of south China from Beijing. The Japanese scholar Kuwabara Jitsuzo, intrigued by north and south China behaving like rival countries, commented: "Northern Chinese people are not very much opposed to foreign races. . . . The rebellion that ended the Yuan dynasty and the revolution that ended the Qing dynasty both erupted in the south, and succeeded by virtue of the south" (Kuwabara 1930, 281–360). He obviously had Japan's continental interests in mind.

The Second Round: Yuan and
the "Southern" Opposition

The revolution was undermined at its very moment of triumph by the conservative north. It was Yuan Shikai, the military strong man of the *ci-devant* Qing regime, who proceeded to bury the republic after having become its first warden. From the very inception of the republic, the two rival regions conducted themselves like belligerents. In October 1911, the first negotiation between the northern and southern forces began in earnest in Shanghai, resulting in the yielding of the presidency to Yuan in exchange for his allegiance to the republic. Reneging on his promise, Yuan refused to assume office in the southern capital of Nanjing. Instead, he went on to use his power base in the north to pursue his dream of unification by force. It provoked the Second Revolution of 1913, which was launched by the Nationalists from the south but failed miserably.

In the aftermath, a Nationalist fugitive in Japan resented the fact that a struggle to determine the republican or antirepublican future of China was obfuscated by the so-called north-south rivalry (Shan 1914). This misdesignation, however, played into Yuan's hands, for he was able to depict the revolutionaries as regional separatists. Yet, Yuan's dream of imperial restoration was finally dashed by the Yunnan revolt of 1915 and 1916, which sent the signal to the southern forces to declare their independence from Beijing—a replay of the 1911 "revolution."

The Third Round: The Nationalists and
the Beiyang Warlords

Yuan's epigones, the Beiyang warlords, together with the southern secessionists, plunged the republic into chaos for a decade. In 1917, Sun Zhongshan, in opposition to the Beiyang government of Duan Qirui, launched the Defend the Constitution movement in Guangzhou. Another round of north-south warfare ensued. In 1918, General Wu Peifu of the Zhili faction of the Beiyang establishment took Wuhan, but Duan gave the province to a member of the Anhui clique. In retaliation, Wu advocated peace talks between the north and the south. What followed was another round of peace negotiation in Shanghai that began in August 1918, only to be aborted in May 1919.

By that time, Cen Chunxuan (a former high official of the Qing dynasty who came to head a regime in the south under the republic) and others had chased Sun Zhongshan out of the Guangzhou government. In 1920, with the collapse of Cen's southern regime, the Beiyang president Xu Shichang unilaterally announced the successful conclusion of the "peaceful unification" of the country. It prompted Sun Zhongshan to launch the second Defend the Constitution movement in Guangzhou later that year. The north-south war raged on. Late in 1924, Sun, upon the invitation of the sympathetic forces of General Feng Yuxiang, went north for another attempt at peaceful unification. After Sun's death at Beijing's Union Hospital, the southern forces of Guomindang launched the Northern Expedition of 1926 and 1927, leading to the unification of China under the Nanjing regime.

The Fourth Round: Nanjing Regime and Its Enemies

Aside from strategic reasons, the new regime's choice of location was also ideologically motivated. The Nationalists, now under Jiang Jieshi (Chiang Kaishek), blamed Beijing and its inhabitants "for the failure of the Republic and expressed concern lest their own movement become contaminated by contact with the old capital" (Strand 1989, 10). Actually, the Nanjing regime had no effective control in the north. A founder of the Chinese Youth Party, Li Huang, reminisced about a tour from 1929 to 1931 to the north where he sensed a pervasive "antisoutherner" sentiment in the post–Northern Expedition era. In his opinion, the southern forces had erred in "naming the revolution 'an expedition against the north,' " thus treating the northerners as "a foreign race," and, having relocated the capital in Nanjing, "renamed Beijing as Beiping," which means literally "levelling the north." All these measures "confirmed in the northerners' minds the arrogance of southerners." He worried that north China's alienation could be exploited by the two predatory neighbors, Japan and Russia (Li 1982, 249).

The Japanese imperialists regarded the north as a separate country, more ready to fall into their grip than into Nanjing's. Having annexed Manchuria by force in the early 1930s, their further designs on north China led to the Marco Polo Bridge incident in July 1937, which started World War II in East Asia. However, Nanjing and Tokyo were not the only contenders in north China. Following their defeat in the south by Guomindang forces, the

Communists entered the region at the end of their Long March. It was in the backward north that the Communists rebuilt their power base and recruited a huge peasant army for the postwar contest for China. The collapse of Japanese power in north China also enabled the Soviets to enter Manchuria, greatly contributing to the postwar Chinese Communist victory.

The North-South Cultural Animus

A 1924 issue of the Chinese version of the *Ladies Home Journal* (*Funü Zazhi*) published a parable: A southern cat brought by its master to the Beijing area learns that northern cats have never heard of fish. Faced with such benightedness, the southern cat cannot hold back its contempt. However, when this more "progressive" cat, bereft of its familiar diet, attempts to catch fishes on its own, it drowns in a brook (Zhang 1924, 1606–1607).

A Tale of Two Cities

Beijing, far from being benighted, was the seat of the May Fourth movement (which began as a student protest on May 4, 1919), although by June the movement's center of gravity had shifted to Shanghai. The shift was symptomatic of upstart Shanghai's challenge to the northern capital's cultural hegemony in the early 1920s. Beijing owed its intellectual leadership to the fact that it had been the seat of government for the previous millennium and, since 1898, also the seat of the National Peking University. In fact, Beijing benefited from the heavy concentration of talents from every province, notably southern ones.

After the May Fourth era, Beijing-based intellectuals continued to snipe at southern flashiness. When China's Dr. Sex, Zhang Jingsheng, turned into a crackpot, Zhou Zuoren attributed the change to the fact that he had moved from Beijing to Shanghai (Leary 1993, 120). Zuoren denigrated Shanghai culture summarily as that of "compradores, rogues, and prostitutes" (Zhou Zuoren 1926, 73). His brother Lu Xun vilified Shanghai intellectuals as "dilettantes and rogues" (Lu 1931, 296). Ironically, they themselves were from the southern province of Zhejiang, but had been longtime residents of Beijing. They were also veterans of the Beijing-based New Culture movement. Zhou belonged to the Literary Research Association, which originated in Beijing. The "roguish" school Lu Xun alluded to was the Creation Society, a Shanghai rival to the Literary Research Association. When, in 1931, Lu Xun castigated the Shanghai literati, he had already taken up residence in the southern metropolis, turning into a Shanghai intellectual himself. Beginning in 1933, an acrimonious squabble between the "Beijing school" and "Shanghai school" of literati erupted, this time started by Su Wen in Shanghai and Shen Congwen in Tianjin. It soon snowballed into a full-scale literary war between northern and southern men-of-letters (Tang Yizhong 1981).

In the years following the Northern Expedition, Beijing, now rechristened "Beiping," declined, while Shanghai emerged as the intellectual center. With the unification of China under a southern regime, the north-south division was sharper than ever. With both the governmental and intellectual centers shifted to the south, north became the synonym of backwardness and chaos. In a 1930 story by the Shanghai-based Communist writer Zhang Tianyi, a decadent intellectual who has led a vacuous life in Beiping is advised by his radical friend to "trade the present epoch [*shidai*] for a new one," and after his friend's execution he decides to look for a new life of engagement by moving to the south (Anderson 1990, 158).

Southern chauvinism was contagious, affecting the deep south as well. Zhu Qianzhi, a student of Peking University in the May Fourth days, had by the 1930s become a professor at the Sun Zhongshan University in Guangzhou, capital of the southernmost province of Guangdong. In a 1932 manifesto, "The Southern Cultural Movement," he adapted Oswald Spengler's notion of civilizational decline to his own purpose. He declared northern culture senile, so that China's regeneration would have to come from the south, especially the extreme south, the Pearl River Valley (Zhu 1980, 492–493)—a wish Liang Qichao had expressed in 1902.

Two Opposing Ethoi

If Liang Qichao was guilty of making an unlikely analogy between the regional divisions in the West and those in China, this practice was perpetuated by Mao Dun who, in his 1929 study of Chinese mythology, likened the two regions of China to the Norse and Mediterranean components of Western civilization (Xuanzhu 1929). It was reiterated by Lin Yutang to the effect that "the southern Chinese differ probably as much from the northerners, in temperament, physique and habits, as the Mediterraneans differ from the Nordic peoples in Europe" (Lin 1935, 17).

Throughout the Republican era and beyond, the thesis of two literary styles or even cultures of north and south persisted. This binarism was even read into the picture of ancient China. Li Changzhi's 1946 study of the Han historian Sima Qian saw him embodying the cultural spirits of both Zhou (north) and Chu (south), with the latter predominating. Li, *à la* Nietzsche and Spengler, asserted that Zhou culture "tended to be quantitative, scientific, rational, and orderly," while Chu culture was "unbridled, leaping, soaring, and free-flowing"; the former was "geometric," the latter "chromatic." In short, "Zhou culture was classical, Chu culture, romantic" (Li 1984, 4). Though not likening the two Chinese regions to the Norse and the Mediterranean, Li set them up as an Apollonian-Dionysian contrariety.

The "classical" and the "romantic" happened to be qualifiers applied by an observer, Cao Juren, to the rival Beijing school and Shanghai school of literati in their debate of 1933–1934 (Tang Yizhong 1981, 449). Regional stereotyping of Chinese literature certainly continued beyond the 1930s. In 1944, a collaborationist in occupied Shanghai wrote about "two kinds" of Chinese literature, northern and southern. The former, with a style more profound and tranquil, had its center in Beijing. Shanghai was the center of the southern school, livelier but coarser and shallower, a shortcoming attributable to its ties with politics (Hu 1944, in Tang 1982, 173–175). The "two literatures" thesis was incorporated by C.T. Hsia in his history of modern Chinese fiction, first appearing in 1961, for an American audience. He used the "time-honored test of Northern and Southern literary sensibilities," to sum up the difference between the Beijing-based Lao She and the Shanghai-based Mao Dun. The former "represents the North, individualist, forthright, humorous," and the latter, "the more feminine South, romantic, sensuous, melancholic" (Hsia 1971, 165).

Southern Supremacy

Whatever virtue the theory of the two *ethoi* had, the Norse-Mediterranean scenario did not quite fit China. In the West, the Mediterranean had been eclipsed by the Transalpine since early modern times. In China, it was the south that had been on the rise in the previous millennium, a fact emphasized by Republican scholars. In the early 1920s, the geologist Ding Wenjiang did a statistical survey of the regional distribution of "historical personages" in the twenty-four dynastic histories. He concluded that before the Song period, China's cultural center was in the north. Since the Southern Song dynasty (1127–1279 C.E.), the two Yangzi "provinces of Jiangsu and Zhejiang have become the cultural center of China." Ding also thought that, due to barbarian invasions, the Han race was less pure in the north (Ding 1923).

The study of geographical distribution of talents was probably inspired by a similar vogue in the West. A study on the geographical distribution of awards given by the Paris *Salon* of 1896 shows that "the rough highlands of Savoy, Alpine Provence, the massive eastern Pyrenees, and the Auvergne Plateau, together with the barren peninsula of Brittany, are singularly lacking in artistic instinct, while art flourished in all the river lowlands of

France." Heinrich von Treitschke did a similar study on Germany (Semple 1911, 19). In China, this pursuit found its practitioners in Liang Qichao, Zhu Junyi, Zhang Yaoxiang, and Pan Guangdan (Liang 1924; Zhu 1925; Zhang 1925; Pan 1927a). Ding differed from them by aiming at macro-history, not case studies.

Fu Sinian, a May Fourth activist and a historian, deemed Ding's statistics faulty, as they were based on republican provincial demarcations. Yet Fu questioned Ding's methodology, not the rise of the south. Fu himself suggested a "first China" ended by the barbarian invasions that toppled the Western Jin dynasty (265–316 C.E.), and a "second China" beginning from the reunification under the Sui and Tang dynasties (581–617 C.E., 618–907 C.E., respectively). He urged scholars to pay attention to the connection between this unique Chinese historical pattern and the formation of the Chinese race (Fu 1924). It is no coincidence that in the same period Arnold J. Toynbee also developed the view of a first and a second China: The first, named "Sinic," originated in the Yellow River basin and was parent to the "Far Eastern," which extended to the Yangzi region and affected Korea and Japan as well (Toynbee 1934, 90). Toynbee thought in terms of civilizations, which he construed as the resultants of both race and environment.

The scholarly consensus on the historical rise of the south was shared by the Japanese scholar Kuwabara Jitsuzo. He also regarded the southward escape of the Jin dynasty, away from barbarian invasions, as the beginning of the south's gradual rise and the decline of the north. The process was completed by the second cycle of barbarian invasions and the southward movement of another native dynasty, this time the Song. Using statistics of provincial distribution of successful candidates of the highest degree in the imperial examinations as a barometer, Kuwabara proved that by the Ming and Qing times, "the north was no longer the equal of the south." He attributed the causes of this historical shift to barbarian invasions in the north and "the migration of superior Han stock to the south," which betrayed a trace of eugenic reasoning. Kuwabara, with Japan's continental interests in mind, asserted that the northern Chinese contained "a lot of alien blood" and therefore were less opposed to alien races. The south, on the other hand, was an asylum for Han people who fled alien oppression, thus it was antiforeign and keen on "racial preservation" (Kuwabara 1930, 283–284, 289–292, 300–301).

Shifting Centers

Meanwhile, Kuwabara's colleague, Naito Konan, in his *Shina Shina ron* (New treatise on China) (1924), presented a theory of the shifting of cultural centers in East Asia. In ancient times, its center was north China. From the Ming dynasty, the Jiangsu-Zhejiang area, formerly inhabited by non-Chinese, became the center. At present, the center in China seems to have shifted to Guangdong, another barbarian region. But, the center of East Asia as a whole has shifted to Japan in the modern times. A product of his time, Naito also theorized in terms of civilizational decline. For him, China had reached modernity during the Song, and at present she is in her decadent phase, a fate to be followed by the West. That leaves a late-comer like Japan to assume the mission of leading a new "universal civilization" (Tam 1980, 172–174). The thesis of cultural centers shifting to formerly non-Chinese regions enabled Naito to think in terms of East Asian civilization as a unit, thus minimizing the significance of Chinese statehood.

While Naito spoke for Japanese imperialism, a Marxian version of shifting centers appeared in Karl A. Wittfogel's *Wirtschaft und Gesellschaft Chinas* (The economy and society of China) (1931). He discerned, in Chinese history, three shifts of "the agricultural centres of production," first from the northwest to the northeast, and then to the Yangzi Valley (Chi 1936, 11). The Wittfogel thesis was elaborated by Ji Chaoding (Chi Ch'ao-ting), who also benefited from the Marxian debates on Chinese social history in the 1920s and 1930s. Ji saw the "key economic area" of China moving from the northwest to the Yangzi Valley, due to the latter's overtaking the former in water control and public works.

Echoes in the West

In the West, the north-south view of China allegedly began with Marco Polo, who called the North, Cathay, and the South, Manji (Cressey 1934, 13–14). But, more recent Western views of the kind were echoes of late Qing and Republican Chinese sentiments. A German scholar, Richard Wilhelm, who had lived in the German concession in Shandong during the transition from empire to republic, concurred with his Chinese colleagues. In his opinion, "the old culture of China blossoms in a northern and a southern form which fertilize each other," and the former had its base in the Yellow River region. The Yellow River is not navigable in its lower reaches; the northern culture is therefore land-locked and "of a continental origin" (Wilhelm 1928, 354; Wusheng 1943, 14). America's doyen of modern Chinese studies, John K. Fairbank, was to develop this insight into a full-fledged theory of two Chinas: the Continental versus the Maritime.

Geography, Temperament, and Race

The Chinese began to pick up theories linking geography and national characteristics in the educational reforms of the late Qing, when they were exposed to a wide range of modern subjects either through Japanese instructors in China or during sojourns in Japan. In 1902, Liang Qichao wrote several articles on the relationship between geography and civilization (Liang 1902b, 1902i, 1902u). In 1903, a Hubei student addressed the issue of geography and "national character" directly, generalizing about the "insular" character of mountain-dwellers and the "expansive" character of plain-dwellers, and asserted that civilizations were products of a "temperate" climate. When it comes to the impact of rivers, he attributed the uncouthness of the northern Chinese to the muddy Yellow River, and the elegance and softness of southerners to the scenic Yangzi (Anonymous 1903a). This impressionistic approach would soon make way for more sophisticated theories.

Regions and Humors

The north-south binarism was eventually wedded to eugenics. As a prelude, in the May Fourth era there was an attempt to tie the north-south binarism to the theory of the four humors. In 1919, the Young China Society's Kang Baiqing wrote a study on the Chinese "temperament" in the spirit of the ancient Greek physician Galen. Galen's theory of four humors—the sanguine, the phlegmatic, the choleric, and the melancholic—was elaborated in modern times by Immanuel Kant, Rudolf Lotze, and Wilhelm Wundt.[1] Kang combined their theories with that of Alfred Fouillée, who defined race as an aggregate of individuals with certain hereditary traits. Fouillée's influence was also evident in Kang's division of national temperament into its static aspect (race, environment) and its dynamic aspect (cultural history). Kang explained the national temperament by a loosely defined concept of ontogeny and phylogeny, seeing the individual as historically shaped by, but also helping to shape, the natural and social environments. Influenced by a recent trend in Western theory, notably Willy Hellpach's, Kang stressed the importance of climate in shaping temperament (Kang 1919, 197–202). Hellpach, a degeneration theorist, had published a popular medical tract in 1902, *Nervosität und Kultur* (Nervousness and culture), which "set the beginning of the age of nervousness in 1880," caused by the speedup of life under industrialism (Kern 1983, 126).[2]

Kang also began drawing ideas from the eugenics movement, such as the statistical study of regional (i.e., ethnic) distribution of crime types and crime rate. For example, the Cantonese had the highest rate of tomb-robbing (Kang 1919, 211–212, 224). He followed Galton's suggestion of studying human types through physiological, especially facial features, and applied it to the nine Chinese regions (Kang 1919, 209–210). Galton adapted his idea of connecting observable physical characteristics and personality from the work of Franz Joseph Gall, the founder of phrenology. The discipline was an attempt to link moral and social behavior with certain cranial features in man, but it is now looked upon as a pseudoscience (Jones 1980, 103–5; Leahey and Leahey 1983, 45–113).

Instead of imagining a unitary national character, Kang examined the physiognomies of nine Chinese regions, seeing in each a different temperament shaped by history and climate. "Regions" are also stereotypes, but of a different order: "Generally speaking, people of the northern provinces are more robust in physique, taller and heavier than the inhabitants of the southern provinces; their faces are longer, their skin darker, their jaws rounder, and their chins carry thicker beard, but their foreheads are narrower, than the southerners" (Kang 1919, 209). Unfortunately, compared to the vigorous northerners of yore, today's northern Chinese have become effeminate, because the choleric temperament is prone to change into the phlegmatic, and the sanguine, into the sentimental (melancholic). A similar fate had befallen the Mongol and the Manchu conquerors of China (Kang 1919, 219, 228–229). According to Kang, the primitive, savage, barbarian, and civilized stages in human history are like infancy, adolescence, adulthood, and old age and are characterized respectively by the sentimental, the sanguine, the choleric, and the phlegmatic (Kang 1919, 234). Kang thus hinted at the equivalence of civilization and decadence.

Terrain and Cranium

Before the rise in the modern imagination of the cultural and ethnic differences between north and south China, this binarism had been established as a geographical fact by Baron Ferdinand von Richthofen. Beginning in 1868, the German geologist made seven tours in China, reaching every province, and laid the foundation on which Ding Wenjiang was to establish the discipline of Chinese geology in the Republican era (Furth 1970, 39–40). For Richthofen, north and south China are geologically distinct. The former, an extension of central Asian deserts, is flat and covered by loess deposited by wind from the West, which also explains its cold and dry winter weather. The rivers in north China, notably the Yellow River, originate in dry areas and are therefore filled with grit. The northern coastal areas, mostly flat and gradually sloping beaches, are equally unconducive to navigation. The southern landscape, a combination of the Yangzi alluvial plains and the eastward extension of Tibetan highlands, is of a more recent formation, thus mountainous and full of ravines. In the south, rivers are fed by melted snow from the highlands, and the hilly coastlines are punctuated by good harbors (Jin 1935, 55–56).

The geographer Jin Qisan, building on Richthofen's geological picture of China, delved into the racial difference between north and south. He alleged that, according to blood tests, the southern races are more "pure" than the northern. The northern Chinese have mixed with invaders from north of the Great Wall, while the Han people in the south were relatively recent immigrants not fully mingled with the aborigines. Northerners are taller than southerners on average. In terms of head forms, the northerners tend to be dolichocephalic (long-headed), the southerners, brachycephalic (round-headed), and central China, mesocephalic (in between).

Defining race through cephalic index originated with the Swedish anatomist, Anders Retzius, and became a fad by the end of the nineteenth century (Boyd 1953, 298). His system was referred to by Yan Fu in 1906 (see chapter 2). In America, William Z. Ripley's *The Races of Europe* (1899) popularized the idea of the three European races—Nordics, Alpines, and Mediterraneans—defined by skull measurements (Haller 1963, 55). The Western fad held such sway that this tripartite scheme, originally tailored for the Europeans, somehow also became the cephalic taxonomy of the Chinese. In his *The Formation of the Chinese People* (1928), Li Chi (Li Ji) divided the dolichocephalic into the dolicho-leptorrhinic and the dolicho-platyrrhinic, with the former prevalent in Shandong and the latter in Gansu and Guangxi. He also saw the brachycephalic elements as dominant in the Yangzi Valley with Jiangsu as the "centre of its purest form." The mesocephalic element, "the cross of the two types," is the "most dominant," presumably in the entire population (Li 1928, 49).

Jin probably adapted his scheme from Li Chi, but it is unclear whether he believed that the cephalic index had anything to do with racial purity. He tried to prove the purity of the southern races through the linguistic diversity in that region. While the northern Chinese language has extended its influence into the southwest through immigration from Sichuan, the languages of the hilly southeastern coastal provinces, namely Jiangsu, Zhejiang, Fujian, and Guangdong, are not only separate from the northern language family, but from one another. Taking into consideration geographical, racial, and linguistic factors, Jin alleged that northern culture was "plain culture," and southern culture consisted of "insular" pockets (Jin 1935, 56–59).

As Jin wrote, more pretentious anthropogeographical views of China were already in existence. In America, Ellsworth Huntington, a Yale University professor, combined human geography with racial theory and used human geography to explain the racial degeneration in north China. He was introduced to China by the eugenicist Pan Guangdan.

Eugenics Since the May Fourth Era

Before we examine the influence of the Huntington-Pan thesis, it is necessary to clarify its historical background: Chinese eugenic thinking since the May Fourth era. In the previous chapter, we showed that May Fourth eugenic thinking, represented by Zhou Jianren, was eclectic. It not only reconciled Galton and Mendel, but also accommodated neo-Lamarckian theories of the inheritance of habits acquired through adaptation to environment.

In 1919, Ding Wenjiang referred to the orthodox eugenics of the Galton-Pearson school by introducing its seven basic principles (Furth 1970, 71). The fourth and the fifth are clearly anti-Lamarckian, as one downplays the importance of "acquired characteristics" vis-à-vis "inherited characteristics," and the other denies the inheritability of habits. The sixth, "reproductive cells are transmitted perpetually," betrays the school's reliance on Weismann's theory of heredity as the transmission of the immortal "germ plasm." The third, "natural selection is the only method of evolution," limits environmental factors to the function of merely selecting for transmission or extinction what is already innate in the organism. The seventh, "a man's individual nature is inherited from countless ancestors; the extent of his inheritance is in direct ratio to the closeness of the ancestor," was stipulated by Galton before the rediscovery of the Mendelian law of biological inheritance in 1900.

Although he was an admirer of Karl Pearson, Ding made only a brief excursion into eugenics. Like other May Fourth intellectuals, Ding dabbled in eugenics as an amateur. Most of them also did so in an eclectic fashion, in the spirit of Zhou Jianren. For instance, the historian Gu Jiegang advocated eugenics alongside "better educational methods," for the improvement of the Chinese race (Schneider 1971, 258). The amorphous nature of May Fourth eugenic thinking explains why even Chen Duxiu spoke positively of it when he was turning Marxist in 1920 (see chapter 3). Toward the late 1920s, eugenics was definitely under fire from Marxism (Schneider 1971, 268). As a result, its popularity among leading intellectuals dwindled in comparison to that of the May Fourth period. On the other hand, like Marxism, it also became more dogmatic and hardened into a movement (Dikötter 1992, 177–179). Its leading voice was Pan Guangdan.

In the 1920s, Pan received his master's degree from Columbia University, having majored in zoology, paleontology, and genetics. For three summers beginning in 1923, he received training at the Eugenics Record Office and the Carnegie Institution, both at Cold Spring Harbor, New York (Quan 1985, 486–487).[3] The Eugenics Record Office, founded in 1910 by Charles B. Davenport, doyen of the American eugenics movement, was at the center of the movement. American eugenics applied Mendel's theories, not the statistical method of Galton and Pearson, yet continued to uphold Galton's social dogma, "that is, race and ancestor worship" (Pickens 1968, 49–50, 53).

Pan also adopted this creed and believed that progress hinged on good heredity. He was an orthodox eugenicist, and his position on heredity was unalloyed Weismannism. In 1924 and 1925, Pan carried on a debate with Zhou Jianren, Sun Benwen, and Guo Renyuan concerning the nature of heredity (Ru 1931). Jianren was a Neo-Lamarckian who stressed the importance of environment; Sun was a "culturalist" sociologist who put a premium on culture; whereas Guo was a behavorist trained at University of California–Berkeley who denied the existence of "instinct"—these three are fairly representative of the spectrum of views on the issue at that time. Adamantly opposed to the Lamarckian notion of inheritance of "acquired characteristics," Pan labelled it "pseudo-scientific" (Pan 1981, 31). He adhered strictly to the principle of "natural selection." Citing the case of the blind fishes in underseas caves (which Liang Qichao had used in 1904 to prove the influence of environment), Pan argued that the underseas caves "selected" only those fishes with defective eyesight to remain and procreate, while those with good eyesight had probably left through some secret passages (Pan 1981, 36).

Geography and Eugenics

Ellsworth Huntington, whose work Pan introduced to the Chinese, was a member of the Galton Society when it was founded in 1918 by Davenport (Haller 1963, 73; Pickens 1968, 53). He believed that "in the strictest sense of the word, races should be defined only in terms of heredity." On the other hand, he averred, geographical factors and social conditions also "have a great deal to do with determining a people's character." They "select certain types for preservation and eliminate others." Thus, in spite of his deceptively eclectic statement that "the character of specific groups of mankind depends on inheritance, physical environment, and social environment" (Huntington 1924, 6), Huntington, like Pan, was rooted in the tradition of Weismann and Galton.

Huntington was president of the Association of American Geographers in 1923. He was president of the American Eugenics Society from 1934 to 1938 and continued as a director until 1947 (Martin 1973, 184, 300). The society was born in 1926 amidst waves of legislation aimed at selective restriction of immigration into the United States, by discriminating against Asians and Latins, in favor of "Nordics." Many of the society's members were involved in providing a eugenic rationalization for the Congress' immigration acts. By the 1930s, under the influence of social reform–minded Frederick Osborn, the society moved away from the racist position of people like Madison Grant (Haller 1963, 155–157, 174–175). Huntington was a cothinker of Grant's with regard to restriction of Latin American immigrants in the 1920s, although he refused to be identified as a "Nordic booster" (Martin 1973, 177). The Nordic cult was the racist scion of a time-honored genealogy of an idea called the "north temperate zone" theory.

The North Temperate Zone Theory

A Time-Honored Thesis

The awareness of the rise of northern Europe *vis-à-vis* the Mediterranean could be traced to the sixteenth-century French historian, Jean Bodin (Bury 1932, 38). It confirmed civilization as a gift of the north temperate zone—a thesis originated by Aristotle and revived by John Locke in modern times. In France, it inspired the political philosopher Montesquieu to attribute the immutability of Oriental cultures to their southern locations and warm climate (Semple 1911, 18). In Germany, the theory was embraced by the philosophers Johann G. von Herder and G.W. Friedrich Hegel. Herder believed that only "well-formed men molded by temperate climes" could have produced the "cultivation and humanity" unique to Europe (Stocking Jr. 1987, 20). Hegel said: "The true theatre of History is therefore the temperate zone; or rather, its northern half" (Hegel 1956, 80).

Aristotle's and Locke's views were known to Liang Qichao as early as 1902 (Liang 1902b, 106–107). Liang's icon, the Swiss political theorist J.K. Bluntschli, also endorsed what he believed to be a time-honored theory that "the hot tropical countries (up to 23° 28') and the cold polar zones (beyond 66° 23') are less favourable to the development of States than the temperate zones which lies between them." Furthermore, "the capitals of nearly all important States lie in the midmost temperate zone, where the average temperature ranges between 8° and 16° C" (Bluntschli 1885, 211, 212). In 1904, Liang Qichao opined that "according to geographers" only the temperate zone could give rise to "advanced and developed polities' (Liang 1904d, 8).

Its Racialist Applications

Not all subscribers to the north temperate zone thesis drew conclusions favorable to the European races. According to the Anglo-Australian Charles Pearson, in his *National Life and Character* (1893), "the higher races," who can live only in the north temperate zone, will be forever barred from effectively colonizing the tropics, leaving the lower and more prolific races—the Chinese, Hindus, Negroes—to take over the rest of the world (Hofstadter 1945, 160).[4] Nonetheless, the north temperate zone theory normally bolstered Nordic superiority, as in Houston Stewart Chamberlain's *The Foundations of the Nineteenth Century* (1911).

Pearson and Chamberlain were contemporaries of Liang Qichao and Kang Youwei. This fad explains Liang's interest in the geographical foundation of "advanced and developed polity." Kang, on the other hand, parroted a white-supremacist version of the north temperate zone theory in his *Datong Shu* (The book of great harmony). It argues that the repulsive looks of the blacks is due to their tropical habitat and its uninviting terrain. Chinese and Englishmen who moved into the East Indies "have turned dark yellow in pigments and their intelligence has also become diminished." In contrast, those Chinese who migrated to Canada, located near latitude 50° north and close to the Rocky Mountains, have given birth to "white, fair, and handsome children." European races located within the temperate zone are largely fair, while inhabitants of southern Italy, Portugal, and Spain tend to be yellow (Kang 1956, 196).

Kang and Chamberlain agreed on Nordic superiority, but their differences were also profound. Kang's *bêtes-noire* were blacks, not Jews. His criterion of racial superiority is shallow, based on the subjective perception of "good looks." He was also oblivious to the hereditarian premise of eugenics and deemed geography the decisive factor. Chamberlain, on the other hand, defended the purity of a good blood line once it had taken shape in history and assumed a distinct racial identity. For him, the Aryans, especially the Teutons, are "the elect," whereas in Kang's Great Harmony, mankind shall erase all "boundaries" by becoming one race: the Caucasian. The underlying difference between the two is that between the Judaeo-Christian notion of the Chosen People and Confucian ecumenism. In Chinese, "great harmony" (*datong*) also connotes "great sameness." It was precisely the corruption of pedigree and degeneration into mongrelism that Chamberlain abhorred. His comment on ecumenism runs: "The raceless and nationless chaos of the late Roman Empire was a pernicious and fatal condition, a sin against nature. Only one ray of light shone over that degenerate world. It came from the north" (Chamberlain 1911, 320).

In the United States, Chamberlain's racial mysticism was echoed by Madison Grant. For Grant, the Nordic peoples were born rulers and conquerors, while the southern races were either peasants or excelling in artistic (i.e., feminine) pursuits (Grant 1918, 227–229). In the 1920s, Ellsworth Huntington worked together with Grant in favoring Nordic migrations into the United States, but his position on the Nordic thesis was rather ambiguous.

Huntington's Version

Huntington started out as a proponent of the north temperate zone theory, a creed of anthropogeography at the time. "The greatest events of universal history and especially the greatest historical developments belong to the North Temperate Zone," avers an authoritative text (Semple 1911, 611). In 1915, Huntington held the opinion that for both work and health, the best climate is one in which "the main temperature rarely falls below the mental optimum of perhaps 38° [F], or rises above the physical optimum of about 64°[F]." Thus ideal conditions would be found where the average annual temperature is around 51 degrees, as in London, Paris, New York, and Beijing (Huntington 1915, 220). He turned from environment to heredity between 1915 and 1923. "During the eight years . . . I saw how both physical and social environment often act as selective agencies which pick out special types of people for preservation or elimination in any given occupation or region. In *The Character of Races* I have set forth this line of reasoning in orderly fashion" (Huntington 1925, viii–ix).

The reasoning in that book is by no means orderly, for it attempts to advocate both geographical determinism and hereditarian fatalism—a vision that is at once more sophisticated and less coherent than Kang Youwei's. Huntington argues that "no matter what the original character" of the race that migrated into Scandinavia, "the process of natural selection" there would tend to preserve "qualities of curiosity, individualism, introversion, self-assertion, and acquisitiveness." But, "some races, such as the Negroes, would be exterminated under such circumstances because they have already acquired opposite qualities under another environment." Thus, "an incompetent race might find the environment repressive where the Norse find it stimulating" (Huntington 1924, 218). The reader gets the impression that environment would make a difference only for races of similar calibre. Provided that all Europeans are equally endowed with "hereditary ability," he opines, the North Sea regions would "always excel eastern and southern Europe," because "on an average the men of genius in the North Sea countries would be more energetic," and enjoy better health in the "cool, bracing climate" (Huntington 1924, 233).

Adverse Environment, Bad Heredity, and the "Chosen People"

It seems that every major theory with a pretension to universal application has foundered on the case of China. Marxism, from its inception in China, had to make room for her "exceptionalism," first through the nebulous "Asiatic mode of production" and later in the oxymoron of a protracted "centralized feudalism." Today, the followers of Max Weber busy themselves in explaining the economic miracle of East Asia by seeing in neo-Confucianism an equivalent to the allegedly *sui generis* Protestant ethic. In the interwar years, the north temperate zone theory was transmogrified by China—into rationalizing why in her case the south is superior to the north in the modern times.

China's Exceptionalism

Huntington visited China in 1923 (Martin 1973, 198).[5] He devoted four chapters of his work, *The Character of Races* (1924), to accounting for the anomaly of China. These chapters were translated by Pan Guangdan in 1929 under the title, *Natural Selection and the Chinese National Character* (Pan 1929b). Huntington says:

> One of the strangest facts about China is that the northern and southern parts of that country invert the usual roles. In most parts of the world a region in low latitudes is less progressive than a corresponding region in higher latitudes, provided the high latitudes are not so cold that life becomes difficult. That is true in Europe, western Asia, India, and North America. It is equally true in the southern continents, where Argentina and Chile lead South America, and South Africa leads Africa. But in China the opposite is true: the south is progressive and the north backward. Except where Europeans have recently settled, no region within twenty-five degrees of the equator probably shows so much real progress as south China, a fact which goes far to show that the Chinese are one of the world's most able races. But between thirty-five degrees and forty degrees from the equator there is perhaps no region save central Asia so backward as north China (Huntington 1924, 158).

Chinese civilization originated in the north temperate zone, but the supremacy of this region seems to be a matter of the past. The north-temperate-zone theory thus fails to account for the anomaly of China in a modern world where "north" and "south" are code words for development and underdevelopment.

North China, the Killing Field

According to Huntington, China's peculiarity resulted from an ensemble of anthropogeographic factors. North China, adjacent to the Eurasian steppes, was subjected in the past to periodic invasions by nomads, caused by the cycles of aridity in central Asia. Each invasion caused a massive exodus of northern Chinese southward or southeastward toward the Yangzi and the Pearl River valleys, or beyond (i.e., overseas). More frequent than barbarian invasions have been natural disasters causing periodic famines, a pattern repeated for more than two millennia. Part of the reason for this is the weather. In north China the rainfall is limited largely to a few months in the summer, and a delay in its arrival requires heavy reliance on irrigation and means potential disaster. This hardly ever happens in the south or in Manchuria. The unfavorable weather aside, the terrain of north China is flat and bare. Huntington observed: "Nowhere, during many years of travel, do I recall a more vivid impression of the absolute levelness of the [north China] plains" (Huntington 1924, 170–171). The ecological disasters of north China have rendered it an easy prey of the Yellow River, perhaps the most destructive ecosystem in human chronicles. Thus the problems of invasion and drought are compounded by devastating floods.

When a cycle of Chinese history culminates in such events, a "natural selection" process is at work, and "an enormous extermination of the less competent parts of the population takes place" (Huntington 1924, 157). The winnowing process allows for survival only of those with the qualities of thrift, parsimony, selfishness, and callousness, which then become dominant traits in the region. The selection process also weeds out the prettiest girls—prospective mothers, best in mind and body—from the region, as they are sold by their families who struggle to survive. If they become concubines of the urban rich, they are lost to rural China; and if they are sold into prostitution, they are lost to the Chinese race as a whole.

Those northerners with more energy and initiative chose neither to perish nor to stay, but to leave the afflicted region altogether. Thus they repeated on a smaller scale the exodus to the south occasioned by the major upheavals of the barbarian invasions. In the Qing and Republican periods, an alternative route of escape was migration to Manchuria. Those migrations were also selective processes, which allowed only the strongest and most resourceful to reach the final destination, and those qualities were also passed on to the progeny.

As a result, only those with "passive qualities of economy, industry, patience, and endurance" rather than "active leadership" are fit to survive in an environment like north China. In other words, good stock has been continuously drained from north China by the migrations out of the region. Huntington points out that the inhabitants of areas in north China perennially afflicted by famine "appear to be little more than morons," while the north Chinese as a whole have become "more and more dull," and "pretty women and girls are far rarer among them than in the south" (Huntington 1924, 190).

The Northern Chinese in Arthur Smith's Eyes

Pan Guangdan corroborated Huntington's observations with those in Arthur Smith's *Chinese Characteristics* (1894), which he partially translated. In 1937 Pan combined the fifteen chapters from Smith with Huntington's four chapters into a larger volume, *National Characteristics and Racial Hygiene*. Smith, an American missionary, spent over twenty years in Shandong, therefore the "Chinese" characteristics he observed were largely north Chinese. Indeed, Smith was quoted by Huntington to illustrate the "moronic" quality of the northern Chinese.

Smith is struck by the "intellectual turbidity" of the uneducated Chinese, for whom "any idea whatever comes as a surprise." A telltale sign of such benightedness is the habit of repeating as a reason for a fact, the fact itself. " 'Why do you not put salt into bread-cakes?' you ask of a Chinese cook. 'We do not put salt into bread-cakes,' is the explanation" (Smith 1894, 85). Smith is also annoyed by the Chinese disregard of accuracy, to the extent that "the regulation of standards is a thing which each individual undertakes for himself" (Smith 1894, 53). The other negative traits described by Smith, namely, mutual suspicion and the absence of sympathy, public spirit, and sincerity, seem to bear out Huntington's observations of the selfishness and callousness of the northern Chinese.

The "positive" traits according to Smith—namely, the absence of nerves, indifference to comfort and convenience, physical vitality, patience and perseverance, content and cheerfulness—also fit Huntington's thesis of the "selection" of the passive-endurance quality by the adverse environment of north China. Smith gives a pithy description of the "virtue" of content inculcated by a hopeless situation: "They [the Chinese] do not cherish plans which seem to them to lead ultimately to 'a good time coming,' and they do not appear to suppose that there is any such time to be expected" (Smith 1894, 162).

South China as the Purer China

To illustrate southern advancement over the north, Huntington cited an official list of the higher metropolitan and provincial officials provided to him in 1910 by a staff member of the American embassy. It showed a much higher ratio of officials from the south with regard to their respective provincial populations (Huntington 1924, 161–162). Pan Guangdan corroborated this observation with the studies of geographical distribution of historical personages, notably literati-officials, by Liang Qichao, Ding Wenjiang, Zhu Junyi, Zhang Yaoxiang, and himself (Pan 1929a, 129–130).

Although the conquerors have invariably infused new, virile blood into the northern Chinese race, "the absence of further selection and the prevalence of intermarriage with stock less highly selected causes a tendency toward reversion to the normal type" (Huntington 1924, 156). In contrast to the nomadic conquerors of the north, "in the southerly migrations the Chinese have intermarried relatively little with aborigines and often exterminated them" (Huntington 1924, 150). Thus, "the part of the population which gives southern China its distinctive character is the most purely Chinese" (Huntington 1924, 166). They are not only the oldest Chinese but the most "selected" stock.

The Flower of the Chinese People

Huntington especially singled out the Hakkas as the "cream of the Chinese." The Hakkas, according to Huntington, are the choicest remnant of three migrations. The first wave moved from their original homeland in Henan to the southern provinces of Zhejiang, Fujian, and Jiangsi when north China was devastated by the barbarians in the fourth century C.E. The second wave moved out from Henan in the ninth century during the fall of the Tang dynasty and settled in Fujian. The Mongol invasion in the thirteenth century affected the whole Hakka region and exterminated a majority of the population. "The chosen remnant whose skill, bravery, and endurance enabled them to survive this terrible period gave rise to the last migration," to the Meizhou region in Guangdong. Throughout a greater part of their odyssey, the Hakkas "kept themselves unmixed with any other race." Huntington noted that the modern Hakkas' energy and cleanliness, their respect for women, and their high level of education are almost unique among the Chinese. He agreed with George Campbell, an authority on the

Hakkas, in predicting that "the Hakkas will play an increasingly important part in the progress and elevation of the Chinese race" (Huntington 1924, 198–199). Huntington also highly evaluated the Chinese in Manchuria who were the best stock from Zhili and Shandong provinces, selected through the ordeals of migration.

Among Huntington's correspondents were the historians Frederick J. Turner and Arnold J. Toynbee. Although Huntington criticized Turner's obliviousness to the "natural selection" occasioned by historical migrations of peoples (Huntington 1924, 243), his own view smacks of the latter's "frontier theory." Huntington shared with Toynbee an interest in the rise and fall of civilizations, and both eschewed mono-causal (either race or environment) interpretations. Toynbee, the more schematic of the two, subsumed both factors under an overarching formula, "challenge-and-response" (Toynbee 1934, vol. 1, part 2, section C, subsections (a) and (b)). Cosy environments are conducive to inertia, whereas adverse environments pose challenges to human societies, evoking their creative *élan* for the task of civilization-building. But if the environment is overly adverse, it would simply cripple the agents' ability to respond—an argument that seems to fit north China. Toynbee opts for the "optimal challenge," which he fails to clarify.

Theorizing in terms of race, environment, and Bergsonian *élan vital* was popular at the time. By the early twentieth century, Henri Bergson had reworked the Nietzschean vision into a theory for the regeneration of civilization by the creative few, whose surging *élan* would burst through the ossified institutions that governed the majority. Although Toynbee published the first three volumes of *A Study of History* in the 1930s, his ideas were formed in the previous decade, when Liang Qichao also theorized about the creative minority's "mental power" countervailing the forces of environment (Liang 1924, 50–51). Inspired by Bergson, Toynbee's philosophy of history is inevitably more voluntarist than Huntington's. Nonetheless, both explain history in terms of the interaction between humans and environment. Like his cothinker, Toynbee also stresses the role of migration, or *Völkerwanderung* (a term borrowed from Friedrich Ratzel), especially in the birth of civilization.

There is an Old Testament aura about the idea of "exodus" as an ordeal giving birth to a "chosen people." Huntington, for example, compared the Hakka settlements in south China to those of the Puritans in early America (Huntington 1924, 197). In a 1935 study of the Huntington clan descended from New England Puritans, *After Three Centuries: A Typical New England Family*, he avers that "any racial group which has undergone a process of selection and segregation will prove superior to its congeners which have not" (Martin 1973, 189). His chronicle of the Hakkas is also similar to his history of the Jews descended from the tribes of Judah and Benjamin. They survived to give rise to a chosen people because they refused to mingle, unlike the Lost Ten Tribes, with the peoples surrounding them (Huntington 1924, 130–134). Toynbee concurred: "The ancient Syriac neighbours of Israel have fallen into the melting-pot and have been re-minted, in the fullness of time, with new images and superscriptions, while Israel has proved impervious to this alchemy—performed by History in the crucibles of universal states and universal churches and wanderings of the nations—to which we Gentiles all in turn succumb" (Toynbee 1934, vol. 2, p. 55).

The Fad of Anthropogeography

Geographical or climactic determinism is basically at odds with Marxian reasoning, which theorizes in terms of society's productive forces. Thus, Karl Wittfogel's Chinese disciple Ji Chaoding (Chi Ch'ao-ting) refuted Huntington and attributed the rise of one region *vis-à-vis* another to an increase in "irrigation activity," due to "the political and economic importance of an area" (Chi 1936, 29). Ji's theory, however, has trouble explaining why in late imperial China, state-sponsored attempts to turn the metropolitan area around Beijing into a "second Jiangnan," i.e., a self-sufficient region (instead of one constantly at the mercy of the undependable supply of southern grains transported via the Grand Canal), repeatedly failed.

In the late 1920s and 1930s, notwithstanding the rise of Marxism as an intellectual trend, anthropogeographic reasoning still had its audience. In the geographical profession, "human geography," or "anthropogeography," was a main force represented by Karl Ritter and Friedrich Ratzel in Germany, Paul Vidal de la Blache and Jean Brunhes in France, and Ellen Semple in the United States. This trend sought to explain history through geography, and was known in China (Hu 1928, 5–15; 1929, 1–8; Ju 1987, 207–208). It was shown in Wang Zhaoshi, one of the "seven gentlemen" of the National Salvation Association jailed by the Nanjing government in 1936 for engaging in anti-Japanese activities. In the late 1920s and early 1930s, Wang was a writer for the journal *Xin Yue* (Crescent moon), where Pan Guangdan published his view on eugenics and his translation of Huntington. The influence of those writings on Wang is evident. He attributed the egotistic "national psychology" of the Chinese to famines, which all their ancestors had experienced. During each famine, those who were more selfish and egotistical (i.e., they refused to share food with others or were ruthless enough to sell their own daughters) had a better opportunity to survive. Therefore, "with each famine, selfishness and egotism [in the Chinese character] tended to deepen" (Wang 1929, 14–16).

In 1929, Fu Shaozeng published his *A Study of the Chinese National Character*, in which the concept is defined by "heredity and environment." Physical environment, or geography, is singled out as the most influential factor. Fu divided the Chinese into four categories: (1) the rice-eating race of the Yangzi and Pearl River Valleys; (2) the wheat-eating race of the Yellow River region; (3) the meat-eating race of Mongolia, Qinghai, and Tibet; (4) the wheat-and-meat-eating race of Manchuria. The first type, living in mild and humid regions, is wealthy and highly literate, but effeminate. The second type inhabits cold and dry regions, is robust, strong-willed, straightforward, and chivalrous. The third type, under a climate that alternates between hot desert storms and cold winds, is largely nomadic and aggressive in character. The fourth type has the advantages of both the second and the third. Like Huntington, Fu also divided "environment" into the physical and the social. The former shapes "natural racial character," and the latter, "habitual racial character." With the second concept, Fu attempted to forge a unitary notion of Chinese culture that puts a premium on obedience, family ethics, and passivity, and denigrates talent, organization, and material progress. But to talk in terms of a unitary national character is to depart from anthropogeography and to fall back on national-psychological reasoning with its own inherent aporia. For example, Fu thought that China's "national spirit" was encapsulated in Confucianism, yet due precisely to Chinese familism, a "universal psychology of the nation" was wanting (Otani 1935, 661–670).

In the 1930s, Huntington-style argument also managed to find its way into history textbooks. In Kenneth S. Latourette's 1934 history of China, chapter 1 has the predictable title, "Geography and Its Influence on the Chinese." Expressing the usual regret for north China's adverse natural environment, the author comes to the conclusion that "frequent famines in the North tend also to lower the quality of the population" (Latourette 1942, 12).

Zhang Junjun's Racial Reform Program

Zhang Junjun was another Chinese follower of Huntington and, like Pan Guangdan, graduated from Columbia University in the 1920s. He majored in psychology and religious philosophy and returned to China to become a professor and the director of the Chinese Association for the Prevention of Tuberculosis. His interest in eugenics, however, dated back to his pre-American days, and in 1923 he had published a book on racial reform

(Zhang 1935, 280). In 1935 he published *Zhangguo minzu zhi gaizo* (Reforming the Chinese race) and its sequel (with the same title) in the following year. During the war years, he published, among other works, *Huazu suzhi zhi jiantao* (An Examination of the racial qualities of the Chinese) (1944).

Exhausted Spirit

Zhang regarded the Chinese as a degenerate race. He wrote at a time when the Japanese menace was hanging like a sword over the head of the Chinese nation. He lamented that there must be something wrong with a nation whose population amounted to a quarter of humanity and yet was about to be conquered by the Japanese, thirty times smaller in population and eight times smaller in territory (Zhang 1935, 181).

In his eyes, the Chinese people lack energy. They are listless and dispirited. The outward signs are slackness, procrastination, egotism, the lack of unity, and the absence of a sense of responsibility. The Chinese are perfunctory and insincere about everything, even their well-cherished family relationships, not to mention public affairs. Improvident, they lack persistence in anything, and any fervor lasts only five minutes. They are short of courage and inclined to cowardice. Among the Chinese males, "nine out of ten have a feminine temperament" (Zhang 1935, 188). They are always succumbing to a situation and seldom dare to face problems head on, for they cannot handle tension and speed. Instead, they tend to be slow and lacking fire. Their spirit is one of dependence, which is the very substance of the Chinese family. The Chinese people also lack sympathy, and their selfishness is boundless. They are without deep conviction about anything and are capable of reconciling contradictory principles without much ado, meanwhile never bothering to spend time to study any of them in depth. Zhang again attributes this propensity to a lack of energy.

Stunted Corporeality

Zhang cited the statistics of a recent survey conducted by the ministry of education concerning 13,485 students, whom he classified as middle-class, who were better off than most people. Among them, those who were physically fully-grown numbered only 6,166, that is, less than half. The ratio in the north was higher. At the Beiping (Peking) University, the figure was 1,097 of 1,632, that is, two-thirds, whereas at Nanjing's Central University, the figure was 278 of 1,285, that is, only a quarter. In terms of nutrition, the survey showed that of 12,095 students, only 5,754, or less than half, were included in the top category A (Zhang 1935, 199–200).

In his 1944 work, Zhang complained that the Chinese team of 139 athletes had failed to win a single medal in the 1936 Berlin Olympic Games, a failure he regarded as a sure sign of racial degeneration (Zhang 1944, 5–6). The reason for this degeneration is the separation of intelligence and physique. The northern Chinese are relatively strong in physique but dull in wit, and it is the reverse for the southern Chinese. The end result is the lowering of both physical and mental qualities of the race as a whole. Zhang was also convinced that physical degeneration was the root of moral degeneration, hence the moral bankruptcy of the Chinese, and that within the nation, southerners were more morally degenerate than northerners.

Zhang assumed the southern superiority in intelligence to be an established fact based on Ding Wenjiang's and Zhu Junyi's statistics on the regional distribution of talent in Chinese history. Using 15,089 famous historical figures as a data base, they calculated that the three southern provinces of Jiangsu, Zhejiang, and Hunan had had a phenomenal growth since the late imperial period, and the total output of talent of the seven provinces of the Yangzi Valley was twice as much as that of both northern and southernmost China put together (Zhang 1935, 30). Zhang, however, disagreed with Ding's multi-causal explanation. He upheld the racialist explanation put forth by Huntington that north China had been depleted of people with superior intelligence through migrations out of the region. Zhang also refuted Zhu Junyi's environmentalist view by stressing heredity, which betrays his Weismann-Galtonian bias.

It is unclear whether Zhang attempted to correlate the Yangzi Valley's superiority in intelligence with the "purity" of the Han stock in that region. He resorted to the technique of using the frequencies of blood groups—O, A, B, or AB—in populations as criteria to classify races, a popular practice in the physical anthropology of his time (Boyd 1953, chapters 8 and 9). According to him, the dominant blood group in Jiangsu and Zhejiang is one that "does not contain agglutinin in the serum," a sign of its "relative purity" (Zhang 1935, 24); but nothing more than a mere allusion is implied in this ambiguous statement. It is also not clear whether Zhang regarded the putative northern inferiority in intelligence as resulting from mongrelism, but there is no mistake about his attribution of their robust physique to the north temperate zone.

The Regional Other

Zhang set up northern and southern temperaments as a binarism. For him, a strong physique contributes to strong moral fiber. Therefore, northerners are straightforward and forthright, "pretty much like the Western peoples" (Zhang 1935, 125). The southerners, especially Jiangsu and Zhejiang provincials, are sly. Northerners value etiquette, are observant of rules and closer to the teachings of ancient sages, in contrast to the flagrant rule-breaking of southerners. Northerners, obedient to the established system and to old custom, keep their promises and have a strong sense of justice. They are also cool-headed and steady. Zhang argues that only people who have a strong physique are capable of facing their surroundings in a forthright manner, hence northerners act while southerners only talk. The latter never fight it out when animosity arises between two parties but instead resort to violent words and posturing—in this respect the most typical are the Hubei provincials. In short, northerners are honest; southerners, hypocritical and phony. However, the former are conservative, unlike the latter, who are eager to make progress, as evident in their activities in Southeast Asia. Northerners are also slow, dull, and cautious, while southerners are nimble and alert. Unfortunately, in Zhang's view, in China the strains pertaining to steadiness and the eagerness to make progress are separated geographically.

Faithful to the north temperate zone theory, Zhang stated that the enervating subtropical zone was uncongenial to the development of higher civilization. If Huntington used the migration of the better northern stock to the south to account for that region's development, Zhang's theoretical innovation was that the excellent northern stock, having resettled in the southern region, was physically undermined by its climate. "China's weakness is due to the Yellow River," Zhang averred, anticipating the 1980s' television-series, *Heshang* (River elegy). Yet the good stock fleeing the wrath of the Yellow River had fallen into the trap of the subtropical zone and become emaciated. They became a "feminized race" (Zhang 1935, 214, 215). Zhang held the view that moral fiber is physically determined and wondered "if a physically weak people can have high morality?" (Zhang 1935, 3)

Zhang's idea of northerners excelling in physique was also inspired by Huntington, who writes, "[T]he people of Shantung [Shandong] and the other famine districts are physically much superior to the quicker and more alert people of the south, where famines are rare or unknown" (Huntington 1924, 185). Huntington, however, did not link physique and moral fiber in Zhang's manner. Huntington, in fact, referred to the traits of selfishness and callousness prevalent in the famine-afflicted north China, while he held a relatively positive view of the south. The southerners' moral degeneration, resulting from their physical degeneration was therefore a theory entirely of Zhang's own invention.

Pseudoscientific Explanations

Zhang in fact presented an impressionistic list of racial qualities under the guise of scientific study. The grounding of those qualities in the "natural selection of genes" was accomplished through flimsy reasoning and loose definitions. For example, he argued that those who had migrated to the south were cleverer, therefore their modern descendants tended to adopt the roundabout approach to cope with the environment, hence their slyness. Zhang went on to assert that forthrightness was the foundation of practical morality, while slyness vitiated it (Zhang 1935, 126). This argument contradicts Huntington in whose opinion natural selection has singled out those who could live up to the challenge of the migratory processes to reach their destinations in the south. It also contradicts Zhang's own allegation that southerners are more eager to seek progress. One wonders how southerners, weak in physique and preferring empty talk to action, managed to have the vitality and venturesomeness to explore Southeast Asia.

Zhang's works, nonetheless, are valuable for the compilation of statistics pertaining to his time. They reveal that on average central Chinese males were shorter and weighed less than their north Chinese counterparts in all age groups, while those in the southern Chinese samples were shorter and less heavy than those of central China. Meanwhile, English males were on average taller and heavier than the northern Chinese (Zhang 1935, 56, 59, 60). The staple of the northerners is wheat, which is richer in protein than the southern staple, rice, and so forth.

Northern physical superiority is also shown in the measurement of "vitality." The 1930 infant mortality rate in the Beiping area was 221 per 1,000, and the deaths of babies in the first month of life amounted to 54.4% of all deaths. However, the southern death rate surpassed the northern by three times. As for the adult mortality rate, the statistics of a Shanghai life insurance company revealed the death rate of southerners to be higher than that of northerners in all age groups, so the former incurred higher premiums (Zhang 1935, 77–78, 80, 81–83).

Zonal Determinism

Zhang correlated vitality with the climate zones of the earth. The "high vitality" countries are all located within 33 to 60 degrees north latitude. Unfortunately for China, the area that is located in the same zone that is almost the size as the United States, with a population of 160,000,000, is most backward, due to the migration of the better stock out of the region. Zhang relied on Huntington's authority: The optimal climate is 38 to 64 degrees, with an average of 51 degrees. Beiping's average is 53 degrees.

Taking all conditions into account, the best place to live and work is Zhifu, Shandong. South China is located within the 33 to 20 degrees north belt, putting it in the same category as Burma, Vietnam, Siam, India, Arabia, Egypt, North Africa, Mexico, and Central America. Although the temperature of Shanghai could match that of London, Paris, New York, or Beiping in winter, for half the year the temperature averages up to a humid 88 degrees. Guangzhou is virtually inside the tropical zone, with an average high of over 71 degrees for ten months out of a year. The southern climate is so enervating that its inhabitants, having used most of their bodily energy to survive in the natural environment, have very little energy left to cope with demanding physical and intellectual tasks, hence the lack of perseverance (Zhang 1935, 85, 88–89, 98, 102, 112–113, 115).

The heat and humidity in the south are conducive to the proliferation of germs and parasites. While malaria is absent in the northwest, it infests the lower Yangzi Valley and part of Sichuan. Hookworms are found in the southern provinces of Jiangsu, Zhejiang, Anhui, Hubei, and Guangdong. *Filariasis* afflicts the Yangzi Valley, especially the lower part. *Schistosomiasis japonica* is commonly known as Yangzi fever, Hankou fever, or Jiujiang fever. *Faciolopsis buski* and *Chlonorchis sinensis* afflict the Yangzi Valley and the southernmost provinces (Zhang 1935, 135–148). An intriguing fact is that although the north is backward and conditions there are less hygienic than in the south, it is less affected by diseases. In the Yangzi Valley the hospitalization rate is twice as high as that of the Yellow River Valley. The lower Yangzi is more afflicted than the upper, and Jiangsu and Zhejiang are the worst in the entire valley. The hospitalization rate in the Pearl River Valley is one and a half times higher than that of the Yellow River Valley (Zhang 1935, 160–161, 164).

Although Zhang was a Hunanese, he had few positive things to say about southern regions in general. He identified the common "zonal" problems as the lack of political acumen, the inability to resist conquerors from the north, and the lack of contribution to science. Even in the United States, the south "has made no contribution whatsoever to American culture" (Zhang 1935, 174). The Mexicans are tumultuous, the Moroccans like to fight (a trait shared by all north Africans), the Arabs are robbers, the Jews are thieves, the Persians are prone to suspicion, the Indians are deluded, the Burmese are treacherous. The Guangdong provincials, in their turn, like to loiter and tend to be pompous and pretentious (Zhang 1935, 175–176).

Desperate Measures

Zhang's solutions to problems ranged from increasing the amount of calcium and vitamin B in baby food to urging the government to induce the migration of talented southerners to north China. A more fundamental measure than social engineering was planned heredity. He advocated intermarriage with the Japanese and Anglo-American races (Zhang 1936, 168). Planned heredity also included legislating marriage prohibitions or castration of the genetically inferior, segregation of those with inherited diseases, and late marriage for the general population (Zhang 1936, 171–175). If the draconian measures go against humanitarianism, Zhang argued, it is because the very idea of humanitarianism is faulty—it allows bad heredity to perpetuate itself in the name of "the right to live." "Honestly speaking," Zhang said, "within our race, perhaps only 40 percent are entitled to 'the right to live,' while the other 60 percent have only 'the right to perish' " (Zhang 1936, 194). In the area of eugenic legislation, Zhang in the interwar years looked upon Nazi Germany as a model.

Zhang's pessimism deepened during wartime. The Japanese invasion had precipitated the third major historical migration of superior stock out of north China (the previous ones took place under the Jin and Song Dynasties). This time, they had moved into the southwest, a region "harmful to racial hygiene" and thus implying racial suicide (Zhang 1944, 7–8). In Chongqing, the wartime capital, the climate was so enervating that only four months out of a year were suitable for intellectual labor. Zhang alleged that Chongqing's "geographical environment" could never produce a Thomas Edison (Zhang 1944, 23). This allegation was made on the eve of the introduction of the air-conditioner for mass consumption in America, which eventually contributed to the development of the U.S. Sun Belt. It seems that Zhang resorted to a zonal determinism that Huntington himself had refrained from. The latter, for example, offered a more complicated explanation to the "anomaly" of pre-Columbian America to account for the fact that Indian civilization did not emerge in the north temperate zone but in Mexico and Peru, further to the south (Huntington 1924, chapter 7).

Zhang's program gives a nation under construction the right to set the standards for, and thus lay claim to, the body of each citizen. In this process, the problematic sectors are culpable of the malformation of the nation as whole—they are to be estranged but also incorporated by taking blame for the failed nationhood project. We find a comparable agenda in Cesare Lombroso's criminology in the newly unified Italy. Its "concepts of atavism and degeneration" articulated "the horror of a largely northern Italian medical and scientific intelligentsia" in the face of a backward south and the rising delinquency of the urban population in the north (Pick 1993, 4). As blame is consigned to both the north and the south and malaise is discerned in the backward as well as the modern, one wonders where is the nation after all?

Lin Yutang's Pseudo-Regionality

Lin Yutang's *My Country and My People* (1935) enjoyed a tremendous success in the United States, thanks to his superb English and witty style. In fact, it is a weaving of popular intellectual themes from his time, and the book is less original than it appears. It served the purpose of acquainting the English-reading world with some of the topics that had engaged Chinese intellectuals for sometime.

The book actually begins its discussion on the Chinese race with the section, "North and South," attesting to Lin's indebtedness to a discourse fashionable since the time of Liang Qichao. The section's opening rhetoric harks back to another source: The discourse on *shidai* with a special reference to relationships between "epochalness" (*shidaxing*) and "timelessness" (*yongjiuxing*), geniuses and the masses—is a rhetoric traceable to Taine and Baudelaire and turned by the Chinese men of letters into a shibboleth.[6] Echoing Liang Qichao's and Bertrand Russell's earlier views on "great men," Lin asserts that "in the study of any period of literature or of any epoch of history," the best approach is to name it after "the individual [genius]" who epitomizes the epoch. Yet, "in dealing with a country the common man cannot be ignored." The answer to his own question as to "who is the common man" in China is: There is no ethnic unity in China, for southerners differ from northerners in the same manner as the Mediterraneans differ from the Nordics (Lin 1935, 16–17). It was a leaf from Mao Dun's 1929 study of Chinese mythology.

Degeneration and Regeneration

The themes woven together by Lin give us a glimpse into the intellectual cliché of his time. Unlike other versions, Lin's north-south scheme is more optimistic on the issue of racial degeneration. In his book "degeneration," another favorite term of the time, becomes the title of the section following the one on "North and South." Lin is ambiguous about the degeneration of the Chinese race. He avers that "it is not dirt but the fear of dirt," such as the Western obsession with cleanliness, "which is the sign of man's degeneration" (Lin 1935, 23).[7] Chinese people are also less sensitive than the white man to cold, heat, pain, and general noise. Lin cites Arthur Smith to prove that "perhaps the one thing that compels admiration from Westerners is our nerves" (Lin 1935, 27). Having expressed his relativism, Lin confirms the view of the Chinese as a degenerate race: "Man in China has adapted himself to a social and cultural environment that demands stamina, resistance power and negative strength, and he has lost a great part of mental and physical powers of conquest and adventure which characterized his forebears in the primeval forests" (Lin 1935, 24).

In Lin's opinion, racial degeneration has largely affected the inhabitants of the southeast coast who are "mentally developed but physically retrograde, loving their poetry and their comforts, sleek undergrown men and slim neurasthenic women, fed on birds'-nest soup and lotus seeds, shrewd in business, gifted in *belles-lettres*, and cowardly in war, ready to roll on the ground and cry for mamma before the lifted fist descends, offsprings [sic] of the cultured Chinese families who crossed the Yangtze [Yangzi] with their books and paintings during the end of the Chin [Jin] Dynasty, when China was overrun by barbaric invaders." This racial degeneration has been offset by the northern Chinese. The latter, "acclimatized to simple thinking and hard living, tall and stalwart, hale, hearty and humorous, onion-eating and fun-loving, children of nature," are "in every way more Mongolic and more conservative" than the southerners. They "suggest nothing of their loss of racial vigor." Small wonder that none of the conquerors of China have come from south of the Yangzi (Lin 1935, 18–19).

Civilization and Barbarism

Lin discerns two major infusions of "Mongolic" blood into the senile Chinese race, each of which concluded a historical cycle that lasted about eight hundred years. The first lasted from the Qin dynasty, to the end of the Six dynasties including major barbarian invasions (221 B.C.E–588 C.E.); the second from the Sui dynasty to the Mongol conquest (589–1367 C.E.). The modern cycle, beginning from the Ming dynasty (1368–1644 C.E), is yet incomplete, but the downward swing has already set in, manifest in the Taiping Rebellion and the removal of the capital from northern to southern China, as had also occurred in the two previous cycles (Lin 1935, 29–30). A conclusion Lin refrained from drawing is that the third reinvigoration of the Chinese race might coincide with the pending Japanese conquest.

According to Lin, "it was this amalgamation of foreign blood that accounted for, to a large extent, the race's long survival" (Lin 1935, 34). In other words, while most historical races had only one life cycle, the Chinese race is unique in having three. This interpretation of Chinese history was actually taken from Gu Jiegang (Schneider 1971, 263–266; Duara 1995, 42–44), whom Lin failed to acknowledge. Later on, during wartime, a similar view was presented by a group of Chinese Spenglerians, the *Zhanguoce* school. The difference is that, for the wartime Spenglerians, China's historical cycles were determined by the inner logic of cultural morphology, whereas the Gu–Lin thesis was based on racial thinking akin to Zhang

Junjun's. Yet, for Zhang, the north-south cleavage meant the divorce of northern physique and southern intelligence, with dire consequences for the racial quality of the nation as a whole. For Gu and Lin, the north-south difference worked favorably for the regeneration of the Chinese race.

The "coming of barbarians" to deliver the civilized world from its decadence was a standard trope in European literature of the *fin de siècle*. The motif was adapted by the Greek poet Constantine Cavafis (aka: C.P. Cavafy, 1863–1933) in his "Waiting for the Barbarians" (1898). The barbarians have not arrived in the Roman capital, as eagerly anticipated by its rulers and populace, "because there are no barbarians any more." The civilized world is bewildered: "And now, what's to become of us without barbarians? These people were some sort of a solution" (Friar 1973, 137).[8] Seen in this light, the boundary between historical and poetic narratives seem to become blurred.

Nature and Artifice

If we probe deeper into the text of *My Country and My People*, we shall see that Lin did not have a geographical theory, his north-south binarism is a mere rhetorical facade for his more fundamental opposition between nature and civilization. For Lin, northerners' racial vigor is intact not because they reside in the north temperate zone, but because they are "children of nature." Contrary to the north-temperate-zone theory, he says: "South in Kwangtung [Guangdong], one meets again a different people, where racial vigor is again in evidence, where people eat like men and work like men, enterprising, carefree, spendthrift, pugnacious, adventurous, progressive and quick-tempered, where beneath the Chinese culture a snake-eating aborigines tradition persists, revealing a strong admixture of the blood of the ancient *Yüeh* [*Yue*] inhabitants of southern China" (Lin 1935, 18–19). It shows Lin's indebtedness to Chinese folk studies' discovery of "local cultures." The "cult of the snake" in Guangdong's Yue culture is referred to by Wolfram Eberhard, a longtime participant in the Chinese folk studies movement (Eberhard 1968, 380).

In the final analysis, what inspired Lin was not anthropogeography but a popular European discourse, which Michel Foucault traces to the late eighteenth century, that civilization, an unhealthy artifice divorced from nature, is conducive to madness (Foucault 1965, 217–220). The nature-artifice binarism that was at the heart of literary Decadence seemed to be more congenial to Lin's thinking—there are hints to that effect in Lin's text. In giving examples of great men who are eponyms of an epoch, Lin "thinks of a Marcus Aurelius or a Lucian in the times of decadent Rome" (Lin

1935, 16), in other words, the Silver Age in classical literature of which the Latin decadence in nineteenth-century France was intended to be a renaissance. In the 1920s, Lin was a writer for *Yusi* (Word threads), and a close associate of the brothers Zhou Shuren and Zuoren (see chapter 3). He also showed the influence of eugenics: At the time when Lin wrote, the American eugenics movement, inspired by Galton's apprehension of cities as harmful to the nation's germ plasm, was also promoting the back-to-the-farm movement (Pickens 1968, 59, 96). Similar trends at the time included the Nazi *Blut und Boden* (blood and soil) movement, the *nohonshugi* (agrarianism) in Japan, and the Rural Reconstruction in China. Lin's eclectic mind made him equate these ultramodern trends with Daoism, to which he was personally inclined. Lin drew the equation mark—despite the intrinsic difference—between Daoism's vegetative naturalism and Western animalism, a virtue he extolled in the "barbarians."

Lin seemed to display Daoist affinity when he applauded the traditional Chinese ruling class for their "natural distrust of civilization" and their preservation of a degree of primitivism. They "not only came from the country but also returned to the country, as the rural mode of life was always regarded as the ideal," an ideal "deeply imbedded in the Chinese general consciousness," which "must account in a large measure for the racial health today." Lin was enthralled with the romantic myth of nature: "For to be close to nature is to have physical and moral health. Man in the country does not degenerate; only man in the cities does" (Lin 1935, 36). Here, we discern the uncredited influence of Pan Guangdan, who claimed that rural life had maintained the Chinese race's vitality, in contrast to the "decadent individualism" of the urban lifestyle (Dikötter 1989, 6)

But, the Chinese with their long history are, after all, an overly "civilized" nation. Their hair, skin, and voice betray the "results of millenniums of civilized indoor living." Chinese men tend not to grow a beard, "a fact which makes it possible for most Chinese men not to know the use of a personal razor." In China, hair on men's chests is unknown. Chinese women have finer skin than European women, but their muscles are considerably flabbier, "an ideal consciously cultivated through the institution of footbinding, which has other sex appeals." Lin compares these examples to that of the famous Xinfeng chicken farms in Guangdong where chickens are shut up for life in a dark coop, without room for movement, in order to produce chicken meat "noted for its extreme tenderness." The Chinese voice has also lost "the full, rich resonant quality" of the Europeans (Lin 1935, 26–27). All these certainly evoke the picture of Orientalist decadence.

Evolution and Eugenics

It seems that Lin sets up a binarism under the name of "north-and-south" to accommodate a series of contradictions. It enabled him to say that the Chinese race, though degenerate, had managed to reinvigorate. It allowed him to combine the sentiment that the Chinese race was senile, characterized by "old roguery" in its attitude toward life (Lin 1935, 52–57), with the belief that China's long history was in fact "a prolonged childhood" (Lin 1935, 40). In pursuing this thesis, Lin cited the "migration zone" theory of the Australian geographer Griffith Taylor, who put the Chinese among the latest strata in the evolution of the human race. Taylor's theory is quite irrelevant to Lin's purpose, because it is about a totally different process with a much larger time scale. It is of some interest to note that Taylor's "migration zone" theory was convincing to both Huntington and Toynbee and was another academic fad of the time.

Lin's north-south scheme is marginal in sustaining the dialectic between nature and civilization. The "coming of barbarians as rejuvenators" played a mere supplementary role as Lin was able to explain China's racial health by the primitivist strain of her native elite. He also attributed China's cultural stability to two indigenous factors: "While the family system accounted for their survival through fecundity, the imperial examination system effected a qualitative selection, and enabled talent to reproduce and propagate itself" (Lin 1935, 35). Lin again failed to acknowledge the source of his eugenic reasoning: Pan Guangdan. The *bêtes-noires* of the May Fourth iconoclasts, China's family system and the imperial examination system were reinstated in the late 1920s by Pan, the eugenicist, who saw in them the causes of China's remarkable continuity as a cultural entity (Pan 1929a, 1–20).

The meaning ascribed by Lin to the north-south scheme is highly arbitrary. The same scheme could, and did, inspire opposite views. For example, Richard Wilhelm saw the "return to nature" as the characteristic of the Daoist south, which did not oppose, but tended to complement, the Confucian north (Wilhelm 1928, 357–358). The same thesis of "Confucian north, Daoist south" had been stipulated by the Japanese art critic Okakura Tenshin much earlier (Okakura 1903, 23–38).

The Persistence of Regional Typologies

In addition to being a rhetorical facade for the tension between nature and artifice, Lin's north-south scheme was also an umbrella for all regional differences. While dwelling on the three major regions at length, he took special note of the Hubei people who "never say die" and are called "nine-headed birds" (cantakerous and argumentative) by other provincials. Lin also highly regarded the Hunan people, "noted for their soldiery and their dogged persistence" (Lin 1935, 19). The practice of using the north-south scheme as an umbrella for region variations was inherited by the Columbia University–trained anthropologist Hu Xianjin (Hu Hsien-chin).

Hu Xianjian's Regional Stereotypes

In the late 1940s, Hu prepared a document on north-south differences for the Research in Contemporary Cultures Projects, conducted at Columbia University (see chapter 6). She used the term "South China" to include the entire rice-growing area from the Yangzi Valley down, and pointed out that geographically and ecologically one may also speak of a "Central China," but "to a Chinese the nation is composed of North Chinese and South Chinese" in terms of social custom (Hu n.d.(a), 1).

Hu reiterated the scholarly consensus of the time: From the time of the Song dynasty (960–1279) the Yangzi Valley has come to dominate China, and the south has since then contributed the largest number of candidates for civil service examinations and controls the largest number of government positions. The south has also taken the lead in literature, scholarship, art, trade, handicrafts, and science. In modern times, in institutions of higher education southerners predominate in both faculty and student bodies (Hu n.d.(a), 7–8).

Hu took note of the remarkable difference between northern and southern temperaments. "Northerners are quiet in movement and slow in mind," while their southern compatriots "are sharp-witted and quick in speech and action." The latter are more volatile and welcome change and progress. Although the southerners tend to quarrel a great deal, their hot temper is easily dissipated. In contrast, in the north, mediation is the norm in such situations, so there is little excitement on the street or in the home. But when a person becomes really angry, he tends to be physically violent. Beiping people are particularly dexterous in mediating between two quarrelling parties, to the effect that Beiping policemen are often assigned to Shanghai, because they can arbitrate between rickshaw pullers and customers most effectively in spite of their unfamiliarity with the dialect and their slower reasoning ability (Hu n.d.(a), 1–4).

Northerners on the whole make more obedient subordinates, while southerners are more insistent on their "rights." North China has contributed the most soldiers to the military, more because of their acceptance of discipline than their stronger physique. Due to the southerners' higher awareness of self-interest, envy and jealousy are much more manifest in south China, and conflicts within the family also tend to be sharper here than in the north. Bargaining in the marketplace is louder and conducted in less good humor in south China. In the north, the well-trained clerk is as a rule more polite to customers (Hu n.d.(a), 4–5).

Hu, an authority on the Chinese concept of "face" (Hu Hsien-chin 1944), also delved into the northern and southern attitudes towards "face." Within the Chinese concept of "face," she distinguished between *mianzi* and *lian*. The south China patterns favor competition and the enhancing of one's prestige in interpersonal relations, thus consideration for *mianzi* becomes all-important. To further those aims, they might disregard *lian* (i.e., becoming shameless) more often than the northerners. In sharp contrast, to the northerners *lian* appears to be a greater concern. In order to build up "face," the southerner tends to treat friends with lavish hospitality in order to impress, even though privately he may be quite frugal. The north Chinese reserves hospitality for close friends, and he tends to hide his wealth behind a show of frugality (Hu n.d.(a), 5–6).

Hu tended to polarize the differences between the women in north and south China. In the south, the woman is "quick-tempered, excitable, voluble, fast in speech and gesture, perhaps more so than men." She is more colorful in her costumes and make-up and also less tolerant of the old family patterns than her northern sister. She is often acerbic in her words and more likely to resort to suicide as a form of protest. In contrast, the north Chinese woman is "comparatively quiet and even-tempered." Even "her gestures are quiet, and she dresses usually in the most inostentatious [unostentatious] manner." She tends to be plain and simple and is more compliant with her husband's family than is the case with her southern counterpart (Hu n.d.(a), 6–7).

Inheriting a discourse popular since the late Qing, Hu also referred to northern and southern art styles. "The art of the North is heavy, static, emphasizing symmetry; that of South China graceful, lively, gay" (Hu n.d.(a), 8). In Hu's opinion, southerners are more artistic on the whole. With regard to the culinary habits of the two regions, the southern cuisine is more refined, and the southerner has a keener sense of taste and smell. Hu also provided details of northern and southern "cleanliness habits." Some of the observations are quite interesting and might elude the non-native ethnologist. For example: "The Southerner thinks the Northerner dirty, because he does not take a bath frequently, while the Northerner thinks the Southerner uncivilized, because he uses the same water for all parts of the body, and even will place his shoes on the table" (Hu n.d.(a), 11). Attitudes concerning the exposure of the body are different as well. The northern Chinese do not mind stripping to the waist in public, but keep their legs and feet covered. Many countrywomen past middle-age even expose their breasts in summer time, and children often go around naked. The southerners, even children, are always dressed but they are not so particular about showing their feet (Hu n.d.(a), 11–12).

Hu also described the two regions' stereotyping of each other with respect to character. The southerners are contemptuous of their northern countrymen, because the latter are considered "slow, stupid, coarse in manners, unimaginative and unresourceful," even though they might acknowledge the northerners' steady and honest character. The northerners, on their turn, consider the southerners crafty and deceptive (Hu n.d.(a), 16).

Hu then delved into the different characteristics of the provinces. Like Zhang Junjun and Lin Yutang, Hu singled out the Hubei provincials for their love of arguments, which earned them the nickname, the "nine-headed birds." She also seems to concur with Zhang that inhabitants of the Yangzi Valley are not as persevering as, and are certainly less reliable than, northerners (Hu n.d.(a), 17). Among the latter, the Shandong people are the most thoroughgoing, persevering, and stubborn; their reputation for reliability also surpasses that of the neighboring Hebei provincials. Yet, the Shandong immigrants in Manchuria, who form the bulk of the Chinese in that region, are different in character. Here she resorted to a Huntington-style argument: "[T]he immigrants are usually those who do not fit into the pattern of their home or village," for they are those who "resent authority and have an adventurous spirit." Thus, "they are considered less reliable and more opportunistic than North Chinese on the whole." To achieve their end, the Manchurians with Shandong origins do not refrain from using violence and trickery if necessary (Hu n.d.(a), 21–22). The natives of Hunan, on the other hand, fight for principle. They are known for taking a strong stand on issues they believe in. The province has produced many of modern China's revolutionary leaders as well as archconservatives (Hu n.d.(a), 18). The natives of another province, Henan, are also feared by their neighbors for their occasional violence. In addition, they are considered to have rather dull minds (Hu n.d.(a), 21).

Stereotypes Die Hard

Traces of north-south typology are found in *Americans and Chinese* (1953) by Francis L.K. Hsu. While treating America and China as two contrasting cultural configurations, Hsu also refers to regional differences within China herself. There, the contrast, understandably, is between the conservative north and the progressive south: " 'Good family' women in households of modest means did appear in public in south and southwest China more often than in north China. In the latter region women went to the fields to bring the midday meal to their fathers, husbands, brothers, but they usually did not work there. In the south, farmers' wives and daughters worked side by side with their men" (Hsu 1981, 65).

The results of a survey published by Wolfram Eberhard in 1965 show that some of the regional stereotypes recorded by Hu Xianjin have persisted. The survey ascertains that in the Chinese perception, there is a "northern type" with its typical traits best represented by the Shandong-Hebei area. These people are considered "straight and honest, simple and enduring." Then there is a "Yangtze [Yangzi] Valley type," most pronounced in Jiangsu-Zhejiang, whose provincials "are clever and sharp, cunning businessmen." There is also the "Southwestern type," centered in Hunan, but also including the southern part of Henan. "These are the emotional Chinese with violent temper" (Eberhard 1965, 598). Provincial stereotypes within China are still very much alive today.

Multiple Chinas

Continental China versus Maritime China

The historian John K. Fairbank has carried the earlier perceptions of north-south differences into postwar American scholarship. His *The United States and China* (1948, revised in 1958, 1971, and 1983), which is in fact a concise history of China, begins with a section on "The Contrast of North and South."[9] It reiterates the observations of Richthofen, Liu Guanghan, and Huntington that north China tends to be dryer and has a more uncertain water supply than the south (Fairbank 1983, 4–5).

We also find a variation of the "conservative north, progressive south" theme in Fairbank's view of the two Chinas: the continental and the maritime. Throughout Chinese history this binarism sees peripheral cultures coexisting alongside the great tradition of the north China core area. Before the encounter with the West, the pastoral region of the northwest periphery had greater impact on Chinese history because it posed a nomadic threat. As a result, it tended to reinforce the dominant "agrarian-bureaucratic" power of the core area. A maritime China, however, had developed since neolithic times but had remained "a subordinate and even marginal appendage of Continental China" until modern times. Fairbank's maritime China refers to the southeastern coastal regions and the Chinese settlers in southeast Asia. In spite of its coastal lines, north China is largely land-locked, because the swampy estuaries of the Yellow and Huai rivers inhibit coastal settlement and seafaring. Fairbank sees the Manchu conquest as "the peripheral culture of Inner Asian tribal nomadism and semi-nomadism reinforcing the anti-seafaring tradition of the Chinese heartland." The situation began to change with the Western intrusion (Fairbank 1983, 9–20).

The Post-Mao Quest for Diversity

In post–Mao China, the crisis of Marxism occasioned a revived interest in national character under the guise of "culture fever" (*wenhua re*). It also witnessed the resurfacing of many a familiar old theme from the past, such as folk studies, evident in the "searching for roots" school of literature and the attention paid to the "great northwest" frontier. The literary fad had its echoes among scholarly circles as well.

In 1986, Tan Qixiang of Shanghai's Fudan University charged that the Chinese had for the past six decades focused on the difference between feudalism and capitalism, and squandered their efforts by confusing this antagonism with the "cultural" difference between the East and the West (Tan 1987, 27–28). Even within Chinese culture, he averred, there have been "epochal" as well as "regional" variations. He cautioned against equating Chinese culture with Han culture, for Confucianism did not dominate in all regions and at all times. In dwelling on regional differences, Tan harked back to Ding Wenjiang, Pan Guangdan, and the like. For example, his statistics show that beginning in the Ming dynasty, a high percentage of imperial grand secretaries and renowned Confucian scholars came steadily from the southeast provinces (Tan 1987, 46–48).

Yellow and Blue

Meanwhile, Fairbank's continental-maritime binarism found an echo in the television series, *River Elegy* or *Heshang* (1988), in which the two Chinas are color-coded in yellow and blue. *Heshang* lays the blame for China's perennial stagnancy on the Yellow River, representing the continental, land-locked, backward north China. The Blue China symbolizes the southeast coastal region, as embodied in the special economic zones, with its urge to march toward the ocean to link up with the rest of the world—it is where the hope of China lies.

Meant for public consumption, *Heshang*'s script makes no pretension to theoretical consistency. It still lingers in Marxism, although it draws ideas from the heterodox Georgy Plekhanov, N.I. Bukharin, and Karl Wittfogel. Notably, the diagnosis of China's stagnancy in terms of the "Asiatic mode of production" and hydraulic despotism is a leaf taken from Wittfogel. *Heshang*, however, bears no resemblance to the Wittfogelian Ji Chaoding's "key economic areas" theory of the 1930s (Chi 1936). More concerned with the critique of a monolithic despotism that has blighted the life of the whole nation, the scriptwriters find no use for Ji's thesis that the key economic area shifted from north China to the Yangzi region through the spread of water control in the post-Han period (after A.D. 220).

Though heavily tinted with geographical thinking, the scriptwriters are not aware of Huntington. Instead, they show a smattering of Toynbeean cliché, imbued with a dose of Bergsonian vitalism. The reason that the Yellow River basin became the cradle of ancient China, according to the authors, was that "its human inhabitants had to face a challenge posed by a natural environment more adverse than that of the Yangzi," a challenge that "aroused the latent creative potential of men" (Su and Wang 1988, 14–15). It is a rehashing of Toynbee's application of the concept of *élan vital* to account for the genesis of civilization. It is a sign of the authors' loss of self-confidence that they took the word of Toynbee, hardly an authority on China, on a matter concerning their own historical geography. Raymond Dawson points out that Toynbee's view "does not fit the geographical facts. The Yangzi valley was swampy and covered with jungle, but the Yellow River basin provided a rich loessal soil, was well watered and not too thickly forested, and enjoyed a climate which was milder in winter than it is nowadays" (Dawson 1967, 86–87).

In *Heshang*, the inevitability of the decline of the Yellow River region is also explained by the Toynbeean thesis that all river-valley civilizations, without exception, have declined (Su and Wang 1988, 21). The Yellow River, however, differs from all the rivers in the world in having become the most disastrous ecosystem in human history. Having served as the "cradle" of Chinese civilization, its periodic floods and ever-changing courses have retarded the growth, and even caused the retrogression, of north China. Thus, "[mother's] nurturing has turned into a licentiousness in wanton destruction, and mother has turned into a tyrant." Worst still, the ancient despotism of the north China core area has persisted and become an incubus on the nation as a whole. The script laments: "Why do we have such a chronic feudal era [i.e. despotism], which is as perennial as the endless floods of the Yellow River?" (Su and Wang 1988, 80, 79). The authors look toward the other peripheral cultures outside of the "cradle," mainly to the south, for China's salvation. The logical choice is the coastal regions, which have the potential—especially in the guise of today's special economic zones—to merge with the world market.

Differing from the racialism of earlier geographical determinists, the

Heshang writers, like Fairbank, impute a socio-cultural connotation to geography. They see a more modern, maritime, and progressive China—one that has taken shape in the last millennium—shackled by an anachronistic despotic incubus, a relic from the aeon of Babylon and Pharaonic Egypt. In Fairbank's words, the dominant "agrarian-bureaucratic" power of the core area has stifled maritime China. In *Heshang*'s images, "land [as opposed to ocean] and despotism" have "suffocated movement, migration, and commerce" (Su and Wang 1988, 37).

Nostalgia or Anti-Nostalgia?

Racial and sociocultural interpretations seem to arrive at the same conclusion. Under their combined influence, one is even tempted to see in the present Communist polity an unprecedented and deadly alliance of China's anachronistic despotism with a peasant mentality that is equally North China–based, an ethos glorifying backwardness. This ethos was exalted by Maoist China in models such as Dazhai and the Red Flag Canal, but has been cast in a totally negative light in post-Mao movies such as *Yellow Earth, Old Well*, and *Judou*.[10] Recently, an American scholar has discerned the emergence of a "southern alternative" to this northern "national identity" of the Mao era (Friedman 1994, 79). Indeed, in 1992, Deng Xiaoping found it necessary to go on a "southern tour" (*nanxun*) to jump-start his policies of "reform and openness" after the backlash of 1989.

A historical corollary of the north-south geographical binarism is the theory of a "second China" succeeding a "first China." It was propounded in 1918 by Fu Sinian (Fu 1918) and adopted by Toynbee, who split Chinese history into the separate lives of two civilizations, the Sinic and the Far Eastern. The former originated in the Yellow River basin, while the "affiliated" Far Eastern civilization encompassed both the Yellow and Yangzi basins. Unlike the "apparentation-affiliation" between the Hellenic and Western Civilizations, the Far Eastern world, from its very inception under the Sui-Tang empire, was possessed by the "ghost" of the "Sinic universal state" (Toynbee 1934, vol. 2, 120).

Heshang presents a similar lamentation, but its sentiments are quite different from Toynbee's and, for that matter, Huntington's. Though differing in theoretical framework, both suggest that those who leave home might gain a new life while those who stay behind are condemned to retardation. *Heshang*'s tone, in contrast, is lugubrious under the guise of anti-nostalgia. In viewing *Heshang*, one cannot help wondering whether the producers are capable of cutting off "mother" even when she has become dead wood, hindering one's further growth.

A Versatile Schematic

With the development of the coastal areas even in north China, the usefulness of the north-south binarism has become increasingly doubtful. In fact, from the start the Communist regime has premised its regional development strategy on an east-west or coastal-inland axis (He 1990, 136–143). Nonetheless, the north-south leitmotif dies hard, as it continues to serve as a versatile schematic to sort out modern history, cultural styles, and even gender patterns.

The schematic found its latest expression in 1994 in the environmentalist Yang Dongping's *Chengshi jifeng* (Urban monsoon). This thick volume delves into the different tempers, lifestyles, fashions, architecture, art, and literature of Beijing and Shanghai in our century. The two cities also serve as the warp and woof of the epic of China's modern transformation, as they have taken turns to become its agent. If modern China's revolutionary changes initially came from the south by the founding of the People's Republic, leadership had unarguably shifted to Beijing, only to be wrested from her again by Shanghai during the Cultural Revolution. Yang's tale of two cities is narrated with pathos but fraught with ambivalence. He sees Shanghai as a "deformity" created by China's modern history—"an amalgam of pride and humiliation, prosperity and sin" (Yang 1994, 121). Shanghai has spawned China's best entrepreneurs and her slickest opportunists. Yang sees the closing chapter on the cultural spirit of old China in the decimation of the pre-liberation corps of Beijing intellectuals by the Cultural Revolution. It was a liquidation equalled in tragic magnitude to the demolition of old Beijing's architectural marvel, the imperial city walls, immediately after 1949. Both destructive actions were executed in the name of progress. Toward the end of his book Yang ponders the rise of Guangzhou as a new rival center in the 1990s—a dream Liang Qichao harbored almost a century ago has finally been realized by the phenomenal growth of the special economic zones in the last decade.

Urban Monsoon also dwells on the regional gender patterns. Its author laments the decline of masculinity in Shanghai, due to the "domestically-inclined, softening tendencies of the urban personality" (Yang 1994, 497). If the more rustic Beijing males are bold and uninhibited, they are also rude and uncouth and tend to assume the persona of the "riffraff" (*pizi*). The same urban, bourgeois milieu of Shanghai, breeding ground of the Chinese Dagwood, has also produced the Chinese Blondie. In Shanghai, femininity has survived radical indoctrination and political campaigns largely through family traditions. Shanghai women know how to flirt and are sure of their feminine charm, but they are also shrewd and materialistic. Never questioning that their realm is the family, after marriage they often succeed in fully domesticating the male partner. In a reversal of gender roles, the Shanghai wife controls the purse strings and lets the husband do most of the household chores. For the effeminate Shanghai male, captivity in the "bird-cage family" is a trade-off for domestic bliss. In stark contrast to Shanghai women, their more politicized Beijing sisters are disdainful of both the feminized male and crass materialism. If Beijing women have maintained a degree of idealism and naïveté in their love affairs, they also resist the wife's role—a defiance assuming the form of "girlish" feminism. Among Beijing's intellectual and professional women, the smoking and divorce rates are higher than they are among their Shanghai counterparts. For the city as a whole, the divorce rate climbed 10 percent annually in the decade of the 1980s (Yang 1994, 511).

Yang sees China in general as moving toward the "strengthening of the female" at the expense of masculinity. In the last half-century, socialism has raised women's status but has also greatly eroded feminine gracefulness and tenderness. Women's "pseudomasculinity" has thrived on the general denigration of femininity as "petit bourgeois" and on the Red Guard movement in particular. Recently, Chinese women's vulgarization has been compounded by imitation of Western ways. Yang paraphrases an American male observer in Beijing to the effect that he would say goodbye to those Chinese women who, aping a misperceived image of American women, "think that they themselves are so open as to be ready to go to bed with any man at any time" (Yang 1994, 517).

Remotely echoing Kang Youwei's and Zhang Junjun's idea of planned migration between zones, Yang proposes the extensive swapping of geographical locations of secondary schooling for both genders. Yang's other pseudoremedy is to look toward the "liberating" forces of the capitalist market. A new trend conducive to both the "restoration of manhood and the liberation of women," he avers, is to acquire the economic ability to hire a baby-sitter. He also misreads as a reconstruction of the "feminine ideal" the appearance of a new type of working-women in the recently emerging business establishments who combines professionalism and "womanly charm" (Yang 1994, 524). Apparently, sex appeal as a means of surviving and advancing in the corporate world is new and refreshing to the Chinese. In all respects, America is the pioneer and the undisputed model.

Notes

1. For a history of the theory of the four humors in eighteenth-century French medicine, see Foucault (1965, chapter 4).

2. Hellpach was later known for his formulation of the concept *Geopsyche,* and the founding of studies called *Ethnophysiognomik* and *Ethnopsychognomik.*

3. Pan's biographer has simplified the facts. In 1904, the Carnegie Institution of Washington set up the Station for Experimental Evolution at Cold Spring Harbor, NY. The station's head, Charles B. Davenport, founded his own private institute—the Eugenics Record Office—in 1910. In 1921, the station absorbed the office to form the Department of Genetics under the Carnegie Institution of Washington. The office continued as a subsection of the department until 1939 when it changed its title to the Genetics Record Office, due to the growing notoriety of "eugenics" (Pickens 1968, 51–52).

4. Pearson's book was cited by Liang Qichao in 1912 (Liang 1912b).

5. Huntington's travels are recorded in his *West of the Pacific* (1925).

6. Details in my manuscript, *The Apotheosis of* Shidai.

7. The contrast between Chinese and Westerners pertaining to cleanliness is still relevant in post-Mao China, where Western residents who venture out from their cosy quarters often find the visit to a native Chinese toilet a most excruciating experience.

8. The motif of barbarian destroyers as deliverers also inspires modern films such as *Zardoz* (1973) and *Conan the Destroyer* (1984).

9. The first edition (1948) begins with the chapter "Our China Problem," which has been deleted since the third edition. Therefore, "The Contrast of North and South" has become the first section of the first chapter.

10. Dazhai was Mao's favorite "production brigade" in Shanxi. He launched campaigns for all of rural China to learn from this model. The Red Flag Canal is also in Shanxi. According to propaganda, the people of this poor rural area used labor-intensive methods and revolutionary zeal to build this irrigation canal.

— 6 —

"The Rock from a Distant Hill"

Edward Said says: "It is therefore correct that every European, in what he could say about the Orient, was consequently a racist, an imperialist, and almost totally ethnocentric" (Said 1979, 204). This statement is certainly valid if we delve into the primal layer of a person's acculturation. A person might learn to respect a foreign culture out of liberal conviction or cosmopolitan pretensions but still find the alien way preposterous if he or she were to embody it. Such observation fits all cultural encounters and is not limited to those between the West and the Orient. Said's statement carries weight because the West and the Orient are not on a par in terms of power and influence, and the Western way claims to be universal.

Western hegemony is a fact and we do see Orientalism in action in plenty, but let us not treat Said's statement as a conclusion. Multiculturalist politics, even in defiance of a dominant culture with universalist claims, is not a methodology for studying culture, including one's own. In fact, it sets up artificial protective barriers for invented identities, meaning the cordoning off of one another's "turf," not the probing of the roots of cultural partiality—other people's as well as one's own. To expose the Western pretension to universalism is also to preclude all other cultural points of view from becoming the absolute criterion. That leaves us with only a "system of difference" of mutual references that are perspectival in nature.

In this chapter we will be dealing with American perceptions of the Chinese national character. These perceptions cannot be reduced to a single motive. Although they are inevitably ethnocentric, some are motivated, paradoxically, by a critique of the dominant American norm. This critique often enlists the support of imaginary Orientalness in the capacity of a "marginal text." This sort of critique is concerned not so much with cultural differences as with gender issues and alternative sexualities. Because of its inversion of the masculine norm, it finds an ally in Orientalness. Regardless of motives, American perceptions provide a fresh angle that is unfamiliar to the Chinese themselves. An outsider's view can often serve as "the rock from a distant hill," which, as the Chinese proverb indicates, is useful in polishing one's jade; in order to do the job, it is perforce hard but also strange. The same application can also be administered to the American side of the dialogue.

Jacques Lacan believes that "speech always subjectively includes its own reply" (Dor 1998, 211). In this light, American perceptions of Orientalness can be treated as inverted mirror images of themselves. Predictably, the imaginary Chinese personality expresses American anxieties about failed individuation in terms of truncated sexual development and impaired capability for aggression. This Orientalist discourse confers power status on China experts and Oriental studies institutions, in particular, Columbia University's Research in Contemporary Cultures, which is the main focus of this chapter. But departing slightly from Said's domination motif, I discern that this Orientalism is also for domestic consumption, for addressing crises within America.

A Foretaste of Multiculturalism

The Study of Cultures at a Distance

Margaret Mead indicated in 1953 that national character studies in America were a recent development, taking "both their form and methods from the exigencies of the post-1939 world political situation," meaning World War II and the Cold War (Mead 1953, 642). Ruth Benedict conducted a study of the Japanese national character during wartime with military sponsorship. The study was published as *The Chrysanthemum and the Sword* in 1946. Resuming the same ties, she launched the Research in Contemporary Cultures (RCC) project at Columbia University in 1947 with a grant from the U.S. Office of Naval Research.

Margaret Mead took over when Benedict died in 1948, and the RCC research project was extended, with different funding, into a series of successor projects at the American Museum of Natural History, New York City. Under the umbrella of RCC and successor projects until 1953, research groups studied the cultures of France, Spain, Czechoslovakia, Poland, Russia, East European Jews, Syria, and China. The RCC alone is probably the largest national-character-studies task force ever gathered, numbering 120 people from fourteen disciplines and sixteen nations (Mead and Metraux 1953, 6). The period from World War II to the early postwar era was the golden age of national-character study, which became "a major area of anthropological interest," but this interest began to wane after 1955 (Inkeles 1997, 5)

Changing Paradigm: Culture over Biology

Benedict and her student Mead were trained in the American school of cultural anthropology founded by Franz Boas. Before migrating from Germany, Boas had been under the sway of geographical determinism, which he later rejected (Harris 1968, 265–267). In its reaction against materialism, biologism, and social evolutionism, the Boasian program eschewed grandiose but ill-founded system-building; instead, it opted for the methodological particularism of ethnographic survey. Though frowning upon generalizations, the Boasian program had a "mentalistic" slant due to neo-Kantian influences. It paved the way for the dismissal of biological determinism and racialist theories by a more liberal "cultural" interpretation of the human phenomenon. Boas was a member of an immigrant minority, and his ideas bolstered the "belief in multiracial democracy, relativity of custom, maximum freedom for the individual . . . and hence, the ultimate openness of society and history" (Harris 1968, 298). Boas' atomistic approach was later modified by the configurationism of Benedict and Mead— not unlike the redress of the shortcomings of behavorism by Gestalt psychology—although it was actually a logical extension of Boas' neo-Kantian idealism.

A Cosmopolitan Stance

Benedict and Mead also brought their mentor's multiracialism to fruition. Benedict formulated the principles of configurationism in *Patterns of Culture* (1934), which stated her belief in the basic unity of humankind. It is a unity latent in a keyboard of all possible human traits and activities, from which each culture selects those it would emphasize and those it would omit; the chosen elements are integrated in a pattern supra-summative to its components and unique to the culture (Benedict 1934, 23–24).

During wartime, Benedict and Mead worked for the goal of global cultural coexistence in the postwar world. In 1942, Mead founded the Council on Intercultural Relations (renamed the Institute for Intercultural Studies in 1944) to facilitate communication among students of diverse national character and to promote a "cultural" approach to contemporary international problems. Its underlying principles were respect for cultural differences and the striving for global cultural "synergy" in a postwar world community. Benedict was a leading member of the institute, which paved the way for her postwar study of "contemporary cultures" (Howard 1984, 267; Caffrey 1989, 328).

Personality as the Metonym of Culture

Culture as Personality Writ Large

Benedict clarified configurationism by the simile of personality, or more precisely, through the metaphor of rational self-mastery: "A culture, like an individual, is a more or less consistent pattern of thought and action," and the ones that are not well-integrated are like "certain individuals" who fail to "subordinate activities to a ruling motivation" (Benedict 1934, 46, 223). The door to Freudian influence was wide open. Freud was an early influence on Mead, and her "conversion" in 1934 to "a modified Freudian theoretical orientation was something of a watershed for American anthropology" (Manson, in Stocking Jr. 1986, 77–78); Yans-McLaughlin, in Stocking Jr. 1986, 189).

The person who was most instrumental in fusing neo-Freudian theory and cultural anthropology was Abram Kardiner, who based his "basic personality" theory on the configurationist premise that culture and personality were similarly integrated. A culture in Kardiner's sense is integrated if all its members share the same childhood experiences that give rise to a certain type of personality formation, which in its turn shapes the over-all pattern of the culture through projections. Kardiner defined a cultural institution as at once a symbolic resolution and a repository of shared anxieties, defenses, and neuroses (Manson 1988, 42–44). When he organized a seminar at the New York Psychoanalytic Institute in 1936, Ruth Benedict, Edward Sapir, and Ruth Bunzel (the future coordinator of the RCC China project) became participants. For Freudianism to be accepted by the Boasians, it had to shed its evolutionism and its dogma of universal instinctual complexes to accommodate their cultural relativism, whereas the Boasians for their part relinquished their stress on history and diffusion. "The result was the American version of synchronic functionalism: culture and personality" (Harris 1968, 393).

The Psychologization of Culture

Meanwhile, Freud was being Americanized by Harry Stack Sullivan, who added a relational nexus (family in general, but notably the mother-son relationship) to supplement Freud's psychic stages of individual growth. The Sullivan factor in American cultural anthropology is noteworthy, for in 1937 he founded the journal *Psychiatry*, which became a long-term forum for the fermenting of the culture-and-personality theory (Bock 1988, 58). Sullivan was connected to Chinese national character studies in more than one way. A decade before the RCC, his Chinese disciple Dai Bingheng (Bingham Dai), also the very first Chinese lay analyst, had applied his relational approach to the pathological cases at Beiping's Union Medical College Hospital (Dai 1984, 281).

Even in its pre-Freudian phase, the culture-and-personality approach had already produced an anthropomorphic image of culture, for Benedict saw "culture" as simply "personality" writ large, and a pathological culture resembled a poorly integrated personality. After the Freudian intervention, this school began to use psychodynamics to explain culture, and personality readily turned into a metonym of culture. In this respect, Kardiner seems to be the exception, for he "assumes that human cultures are projections of the conflicts and sufferings of childhood, and their symbolic solutions, in such a way that childhood experience is assigned a definitely causal role in history." All the other students rejected this approach "in favor of one in which human society is seen as a self-perpetuating circular system within which specific causality cannot be assigned to any part" (Mead 1951, 78). If personality does not have a causal relationship with culture, it becomes its metonym.

One way or another, the school underlined the central place of individuality in American thinking. This strain was most pronounced in the work of another pioneer, Edward Sapir (who was also Bingham Dai's teacher). Even the Benedictian concept of "culture" was too collectivist for Sapir's taste:

> The study of culture as such . . . has a deep and unacknowledged root in the desire to lose oneself safely in the historically determined patterns of behavior. The motive for the study of personality . . . proceeds from the necessity which the ego feels to assert itself significantly. (Bock 1988, 43)

Its multiculturalist claim notwithstanding, the culture-and-personality study of the Chinese unavoidably contained a few assertions of the American "ego" at the expense of Chinese "culture."

Chinese Childhood and Sexual Growth

The RCC's China Group initially concentrated on Chinese immigrants exclusively from a small area in Guangdong, in New York's Chinatown. The ratio of women was very low, compelling the researchers to turn to young female students, most of whom came from urban areas in central and northern China. In a later phase the researchers also got in touch with a group of recently arrived war brides from the villages and urban middle classes of central China. The samples represented all social classes except poor peasants, industrial workers, and seamen. Most of the 158 informants used were under forty years of age, presumably conveying a picture of the Chinese people as they were between 1910 and 1947 (Bunzel 1950, 3–4).

The convener of the RCC China Group was Ruth Bunzel, an anthropologist and a lecturer at the New York Psychoanalytic Institute in the 1930s (Barnouw 1979, 115). As noted above, she was also a participant in Abram Kardiner's seminar at that Institute. Bunzel wrote a report in 1950 concluding the three years' work of the RCC China Group. We will refer to her report as the "synoptic view," to distinguish it from the individual views of group members.

The Ambivalent Early Chinese Childhood

The RCC methodology dictated that it understand Chinese culture through child training. An RCC member, the Chinese anthropologist Hu Xianjin (Hu Hsien-chin) saw the foundation of a secure Chinese personality being laid in early childhood, through sleeping with mother and other adults, late weaning, and the habit of disposing of excreta with direct help from mother (Hu 1946, 1; Bunzel 1950, 83, 92). Hu inspired Bunzel to assert, with a trace of envy, that Chinese training is "not a control of the instinctual life but an adaptation to it" (Bunzel 1949, 1).[1]

Hu's picture of the formation of a "secure" Chinese personality is relatively tension-free, although she sees signs of latent rebellion from the age of five years onward. Bunzel, however, discerns tension between succoring and the need for individuation from the very beginning, using evidence little known to the Chinese themselves: For example, a pregnant Chinese woman would go to a funeral wearing two sets of mourning clothes, and a Chinese infant sleeping together with mother and father is wrapped in his own quilt and "does not share his mother's cocoon" (Bunzel 1950, 84–85).

The budding of separation-individuation apparently falls short of fruition, and the researchers became more ambivalent on the subsequent stages of Chinese individuation. Growing up in an extended family, the Chinese child from very early on learns the nomenclature of relatives. But, "there is no training in achieving independence or self-reliance" (Hu 1946, 19–20). Chinese practices are inimical to autonomy and the growing child is deprived of chances to explore his surroundings. The toddler is given few opportunities to manipulate toys, instead he is trained to "look at" things, in sharp contrast to the American way of "learning to do things to objects" (Bunzel 1950, 94–95). This tactile deprivation in Chinese infancy persists in the next stage of life in "the restraint of motor activity in general." Quarrelling among siblings and with schoolmates is always discouraged, and a boy who defends himself by fighting earns a penalty instead of sympathy (Bunzel 1950, 107–109). His body belongs to the family, for continuing the family line through procreation—he has no right to expose it to danger (Bunzel 1950, 82).

Individuation Aborted

The RCC also applied to the study of the Chinese the theory of "gender role identities," a study that was initially rooted in biology-based "sexology," but like culture-and-personality in anthropology, had come under the "Freudian" rubric by mid-century. Regardless of the scanty comments by the master himself on the subject, since that time "the 'psychoanalytic' idea that has been the most widely disseminated and deeply accepted in American culture is the concept of sex role identity." By then, it had also attained the status of dogma with regard to the definitions of "normal" masculinity and femininity (Peck 1982, 40, 157–158).

In China, gender roles as such seem to be overshadowed, or even deliberately confounded, by generational ones. "It is the mother who picks a daughter-in-law to serve herself, rather than the father who picks a bride for his son." All informants for the RCC China Group reiterated that men could not defend their wives against their mothers. The personal satisfaction and happiness of the married couple are not top priority, and public expressions of strong affection between them are discouraged. Chinese people inhibit romantic love by presenting sex to the boy as dangerous and destructive (Bunzel 1950, 148–158, 160, 164, 165).

The Western child learns gender role from a single man or woman, i.e., father or mother, whereas the Chinese child growing up in the extended family learns from all its men and women in complex social contexts. For the boy, the female images deposited in his psyche in the first six years are largely protective and succoring. During those blissful years, of all the familiar women, only mother in her disciplinary mood is threatening. Punishment, as a rule administered by the mother, comes with little predictability as it depends on the temper of mother who frequently takes out on her child "her irritation with her husband, mother-in-law, or her exasperation with the whole family situation" (Bunzel, 1950, 110–111). Meanwhile crones in the household tell folk tales of beautiful women who are ghosts or fox spirits and how they destroy men through love. They become his picture of the outside or strange woman. Together, these images form "the world of women as the young child sees it, succoring but punishing (more succoring than punishing), actually protective, but potentially dangerous." On the other hand, the Chinese father is depicted as nonthreatening, and the boy sees his father subservient to his grandfather and grandmother, even though "she is only a woman" (Bunzel 1950, 165–167). In short, the Chinese father is not a role model for the male gender.

Regarding Chinese personality growth, Bunzel's tone is at once nostalgic and antinostalgic. She charges that Puritan America is paying too exorbitant a price for individual independence, especially in an "unnaturally" regimented childhood. In contrast, the Chinese attach "no shame" to "pregenital sexuality in children." There is also "no guilt" in women masturbating boy babies to quiet them, i.e., there is no hysteria about sexual abuse of children. Also absent is "guilt or deprecation of overt homosexuality of young boys" (Bunzel 1948, 6).

In spite of Bunzel's half-hearted idealization of the Orient, the blissful pregenital license of the Chinese seems to incur a high price, which they would have to pay in their later lives—according to another part of the RCC's reasoning. Evidently early childhood experience ill prepares the Chinese boy to face the adult masculine world, a grown-up world where "women become less satisfying." Furthermore, "the cultural formulation of male superiority is threatened by his subordination to his mother and his years of complete dependence on her," to the effect that "he can never quite free himself from the fear-dependence constellation which this overwhelming female figure has fostered in him" (Bunzel 1950, 168; Muensterberger n.d., 7–13). Layers of ambiguous gender images deposited in the Chinese male psyche explain why the American macho ideal is absent in China.

The Chinese Reversal of Gender Roles

Female professionals were heavily represented in the RCC projects: Ruth Benedict and Margaret Mead, Rhoda Metraux, Jane Belo, Martha Wolfenstein, Hu Xianjin, Theodora Abel, Elizabeth Hellersberg, Virginia Heyer, Gitel Poznanski, and Ruth Bunzel herself. In the latter's synoptic report, a feminist voice resenting America is detectable. It states that Chinese professional women are "shocked at the discrimination against women" in the United States, for in China a woman professional is simply a "strong character," not stigmatized as a "masculine woman." They are not "hampered by confusion as to their sexual identity" like their American sisters. In

China, "the cultural ideals do not require men to be strong, women weak; it merely requires that women obey; men, too, in suitable contexts must obey" (Bunzel 1950, 143, 145, 153).

Chinese girls also grow up in the same environment as the boys, but what makes the difference is the girl's relationship with males, chiefly her father and older brothers, who are often protective and caring. If a girl happens to be the oldest child, she helps her mother with the younger children, and becomes "second in command to the mother only." So, in spite of the formal emphasis on the greater importance of the boy, the girl often "sees her role in relation to the world of men as not one of simple subordination, but as one in which she is formally subordinate but potentially possesses considerable power" (Bunzel 1950, 168, 170; Hu n.d.(b), 2–3). This passage, though couched in Harry Stack Sullivan's "relational" terms, has less to do with psychoanalytical insights than with who has power and control.

To the surprise of the RCC researchers, Chinese female informants were less shy and more articulate than male ones. The women, in general, were "more willing or perhaps more able than men to describe actual behavior." The Chinese men, on the other hand, were more ready to talk about "their sexual difficulties" (Bunzel 1950, 173). After a longer period of acquaintance, the interviewers learned about the male informants' "preference for masturbation (manual), their insecurity in approaching girls," and their hope that "mother will find the right girl" (Muensterberger 1948, 2). Among the foreign student group, young Chinese women often took the initiative to approach members of the RCC Projects to look for jobs and to seek help in straightening out immigration tangles. The married women often acted on behalf of their husbands in confronting those problems; during interviews, they tended to speak for their men, who most of the time remained silent (Bunzel 1950, 174). The pattern that emerged in Chinatown showed that men approached the social workers because they felt rejected and unloved; the girls, on the other hand, merely used the social workers as "a service agency" for help in carrying out plans to conceal illegitimate pregnancies from their parents, and "none of them thought they had any personal problem."[2] The American-born females were able, "as American mores demand, to express hostility and to face their sexual problems." The American-born males felt that "they are unable to cope with the American-born girls and want to marry China-born girls, although none are available" (Bunzel 1950, 175, 179).

Both the foreign-student pattern and the Chinatown pattern were confirmed by Theodora Abel and Francis L.K. Hsu's analysis of Chinese responses to the Rorschach ink-blot cards. It showed that both the China-born and American-born females displayed a greater ego-strength than their male counterparts in adapting to the environment as well as in resolving their intrapsychic conflicts (Abel and Hsu 1949; Abel and Hsu, in Mead and Metraux 1953, 329–340). Bunzel saw "the castration fantasies" of Chinese men as betraying "a general sense of inadequacy." They always want to return home, to mother, to China, even "their art and poetry are nostalgic." Bunzel looked forward to a future China that was to become strongly female-oriented (Bunzel 1950, 180).

Bunzel's report nonetheless displays certain ambivalence: The "feminist" voice is at times drowned out by the "macho" anxiety about a domineering female. If Bunzel's synopsis of early Chinese childhood echoes Hu Xianjin and her envy of the Chinese professional women's freedom from gender stigma speaks for the RCC female team members as a whole, then the section on sexuality shows the handiwork of Warner Muensterberger, Virginia Heyer, and John Weakland. The trio was the anti-Momist contingent in the China Group, but we cannot rule out the possibility that Bunzel herself shared the same anxiety, for the stunting of individual growth, regardless of gender, went against certain basic American values.

The "Castrating Mother"

The RCC study of China contained more than one voice: Coeval with the mid-century matricidal high tide in American culture (see below), it somehow managed to uphold to a certain degree the credo of cultural relativism; while looking askance at the state of Chinese masculinity, at the same time it envied women's strong position in China. However, only a part of the results of the RCC China Group was published—by Heyer, Muensterberger, and Weakland—thus skewing the picture of the Chinese personality in the direction of a shrill anti-Momism. It suggested that Chinese nonrepression of pregenital license was degenerate, symptomatic of the stunting of genital or advanced sexuality.

Rewarding Passivity

Virginia Heyer, in her 1953 article, states that in a Chinese story, the hero, unlike his macho Western counterpart, is always an effeminate scholar, while the other character type, the military man, plays only an auxiliary role. The scholar is passive, nonassertive, always a victim, but he is rewarded precisely for those qualities. As the hero tends to let "events happen to him," the heroine is by default the active partner who initiates the love affair. A popular figure is the "swordswoman" who saves and protects her man, and this type is only a step from the dangerous seductress, attractive and sexually available: The fox maiden, snake woman, or banana spirit. "The result of sexual relations with a woman of this type is exhaustion or illness and often death." These fantasies reveal Chinese men's sense of inadequacy in the face of the phallic woman. For the Chinese, the "good" woman is the motherly type, underlining "the man's desire to regress to infancy when he is married, and the woman's preference for a mother's role to a wife's role." The fantasized "castrating woman" results from "a split in the complex attitude of the Chinese son to his mother," whose menacing side he projects onto the "outside" woman. The outsider image also falls upon the wife when the husband remains mamma's boy (Heyer 1953, 221–234).

Heyer not only ignored RCC's synoptic view that a strong woman in China was not a "phallic woman," for her a "scholar" was perforce a weak male. A different voice is audible from the unpublished materials: In her analysis of the novel, *The Romance of the Three Kingdoms*, Hu Xianjin pointed to brain's supremacy over brawn in China: It is "the strategist behind the fighter who directs and wins the battle" (Hu 1947b, 3). The "scholar" is but one facet of the Chinese ego ideal. In traditional China, the greater part of the male population undertook martial art training, and "girls received it occasionally" (Hu 1947a, 15).

The Maternal Conspiracy

Hu's view was not published; meanwhile Warner Muensterberger reinforced Heyer by stressing mother's power in the nominally patriarchal Chinese family. Chinese child-upbringing controlled by mother fosters personality traits such as oral indulgence, dependency, and passivity. It results in "food" being "the principle link between people" in Chinese adult life. The Chinese "longing to remain sheltered and passive" also explains "the institution of rest (*hsiu-hsi*)[or *xiuxsi* in pinyin]." These traits are magnified in the male personality, due to mother's ambivalent attitude rooted in her own "penis wish" and "penis envy." She whimsically alternates between overprotection-overindulgence and demands-prohibitions. The effect is to "de-autonomize" the Chinese male's "ego functions," making him anxiety laden when confronted with the adult sexual task. Defense against such anxiety assumes forms of regression to early childhood such as seeking refuge in oral forms of gratification and the masochistic wish to be "castrated." Muensterberger includes opium-smoking and gambling among symptoms of oral indulgence and masochism, the same psychological roots that also explain "homosexuality" (Muensterberger 1951).

Muensterberger's mother-bashing departs remarkably from Bunzel's synoptic view, which states that Chinese culture inhibits romantic love to ensure the stability of the patriarchal family. However, Muensterberger's article, published in 1951, is already very much subdued compared to his unpublished RCC writings, in which he speaks more freely. In the latter, the Chinese female has an exaggerated "penis wish." She "grows up into what is psychoanalytically described as the castrating woman." Her "genital desire" is "strongly repressed," so in "her sadistic fantasy the male genital becomes the object for reparation." This wish "is largely fulfilled when she is the mother of a son through whom she can act." She overindulges her son to such an extent that "no situation in the future will offer comparable protection and security." As a result, the Chinese male can never "renounce orality for the ensuing levels of development" that befit "an integrated, as well as independent adult." Making the son weak is "the way in which the mother realizes her castration wish." As "the female is also fixed at the oral level," where girls and boys used to be equal, her reducing the male to the same level is her way of "getting even" (Muensterberger n.d., 6–11).

For Muensterberger, Chinese culture was simply a milieu that, unlike America, allowed an international maternal conspiracy to have a field day. This conspiracy-allegation was grounded in the Freudian dogma of woman's "penis envy." Chinese RCC members, namely Hu Xianjin and Liu Jinghe (a female research subject), conceded that Chinese men were "spoiled and pampered" by women (Hu 1949, 1). But Bunzel's synopsis on early Chinese childhood, drawn largely from the Chinese members of the research project, refers only to the girl's jealousy of her younger brother because she is required to yield to him in material terms; yet it does not prevent the brother-sister relationship from becoming the warmest in the family.

A Matter of Power and Control

For Muensterberger, "when a Chinese uses a go-between, he is avoiding contact with a (castrating) situation of reality, and is using the good mother to help him escape, sacrificing his masculinity in order to be accepted as he was in infancy" (Muensterberger n.d., 13–14). John Weakland's 1950 article seems to bear out this point—it cites the single case of a thirty-year old Chinese informant who went through marriage and business transactions by manipulating Weakland into making the major decisions for him. It led Weakland to ponder on the separation of desire and effort, passion and action in Chinese culture. But Weakland located these patterns squarely within the general Chinese child-training practice, with the mother playing a crucial but not overarching role, which was closer to the synoptic position (Weakland 1950).

Weakland later conducted a study of the fear of "depletion" for an RCC successor project, the CPC (Chinese political character), and published the results in 1956. He also resorted to the Freudian concept of orality, noting the plethora of oral imagery in Chinese descriptions of male genital sexuality. The Chinese people believe that in a sexual act the male semen is easily depleted while the nourishing female "essence" is inexhaustible. Weakland ascribed such myths to the male's psychological dwarfing by mother. Unlike Muensterberger, Weakland thought that Chinese childhood was not all blissful: The "oralization" of male genital sexuality may have resulted from the power mother exercises in feeding, which encourages passive receptivity while it penalizes active demands (Weakland 1956). Weakland's view in this instance is a far cry from Bunzel's synoptic position, which is that in feeding, the Chinese mother usually goes along with, and is sometimes at the mercy of, the "natural" demands of the child though she might punish arbitrarily to vent her frustration at the general family situation. There is also a subtle difference between Weakland's concern with maternal "power and control" and Muensterberger's "getting even" argument, although both betray the same obsession with power and dominance.

Fear of Passivity and "Depletion"

Heyer, Muensterberger, and Weakland also stigmatized "passivity," which the Chinese RCC members found objectionable. Bunzel's report reveals that "our Chinese colleagues objected strenuously whenever the word 'passivity' was used in connection with the Chinese preferences for a life of contemplation" (Bunzel 1950, 26).[3] A 1948 study of the American national character by Geoffrey Gorer, a British member of the RCC, throws light on this issue. Gorer sees most American men under pressure to convince their fellows and themselves "that they are not sissies, not homosexuals," by shying away from "feminine" interests such as art and literature. In fact, in America, "all intellectual pursuits and interests are somewhat tainted" (Gorer 1964, 129). Small wonder that the "scholar," the Chinese hero *par excellence*, was suspected of latent homosexuality. In the 1950s, McCarthyites even alluded to an intellectual *per se* as a cross between a "faggot" and a "commie," both equally *un-American* (Hofstadter 1966, 9–10). Ironically, Nathan Leites of the RCC Russian project saw the Bolshevik apotheosis of activism in the same light: As a psychic defense against the Russian intellectuals' passivity and femininity (Leites 1953). His psychologizing of a Cold War enemy betrayed a deep-seated American anxiety about passivity (read: feminization) as a telltale sign of latent homosexuality.

The Sapping of Virility

The dominant discourse of the time was so powerful that even the heavy presence of female professionals in the RCC did not help to refute the "castrating mother" thesis, nor did it lift the opprobrium of passivity. The concern at the time, it seems, was not gender but the stunting of individuality. It is in this light we should read the following excerpt from the minutes of an RCC-CPC meeting in 1951, presided over by Margaret Mead, with Ruth Bunzel, Rhoda Metraux, Nathan Leites, John Weakland, and Martha Wolfenstein present:

> MM: To go back for a minute, on this question of double projection of activity and passivity sort of things, of which Rhoda gave the example of a paper toy which the child mustn't touch. And then Bunny [Bunzel] gave the point of the [Confucian] doctrine of rectification of names. Again a reversal projection point . . .
> RB: The adult holds it [the paper toy] and makes it move.
> RM: The Chinese child is supposed to look at it. If Daniel [Rhoda's boy?] saw it, he'd grab at it.
> MW: You're sure it isn't supposed to be a frightening image?
> RM: Oh, no.
> MW: So what is dangerous really is the destructiveness of the child.
> MM: If you make the image of projected destructiveness exceedingly fragile, it has a double position in it.
> JW: The Chinese old image of the beautiful woman is exceedingly fragile, too.
> MM: And frightening.
> JW: And very dangerous if you reach for it.
> RB: The more beautiful and delicate the more dangerous she is.
> MM: That might throw some light.
> NL: What is the process of its being dangerous? What will happen?
> RM: Nobody knows.
> MW: In what words is the child told it's dangerous?
> NL: How will the beautiful woman be destructive?
> JW: She takes away one's strength.
> RB: Saps virility and life.
> JW: We also find other points on that. In one shadow play about a beautiful woman who turns out to be the White Snake.
> MW & NL: Mrs White!
> NL: A story by Wylie. (Minutes 1951a, 4–6)

In the manner of a psychoanalytic free-association session, the conversation tells more about American anxieties over the sapping of virility than about the Chinese personality. The excerpt begins with Chinese child-training's inhibition on touching, hence the inculcation of passivity, then proceeds to the "castrating female," concluding with Philip Wylie the American crusader against Momism (see below). Most Chinese would assign a common-sense instead of a convoluted reason for not allowing the child to touch a toy, as in the opinion of Hu Xianjin: "If the thing is unbreakable and if it cannot hurt the baby it is given to him. If this is impossible, it is taken out of his sight and another toy or object substituted" (Hu 1946, 6). Yet Hu's voice, albeit a native one, carried little weight.

Cold War and Cold Sex

Beginning with *Coming of Age in Samoa* (1928), Mead had published a series of immensely popular books on the sexual mores of Pacific islanders. They questioned the Western norm's claim to universality and lent support to the Boasian emphasis on culture over biology. Mead used the Samoans' amazingly uninhibited sexual patterns and their relatively tension-free adolescence as scientific supports for the "sexual revolution," which was then in the offing among middle-class Americans (Harris 1968, 408). Unlike these conscious and studied manifestos of cultural relativism, Mead in her off-guard mood, as revealed in the unpublished minutes, seemed to inject American-style tension and anxiety into Chinese childhood and adult sexuality.

The RCC projects happened to coincide with the onset of the Cold War and the "fluoridation scare" in the United States (Heilbroner 1956; Reinemer 1955). This paranoia was caricatured in the British film classic, *Dr. Strangelove* (1964): General Jack Ripper orders an unauthorized nuclear attack on the Soviet Union, convinced that the commies have managed to poison the nation's "precious bodily fluids," evident in his own "fatigue" in the company of women. Incidentally, Weakland also discerned "depletion" phobia in Chinese Communist perceptions of the imperialist threat (Weakland 1951b, 1–2). At the same time he employed the "intrusion" imagery, betraying fears of homosexual "penetration" of the male body by an enemy (Weakland 1951a, 1–4). His Chinese colleague Hu Xianjin, on the other hand, indicated that the Chinese tended to imagine external threats as cannibalism (Hu n.d.(c)).[4]

The "castrating mother" thesis went on to inspire clinical studies of those "culture-bound" psychoses found only among Chinese males, namely "koro" and "frigophobia." Koro is the irrational fear of the shrinking and eventual disappearance of the penis, which would result in death. Frigo-phobia is the morbid fear of cold even in warm weather. The two share "a core symptom of extreme fear of loss of bodily energy or vitality." Again, all fingers seem to point to mother, for "lack of maternal care in childhood is frequently reported by Koro patients, and maternal overprotection by Frigophobia patients" (Rin 1966, 21).

The Impaired Ability for Aggression

The Neglected Father

In American studies of the Chinese national character, a corollary to the thesis of stunted sexuality is the impaired ability for aggression. In the 1960s, Lucian Pye and Richard Solomon, political scientists, concluded that Chinese people could not properly handle aggression. It resulted from their study of the "authoritarian personality," a topic made voguish by the Frank-furt School, China's Cultural Revolution, the Vietnam War, and campus revolts. Unlike the RCC projects, Pye and Solomon blamed the impairment on "father," whom they deemed central to the Chinese authoritarian per-sonality. Both men were acquainted with the RCC China projects. Like theirs, and unlike the social psychology of the Frankfurt School, Pye and Solomon's "political culture" is psychodynamic and caters to the American interest in sexuality and gender.

The shift of attention to the male parent corrected the one-sided picture of the RCC, which placed the Chinese father in limbo, where he belonged with Dagwood, the ineffectual father in mid-century America. The RCC research subjects from New York City Chinatown were also atypical: Their fathers had migrated to the United States and sent for their sons only after thirty years' absence, which means that they grew up under a single parent, the mother (Bunzel 1948, 3). In short, the skewed samples of the RCC were the products of the Chinese Exclusion Acts repealed only in December 1943. In 1948, in his *Under the Ancestors' Shadow*, Francis Hsu had already redressed the skewed RCC picture before it even appeared by pointing to the obvious: Chinese society was, after all, patriarchal. With an intent dif-ferent from Hsu's, Pye and Solomon used the father figure, as RCC had used the mother, to express the same paranoia about feminization and gender-role reversal.

Filial Piety = Moral Masochism

The "oppressive demands of filial piety," Pye wrote in 1969, compels the Chinese to find self-esteem in "yielding submissively to the cruelties of his authoritarian father." It results in a personality based on "moral maso-chism"—the penchant to harbor a sense of narcissistic omnipotence by wallowing in the victim's role. By so doing, he turns impotence into moral superiority. In fact, the Chinese individual abdicates the responsibility of controlling his own fate and avoids confronting his own aggression by al-ways accusing the opposing party of being the "aggressor" (Pye 1969, 75–79). Pye disparaged modern China's anti-imperialist movement by likening it to a "crybaby" syndrome (Pye 1969, 73). A twist in Pye's narrative of the Chinese character is that modern Chinese rebellion, of which the Cul-tural Revolution is typical, is not an assertion of manhood but an expression of "disappointment" at a weak and "inadequate authority" (Pye 1969, 242).

Pye's pupil Solomon saw the father-son relationship as prototypal in Chinese culture: "The pattern of authority and deference the son learns in dealing with his father is primary: yet this 'submission-dominance' style influences most other relations between males." Relationship between peo-ple of equal social status is an "underdeveloped" area among the Chinese (Solomon 1971, 54, 125–126). They need intermediaries in social transac-tions in much the same way as a Chinese child uses mother as a cushion against an emotionally distant and punitive father, thus evading the task of growing up himself.

Sexualizing and Gendering Passivity

For our purpose, it is sufficient to discern that Pye's concept of moral mas-ochism, as applied to the Chinese, is directly lifted from Freud's "The Eco-nomic Problem of Masochism" (1924), where Freud describes masochism in the male as placing "the subject in a characteristically female situation" signifying the state of "being castrated, or copulated with, or giving birth to a baby." Moral masochism is a desexualized variant, but "the wish to be beaten by the father stands very close to the other wish, to have a passive (feminine) sexual relation to him" (Freud 1924, 162, 169). If Pye saw the Chinese people settling in the "normal" position of woman, Solomon's dominance and submission terminology seems to be adapted from American "kinky-sex" practices where conventional male and female roles are delib-erately reversed.[5]

In America, the immediate postwar era witnessed a censure of relativism, especially cultural relativism in anthropology, and the rise of a more affir-mative attitude toward Western values *vis-à-vis* the totalitarianism of the Eastern Bloc (Novick 1988, 286–288). In this Cold War atmosphere, the RCC-type cultural relativism was on the wane—already discernible in the later-phase RCC publications by Heyer, Muensterberger, and Weakland—allowing Pye and Solomon to affirm Western superiority in a most unabashed manner. The difference between the RCC and Pye-Solomon team is minimal in the face of their common concern, which was to cast individuals in gendered terms—at a time when individuality seemed to be exemplified by the male gender alone.

Individuation as Parenticidal Drama

It is interesting to contrast the Pye-Solomon thesis with Tu Wei-ming's New Confucian view of the father-son relationship. Where the latter discerns nonadversarial and fiduciary relations, the former sees *only* emasculation, stunted psychological growth, sado-masochism, and the authoritarian personality. Pye and Solomon were discredited by American critics for their unsound methodology and State Department affiliations, but no one ever questioned their truism that a man must come into his own by asserting himself against his father.

"The King Must Die"

In America, the Oedipal stance is a precondition to male growth. Without passing the test of defying the father, the individual is not prepared to face the more strenuous fratricidal game, or competition in the adult world of equals. To surpass father is to believe in the young generation's moral superiority over the old. Being overshadowed by father implies stagnancy and death; the son should learn skills from the father figure in order to beat him. Understandably, father is also the role model, and he, as the king, must die to make way for the heir apparent. The slain father is to be emulated and placated, and the prodigal son often returns to father's ideal of justice after worsting him; that is, he succeeds where the father has failed. Before the outbreak of the "child abuse" epidemic, father in male patricidal fantasies was rarely portrayed as evil, but even in the case of Darth Vader (Dark Father or Death Father), Luke Skywalker still strives to win him back to the side of the Light.[6]

In stark contrast, as I shall show below, the slain "mother" has no redeeming value, she embodies forces of darkness pure and simple. The damage caused by failing to surpass one's role model is minor compared to the one inflicted by the "castrating" mother who sabotages the boy's development into manhood. As the movie *Rebel Without A Cause* (1955) shows, the male patricidal urge is also directed at a father henpecked by the mother, a father who fails to provide a male role model for the son. This line of reasoning reminds us of Lucian Pye's argument that malformed manhood tends to become resentful toward a weak and "inadequate authority." In the terms of the gender role identity theory, an "unmanly" father is not a gender role model. It also leads to the collapse of the Freudian triangle, as the son can no longer have a contest with the father for the mother to prove his manhood, for both parties are absent in their role and devoured by the mother. The unravelling of the triangle threatens not only manhood but also the prospect of heterosexuality.

The Campaign against Momism

There were indications that matriphobia was on the rise by the 1940s and that it was related to the fear of feminine contamination. Some studies traced the fear back no further than the *fin de siècle*, when sexuality, free from the Victorian straitjacket, was emerging as a major discourse in the West. In America, it was also a time when both mother at home and the female teacher at school began to play a larger role. The resulting "concerns about feminization were a major factor in the rapid rise of the Boy Scouts." Alarm over feminization was heightened to collective shock when nearly half of the World War I recruits were found to be physically and mentally unfit for military service. In the interwar years, Lewis Terman and Catherine Miles, who devised the IQ test, also invented the "masculinity-femininity" (MF) scale based on the same model and found homosexuality the crucial deviation. Their scale still drew from early twentieth-century bio-sexological taxonomy, until the postwar era, when the rise of psychody-namic thinking ushered in new scales of measuring male development. It was now defined as a departure from FF (total identification with mother) to MM (full masculinity) (Peck 1987, 23–25, 32–33). By that time, the so-called sexual-role-identities paradigm was in full sway, and deviations were inevitably characterized as psychopathological. In the field of psychoanal-ysis there was a parallel development: The interwar years also saw the formulation of Harry Stack Sullivan's theory of the "schizophrenogenic mother."

All these trends inevitably found an echo in literature. It was the writer Philip Wylie who first launched a diatribe against "Momism" in the early forties. He evoked the authority of Freud to condemn "mother-love-in-action" as "an incestuous perversion of a normal [maternal or heterosexual?] instinct" (Wylie 1942, 185). Wylie's characterization of Mom is full of venom:

> She is a middle-aged puffin with an eye like a hawk that has just seen a rabbit twitch far below. She is about twenty-five pounds overweight, with no sprint,

but sharp heels and a hard backhand which she does not regard as a foul but a womanly defense. In a thousand of her there is not sex appeal enough to budge a hermit ten paces off a rock ledge (Wylie 1942, 189).

It strikes us that Wylie *sexualizes* the image of mother by relentlessly harping on her fading sexual appeal—even her caprices "are of a menopausal nature." Mom cannot compete with younger women because "she contrasts so unfavorably with them." In order to remain in control, she subverts "her boy" through protection and love, retarding him from "his progress toward maturity," thus "Mom steals from the generation of women behind her . . . that part of her boy's personality which should have become the love of a female contemporary." Even the revolt against father can play into Mom's hands: "Mom's boy will be allowed to have his psychobiological struggle with dad," but if it is done "under mom's ruinous aegis it . . . leads to more serfdom for the boy" (Wylie 1942, 186, 189, 190, 191, 195–197).

By Wylie's time the psychodynamic (e.g., Freudian) approach had become ascendant, as evident in the anthropological culture-and-personality school as well as the "gender role identity" paradigm in gender studies. The Freudian family romance sets up an Oedipal triangle where the boy establishes his sexual oppositeness to mother by competing with the father. What enraged Wylie was the wrong alignment of the triangle: The boy's failure to grow into mature heterosexuality because he is devoured by the mother, so much so that his Oedipal confrontation with father is also a sham. In Freudian logic, once the neurotic Oedipal triangle is simplified into the "we have each other" dyad of the mother and the son, the situation becomes psychotic. Within the Freudian framework, the turning from Freud's focus on neurosis to the study of psychosis had begun in earnest under Harry Stack Sullivan. In his relational approach, Sullivan laid the blame on the unhealthy American family situation, where the curb on the husband's extramarital sexual life was weak, and the wife sought revenge in "raising the boy so he won't be like his father" (Sullivan 1974, 94). Sullivan thus attributed "schizophrenic disorders" to "persisting immature attitudes subtending the mother and son relationship," which also caused the son to harbor "homosexual cravings" (Sullivan 1974, 327).

From the Oedipal to the Matricidal

The RCC was coeval with the transition from the motif of Oedipal triangle to that of matricide in the American popular-culture imagination. Martha Wolfenstein and Nathan Leites' 1950 psychoanalytic study of American movies does not have a single reference to the matricidal genre. It mentions family comedies featuring the ineffectual, Dagwood-type father allied with the son against "the colorless, slightly unpleasant, emotionally impactless mother," of whom "they are both a little afraid" (Wolfenstein and Leites 1950, 157). Their study indicates another popular motif, which had this triangle realigned, with the son (e.g., a young adventurer) invariably killing the father (e.g., a crime boss) and taking over the mother (his mistress). The book omits Alfred Hitchcock's *Spellbound* (1945), because, in spite of superficial resemblance to the Freudian family romance, it actually destabilizes the Oedipal triangle: It was the "mother" who played the active role to protect the weak "son" from the "father." In the story, the amnesiac young director of a psychiatric institute is framed for murder by the aging ex-director who refuses to retire, but a loving, pretty woman doctor comes to the hero's rescue. Such frank depiction of a male in his most helpless (powerless) state to be rescued by the maternal female was akin to a Chinese love story plot *à la* Virginia Heyer—it was to become unthinkable half a decade later due to the mounting crisis of masculinity.

If the mobster is the perennial "macho" persona in America's popular imagination, then a new and disturbing departure occurred in *White Heat* (1949). "In it, James Cagney, as a mother-fixated gangster, sits on his mother's lap, suffers from crippling migraines only she can cure, has a psychotic breakdown when he learns of her death, and meets a fiery end atop an exploding gas tank while shouting, 'Made it, Ma! Top of the world!' " (Thurer 1994, 270). The first mother-possessed serial killer made his debut in Ira Levin's 1953 novel, *A Kiss Before Dying* (movie, 1956; remake, 1991). In this melodrama, a young man plots to marry into the family of a rich industrialist. He courts the three daughters of a copper magnate in succession, murdering two of them when the plan goes awry, for he has no love for them, acting solely to satisfy his mother's "phallic" wish for social climbing.

The same year (1955) that produced *Rebel Without a Cause* also gave us *Marty*. The story admonished a man to break out of the stranglehold of mother and male peer group to proceed to mature heterosexual love. In *Suddenly, Last Summer* (Broadway show, 1958; movie, 1959), Tennessee Williams portrays a Southern matriarch who, in order to maintain herself as the only woman in her son's life, turns him into a homosexual and causes his violent death (Williams 1976).

The Sexual Revolution Magnified the Problem

The sexual mores were changing at the time. Major landmarks: Alfred Kinsey's immensely popular report on female sexuality was published in 1953;

Playboy magazine appeared in the following year; the birth control pill was invented by the mid-1950s. The pill's legalization in 1960 paved the way for the liberation of feminine sexuality, and the number of users had jumped sixfold by 1963 (Halberstam 1993, 48). By the 1960s, the sexual inadequacy of the "Mamma's boy" became glaring, and his shriek of rage precipitated an avalanche of matricidal fantasies.

In 1960, Hitchcock produced his film classic, *Psycho*, the story of Norman Bates, who has murdered his "schizophrenogenic" mother. Assuming the personality of the murdered mother, the man-child dresses up as a transvestite to kill young women to whom he feels attracted. American matriphobia was melded with aversions to communism and Asians in *The Manchurian Candidate* (1962), a spy yarn and matricidal fantasy rolled into one. Sounding the Wyliean alarm that America is controlled by Mom—in Wylie's words, Mom "has become the American pope" (Wylie, 1942, 195)—the film shows that in their twisted memories, the returned Korean-War POWs recall the brain-washing sessions in Manchuria as a garden tea party and their Chinese and Russian captors as middle-aged American ladies who patronize them as schoolboys. In the story, the man-child Raymond Shaw also kills his mother, but this time she is an "un-American" communist agent, and matricide becomes a patriotic act. Meanwhile, the matricidal serial killer character was perpetuated with less fanfare in *The Strangler* (1964) and *No Way to Treat a Lady* (1968).

A mother all wrapped up in herself attained the status of symbolism in *Lady in a Cage* (1964). The throne-like elevator of the Southern matriarch, regal as the Byzantine Empress Theodora descending, *dea ex machina*, upon her court in *Suddenly, Last Summer*, turned into a cage. If the sexual revolution highlighted the inadequacy of the man-child, it also exposed maternal fixation on the son as the misdirection of repressed sexuality.

The matricidal decade had an endnote in Philip Roth's novel *Portnoy's Complaint* (1967) and the movie *The Midnight Cowboy*, (1969). The guilt-ridden Portnoy tries very hard to be "Mommy's best little boy" by spending his adolescence in endless masturbation, and when he finally falls for a coreligious woman in a pilgrimage to Israel, he turns impotent. *The Midnight Cowboy* contains random flashbacks from the traumatic past of a male hooker, juxtaposing scenes of gang rape and mother's obscene mien, strongly hinting at childhood sexual abuse, probably one of the earliest in cinematic representation. "Thus the women of America raped the men, not sexually, unfortunately, but morally," lamented Wylie as early as 1942 (Wylie 1942, 188).

Matricide as "Party Line"

The 1960s abounded in pathological portrayals of power-hungry men with a mother-fixation. The interpretations of Hitler in *Hitler* (1962) and Commodus in *The Fall of the Roman Empire* (1964) fall within this category. In the same vein is a fictional Southern presidential candidate in Gore Vidal's *The Best Man* (1964), who is overly (also blindly) aggressive, but reverent of mother, and, while in the service, was suspected of being a homosexual. In fact, in 1960, Daniel Bell had reintroduced Nathan Leites' view of Bolshevism by detecting in Lenin's exaggerated emphasis on activism a defense against "latent homosexuality" (Bell 1965, 330). Here the artificial boundary between the narratives for entertainment and serious scholarship virtually disappeared. In the same decade, the Egyptologist Donald Redford debunked the monotheism of Pharaoh Akhenaton by alluding to his being a "faggot." Redford speculated that Akhenaton probably grew up under mother's influence, thus strongly hating his father, whose work he attempted to undo. It resulted in his deficiency in the "manly" pursuits of international politics and warfare, but excellence in "feminine" forms of daydream such as art and poetry: The contention was that a faggot's mythopoeic daydream should not be honored as seminal monotheism (Redford, in Sowards 1992). In a 1963 work on the history of Japan, George Sansom also attributed Shogun Tokugawa Tsunayoshi's eccentricities to maternal influences (Sansom 1963, 130–134). The "mother-fixation" narrative was symptomatic of the 1960s in the same manner as the "child abuse" narrative in our time. It came as no surprise when, in 1965, Senator Daniel Patrick Moynihan delivered his report on the African American ghettos, it traced the origins of pimps and drug-traffickers to their having grown up under the shadow of mother, in the absence of father (Strickland and Ambrose 1985, 551).

The after-effect of anti-Momism on American judicial reasoning lingered beyond the 1960s. In *Judgment at Nuremberg* (1961), a victim of the Nazi castration law serves as a witness for the prosecution. The defense strategy is to cite the castration laws in the United States and to prove that the witness' fate was determined by a diagnosis of feeble-mindedness, not political considerations. When the witness does not respond to questions but displays his mother's photo instead, the court yields to the defense's opinion of the witness as "not in control of his mental faculties," over the latter's protest that he has been reduced to the current state by his tragedy. In the case of the "Boston strangler" of the 1960s, the police speculated, without solid evidence, that the killer's rage was caused by his hatred for mother. In the 1970s, David Berkowitz of "Son of Sam" notoriety is reported to have been clinging toward his stepmother, to have poisoned her parakeet to eliminate competition, and to have thought that he had cursed his mother to death. Kenneth Alessio Bianchi of the "hillside strangler" case of the late 1970s feigned multiple personality disorder and managed to fool four psychiatrists, including one hired by the court, by claiming childhood mistreatment by his mother. The case of Fred Coe, the serial rapist of Spokane in the late 1970s, was similarly envisaged: in 1983, Jack Olsen wrote a book about it, called *Son*, when it was televised in 1991, it became *Sins of the Mother*.

Although "mother" is no longer the main target in the prevailing gender ideology of today, matricidal yearnings have nonetheless set the prototype for the narrative incriminating a significant other, and this kind of narrative has become a rage by our time. As long as the motif of individual *will to power* persists, this line of reasoning will continue to thrive. The irony is that a line of reasoning that began with the concern for healthy personality growth has ended up preaching that victimhood is at the root of the human condition.

China as a Foil

In Lacanian psychology, the earliest self is formed when the child sees its specular image reflected in a mirror or the imitative gestures of others. In short, it is only through the Other that the emergent individual is constituted. This act lays the foundation of an ego structure in which "an ego is always an alter ago and vice versa" (Dor 1998, 95, 207). Lacan sees speech as not originating in the ego but in the Other, and in this sense, narrative about Self is circumscribed by the Other. There is no intrinsic reason that an alterity should be an antagonism at all, but where the adversary principle is the dominant cultural outlook, this equation becomes inevitable. As a cultural artifact, American masculinity is constituted by an imaginary opposite: A femininity construed as all that ought to be suppressed in the definition of masculinity.

The decade of the 1960s was the most tumultuous phase in the genealogy of the gendered, sexed, and psychologized individual as exemplified in the male. It was coeval with Maoist China where the individual was politicized, unsexed, and genderless. The introduction of the Chinese as a foil, as in the case of RCC, also accentuates the generational dimension of the problematic in lieu of gender. Where traditional Chinese values still linger, a person uninterested in the opposite sex is often pushed by the parents into marriage to continue the ancestral line, as reflected in Lee Ang's movie *The Wedding Banquet* (1993). In sharp contrast, for the sexed individual of America the older generation can be an emasculating factor. Edward Albee's play, *The American Dream* (1960), tells a parable: In a family, when a baby boy began to stare and "only had eyes for its Daddy," the mother gouged his eyes out; when he began to develop an interest in his penis, the parents had him castrated (Albee 1960, 61–62).

Albee wrote at a time when the son not only blamed the father for being an inadequate gender role model, but virtually accused him of colluding with the mother to take away his manhood. If the American reasoning defies Chinese understanding, it is because its logic is individualistic: Sexuality not only does not concern ancestors, it is a meter gauging who has the upper hand even between two generations—or partners, for that matter.

Ramifications of the Matricidal Syndrome

Understandably, in the wake of the sexual revolution, the sexed individuality with all its fears about "castration" was no longer the male monopoly. In the film *Carrie* (1976), it is the daughter who kills the mother for retarding her sexual growth. The motif of mother causing psychological damage to the daughter also informed the films *Sybil* (1976) and *Frances* (1982). Long before these offshoots of the male "psycho" genre, Hollywood had already censured the mother who tried to run the daughter's life, but these yarns of an earlier vintage were about rescuing the young maiden from the older generation's stranglehold so that she could consummate heterosexual love with a man.[7] With the advent of the female "psycho" genre, the emphasis shifted to women's personality growth.

It was simply one step from generational rift for women to effect a gender schism: to free themselves also from male-centered heterosexuality. In more recent years, the new parenticidal drama has come to focus on the rapist-father. Instead of the castrating mother taking away the son's sexuality, now it is the male parent who conduces nymphomania and multiple personality disorder. The Oedipal triangle has been rendered meaningless by the disintegration of the nuclear family anyway. Even though the individual continues to be imagined in psychological terms, Freud is now discredited for using the theory of childhood sexual fantasies as a cover-up for real molestations.[8]

The RCC's China Group uses the mother-son relationship to account for the Chinese male's inadequacy in handling mature relationships, whereas the Pye-Solomon team sees in the authoritarian father-son nexus the prototype of all Chinese relationships that are detrimental to equality. The same can be said about American parenticidal and fratricidal (competition among equals) narratives providing models for the more recent "sleeping with the enemy" genre. The putative Chinese personality under American gaze is to be understood within a "system of difference," in the sense that the Chinese individual is less aware of domination and victimization, hence more oblivious to his or her rights by American standards. If the Chinese perspective were to be the center of all coordinates in the same "system of difference," the American individual's impetus to differentiate itself from others would have appeared so sharp that its boundary is a string of paranoia. This becomes even more apparent in the filicidal and fan-killing genres.[9] Unlike the parenticidal and spousecidal fantasies, they can no longer use antidomination as a pretext and are therefore pure expressions of the fear of clinging, attachment, invasion of privacy, and the loss of individuality.

The Morbidity of Domineering and Clinging

The RCC China Project also brings to our attention the long-forgotten figure of the "phallic woman." In 1950, when the RCC's Ruth Bunzel resented America for attaching the stigma of "masculine woman" to female professionals, such a caricature was rampant. The era's most notable diatribe against the "phallic woman" was Lundberg and Farnham's *Modern Woman: The Lost Sex* (1947). It charged modern society with vitiating conventional family and gender roles, causing widespread failure on the part of women to resolve "penis envy" in their growth. It was not the mature man, but the defective "phallic-narcissistic" male who failed as father that modern "masculine-aggressive" women had taken as model. This neurosis was most pronounced in the career woman and the feminist, but it also afflicted those wives and mothers who, falling short of mature femininity, caused family dysfunction. "Just what have these women done to their sons? The have stripped them of their male powers—that is, they have castrated them" (Lundberg and Farnham 1947, 319).

The Phallic Woman in Popular Culture

Beginning in the 1940s, American popular culture, notably films, also mass-produced fear of the phallic woman. In *Lady in the Dark* (1944), the heroine, a loveless, domineering career-woman, feels incomplete and seeks analysis, and learns that she can be "cured" only by a man who can dominate her. William Inge's play, *The Dark at the Top of the Stairs* (written, 1945; published, 1958; movie, 1960), sets up two dysfunctional couples as foils: Cora and Rubin, Lottie and Morris; the women in both cases are housewives. Initially, Cora and Rubin are estranged, the wife is not receptive and the husband hides his unemployment out of male pride, but at the end they make up as she relents and he opens up. The second pair has never worked: Lottie is bossy and cracks sexual jokes, to the envy of her sister Cora, who later learns to her amazement that Lottie is sexually blank, that her bossiness is in fact a compensation for Morris' non-dominating character, and that she prefers beatings from him to the present emptiness. Inge also extols Cora's virtue as mother, who let her son deal with taunts of sissiness from a schoolmate by exerting violence on his own (Inge 1958).

In the 1954 western, *Johnny Guitar*, Mercedes McCambridge plays an evil phallic woman who cannot tolerate being reminded of her womanhood. A character named the Dancing Kid "makes her feel like a woman, that frightens her," and she finally shoots him. Yet she bears a deep hatred for the heroine (Joan Crawford) with whom the Kid has a real affair going. To settle the score, she has a duel with the heroine and gets killed. In the story, the Joan Crawford character also displays certain "phallic" aspects: She wears cowboy garb and is gun-toting, but whenever she changes into dresses she turns "feminine." In contrast, the McCambridge character is always in a gunfighter's outfit. In this simplistic stereotyping, she is beyond "redemption" by heterosexual romance, the great American institution.

The movie *The Bad Seed* (1956) presented an interesting case of the phallic woman figure. The story rejected the dominant psychodynamic view of personality and opted for Lombroso's "born criminal" thesis. In theory the script should have stood aloof from gender politics, for what is wrong with a person in hereditarian reasoning is faulty genes, not gender inversion. As it turned out, the "bad seed" in question is an eight-year old girl, born of a mother who was the abandoned child of a female serial-killer. The woman who adopted her is a sound person, so is her husband, an army colonel who has the most robust Nordic features. Among the victims of the little monster's serial killings is a boy of the same age. To explain why a male could be physically worsted by a female peer, the script grants him an unimpressive father and an alcoholic mother. The evil girl kills this boy in order to snatch an award she has lost to him at school in the shape of a military medal—a snipe at the phallic woman who covets a male insignia that is not rightfully hers.

In the last episode of *Star Trek* (June 1969), an old flame of Captain Kirk's who failed to assume a command of her own manages to switch bodies so that she would become the great captain while he is trapped inside a woman's body; once in power, she sentences him to death. Body-snatching was a hysterical Cold War idiom about the subverting of individuality. In the gendered version, the switch sounded the knell of heterosexual romance. The phallic woman, the female double of the mother-possessed man-child, was equally conducive to the death of the heterosexual partner.[10]

Sleeping with the Enemy: Male Version

It is not hard to understand the stigmatization of the career woman as the "phallic woman." World War II, by opening the job market to women on an unprecedented scale, had changed permanently the power relationship between genders, "even though its full impact was to take two decades to manifest itself" (Costello 1985, 264; Chafe 1990). What strikes us was the penchant for using sexual pathology to vent the anxiety over the destabilization of gender roles, for both the feminized male and phallicized female were symptomatic of stunted sexual growth. Even more perplexing is the fact that postwar American culture not only refrained from promoting the housewife over the career woman, but also demonized the woman who played her home-bound role only too well: The "clinging" wife/mother.

If we trace the trajectory from *Spellbound* to the matriphobia of the 1950s, it seems that the former presented the all-loving woman in the most positive light, until alarm began to surface to the effect that such "caring" readily undermined the male individuality. Already, in the same year (1945), the film *Leave Her to Heaven* depicts a clinging wife killing people around her husband in order to have him all to herself, and she nearly ruins his career as a writer. In her mother's words: "There's nothing wrong with Ellen. She just loves too much." As she repeats on the husband what she did to her deceased father, the implication is that she has a retarded personality.

Then a split of the feminine imagery occurred in Bernard Malamud's novel, *The Natural* (1952). In the story, a potential baseball superstar is gunned down by an evil woman before his debut. Having regained his potency after a diapause of fifteen years, he is led to corruption by another bad woman, but at the end he is regenerated by a reencounter with his high-school sweetheart. On the surface, the deadly threat is not from homey quarters, yet the split female imagery is too reminiscent of Virginia Heyer's discernment in Chinese stories of ambivalent male projections that split early childhood imagery of mother into the homey woman who heals and the outside woman who arouses but kills.

Clifford Odets' script of *The Country Girl* (a 1952 movie) consolidated the conflicting male yearning and blaming in one woman: A playwright who helps a former stage actor to rebuild his career blames the actor's depressive wife for turning him into a weakling, only to learn that she is actually dragged down by her husband, yet determined to stick with him through thick and thin. At the end the hero is even enamored of this woman for her wifely "virtues." In *Rhapsody* (1954), a spoiled rich girl is jilted by her fiancé, who practices very hard to become a violinist. He succeeds, while she marries a piano student who succumbs to her possessiveness and ends up with his career wrecked. Her former fiancé chides her for ruining a genius, therefore she forces herself, against all boredom, to accompany him in his piano lessons and sees to it that he achieves success and fame at the end.

The Shrike, a 1955 film based on Joseph Kramm's Pulitzer Prize-winning play (1952), used the ubiquitous image of a pair of scissors to symbolize the emasculation of man by woman. A nonachieving wife of a successful stage director is jealous of her husband's success and systematically undermines his career, finally landing him in a mental ward. As a foil, the story also sets up a sympathetic girlfriend who refuses to play mother to the hero and urges him to "direct" as a real director-in-charge should. The split of evil and good femininity is also evident in *The Man in the Net* (1959), in which a selfish wife attempts to fulfil her phallic wish by urging the husband to stop painting in order to take up a lucrative job. In contrast, a second woman assists in the hero's effort to clear himself of his wife's murder by a third party and to become a successful artist.

Evidently, the "uncaring" woman is as much censured as the clinging one. The accusation of a mother seeking her own pleasure to the detriment of the son is heard from the mouth of the character Hal in William Inge's *Picnic* (1953) and the character Perce in Arthur Miller's *The Misfits* (1957). In Daniel Keyes' *Flowers for Algernon* (1959), Charlie's mother cares only about appearance and has the "mentally challenged" hero sent away from home in his adolescence. It may be argued that both clinging and lack of caring are selfish and have nothing to do with true love. In this regard the career woman whose priority is not marriage should cause little harm—her threat is in the form of a challenge. On the other hand, the home-bound woman, phallic or weakling, is trapped in an intimate situation where she could fulfil her wishes only through or at the expense of significant others. If separation-individuation is the American norm, the "selfless" woman should pose a greater threat than the "selfish" one.

Thus it turned out that in mid-century it was not in the public domain but on the sacred ground of the great institution of romantic love that the most threatening danger was detected. And the "sleeping with the enemy" genre was first invented from the male angle, before it is used against men in our time. It accentuated a fear that nurturing was a trap, tenderness could kill, and intimacy that blurred ego boundaries signaled the death of individuality. Joseph Kramm compared the wife who consumed her husband to a shrike, "an innocent-looking bird with a sharp beak who likes to impale a victim on a thorn."[11] Three years later, this predatory imagery reappeared in Tennessee Williams' *Suddenly, Last Summer*, demonizing mothers as "creatures of the air" preying on "creatures of the sea that had had the bad luck to be hatched on land and weren't able to scramble back into the sea fast enough" (Williams 1976, 19). At around the same time, Daniel Keyes also characterized "mother" as follows: "All I could think of was a hawk ready to swoop down" (Keyes 1959, 243). Recall that the image of a predator from the air originated with Philip Wylie, who caricatured the mother thus: "She is a middle-aged puffin with an eye like a hawk that has just seen a rabbit twitch far below" (Wylie 1942, 185). This male fear of the threat from above was allayed only in Norman Bates' affection for birds because of their harmless *passivity*, which allowed him to stuff them in pursuit of his hobby of taxidermy.

The Hysteria toward Clinging

While American popular culture idealizes heterosexual romance, its reaction against "clinging" verges on the hysterical so much that the clinging party is always demonized and, as a rule, killed. *Fatal Attraction* (1987) is but one example among countless productions that demonize not just women but any one who refuses to let go and needs to be killed off. The justification to execute a "clinging" person is singularly American. Released in the same year as *Fatal Attraction*, the Hong Kong production *Yanzhi kou* (The rouge locket) channels the audience's sympathy toward the clinging woman, who dies in a double suicide, and condemns the male character who survives her murder attempt, meaning his failure at reciprocity. In the Spanish movie *Tie Me Up! Tie Me Down!* (1990), a woman is kidnapped by a secret admirer and subjected to bondage for days. Unlike the typical American ending in retributive violence and recovery of the unattached status, the Spanish heroine is moved by the offender's obsession, decides to marry him, and brings him home to meet mother.

American popular culture is also unique in featuring filicidal fantasies and the genre of killing the invading fan. The story of *The Paper Boy* (TV, 1994) combines the filicidal motif with phobia toward the fan. A boy of twelve turns serial murderer in order to attach to a woman whom he fancies as his foster mother. In sharp contrast to an East Asian story in which an orphan seeking motherly love that is as a rule found, the American heroine has the boy eliminated toward the end.

The American fear of boundary-blurring that threatens to subvert individuality is present in any quarter, yet its prototype is matriphobia. In the mid-twentieth century it was the maternal woman who, thanks to the matricidal high tide, happened to epitomize the whole threat: She was not just a menace to manhood but to everybody. In *Hot Spell* (1958), a housewife who has never grown up wastes her efforts on turning the clock back to an earlier family "unity," eventually causing her husband's death in a traffic accident as he is running away with a young mistress. At the end, she repents when, intending to cling to her grown-up son and daughter, she realizes her own immaturity. Her final awakening is compared to the lifting of the hot spell that has dominated the region throughout the duration of the plot.

In mid-century, woman seemed to be at the root of family dysfunction; she was responsible for it as in *Hot Spell*, or was charged to fix it as in *The Dark at the Top of the Stairs*, not to mention the countless stories in which she brought grief to her man. By the end of the century, in poetic justice, the target has shifted to the male head of the family, namely, in *The Ultimate Lie* (TV, 1996), *Affliction* (1998), and *American Beauty* (1999). In the last-mentioned, the husband/father character is rendered inconsequential as every member of the family is "individuating," that is, going his or her own way. Thus the mother in *Hot Spell*, blamed for causing family dysfunction four decades ago simply by wishing to maintain "family unity," seems to have her final and sweet revenge.

A tenuous, intertextual link between matricidal and fan-killing fantasies still lingers in our time. In *Misery* (1990), a disabled romance writer is held captive by his "number one fan," a deranged woman, and their conversation refers to Liberace, an entertainer whose mother always sat in the front row at his performances. One wonders whether this morbid fear of clinging and attachment could countenance "Oriental" codependency.

The Trope of the Mental Ward

A postcolonial critic of nineteenth-century Eurocentrism tabulates a dichotomy between core and periphery, pitting Western rationality, mind, adulthood, and sanity against the non-Western emotion, body, childhood, and insanity (Blaut 1993, 17). By the postwar era, this hierarchy had been flattened into a superficial respect for cultural "differences." Domestically, the cultural norm of separation-individuation was far from being relativized, for mental adulthood remained a struggle against the dark forces of "feminine" emotionality.

The Dark Female

Indeed, behind the caricature of the phallic woman and the demonization of mother in the 1950s was a more deep-seated sentiment of feminine evil.

All About Eve and *Born To Be Bad*, both of 1950, show how women worm their ways into the confidence of their targeted victims, thus usurping power, wealth, fame, and social position. Even "bad guys" would confront opponents *mano a mano*, whereas nefarious women resort to guile, feigning care, love, devotion, and compassion—precisely as a mother would do to maintain power and control.

If femininity embodied the forces of darkness or, in modern terms, irrationality incarnate, then its most fitting metaphor, nay, its logical habitat, was the lunatic asylum. In Tennessee Williams' *A Streetcar Named Desire* (1947), the heroine Blanche falsifies her disreputable past and moves in with her sister Stella and brother-in-law Stanley. While living off the couple, she feeds them lies extolling her moral superiority, which is actually a delusion of grandeur. Here Williams treats femininity as morally equivalent to a pimp. His view of masculinity, in the person of the brutish Stanley, is equally unflattering, yet (as truth should be brutal) singularly suited to pulverizing Blanche's lies. Perhaps heeding advice from the good doctor, Carl G. Jung, to the effect that the only way to argue with an illogical woman is with "a beating or rape" (Jung 1959, 15), Williams let Stanley do exactly those things to Blanche before packing her off to a mental hospital.

In mid-century, demonic imagery bolstered modern psychiatry in *Possessed* (1947), the story of a clinging woman losing her mind over unrequited love; she shoots the man and ends up confined to a mental ward. In *The Snake Pit* (1948), which portrays an all-female lunatic asylum, the serpentine allegory of primordial evil is from the Book of Genesis, yet *fin-de-siècle* mannerism prevails: Inmates virtually wiggle and collapse around male doctors who are composed, dominant, and well in control. One scene shows a huge and authoritative portrait of Sigmund Freud in a doctor's office gazing down paternally upon the psychotic heroine. Another motion picture, *The Three Faces of Eve* (1957), is about a woman patient, Eve, with multiple personalities. Her psychosis originated in a childhood trauma, trivial by comparison to today's epidemic of childhood sexual abuse: Mother drags Eve the child from her playing so she may kiss grandmother's corpse good-bye at a funeral service. The message is clear: Madness is the making of three generations of Eves, epitomizing the descent of woman. Eve's redeemers are, predictably, sagacious male doctors: Dr. Luther and Dr. Day.

If the nocturnal female symbolizes the forces of chaos, then man's triumph over nature is a morality play of masculine principle overcoming the feminine, reason vanquishing unreason. Elia Kazan's *Wild River* (1960) is about the antagonism between a young man representing the TVA and an old lady who refuses to evacuate her home, thus obstructing the building of a dam. Since the river is irregular, she lectures, it should be left that way. At the end, she is forcibly evicted and dies, and the last scene uses a circular focus to zero-in on the dam that is finally built.

Mental Ward as a Symbol of Victimization

In contrast, Joseph Kramm's *Shrike* uses the mental ward to symbolize man's victimization by woman. The year 1962 saw the publication of Ken Kesey's *One Flew Over the Cuckoo's Nest*, in which the malaise of feminization is symbolized by the lunatic asylum. In an all-male mental ward controlled by Big Nurse, her authority is challenged by McMurphy who urges fellow intimates to reassert their manhood. As a penalty, he is lobotomized, whereas a single inmate, a native American, symbol of earthy vitality, escapes. The mental ward alludes to present-day America, an increasingly effete society that castrates nonconformists. *One Flew Over the Cuckoo's Nest* reverses the metaphor of *Wild River*. The latter, in the spirit of the Enlightenment, celebrates the triumph of masculine reason over Mother Nature. Kesey, following the decadent reasoning of the *fin de siècle*, pits robust nature against effete civilization. In both cases, the feminine is the negative Other.

Behind Kesey's anxieties we once again discern the ubiquitous Harry Stack Sullivan. As the director of Clinical Research at Sheppard-Pratt Hospital from 1923 to 1930, Sullivan dismissed all nurses from a ward of all-male schizophrenic patients, because a "registered nurse may become the prototype of the high-status female in an inferior male society." He not only replaced them with male attendants, but made sure that "no woman was ever allowed on this ward" (Perry 1974, xvi–xvii).

Foucault avers that when the lunatic asylum first emerged in the Age of Reason it changed the description of the mad person to "a latecomer in the world of reason" (Foucault 1965, 249). The Dark Female, as a cultural artifact, pertained to a historical era when women were excluded from the public domain. With the changing social context of our time, the imperative of rational self-mastery required of the public domain is no longer the prerogative of one gender. In fact, with women entering the public domain and exiting conventional heterosexual relationships, the popular culture of our time has come to cast man as the "clinging" party in the person of the stalker or the ex-husband/boyfriend who runs amok. Men who continue to prove their manhood through sexual exploits or simply engage in traditional courtship are increasingly cast in the light of the "out of control" transgressor. In cinematic representations, it is the man's turn to be locked away in a mental ward—or simply blown away.[12]

Rational Control Enables Dominance,
Now Ungendered

I find the best symbolic representation of this reversal in Thomas Harris'
novel, *The Silence of the Lambs* (1989)—a movie released in 1991 that
won five major Oscar awards. The story depicts the heroine Clarice Starling
on the side of justice, not afraid to use violence in its defense, and having
the courage to face danger alone—in short, she is fully in charge of the
public domain. One male antagonist, Hannibal Lecter, nicknamed the Cannibal, is caged in a maximum-security mental institution, formerly the trope
for "out of control" feminine emotionality. The other male antagonist, the
psychotic killer Buffalo Bill (Jame Gumb), is a transvestite whose application for a sex change has been rejected three times. A schizophrenic
trapped in his autistic emotionality, this "male" predator is in a private
domain of his own. The gender-confused killer uses a moth as his *imago*,
which implies sexual metamorphosis and alludes to childhood sexual
abuses. Hannibal Lecter explains: "It's a term from the dead religion of
psychoanalysis. An imago is an image of the parent buried in the unconscious from infancy and bound with infantile affect," but "the significance
of the chrysalis is change," and the pathological killer "thinks he wants to
change [his sex]" (Harris 1989, 163).

This ostensible reversal of gender roles retains the old definition of femininity being *emotionality out of control.* Now it seems that being rational
and ultimately in control is the norm for both genders in America, and the
new contest is to see who beats the other to it. So, the gender issue after
all is about power, dominance, and ascendancy, not sexual organs. Here
Havelock Ellis' study of "sexual inversion in men" is most illuminating.
For illustration, Ellis used the genetic studies of moths. The hybridized
offspring of two different species of moths often have difficulty in maintaining gender stability—the male tends to shift in the direction of female,
and vice versa. In this phenomenon of *intersexuality*, the male case is "turning from the strong to the weak," and the female one, "turning from the
weak to the strong" (Ellis 1987, 290).

The Silence of the Moth

Yet Thomas Harris' notion of evil resulting from gender instability has
relevance only in the American context. Indeed the moth emblematic of the
killer is found anywhere from Canada to the Gulf of Mexico in the novel
(Harris 1989, 105). In the film version, however, it becomes a rare species
found exclusively in *Asia.* When the heroine finally shoots the killer, the

camera shows a close-up of a corner of his ceiling, where a Japanese-style bamboo-and-paper spiral is rotating, featuring an Oriental painting of a moth. The production, eager to depict the reversal of power relations between the genders, unintentionally offended those who were in between. Outside the 1992 Oscar award ceremony in Los Angeles, luckily the film was picketed *only* by members of the gay rights movement. Also falling within the "third sex" are the Orientals, who often receive feminized representations in American popular culture.

In 1925, Charlie Chan made his historical debut in Earl Derr Biggers' novel in the following words: "He was very fat indeed, yet he walked with the light dainty step of a woman" (Hanke 1989, xi). A Chinese film critic also observes: "[As for] the imagery of the Chinese in early American movies . . . the men are usually depicted as devoid of Hollywood's most important factor, *sexual* characteristics, or simply feminized. . . . The silver-screen Charlie Chan is humble and obsequious, highly affected, notable in his lack of machismo, displaying traits that are feminine" (Li 1997, 16, 17).

In the wake of Charlie Chan, Oriental males often appeared on the screen as gender-neutral or eunuch-like, namely, in *Red Dust* (1932) and *Reflections in a Golden Eye* (1967). A scene in the former shows Clark Gable's Asian (Chinese or Vietnamese) servant ironing woman's underwear, getting excited, gleefully holding it above his head and giggling like a clown. The second production depicts an American woman's Chinese servant as a toady, who grimaces in feigned agony while his mistress is taking a bad-tasting medication. The only convincing way to cast a modern American citizen in the same role of slavish servant is to use a homosexual character, e.g., the assistant to the Defense Secretary in *No Way Out* (1987).

Serial (1980) alluded to Chinese asexuality in an inverted manner: When suburbanite yuppie wives whose sexual lives are dysfunctional hear a black housekeeper saying that she had seven orgasms the night before, they begin to wonder whether ethnic stereotypes are true after all, only to learn that her husband is named Wong. *Dreamscape* (1984) used Asians in a dream symbolism expressing anxieties about impotence. In this science-fiction story, a short, bald husband having "bedroom problems" with his voluptuous wife seeks help from a dream-study institution. In the sleeping state he is wired to an agent, thus enabling the latter to enter into his dreamscape. The scene shows the wife's bedroom, initially with two men sitting on the bed. After the husband chases them away, several priests crawl out from under the bed like cockroaches. Detecting objects lurking behind the curtains, he proceeds to expose them, only to find two Asians. At this point, the dream-subject exclaims: "Even you!" In the woman director Lizzie Borden's *Working Girls* (1986), a docudrama about one day in a New York brothel, a Chinese customer is depicted as lazy and passive. *Demolition*

Man (1993) is a futuristic yarn about the U.S. West Coast becoming like Japan, with a low crime rate and people overly courteous (using the sinister Tokyo Rose–style "Greetings and salutations") and men wearing kimonos fainting at the sight of violence—this effete civilization is "redeemed" by resurrecting a criminal and a cop capable of twentieth-century style violence.

Chinese males that have been depicted in a more positive light, namely Bruce Lee and Keith Carradine's portrayal in *Kung Fu*, remain nonsensual if not outright desexualized. In *The Replacement Killers* (1998) and *Romeo Must Die* (2000), Chow Yun Fat and Li Jet's lack of sexual chemistry with their respective leading ladies actually causes something that rarely happens in an American plot: The hero and the heroine become good friends.

The logic of sexual inversion and the fuss over inadequate gender artic-ulation through explicit sex make sense only when the genders are polarized in every respect: temperament, character, psyche, and above all, in their psychical contents attuned to rival social domains. The sharp demarcation between the "masculine" public domain and the "feminine" private domain is less applicable to Chinese culture if we admit Frederic Jameson's critique of Western bifurcation of the instinctual and the public domains. This bi-furcation is culture-bound, for he discerns the fusion of the two in Chinese texts, even though the libidinal contents therein revealed pertain to the oral zone instead of genital sexuality (Jameson 1986). By implication, the intru-sion of oral libido into the rational public domain is, for the Chinese, not necessarily disruptive.

Chinese as Marginal Text

From Pathology to Paragon

When RCC's Ruth Bunzel expressed her envy that the Chinese attached "no shame" to "pre-genital sexuality in children," she was on the same track as Bingham Dai, the Chinese student of Harry Stack Sullivan and Edward Sapir. Dai discerned—in Freudian terms—in Chinese pathology rampant "pregenital" sexual license, the absence of a latency period, and the non-repression of infantile incestuous fantasies (Dai 1944; 1957). Within the Freudian framework, the turning from Freud's focus on neurosis to the study of psychosis had begun in earnest under Sullivan. Dai's innovation was to show that this vertical shift from the "genital" to the "pregenital" in the Freudian entelechy can also occur in a horizontal, or cross-cultural, manner. Today Dai is totally forgotten even by scholars of Chinese Freudianism.[13] He was the first to apply the "pregenital" thesis to the Chinese and can serve as a foil to similar American attempts to question genital primacy.

In 1946, Weston La Barre, Bingham Dai's colleague at Duke University, constructed a full-fledged East-West culturology out of Dai's writings. He also commented, with envy and relish, the oral indulgence, the easy-going toilet training, and the low degree of anxiety among the Chinese. Although he knew nothing about Chinese sexuality, he divined that the Chinese had "none of the puritanism and the anti-sexual tradition of the Platonist and Christian West" (La Barre 1946, 375–379).[14] La Barre later wrote an article publicizing the RCC projects in *The Scientific Monthly* (La Barre 1948).

Dai and La Barre presaged the advocacy of "polymorphous perversity" by Herbert Marcuse (Marcuse 1955) and Norman Brown (Brown 1966) in the "sexual revolution" of the 1960s. Intending to burst the confines of genital sexuality, these two prophets of sexual liberation declared the whole body to be an erogenous zone, just like that of the infant at the mother's bosom. By extension, this love's body would usher in the eroticization of society as a whole, a utopia that was just around the corner. If Marcuse and Brown sought to liberate repressed eros from the regimen of capitalism, Julia Kristeva saw an alternative in Maoist China. She used the Chinese to castigate the monotheistic West:

> No other civilization . . . seems to have made the principle of sexual difference so crystal clear: between the two sexes there is a cleavage, an abyss. . . . For without this gap between the sexes, without this localization of the polymorphic, orgasmic body . . . in the other sex, it would have been impossible, in the symbolic sphere, to isolate the principle of the One Law. (Kristeva 1977, 19)

In her revolt against Western monotheism in religion, heterosexual dogma in gender relations, and genital primacy in sex, Kristeva looked upon China as an alternative. Arguing in a Marxian vein, Kristeva saw China's transition from a matrilinear society to the patriarchal "feudal order" as less complete than in the West, for it retained "the forms of the previous system." The Chinese language also seemed to have retained the "psycho-corporeal imprint of the mother's body," and she wondered whether it manifested an "archaic" psychic stratum lost in the more abstract Western syntaxes (Kristeva 1977, 46, 55–56). It went a long way to explain the centrality of mother in the Chinese family and the power of women under Maoist socialism.

The Lost Horizon

When Kristeva pondered the "pre-Oedipal, pre-syntactic, pre-symbolic" nature of the Chinese language, she was also in a Lacanian mood. For radical and amateur Lacanians, it is the paternal symbolic order that enforces the artificial heterosexual norm. They see a way of resistance in retracing the *jouissance* of the mirror stage when the child is at one with mother.

The clinical Lacanians are less optimistic, for Lacan's theory discerns bereavement even in the mirror stage, when infant and mother are allegedly one. For Lacan, "the original satisfaction in which the child was filled with *jouissance*" was a condition "he had neither asked for nor expected." The uniqueness of this *jouissance* is that "it is *not* mediated by a demand." Once a demand mediates the second experience of satisfaction, the child is confronted with "the register of loss" (Dor 1998, 191–192). Yet the Lacanian *jouissance* (which includes both pain and pleasure), as an imposition one "neither asks for nor expects," can only be "rape" in the rationalistic-individualistic-legalistic adult. It implies a state of passivity bordering on the total disorganization of self, pertaining to the realm of emotions where rational self-possession is in abeyance, as evident in the common etymological root of *pathology*, *pathetic*, and the *pathic*, the last-mentioned being the passive party in sex, notably a catamite.

Even Norman Brown, who went further than Marcuse in advocating the total breakdown of all sexual organization of the body, sees the danger in such a state: "the infant's objective dependence on . . . maternal care promotes a dependent attitude toward reality and inculcates a passive (dependent) need to be loved, which colors all subsequent interpersonal relationships. This psychological vulnerability is subsequently exploited to extract submission to social authority and to the reality-principle in general" (Brown 1985, 25). Brown cannot escape the paranoid "adult" mindset, and he would certainly show distaste for a situation like Maoist China where the entire populace was urged to venerate the Communist Party as mother.

For Lacan, the primordial self is already the product of the Other, first one's specular image and then the omnipotent mother. Although the specular image helps to form the ego, it also highlights the infant's lack of bodily coordination, and in this sense threatens the subject with fragmentation. The child then goes on to identify with the mother's unconsummated (and unfulfillable) desire and always feels a lack. "The mirror stage shows that the ego is the product of misunderstanding (*méconnaissance*) and the site where the subject becomes alienated from himself" (Evans 1997, 116). Unlike Brown and Marcuse who yearned for a unsullied *natural* state, Lacan saw the very unconscious itself already structured like a language. His line of thinking resonates with postmodernism, which presides over the symbolic milieu's triumph over the natural and sees the self as always a decentered self. It also suits the spirit of the 1990s, which tends to see the damaged syndrome as the human condition and selfhood as victimhood.

From Redoubt to Receptacle

This is not the place to inquire whether the "sexual revolution" has achieved the eroticization of American society or whether "boundaries" have become more inflexible, turning a sexual encounter of any sort into a mine field, exposing an ever greater part of privacy to policing by the state. We are more concerned with the part the Chinese "marginal text" plays in the subverting of the Western heterosexual norm. This subversion is an inversion: What was formerly adjudicated as a lower stage in the evolutionary, developmental, or psychodynamic sense is now declared equal if not superior. This inversion in fact reaffirms the dominant discourse in an oblique manner. Yet a degree of complicity is inevitable when people are used to certain deep-seated modes of discussing sexuality and gender. In Foucault's observation, "discourse can be both an instrument and an effect of power, but also a hindrance, a stumbling block, a point of resistance and a starting point for an opposing strategy" (Foucault 1990, 101). This observation is also applicable to the alliance between "Chinese cognition" and feminine epistemology.

In mid-century, Elizabeth Hellersberg did a study of Chinese apperception for the RCC China Project. She praised the Chinese flair for the "total vision," thanks to tactile restrictions in childhood, which reduces them to watching only. The Chinese compensate for this deprivation "in the quiet contemplation in front of the large world," which gives them the feeling of security in space. The drawings of Chinese test subjects often depict a convergence toward the middle or "the viscera," unlike the Western perspective which "draws the spectator forcibly far beyond himself." For Hellersberg, the spatial tension in Western perspective is indicative of "the suppression of visceral needs and instincts" (Hellersberg 1949, 14–16, 19; n.d., 7, 9–10). The implication is that the Chinese are more in harmony with nature. Although Hellersberg's tone was sympathetic, tactile deprivation is associated in the West with passivity and deficiency in instrumental rationality. This thesis also had Cold War undertones, for tactile deprivation did not seem to be peculiar to the Chinese. RCC member Geoffrey Gorer believed that "the restriction of the other parts of its body forced the Russian child to depend upon vision for his main contact with the world" (Harris 1968, 445).

Cold War sentiments were soon outgrown, and the same thesis was free to serve other purposes or stand on its own. In the field of Chinese literary criticism, Andrew Plaks arrived at the same thesis of "total vision." He granted equal status to what he called the "Chinese narrative" even though, contrary to the linear Western plot, it eschews both climax and closure; instead, it ramifies in many directions, each overlapping with the others in a web of interconnectedness (Plaks 1977).

In 1970, Germaine Greer appealed to Daoist wisdom in questioning the philosophy of dominance: "Women, because they are passive and condemned to observe and react rather than initiate, are more aware of complexity. Men have been forced to suppress their receptivity, in the interest of domination. One of the possible advantages of infantilization of women is that they might after all become, in the words of Lao-Tse [Laozi], 'a channel drawing all the world toward it' " (Greer 1970, 109). Although Greer was still bitter about "passivity" and called *yin* a "condemned" state that was at odds with the complementarity of *yin* and *yang* in Chinese cosmology, she sought an alliance between western feminism and Chinese philosophy.

The Blurring of Rational Ego Boundaries

In 1976, Dorothy Dinnerstein pursued a line of thought similar to Hellersberg's. The latter had observed that Western perspective "draws the spectator forcibly far beyond himself," leading to "the suppression of visceral needs and instincts"—it implied a critique of Western instrumental mentality. Dinnerstein, in the context of reversing the Freudian thesis of "penis envy," saw in the girl who stepped into her mother's role the more accomplished gender, whereas the boy struggling to pull away as the traumatized one. She quotes Simone de Beauvoir: "[F]rom the fact that she [woman] is passive, she experiences more passionately, more movingly, the reality in which she is submerged than does the individual absorbed in an ambition or a profession." Woman, Dinnerstein continues, is able to feel the emotional richness of life because her "sameness of gender" with "the earlier nurturing adult" enables her "to embody this intuition," whereas man's difference prepares him "for the historic undertaking to whose pathology the intuition points" (Dinnerstein 1977, 222, 225).

The fragility of the male gender role was reiterated by Nancy Chodorow in 1978: The daughter does not alienate herself from her original identification with mother, hence the bond between them remains intimate, whereas the son, forced by patriarchy to turn to father, is caught in abstract cultural roles and loses touch with the richness of emotional life. Unlike the boy's "active attachment" to mother that is required to establish his "masculine oppositeness to her," girl's attachment sustains the ambivalence of "boundary confusion." Yet it is exactly "from the retention of preoedipal attachments to their mother, growing girls come to define and experience themselves as continuous with others" (Chodorow 1978, 97, 169).

In 1981, Mary O'Brien contrasted the precarious sense of man-made history to women's reproduction that mediates between nature and history, thus constituting real continuity. In sexual intercourse, the male leaves behind his sperm in the female body and turns "abstract," he polarizes subject and object, a gap he closes through domination (O'Brien, 1981). As a former midwife from working-class Liverpool, England, and a Marxist, O'Brien presents a view different from main-current feminism, which prefers individuation to the enthralment with nature in the name of "continuity." Her characterization actually better suits the Chinese concept of continuing the ancestral line and immortality through procreation.

Care versus Instrumental Rationality

These thinkers, in promoting female naturalness over against male artifice, cleared the way for a full-fledged feminine epistemology, as in Sara Ruddick's "maternal thinking" (Ruddick 1980), and Carol Gilligan's *In A Different Voice* (1982). They elaborated on womanly thinking, based on "love" or "caring," wherein intellect was less divorced from feeling, more attuned to open and complex situations, unlike the abstraction and linearity of masculine logic. Gilligan targeted Lawrence Kohlberg's stages of moral development for criticism, for the schema is not only linear, it places woman on a lower stage for not using abstract principles in their reasoning. Coincidentally, in the 1970s, Alfred Bloom, having administered the Kohlbergian test to Hong Kong Chinese, also concluded that the Chinese surrendered self-decision and "social-principledness" for the sake of social harmony (Bloom 1977). In its critique of abstract principles, Gilligan's feminine cognition sees real human beings in concrete situations and ponders on all the possible consequences of action, thus presenting an alternative "ethic of care" (Gilligan 1982, 30).

Care has been given a status inferior to justice in the Western philosophical tradition. Justice, being more rational, metes out to different parties what each deserves, thus allowing society to work smoothly like a machine, whereas care is emotionally motivated and suited only to personal relationships. Martin Heidegger attempts to turn the tables by elevating "care" above means-end calculation, which, according to him, separates beings from their primordial matrix. To care for an individual being is to recognize him or her as a part of the whole in a state of harmony. "Heidegger emphasized the practical dimension of human existence by defining the very being of *Dasein* as 'care.' To be human means to be concerned about things and to be solicitous toward other people" (Zimmerman 1996, 247). This alternative epistemology is not particularly gendered, but is critical of Western instrumental rationality in general. As a champion of this suppressed alternative, Gilligan is going against the grain, for matricidal America has a most jaundiced view of "care" as either an attempt at controlling, or dependency on the good will of, others.*

Some Consolations

Nonetheless, thanks to dissident voices in the West, the Chinese perspective is finally given some recognition. This "Chinese" perspective, needless to say, is Western. Yet we cannot charge it with distortion, for this would imply that existing somewhere is *the* original Chinese perspective, which is retrievable through another representation. This position is oxymoronic: A representation that is not a copy but the thing itself. A Lacanian schema might get us out of the logjam. It distinguishes between "the little other" and "the big Other." The little other is that part of the other that we address in our speech; it then becomes part of self. In this sense, "speech always subjectively includes its own reply." The big Other is the radical alterity—it is beyond language, ineffable, not subjected to appropriation. Yet its existence is assumed, for once the big Other is no longer present, the language used by self becomes hallucinatory or psychotic.

Western dissidents use the Chinese "marginal text" to help to delineate the boundaries of their suppressed identities, to set themselves apart from the dominant heterosexual norm. It serves a certain purpose in a "system of difference" that polarizes genders. The same text, situated in another "system of difference," namely cross-cultural studies, would highlight those Chinese traits most striking to the Western eyes: The Chinese realize their human essence by emotional investments in other people rather than through strengthening ego-boundaries; the homogenization of male and female by the singular obsession with progeny; a private domain less invaded by rationalistic-legalistic precepts, a more emotive public domain and a mode of transaction that allows *guanxi* (interpersonal ties) to adulterate the rational principle of impersonality.

---

*The preview of the fan-killing film *Single White Female* (1992) runs: "Someone who cares, someone who shares, someone who borrows, someone who steals, someone who would like to kill to become her!" The logic deducting killing from caring is truly astounding.

Notes

1. She apparently still subscribed to the "nature versus civilization" idea, an intellectual cliché popular since the nineteenth century. In this formula, "instinct" represents nature, and civilization symbolizes artifice and decadence.

2. Bunzel points out that the findings of social workers in Chinatown remotely echo the study of psychoses in China by Bingham Dai (Dai 1941).

3. An excerpt from the minutes of a group meeting reveals: "Ruth Bunzel: That is the word that got all the Chinese in our group, and the Chinese informants, most angry, talking about passivity" (Minutes 1951b, 7).

4. In the late Qing period, rumors abounded about Western missionaries using children's bodily organs to manufacture medicine. Maoist propaganda also accused U.S. imperialism and Soviet "social imperialism" of attempting to swallow China like a piece of pork.

5. In kinky sex, "the attraction for men and for women differ, as might be expected, since the men are drawn to submission, and the women to dominance" (Scott 1992, 7).

6. The summary is based on Arthur Miller's *All My Sons* (1948) and *Death of A Salesman* (1949), John Steinbeck's *East of Eden* (1952), James Clavell's *Taipan* (1966), and movies like *Elephant Walk* (1954), *Attack!* (1956), *12 Angry Men* (1957), *The Big Country* (1958), *The Trap* (1959), the *Star Wars* series (1977, 1980, 1983, 1999), *Apocalypse Now* (1979), *Paris, Texas* (1984), *The Flamingo Kid* (1984), *Brotherhood of the Rose* (TV, 1989), *Flashback* (1990), *Point Break* (1991), *Backdraft* (1991), *Hackers* (1995), *Assassins* (1995), *Mission: Impossible* (1996) *Lone Star* (1996), and *The Truman Show* (1998). In three recent productions, *Star Trek: Generations* (1994), *The Mask of Zorro* (1998), and *Man in the Iron Mask* (1998), the "father" character has to die a heroic death to yield the stage to his younger-generation double.

7. In *Hard, Fast, and Beautiful* (1951), a mother who controls the career of her tennis-champion daughter in the name of "caring," is actually self-serving and parasitic. The unhappy daughter finally breaks free of mother's stranglehold and proceeds to heterosexual marriage. In *Four Girls in Town* (1956), a woman pushed by her "phallic" mother to have an acting career at the expense of her marital aspiration is rescued by her boyfriend. The latter confronts the future mother-in-law: "In your native Minnesota there are a thousand lakes, why don't you pick one of them and jump into it!" In *A Summer Place* (1959), a frigid and hysterical mother humiliates her daughter—by summoning a physician to confirm her virginity—after she has spent an innocent night outside with a boy due to unforeseeable conditions. In *Gypsy* (1962), the mother pushes the daughter into the career of a striptease performer and seeks to control her after she became a star. In Tennessee Williams' *This Property is Condemned* (1966), a greedy mother peddles her daughter to a man of means and causes her to die in sorrow.

8. For cinematic representation of incestuous rape, *Peyton Place* (1957), about rape by the stepfather, was an isolated case. The appearance of *Chinatown* (1974), the story of father raping, impregnating, and killing the daughter at the end, in the same year as the Child Abuse Prevention and Treatment Act, was also coincidental. For a new narrative to emerge, the old Freudian one of a daughter fantasizing about father giving her a penis needed to be discredited, and this was duly done by early 1980s from within the Freudian community (Masson 1984). Cinematic representation managed to pick up by the mid-1980s, namely in *Something About Amelia* (TV, 1984), which, far from demonizing the father, depicts him as having curable emotional prob-

lems. In the less realistic *The Calendar Girl Murders* (TV, 1984), the female serial killer still has a crush on father, whereas *Black Widow* (1986) hinted at the father complex of both the serial murderer of old and wealthy husbands and her investigator but left its nature ambiguous. Sexual abuse (but still by a step-father) achieved frank representation in *Nuts* (1987), as the formative experience of a hooker. The classic statement was perhaps the TV series, *Twin Peaks* (1990–1991), in which the bedeviled father rapes and kills the daughter. The incest issue was politicized in *Stop At Nothing* (TV, 1990) and *Liar! Liar!* (Canadian TV, 1993) and exploited in *Scissors* (1991) and *Benefit of the Doubt* (1992). Meanwhile, the saga of Eileen Franklin taking her father to court was televised in 1992 as *Fatal Memories*; the real crimes of a North Carolina housewife who poisoned her father, husband, boyfriend, and second husband were televised as *Black Widow Murders: The Blanche Taylor Moore Story* (1993). Movie stories carrying an "incestuous rape" subplot includes: *Final Analysis* (1992), *Forrest Gump* (1994), *Dolores Claiborne* (1995), *U-Turn* (1997), and *The Cider House Rules* (1999).

9. For fan-killing, see later in the text. As for the filicidal or "bad seed" genre, with no reigning authority to thrash, this genre has no resort but to fall back upon the academic antithesis to the bad mother theory: The "bad child theory"—for this theory, see Fine (1979, 158). This genre peaked in the 1970s after the release of *Rosemary's Baby* (1968), when the first postwar generation (the baby-boomers) faced the prospect of becoming parents themselves, which threatened their immortality as the Eternal Rebel. The decade produced *The Exorcist* (1973), *The Omen* (1976), *Demon Seed* (1977), and *Damien—Omen II* (1978), among others. This genre has also continued to the present, and among the better-known is *The Good Son* (1993).

10. At a time when heterosexuality was not yet problematized, it was the individual who did not live up to the norm who became problematic. In Hitchcock's *Marnie* (1964), a woman who is phobic about sex with a man due to a childhood trauma is "rescued" by the loving husband who confronts her with her suppressed memory.

11. This line is not in the original play, but in the film version, which spells it out for the unknowing audience.

12. Cf. *Lipstick* (1976), *Someone's Watching Me* (1978), *Victim* (TV, 1982), *Seduction* (1982), *Extremities* (1986), *Lady Beware* (1987), *Lower Level* (1990), *Invasion of Privacy* (1992), *Nightmare in the Daylight* (TV, 1992), *Kiss of a Killer* (TV, 1993), *A Kiss Goodnight* (1994), *It Was Him or Us* (TV, 1995), *Eye of the Stalker* (TV, 1995), *Stalked* (1995), *The Abduction* (1996), *Closer and Closer* (TV, 1996). In *Murder: By Reason of Insanity* (TV, 1985), *Dead by Sunset* (TV, 1995), and *Dancing in the Dark* (1995), all fact-based, it is the male—estranged husband or rapist father-in-law—who is, or should have been, locked away. Some of these stories overlap with the "sleeping with the enemy" genre.

13. It is a pity that this earliest Chinese lay analyst is left out of Zhang Jingyuan's study of Chinese Freudianism. She observes that Chinese psychologists trained in the United States were inimical toward Freud because "the American academic psychological community was enamored of behaviorism" in the interwar years. While the first half of this statement is fairly accurate, the second half ignores the all-important Harry Stack Sullivan. As an example of the returned students' hostility toward Freud and his ilk, she refers to the University of California (Berkeley)-trained Guo Renyuan's critique of the instinct theory, including Freud's notion of the unconscious (Zhang 1992, 25–26). She is oblivious to coeval Freudian revisionism in America, for Sullivan also shifted his emphasis from instinct to interpersonal relationships, notably the mother-son nexus.

14. Dai said he was not responsible for his colleague's unrestrained speculations—private correspondence from Dai, February 8, 1990.

Epilogue: Toward a Postnational Age?

My study begins with the imagining of modern nationhood and concludes with the invention of postmodern individuality. The remaining task is to determine whether this historical trajectory is Chinese, Western, or global. Today, the imagining of both nation and individual are subsumed under the postmodern politics of self-fashioned identities. On the collective level, it enables non-Western nations to stage a "postcolonial" critique of the grand narrative of unilinear progress that privileges Eurocentrism. On the personal level, it liberates the individual from established social and sexual norms that are familistic, patriarchal, procreationist, and heterosexual. Postmodernism seems to be the meta-grammar for an emerging global culture based on diversity and equity. Few have noted the incompatibility of the politics of nationality with the politics of individuation.

The Options We Have

Nation-building has been high on the world-historical agenda of the past two centuries. In our time, the most intense phase of nationalism, beginning in the nineteenth century, is over (Gellner 1983, 121).[1] Most of today's theorists on nation are so taken with the post–Cold War resurgence of nationalism that they are oblivious to the other megatrend: the denationalization and privatization of the individual symptomatic of all developed societies. Both trends have particular cultural roots—the nation-state from modern Western Europe and the psychologized, sexualized, and gendered individual from contemporary America—yet both have managed to become universal. Nationality and individuation are two different orders of things.

One seeks to embed the individual in an imagined community; the other lets the individual imagine that he or she can be free of any ties and conventions.

In the wake of Edward Said, an Islamic "postcolonial" critic, Ziauddin Sardar, tries to discredit the postmodern politics of choice from within. He charges that: "Postmodernists regularly generalise a purely western trend (and even here there are doubts) and present it in global terms." It is the postmodern notion of the "social construction of reality" that licenses its allegation of the breakdown of belief systems to make way for a shapeless global culture (Sardar 1998, 21, 23). He is pleased that the sense of community is largely intact in the rest of the world. The trouble is that the so-called communal integrity can be a "social construction" as well, and his picture of the communalized individual harbors the danger of sliding from description to prescription and eventually to proscription.

"Three in the Morning, Four in the Evening"

As the case of our Islamic critic testifies, today, even in resisting Western hegemony, the non-West has to adhere to the dominant doctrinal protocols if it is to stage any resistance at all. Resistance by way of complicity is most typical of the "postcolonial" mindset (Liu 1995, 256). Third World critics are led to believe that the politics of "anthropological space" has placed the non-West on a par with the West. This spatial politics, they are told, is "postcolonial," for it deconstructs the linear temporality of the modernization paradigm, which privileges the West. This switch from time to space reminds us of a parable by the Chinese sage Zhuangzi: A group of monkeys are given three nuts each in the morning and four in the evening, when they complain about the smaller morning allowance, their master simply switches the two portions and the monkeys are placated. Indeed, in the postmodernist politics of space, "all spaces are equal, but some are more equal than others."

Like it or not, the non-West is trailing the Western trajectory whether it imagines itself in the act of catching up or in the act of resisting. It is no consolation to argue that this trajectory, though unilinear, does not necessarily stand for "progress"—even though this judgment is truer to the spirit of Foucault, who sees the displacement of one discourse by another as a matter of changing power relations. Setting all such misgivings aside, to follow the aforementioned trajectory is a "must," if one is to survive and not to be left out by global trends. The only remaining concern, if one may choose to believe, is the right timing.

Given that a few Chinese intellectuals have already "advanced" into postmodernity, the majority today are still obsessed with "modernizing" their country. They insist on the universal validity of the European Enlightenment, which the First World postmodernists have managed to localize as a Eurocentric, rationalist, masculine, domination-driven, and "modern" phenomenon. Today, at the center, the negation of the Enlightenment is couched in terms of a countermovement, which shifts the emphasis from a compartmentalized instrumental reason to the whole body with polymorphous desires, i.e., in the direction of the emotive and the feminine. This cognitive constellation is alleged to be in greater harmony with human interconnectedness than is masculine domination, thus allowing more diversity. It really does not matter whether this gender binarism is originally rooted in the Platonic and Christian split of mind and body, making very little sense outside of that tradition, for both gendered versions of the Enlightenment have become global trends.

A Hegemony That Compels Diversity

In challenging the rationalist canon, the postmodern critique of the Enlightenment offers alternatives and champions diversity. By claiming to be a cognitive constellation superior to, thus superseding, the Enlightenment and like the latter applicable worldwide, it cannot help vindicating the grand narrative of unilinear progress as inescapable. If the new cognitive constellation becomes intolerant of other disagreeable views and does not allow them to see the daylight, then we have a new power establishment becoming monolithic in its own turn. One may even argue that the postmodern politics of diversity has turned into a canon, making diversity compulsory, provided that "diversity" is packaged in the preapproved discursive format.

Thus, "modernity or postmodernity?" becomes a matter of which regime one favors. To the consternation of those non-Western intellectuals still concerned with "modernizing" their country, the trendy "postmodern" identity politics has enabled their "antimodern" opponents to bracket the issue of backwardness in the name of "postcolonial" identity politics. It is an application of the American therapeutic wisdom "you are great the way you are" on an international scale.

Under this new regime, the legitimate claimant of an identity is theoretically conceded the sole right to self-representation. Who would bother to make such a claim but a reflective intellectual stratum, and even in those quarters, this book has shown that, for a century, the claim could hardly be made without the help of theories imported from the West. Today, what matters are the unreflective consumers of mass culture. The question truly remains: Who in reality is holding the global palette to depict national diversity? With regard to our subject—national character—the stereotyping of one another by nations is in large part mediated by Hollywood. The world's perceptions of Germans and Russians have been for a long time the products of American World War II and Cold War movies.[2] In Roman Polanski's *Rosemary's Baby* (1968), the sole Japanese member of a New York satanic cult is the one who shows off his camera by clicking away at the newborn demon child. In the wake of the Japan Miracle, a Third World national who had never met a Japanese in person, or who had seen Japanese tourists with cameras of the latest design hanging from their necks but failed to register the fact as their identity tag, was likely to pick up the clue from American cinematography.

According to Alvin Toffler, in our time, power derived from knowledge and information is of the highest grade compared to the low-grade power of violence and the medium-grade power of wealth (Toffler 1991, 15–16). This upgraded hegemony is implemented through today's high-tech mass media, making the postmodern the era of symbolic domination *par excellence*. Today, not only non–American cultural productions are marginalized in their home countries, this condition applies even to Europe. The French may be proud of their culture but, thanks to the global domination of Americanism, today's French children and crime suspects appear to be more conversant with the American judiciary system than their own.[3] American representations—of themselves and others—are truly omnipresent. Yet the fact remains that peoples in the world would not have the chance to be constantly exposed to the imagery of Others and become more receptive to their strangeness at all but for the American mass media.

The Postnational Condition and the Ahistorical Individual

The "postcolonial" hullabaloo notwithstanding, alongside the liberation of the individual, today's "nationalism" is looked upon as a throwback in more sophisticated circles. In this respect, America is again setting the trend for the whole world in postnational individuation. There, the increasingly private individual is the main catalyst of denationalization. If, according to Benedict Anderson, print as the early modern form of mass communication was crucial to nation-building, then the American postliterate mass media play a comparable role in the cult of the private person.

As befitting the "postcolonial" condition, Americanism's global appeal is now no longer presented as an imperative to "modernize," but an endorsement of similar trends in the cultural peripheries. If we mean by "denationalization" the waning of national consciousness under ultramodern conditions, then America is not shaping other societies, merely lending prestige and authority to the trend. In fact, Hong Kong, due to its peculiar historical conditions, has even predated America in denationalization, although, coming from a colonial background, it has little appeal as a model. Having endured one-and-a-half centuries of colonial rule, Hong Kong is a good example of a modernized people without national consciousness. The Hong Kong Chinese certainly have not turned British, but since reunification there has been an awkward gap between them and the "national" Chinese of the Mainland. Unformatted by the Marxist "national" form, Hong Kong's Chinese culture is an amalgam of local traditions and Westernism. By "national" form I mean the national scaffold imposed on prenational traditions by the historical task of nation-building. In that process, a unitary national consciousness was forged, often by the modern state posing as the historical nation.

Postnational, Posttraumatic, and Postliterate

A national heritage thus composed is made up of something old, something new, and something borrowed. To fashion a "nation" out of a defunct ecumenical empire and the myriad fragmentary local traditions embedded in it, early Chinese nationalists had to cast it in the mold of the Western nation-state. As shown in chapter 1, they reshuffled classical tradition and imperial history to select elements to be pieced together as a "national" genealogy— in short, to refit the old into the new and foreign "national" mode. In the staging of their own revolution they also tried out English, French, and American scripts. So schoolchildren in the Republican era not only learned about Sun Zhongshan, Huang Xing, and the Wuchang Uprising, but also acquired a smattering of modern English, American, and French history. China's nation-building also consulted such models as the Italian *Risorgimento* and the unification of Germany, with cross-references to Gandhi and Kemal Ataturk. On top of these, schoolchildren in Communist China were inculcated with the legend of its founders and martyrs, but since the script was Russian this time, they also became conversant with Lenin and Stalin, as well as the world communist movement. (Seen in this light, obliviousness to one's own national heritage does not make one a cosmopolitan, but more likely a "world-class" cultural illiterate.)

Since the nation-building period was also traumatic, the common national narrative it forged inevitably also includes something blue. In the early postwar era, the humiliation of the Opium War and the epic of resisting Japanese invasion were still deeply etched into every Chinese schoolchild's consciousness. Now these "national calamities" (*guonan*) have faded, and among those Chinese free from the national narrative, these events are as good as foreign. As for Americans, their last *guonan* was ancient, at the time of the Civil War, if not earlier. A recent trauma was the Vietnam War, but it in no way approached the magnitude of China's war with Japan, and it is doubtful whether even half of the nation cared to know the exact location of Vietnam even during the thick of the war.

Since advanced societies have left the posttraumatic phase of nation-building far behind, their citizens could thrive under the nation's aegis without being overly obsessed with it. Their interests are denationalized, mostly turning private and occasionally cosmopolitan, with the least attention paid to "nation," which is taken for granted. Liberation from the national matrix can mean many things. For one thing, advanced societies have become immune to the kind of nationalist fanaticism characteristic of most of today's Balkan countries, which bear a retrograde outlook. The fading of the "national" mainframe also releases a multiplicity of private expressions, hence the democratization of culture. Yet for the majority of people, the nemesis is the liberation from national history and national geography. These mainframes are not customized to format the postnational private self and thus become irrelevant.

An American talk-show host, Jay Leno, once interviewed pedestrians in the street, all college-age youths looking smart and well adjusted. When asked about America's role in World War I, one young person answered that "since it happened in the nineteenth century, it was a long time ago." A man who was asked to identify Benedict Arnold answered with another question: "Isn't it a type of omelette?" Leno then turned to another passerby for the origin of the Statue of Liberty. After searching her brain, she replied that it was a gift from George Washington to the American people and when pressed further came up with the answer: "We the people gave him the cement and he built it himself." In other words, the Statue of Liberty is in danger of becoming the Egyptian Sphinx—an enigma whose origin is a matter of educated or not-so-educated guesses.

Postnational society tends to become postliterate. In the United States, exposure to immigrants from every part of the world does not appear to enhance the general interest in world knowledge. The crux of the matter lies in ignorance of one's own national habitat. It is futile to ask someone to identity France or Russia, let alone China, if that person is indifferent to the location of the fifty states and creatively relocates Hawaii in the Gulf of Mexico. Curiously, it is often foreign students, already equipped with a geographic sensitivity through knowledge of their own countries and continents, who are more conversant with American geography.

In the nineteenth century, when print culture dominated and the modern mass media were not yet born, it was easier to imagine an American "national" culture. Works that informed a common national heritage were few, among them the lives of the founding fathers (Hirsch 1988, 89–90). In fact, the nineteenth-century American veneration of the founders is reminiscent of the Republican or Communist Chinese cult of revolutionary leaders and martyrs. Today, it is not only in American popular culture that mobsters and drug-dealers appear more frequently as role models than do national heroes. The party-controlled film studios and television stations in Guomindang Taiwan have from the start refrained from dramatizing Sun Zhongshan and the Republican Revolution, simply because they do not sell.

Another "End of History" Scenario?

The nation's autobiography produced by the classical period of nationalism, the nineteenth and most of the twentieth centuries, is now consigned to oblivion. It is simply snowed under by the contemporary mass media, which are mammoth shopping malls of images for consumers. Unlike the nation-building narratives, which coincided with the reigns of Romanticism and Realism, the postmodern cultural product is a collage of dismembered images from the cultures of all ages and places, or in a postmodernist critic's words, a ceaseless reshuffling of "the fragments of pre-existing texts" (Jameson 1991, 96).

Take *Star Wars: The Phantom Menace* (released in 1999) for instance: the Jedi knights are modelled after the samurai; the queen wears a harlequinade facial makeup with the attire of a Mongolian princess but resides in a palace of neo-Classical style surrounded by Renaissance courtiers; the arch-villain has a Peking opera mask that carries the horns of a Japanese *oni* (demon)—framing all these fragments is the universalism of contemporary high-tech in its futurist garb. As an ahistorical hybrid, the postmodern cultural product frees the consumer from national narratives and historicity *per se*. In postmodernity, when historical heritages are flattened out into ethnic theme parks, space does triumph over time and the individual is free or trapped (depending on your viewpoint) in the eternal present.[4]

Yet postnational society does not shed its nationhood and certainly not its culture. Instead, "national culture" is now typified in the private lives of citizens carrying local color. If the rest of the world, in various degree of denationalization, is to follow the American model, "culture" might become simply a highly individualized "way of life." Chinese societies have shown an inkling of travelling along the same path. At this point, though, the increasingly private lives of their citizens still fall short of the "American way of life." Although the traditional family based on continuing the ancestral line and practicing filial piety is on the wane, the impulse for the individual to "exit" from others in order to "exist"—to be in the "wilderness" alone, so to speak—is rather weak if not totally alien. In short, Chinese people are late in arriving at the compulsory diversity ordained by the postmodern canon. Although there are signs of their also veering toward the age of national obliviousness, there is no studied avoidance of a common cultural language (or what is left of it) to evade communication lest one's private and separate reality would be encroached upon or, worse, subverted by other people. Cultural literacy is not simply an aptitude; it is an affective-communicative milieu as well. It can hardly be sustained if people's dread of having something in common with one another becomes so hysterical that the threat to self is not just the engulfing nation, but the claustrophobic nuclear family or any minimalist "we" group of two as well.

If one chooses to promote American-style separation-individuation as the new universalism, certain opposing arguments need to be countered. People may contend that in the manufacturing of the postnational individuality, the psychologized, sexualized, gendered format of contemporary America is not the only option. Yet so far it is the only one fully articulated with its algorithms in place while being privileged by the global mass media, compared to potential competitors—if there are any. Chinese "individuality," as in Lu Xun's advocacy, is thinkable only in its battle against society, which is perforce the expression of the exceptional few. Contemporary American separation-individuation is mass-based and consumer-oriented—a routinized rebellion that does not require a cause—and fundamentally conforming to the general culture.

At this point, American sexual politics do provide more personal space to those non-Westerners who adopt them. But most likely they only put a respectable First World stamp on what had preexisted indigenously. It remains to be seen whether the non-Western practitioner also grasps the spirit behind the politics, a spirit Foucault sees as latent in the Christian view of self, "where individuals seek the deep truth of their being in their 'sexuality' " (Best and Kellner 1991, 62). As the ultimate truth about self, this "sexuality" has little to do with procreation and concerns partners only when they are relevant to one's "hermeneutics of desire." Non-Westerners may adopt American lifestyles, but it is moot whether they will treat sexuality as a form of self-knowledge.

Concerning self-fashioned identities, two rival scenarios can be projected for the twenty-first century. One is nativist revival bearing a nationalist or religious stamp to arrest the further disintegration of community—a scenario that cannot be ruled out entirely even for America, where cultural politics aiming at reinventing collective identities are already in place. A collective identity is a powerful weapon of the underprivileged to agitate for more power and representation, but can also serve those who wish to stabilize those structures that shape the individual in terms of nation, history, culture, family, and other time-honored restraints. The opposing scenario sees in the highly individualized and privileged "American way of life" a foretaste of an advanced stage of world society in which the individual is free from the tyranny of "nation," and free to pursue one's lifestyle by picking up dismembered fragments from any social and cultural matrix— the only limit being one's own ignorance of the wares available from the transnational emporium. This alternative, by blurring national boundaries, seems to be the closest thing to a global culture, although it is doubtful whether this new formation is not in itself a different order of homogenization.

Notes

1. Indeed, Gellner made this judgment before the onset of postmodern multiculturalism in America and the breakup of the Soviet Union and Yugoslavia. Yet even from our vantage point, the real nationalist tidal wave of our time should have been the decolonization era of the 1950s and 1960s, had it not been overshadowed by the transnational ideologies of the Cold War. What is happening in the former Eastern Bloc today is not nation-building in the classical sense, but the parting of ways among nationalities many of whom were in fact configured by the Soviet system of federation. As for American multiculturalism, it is a projection of the craze of separation-individuation onto a bigger canvas—meanwhile, the American individual remains atomized and denationalized as ever.

2. In the mid-1990s, I saw a woman from Hong Kong meeting a handsome Russian young man at a conference; in a fit of surprise she told him that he was not what she expected a Russian to look like. Apparently, she had been brainwashed by American Cold War image-making in Hong Kong cinemas decades before.

3. "French politicians have complained that there are so many American crime shows on television that French children often know more abut the U.S. legal system than about their own. Arrested suspects have been known to show up at police stations demanding rights, such as *habeas corpus*, that do not exist in Napoleonic Code" (Tempest 1993, 11).

4. Frederick Jameson observes that "a certain spatial turn has often seemed to offer one of the more productive ways of distinguishing postmodernism from modernism proper," and this great transformation amounts to the "displacement of time" and the "spatialization of the temporal" (Jameson 1991, 154, 156). From this perspective, linear temporality is not time itself, but only a reading of time.

Bibliography

Abbreviations

CPC	*Chinese Political Character*
DFZZ	*Dongfang Zazhi* (Eastern miscellany)
DLZZ	*Dili Zazhi* (Journal of geography)
ESYSJ	*Ershiyi Shiji* (The twenty-first century)
FNZZ	*Funü Zazhi* (Women's journal)
GMRRBHB	*Guomin Riribao Huibian* (Essays from the National Daily Gazette)
HBXSJ	*Hubei Xueshengjie* (The Hubei student circle)
Heji	*Yinbingshi Heji* (The combined collection of the Ice-Drinking Studio)
JDSYJ	*Jindai Shi Yanjiu* (Studies in modern history)
JHLSZX	*Jinhua Lun yu Shanzhongxue* (Evolution and eugenics)
LDZWJ	*Li Dazhao Wenji* (The collected works of Li Dazhao)
LXQJ	*Lu Xun Quanji* (The complete works of Lu Xun)
MMP-RCC	*Margaret Mead Papers-Research in Contemporary Cultures*
QNZZ	*Qingnian Zazhi* (Youth magazine)
XMCB	*Xinmin Congbao* (New people's magazine)
XQN	*Xin Qingnian* (New youth)
YFJ	*Yan Fu Ji* (Yan Fu's works)
YXYB	*Youxue Yibian* (Translation Series of overseas students)
ZJDYD-YTDS	*Ziji de Yuandi—Yutian de Shu* (My own garden—writing on a rainy day)

Abel, T.M. and F.L.K. Hsu. 1949. "Responses of China-born and American-born Chinese to the Rorschach Test." *MMP-RCC*, G-29, v. 29, Ch-679.

———. 1953. "Some Aspects of Personality of Chinese as Revealed by the Rorschach Test." In Mead and Metraux 1953, pp. 329–340.

Abosch, David. 1964. "Kato Hiroyuki and the Influence of German Political Thought in Modern Japan: 1868–1883." Ph.D. diss., University of California, Berkeley. University Microfilms, Inc., Ann Arbor, MI, no. 65–2938.

Albee, Edward. 1960. *The American Dream*. New York: Coward-McCann.

Alitto, Guy S. 1979. *The Last Confucian: Liang Shu-ming and the Chinese Dilemma of Modernity*. Berkeley: University of California Press.

Allport, G. 1968. "The Historical Background of Modern Social Psychology." In *The

Handbook of Social Psychology, vol. 1, 2nd edition, ed. Gardner Lindzey and Elliot Aronson, pp. 1–80. Menlo Park, CA: Addison-Wesley.

Anderson, Benedict. 1991. *Imagined Communities: Reflections on the Origin and Spread of Nationalism*, Rev. ed. London and New York: Verso.

Anderson, Marston. 1990. *The Limits of Realism: Chinese Fiction in the Revolutionary Period*. Berkeley: University of California Press.

Anonymous. 1903a. "Dili yu guomin xingge zhi guanxi" (Geography and its relationship with national character). *HBXSJ*, no. 3:1–6.

Anonymous. 1903b. "Guomin jiaoyu" (National education). *HBXSJ*, no. 3:1–9.

Anonymous. 1903c. "Guomin weisheng xue" (The study of national hygiene). *HBXSJ*, no. 5:1–6.

Anonymous. 1903d. "Minzu jingsheng lun" (On the national spirit). *Jiangsu*, no. 7: 1–12; no. 8:1–10.

Anonymous. 1903e. "Minzuzhuyi" (Nationalism). *Jiangsu*, no. 7; 11–21.

Anonymous. 1903f. "Minzuzhuyi zhi jiaoyu" (Nationalist education). *YXYB*, no. 10: 1–9.

Anonymous. 1903g. "Shehui jiaoyu" (Social education). *YXYB*, no. 11:1–10

Anonymous. 1903h. "Shixue zhi genben tiaojian" (The basic conditions of historiography). *Han Sheng* (The voice of Han), no. 6:1–6; nos. 7–8:1–9.

Anonymous. 1903i. "Zhen nuli" (Exhortation to the slave). *GMRRBHB*, nos. 2–8: 0016–0026.

Anonymous. 1904a. "Lun nanbei zhi chengjian suoqi" (On the origins of the north-and-south regional bias). *Dongfang Zazhi*, no. 10: 233–241.

Anonymous. 1904b. "Zhongguo hun" (The Chinese soul). *GMRRBHB*, no. 1:0078–0084.

Anonymous. 1913. "Zhidu yu minxing" (Institutions and national character). In *Minli Bao* (People's stand), January 5 issue, reprinted in *Minguo Huibao* (Republican digest), pp. 8–9. Collected in *Zhonghua Minguo Shiliao Congbian* (Collected historical material of the Republic of China) A27, ed. Qin Xiaoyi. Taibei: Zhongguo guomindang zhongyang weiyuanhui dangshi weiyuanhui, 1976.

Anonymous. 1915. *Junxian Wenti Wendian Huibian* (Collected telegrams on the issue of constitutional monarchy). Beijing: Zhengmeng Shuju.

Ayers, William. 1971. *Chang Chih-tung and Educational Reform in China*. Cambridge, MA: Harvard University Press.

Azuela, Mariano. 1967. *Los De Abajo*. Mexico: Fondo de Cultura Economica, sexta edicion.

Bao Shaolin. 1992. "Ouzhou, riben, zhongguo de guominxing yanjiu: xixue dongjian de sanbuqu" (National character studies in Europe, Japan, and China: The trilogy of Western learning's coming to the East). *JDSYJ*, no. 67:37–46.

Barker, Ernest. 1948. *National Character and the Factors in Its Formation*, 4th ed., rev. London: Methuen.

Barnouw, Victor. 1979. *Culture and Personality*, 3rd ed. Homewood, IL: Dorsey.

Bauer, Wolfgang and Hwang Shen-chang, eds. 1982. *German Impact on Modern Chinese Intellectual History: A Bibliography of Chinese Publications = Deutschlands Einfluss auf die Moderne Chinesische Geistesgeschichte: Eine Bibliographie Chinesischsprachiger Werke*. Wiesbaden: Franz Steiner Verlag.

Befu, Harumi. 1993. "Nationalism and *Nihonjiron*." In *Cultural Nationalism in East Asia: Representation and Identity*, ed. H. Befu, pp. 107–135. Berkeley: Institute of East Asian Studies: University of California at Berkeley.

Beijing shifan daxue lishixi zhongguo jindaishi zu, ed. 1977. *Zhongguo Jindaishi Ziliao Xuanbian* (Selected materials on the modern history of China). Beijing: Zhonghua Shuju.

Bell, Daniel. 1965. *The End of Ideology: On the Exhaustion of Political Ideas in the Fifties*, rev. ed. New York: Free Press.

Benedict, Ruth. 1934. *Patterns of Culture*. Boston and New York: Houghton Mifflin.

Bernal, Martin. 1976. "Liu Shih-p'ei and National Essence." In *The Limits of Change: Essays on Conservative Alternatives in Republican China*, ed. Charlotte Furth, pp. 90–112. Cambridge, MA: Harvard University Press.

———. 1987. *Black Athena: The Afroasiatic Roots of Classical Civilization*, vol. 1. New Brunswick, NJ: Rutgers University Press.

Best, Steven and Douglas Kellner. 1991. *Postmodern Theory: Critical Interrogations*. New York: Guilford.

Blaut, James Morris. 1993. *The Colonizer's Model of the World: Geographical Diffusionism and Eurocentric History*. New York and London: Guilford.

Bloom, Alfred H. 1977. "A Cognitive Dimension of Social Control: The Hong Kong Chinese in Cross-Cultural Perspective." In *Deviance and Social Control in Chinese Society*, ed. Amy A. Wilson, Sidney L. Greenblatt, Richard W. Wilson, pp. 68–79. New York: Praeger.

Bloom, Allan. 1987. *The Closing of the American Mind*. New York: Simon and Schuster.

Bluntschli, J.K. 1885. *The Theory of the State*. Authorized English translation of the 6th German edition. Oxford: Clarendon.

Bock, Philip. 1988. *Rethinking Psychological Anthropology: Continuity and Change in the Study of Human Action*. New York: W.H. Freeman.

Bond, Michael Harris. 1991. *Beyond the Chinese Face: Insights from Psychology*. Hong Kong: Oxford University Press.

Boring, Edwin G. 1968. "Wilhelm Wundt." In *International Encyclopedia of the Social Sciences*, vol. 16, pp. 581–586. New York: Macmillan and Free Press.

Boyd, William C. 1953. *Genetics and the Races of Man: An Introduction to Modern Physical Anthropology*. Boston: Little, Brown.

Breisach, Ernst. 1994. *Historiography: Ancient, Medieval, and Modern*. 2nd Edition. Chicago: University of Chicago Press.

Bridgwater, Patrick. 1974. *Kafka and Nietzsche*. Bonn: Bouvier Verlag Herbert Grundmann.

Brown, Norman O. 1985. *Life Against Death: The Psychoanalytical Meaning of History*, 2nd ed. Middletown, CT: Wesleyan University Press.

———. 1966. *Love's Body*. New York: Random House.

Bunzel, Ruth. 1948. "Themes in Chinese Culture" (an extract from the General Seminar minutes of March 18). *MMP-RCC*, G-23, v. 8, Ch-686.

———. 1949. "A Note on Urination and Training in Chinese Infants." *MMP-RCC*, v. 8, Ch-661.

———. 1950. *Explorations in Chinese Culture*. Research in Contemporary Cultures, Columbia University, New York, mimeographed copy, East Asian reading room, Columbia University.

Burke, Peter. 1990. *The French Historical Revolution: The Annales School 1929–89*. Stanford, CA: Stanford University Press.

Bury, J.B. 1932. *The Idea of Progress: An Inquiry into Its Origin and Growth*. New York: Macmillan.

Caffrey, Margaret M. 1989. *Ruth Benedict: Stranger in This Land*. Austin: University of Texas Press.

Calinescu, Matei. 1987. *Five Faces of Modernity: Modernism, Avant-Garde, Decadence, Kitsch, Postmodernism*. Durham, NC: Duke University Press.

Canetti, Elias. 1962. *Crowds and Power*, trans. Carol Steward. New York: Viking.

Caponigri, Robert. 1948. Introduction to *Perpetual Peace: A Philosophical Essay*, by Immanuel Kant. New York: Liberal Arts.

Carey, John. 1992. *The Intellectuals and the Masses: Pride and Prejudice Among the Literary Intelligentsia, 1880–1939*. London and Boston: Faber and Faber.

Carroll, John. 1974. *Break-Out from the Crystal Palace—The Anarcho-psychological Critique: Stirner, Nietzsche, Dostoevsky*. London: Routledge and Kegan Paul.

Chafe, William H. 1990. "World War II as a Pivotal Experience for American Women." In *Women and War: The Changing Status of American Women from the 1930s to the 1950s*, eds. Maria Diedrich and Dorothea Fischer-Hornung, pp. 21–34. New York: Berg.

Chamberlain, Houston Stewart. 1911. *The Foundations of the Nineteenth Century*, trans. John Lees. London and New York: J. Lane.

Chang Hao. 1980. "Intellectual change and the reform movement, 1890–8." In *Cambridge History of China*, vol. 11, Part 2, ed. John K. Fairbank and Denis C. Twitchett, pp. 274–338. Cambridge: Cambridge University Press.

———. 1971. *Liang Ch'i-ch'ao and Intellectual Transition in China, 1890–1907*. Cambridge, MA: Harvard University Press.

Chang Hui. 1922. "Women weishenmo yao yanjiu geyao" (Why should we study folk songs?). *Geyao* (Folk song), no. 3:1–3.

Chang Naide. 1920. "Dongfang wenming yu xifang wenming" (Eastern civilization and western civilization). *Guomin* (Citizen) 2, no. 3, in Chen 1985, pp. 266–278.

Chang, Y.H., H. Rin, C.C. Chen. 1975. "Frigophobia: A Report of Five Cases." *Bulletin, Chinese Society of Neurology and Psychiatry* 1, no. 2:9–13.

Chatterjee, Partha. 1993. *The Nation and Its Fragments: Colonial and Postcolonial Histories*. Princeton, NJ: Princeton University Press.

Chen Changheng. 1919. "Jinghua zhi zhenxiang" (The truth about evolution). *DFZZ* 16, nos. 1–2, collected in *JHLSZX*, pp. 1–31.

Chen Changnian. 1994. "Gengzi qinwang yundong de jige wenti" (Problems of the 1900 loyalist movement). *JDSYJ*, no. 82:92–107.

Chen Duxiu. 1915a. "Dikangli" (The power of resistance). *XQN* 1, no. 3:1–5.

———. 1915b. "Dong xi minzu gengben sixiang zhi chayi" (The basic divergence between Eastern and Western nations). *XQN* 1, no. 4:1–4.

———. 1915c. "Falanxiren yu jinshi wenming" (The French and modern civilization). In *Duxiu wencun* (Collected essays of Duxiu), vol. 1, pp. 11–16. Hong Kong: Yuandong Tushu Gongsi, 1965.

———. 1915d. "Jinggao qingnian" (Call to youth). *QNZZ* 1, no. 1:1–6

———. 1915e. "Jinri zhi jiaoyu fangzhen" (Today's educational guidelines). *QNZZ* 1, no. 2:1–6

———. 1916a. "Wo zhi aiguozhuyi" (My patriotism). *XQN* 2, no. 2:1–6

———. 1916b. "Xin qingnian" (New youth). *XQN* 2, no. 1:1–4

———. 1916c. "Yijiuyiliu nian" (The year of 1916). *XQN* 1, no. 5:1–4.

———. 1916d. "Yuan Shikai fuhuo" (The resurrection of Yuan Shikai). *XQN* 2, no. 4:1–3.

———. 1917a. "Fupi yu zunkong" (Monarchical restoration and Confucius-worship). In *Duxiu wencun* (Collected essays of Duxiu), vol. 1, pp. 161–168. Hong Kong: Yuandong Tushu Gongsi, 1965.

———. 1917b. "Wenxue geming lun" (On the literary revolution). *XQN* 2, no. 6:1–4

———. 1920. "Maersesi renkou lun yu zhongguo wenti" (Malthus' population theory and China's population problem). *XQN* 7, no. 4:1–9.

Chen Duxiu and Ou Shengbai. 1921. "Lun wuzhengfuzhuyi" (On anarchism). *XQN* 9, no. 4:1–32.

Chen Gaoyuan. 1992. "Lun jindai zhongguo gaizao guominxing de shehui sichao" (On modern Chinese social thoughts for the reform of national character). *JDSYJ*, no. 67:1–21.

Chen Jiayi. 1919. "Wozhi xin jiu sixiang tiaohe guan" (My view on the reconciliation between the new and the old). *DFZZ* 16, no.11:6–14.

Chen Qi. 1990. "Liu Shipei de jinguwen guan" (Liu Shipei's view on the new and old texts). *JDSYJ*, no. 56:93–111.

Chen Shen. 1913. "Lun guohun shangshi zhi kediao" (The loss of the national soul is lamentable). *Yongyan* (Justice) 1, no. 24:1–9.

Chen Song, ed. 1985. *Wusi qianhou dong xi wenhua wenti taolun wenxuan* (Selected essays from the debates on the issues of Eastern and Western cultures during the May Fourth era). Beijing: Zhongguo Shehui Kexue Chubanshe.

Chen Wanxiong. 1982. *Xin wenhua yundong qian de Chen Duxiu, yibaqijiu nian— yijiuyiwu nian* (Chen Duxiu before the New Culture movement, 1879–1915). Hong Kong: The Chinese University of Hong Kong Press.

———. 1992. *Wusi xinwenhua de yuanliu* (The origins of May Fourth's new culture). Hong Kong: Sanlien Shudian.

Chen Xiaomei. 1995. *Occidentalism: A Theory of Counter-Discourse in Post-Mao China*. New York, Oxford University Press.

Chi Ch'ao-ting (Ji Chaoding). 1936. *Key Economic Areas in Chinese History, As Revealed in the Development of Public Works for Water-Control*. London: George Allen and Unwin Ltd.

Chodorow, Nancy. 1978. *The Reproduction of Mothering: Psychoanalysis and the Sociology of Gender*. Berkeley: University of California Press.

Chow Kai-wing. 1997. "Imagining Boundaries of Blood: Zhang Binglin and the Invention of the Han 'Race' in Modern China." In Dikötter 1997, pp. 34–52.

Chow Tse-tsung. 1960. *The May Fourth Movement: Intellectual Revolution in Modern China*. Cambridge, MA: Harvard University Press.

Chuandao and Kaiming. 1925. "Ren de jiaomai" (The hawking of human flesh). *Yusi* (Word threads), no. 17:7–8.

Chuangfu (Du Yaquan). 1912. "Gonghe zhengti yu guomin xinli" (The republican polity and the national psychology). *DFZZ* 9, no. 5 (November 1):1–4.

———. 1916. "Zailun xinjiu sixiang zhi chongtu" (Again on the conflict between new and old thoughts). *DFZZ* 13, no. 4:1–6.

———. 1917 "Zhanhou dongxi wenming zhi tiaohe" (The postwar reconciliation of Eastern and Western Civilizations), *DFZZ* 14, no. 4:1–7.

———. 1919. "Xinjiu sixiang zhi zhezhong" (The synthesis of new and old thought). *DFZZ* 16, no. 9:1–8.

Clowes, Edith W. 1986. "Literary Reception as Vulgarization: Nietzsche's Idea of the Superman in Neo-Realist Fiction." In *Nietzsche in Russia*, ed. Bernice Glatzer Rosenthal, pp. 315–329. Princeton, NJ: Princeton University Press.

Cohen, Paul A. 1987. *Between Tradition and Modernity: Wang Tao and Reform in Late Ch'ing China*. Cambridge, MA: Council on East Asian Studies, Harvard University Press.

Coker, F.W. 1967. *Organismic Theories of the State*. New York: AMS.

Costello, John. 1985. *Virtue Under Fire: How World War II Changed Our Social and Sexual Attitudes*. Boston: Little, Brown.

CPC. Abbreviation of *Chinese Political Character*.

Cressey, George Babcock. 1934. *China's Geographic Foundations: A Survey of the Land and Its People.* New York and London: McGraw-Hill.

Croll, Elizabeth. 1978. *Feminism and Socialism in China.* Boston: Routledge and Kegan Paul.

Cui Zhihai. 1984. "Liang Qichao 'xinmin shuo' de zai renshi" (A new understanding of Liang Qichao's "On the New People"). *JDSYJ*, no. 52:84–95.

Dai, Bingham (Dai Bingheng). 1941. "Personality Problems in Chinese Culture." *American Sociological Review* 6, no. 5:688–696.

———. 1944. "Divided Loyalty in War: A Study of Cooperation with the Enemy." *Psychiatry* 7, no. 4:327–340.

———. 1952. "A Socio-Psychiatric Approach to Personality Organization." *American Sociological Review* 17, no. 1: 44–49.

———. 1957. "Obsessive-Compulsive Disorders in Chinese Culture." *Social Problems* 4, no. 4:313–339.

———. 1984. "Psychoanalysis in China Before the Revolution; a Letter from Bingham Dai." *Transcultural Psychiatric Research* 21, no. 4:280–282

Davis Jr., Michael M. 1968. *Psychological Interpretations of Society.* Reprint of a 1909 edition. New York: AMS.

Davis, Winston. 1996. *The Moral and Political Naturalism of Baron Kato Hiroyuki.* Berkeley: Institute of East Asian Studies, University of California.

Dawson, Raymond. 1967. *The Chinese Chameleon: An Analysis of European Conceptions of Chinese Civilization.* London: Oxford University Press.

Derrida, Jacques. 1978. *Writing and Difference.* Chicago: University of Chicago Press.

DFZZ. Abbreviation of *Dongfang Zazhi* (Eastern miscellany).

Dijkstra, Bram. 1986. *Idols of Perversity: Fantasies of Feminine Evil in Fin-de-Siècle Culture.* New York: Oxford University Press.

Dikötter, Frank. 1989. "Eugenics in Republican China." *Republican China* 15, no. 1: 1–17.

———. 1992. *The Discourse of Race in Modern China.* Stanford, CA: Stanford University Press.

———. ed. 1997. *The Construction of Racial Identities in China and Japan: Historical and Contemporary Perspectives.* Honolulu, Hawaii: University of Hawaii Press.

Ding Weizhi. 1995. "Wanqing guocuizhuyi shulun" (A discussion on the late Qing's National Essence). *JDSYJ*, no. 86:1–15.

Ding Wenjiang. 1923. "Lishi renwu yu dili de guanxi" (The relationship between historical personages and geography). *DFZZ* 20, no. 5: 125–133.

Ding Wenjiang and Zhao Fengtian. 1983. *Liang Qichao nianpu changpian* (The long version of a chronological biography of Liang Qichao). Shanghai: Renmin Chubanshe.

Dinnerstein, Dorothy. 1977. *The Mermaid and the Minotaur: Sexual Arrangements and Human Malaise.* New York: Harper Colophon Books.

Dirlik, Arif. 1978. *Revolution and History: The Origins of Marxist Historiography in China, 1919–1937.* Berkeley: University of California Press.

———. 1989. *The Origins of Chinese Communism.* New York: Oxford University Press.

———. 1996a. "Chinese History and the Question of Orientalism." *History and Theory* 35, no. 4:96–118.

———. 1996b. "Reversals, Ironies, Hegemonies: Notes on the Contemporary Historiography of Modern China." *Modern China* 22, no. 3:243–284.

Dor, Joël. 1998. *Introduction to the Reading of Lacan: The Unconscious Structured Like a Language.* New York: Other Press.

Duara, Prasenjit. 1995. *Rescuing History from the Nation: Questioning Narratives of Modern China*. Chicago: University of Chicago Press.

Duxiu. 1920. "Suiganlu bashisi: xuwuzhuyi" (Random thoughts 84: Nihilism). *XQN* 8, no. 1:1.

———. 1921a. "Suiganlu yiyiba: fankang yulun de yongqi" (Random thoughts 118: The courage to go against public opinion). *XQN* 9, no. 2:3.

———. 1921b. "Suiganlu yiyiwu: zhongguo shi de wuzhenfuzhuyi" (Random thoughts 115: Chinese-style anarchism). *XQN* 9, no. 1:5–6.

Eberhard, Wolfram. 1965. "Chinese Regional Stereotypes." *Asian Survey* 5, no. 12: 596–608

———. 1968. *The Local Cultures of South and East China*. Leiden: E.J. Brill.

Editorial. 1905. "Lun zhongguoren de tuihua" (On the degeneration of the Chinese). *Jingzhong Ribao* (The alarm bell daily), no. 330:1.

Ellis, Havelock. 1987. *Xing xinlixue* (The psychology of sex), trans. Pan Guangdan. Beijing: Sanlian Shudian.

Elman, Benjamin A. 1984. *From Philosophy to Philology: Intellectual and Social Aspects of Change in Late Imperial China*. Cambridge, MA: Council on East Asian Studies, Harvard University Press.

Engelbrecht, H. C. 1968. *Johann Gottlieb Fichte: A Study of His Political Writings with Special Reference to His Nationalism*. New York: AMS.

Esherick, Joseph W. 1976. *Reform and Revolution in China: The 1911 Revolution in Hunan and Hubei*. Berkeley: University of California Press.

Evans, Dylan. 1997. *An Introductory Dictionary of Lacanian Psychoanalysis*. London and New York: Routledge.

Fairbank, John King. 1983. *The United States and China*, 4th ed. Cambridge, MA: Harvard University Press.

Fairbank, John K., and Denis Twitchett, eds. 1980. *The Cambridge History of China*, vol. 11, part 2. Cambridge: Cambridge University Press.

———, eds. 1983. *The Cambridge History of China*, vol. 12, part 1. Cambridge: Cambridge University Press.

Fan Wenlan. 1957. "Zi qin han qi zhongguo chengwei tongyi guojia de yuanyin" (The causes of China becoming a unified nation since the Qin and the Han). In *Han minzu xingcheng wenti taolunji* (Discussions on the problem of the formation of the Han nation), ed. Lishi yanjiu bianjibu, pp. 1–16. Beijing: Sanlian Shudian.

Fang Hanqi. 1981. *Zhongguo jindai baokan shi* (A history of modern Chinese newspapers and journals). Taiyuan: Shaanxi Renmin Chubanshe, 2 vols.

Farquhar, Judith B., and James L. Hevia. 1993. "Culture and Postwar American Historiography of China." *Positions* 1, no. 2:486–525.

Feisheng. 1903. "Guohun bian" (Treatise on the national soul). *Zhejiang chao* (The Zhejiang tide), no. 1:1–17; no. 3:19–40.

Feng Zuyi. 1994. "Cong 'buren' zazhi kan Kang Youwei minchu de zhengzhi zhuzhang" (A look at Kang Youwei's political views in the early republic based on the journal *Compassion*). *JDSYJ*, no. 81:57–73.

Fine, Reuben. 1979. *A History of Psychoanalysis*. New York: Columbia University Press.

Fitzgerald, John. 1996. *Awakening China: Politics, Culture, and Class in the Nationalist Revolution*. Stanford, CA: Stanford University Press.

Fogel, Joshua A. 1984. *Politics and Sinology: The Case of Naito Konan* (1866–1934). Cambridge, MA: Council on East Asian Studies, Harvard University Press.

Foucault, Michel. 1965. *Madness and Civilization: A History of Insanity in the Age of Reason*, trans. Richard Howard. New York: Pantheon.

————. 1990. *The History of Sexuality*, I: *An Introduction*, trans. Robert Hurley. New York: Vintage.

Freud, Sigmund. 1924. "The Economic Problem of Masochism." In *The Standard Edition of the Complete Psychological Works of Sigmund Freud*, trans. under James Strachey. London: Hogarth, 1961, vol. 19, pp. 159–170.

Friar, Kimon, trans. 1973. *Modern Greek Poetry*. New York: Simon and Schuster.

Friedman, Edward. 1994. "Reconstructing China's National Identity: A Southern Alternative to Mao-Era Anti-Imperialist Nationalism," *Journal of Asian Studies* 53, no. 1: 67–91.

Fu Sinian. 1918. "Zhongguo lishi fenqi zhi yanjiu" (A study on the periodization of Chinese history). In *Fu Mengzhen xiangsheng ji* (The collected works of Mr. Fu Mengzhen), 1952, vol. 1, Part 1(a), pp. 54–61. Taibei: Guoli Taiwan Daxue.

————. 1919. "Baihua wenxue yu xinli de gaige" (The vernacular literature and the psychological reform). In *Fu Mengzhen xiangsheng ji* (The collected works of Mr. Fu Mengzhen), 1952, vol. 1, Part 1(a), pp. 117–126. Taibei: Guoli Taiwan Daxue.

————. 1924. "Ping Ding Wenjiang de 'lishi renwu yu dili de guanxi' " (A critique of Ding Wenjiang's "The relationship between historical personages and geography"). In *Fu Mengzhen xiangsheng ji* (The collected works of Mr. Fu Mengzhen), 1952, vol. 1, Part 1(j), pp. 96–102. Taibei: Guoli Taiwan Daxue.

FNZZ. Abbreviation of *Funü zazhi* (The women's journal).

Furth, Charlotte. 1970. *Ting Wen-chiang: Science and China's New Culture*. Cambridge, MA: Harvard University Press.

————. 1976. *The Limits of Change: Essays on Conservative Alternatives in Republican China*. Cambridge, MA: Harvard University Press.

————. 1983. "Intellectual change: From the Reform movement to the May Fourth movement, 1895–1920." In *Cambridge History of China*, vol. 12, Part 1, ed. John K. Fairbank and Denis Twitchett, pp. 322–405. Cambridge: Cambridge University Press.

Gao Like. 1992. "Fuzeyuji yu Liang Qichao jindaihua sixiang bijiao" (Comparing the modernization thinking of Fukuzawa Yukichi and Liang Qichao). *Lishi yanjiu* (Historical studies) 2:163–173.

————. 1994. "Chongping Du Yaquan yu Chen Duxiu de dongxi wenhua lunzhan" (A re-appraisal of the eastern-western cultures debate between Du Yaquan and Chen Duxiu). *JDSYJ*, no. 82:144–163.

————. 1996. "Du Yuanquan de zhongxi wenhua guan" (Du Yaquan's view on Chinese and Western cultures). *ESYSJ*, no. 34:52–62.

Gao Shan (Zhou Jianren). 1922. "Liangge yichuanxuejia de bainian jinian" (The centennial anniversary of two geneticists). *DFZZ* 19, no. 12:96–99.

Gao Yihan. 1915a. "Gonghe guojia yu qingnian zhi zijue (zhi er)" (The republic and the self-consciousness of the youth (part 2)). *QNZZ* 1, no. 2:1–6.

————. 1915b. "Minyue yu bangben" (The social contract and the foundation of the state). *XQN* 1, no. 3:1–6:

————. 1917. "Yijiuyiqi yuxiang zhi geming" (The revolution projected for 1917). *XQN* 2, no. 5:1–5.

Gellner, Ernest. 1983. *Nations and Nationalism*. Ithaca, New York: Cornell University Press.

Gilligan, Carol. 1982. *In A Different Voice*. Cambridge, MA: Harvard University Press.

Gilman, Richard. 1979. *Decadence: The Strange Life of an Epithet*. New York: Farrar, Straus and Giroux.

Gluck, Carol. 1985. *Japan's Modern Myths: Ideology in the Late Meiji Period*. Princeton, NJ: Princeton University Press.

GMRRBHB. Abbreviation of *Guomin riribao huibian* (Essays from the National Daily Gazette). Taibei: The Committee for the Compilation of Party-History Materials, the Central Committee of the Chinese Nationalist Party, 1968.

Gong Chu. 1978. *Gong Chu jiangjun huiyilu* (General Gong Chu's memoirs), vol. 1. Hong Kong: Mingbao Yuekan She

Gong Nuli Lishan. 1901. "Shuo nuli" (Discourse on slave). *Qingyi Bao* (The pure opinion journal), no. 80:5101–5108.

Gorer, Geoffrey. 1964. *The American People: A Study in National Character*, rev. ed. New York: Norton.

Granet, Marcel. 1950. *Chinese Civilization*. London: Routledge and Kegan Paul.

Grant, Madison. 1918. *The Passing of the Great Race, or the Racial Basis of European History*. New York and London: Scribner.

Greer, Germaine. 1970. *The Female Eunuch*. London: MacGibbon and Kee.

Grossman, Joan Delaney. 1973. "Genius and Madness: The Return of the Romantic Concept of the Poet in Russia at the End of the Nineteenth Century." In *American Contributions to the Seventh International Congress of Slavists, Warsaw, August 21–27, 1973*, vol. 2, pp. 247–260. The Hague/Paris: Mouton and Co.

Guangsheng. 1917. "Zhongguo guominxing jiqi ruodian" (The Chinese national character and its weaknesses). *XQN* 2, no. 6:1–11.

Guanyun. 1903. "Zhongguo renzhong kao" (A historical investigation into the origins of the Chinese race). In *XMCB*, nos. 40–41 (November):1–8.

———1904. "Zhongguo renzhong kao (xu)" (An investigation into the origins of the Chinese race [cont'd]). In *XMCB*, no. 55 (October):1–11.

———. 1904–1905. "Gongtong ganqing zhi biyao lun" (On the necessity of common feelings). *XMCB*, no. 57:1–8; no. 58:1–12; no. 59:1–7; no. 60:1–15.

———. 1906. "Lun zhongguoren chongbai Yue Fei de xinli" (On the Chinese psychology of worshipping Yue Fei). *XMCB*, no. 72:10–28.

Guignon, Charles B. 1996. "Authenticity, Moral Values, and Psychotherapy." In *The Cambridge Companion to Heidegger*, ed. Charles Guignon, pp. 215–239. New York: Cambridge University Press.

Guyin. 1904. "Tuihua lun" (On degeneration). *DFZZ*, no. 11:257–259.

Halberstam, David. 1993. "Discovering Sex." *American Heritage* (May–June 1993): 39–58.

Hall, Ivan Parker. 1973. *Mori Arinori*. Cambridge, MA: Harvard University Press.

Haller, Mark H. 1963. *Eugenics: Hereditarian Attitudes in American Thought*. New Brunswick, NJ: Rutgers University Press.

Hanke, Ken. 1989. *Charlie Chan at the Movies: History, Filmography, and Criticism*. Jefferson, NC: McFarland.

Harris, Marvin. 1968. *The Rise of Anthropological Theory*. New York: Crowell.

Harris, Thomas. 1989. *The Silence of the Lambs*. New York: St. Martin's Paperbacks.

HBXSJ. Abbreviation of *Hubei xueshengjie* (The Hubei student circle).

He Bochuan. 1990. *Shan'ao shang de zhongguo—wenti, kunjing, tongku de xuanze* (China in a depression of a mountain range—problems, predicaments, and painful choices). Hong Kong: Sanlian Shudian.

Hegel, Georg Wilhelm Friedrich. 1956. *The Philosophy of History*, trans. J. Sibree. New York: Dover.

Heilbroner, R.L. 1956. "The Great Flouridation Scare." *Reader's Digest* 69 (412):123–126.

Heji. 1989. Abbreviation of *Yinbingshi Heji* (The combined collections of the ice-drinking studio). Beijing: Zhonghua Shuju.

Heller, Peter. 1966. *Dialectics and Nihilism: Essays on Lessing, Nietzsche, Mann, and Kafka*. MA: University of Massachusetts Press.

Hellersberg, Elizabeth. 1949. "Visual Perception and Spatial Organization as a Means to the Understanding of Some Chinese Phenomena (An Experimental Approach)." *MMP-RCC*, G-26, v. 19, Ch-662.

———. n.d. "The Use of Visual Material for the Understanding of Some Psycho-dynamics of the Chinese." *MMP-RCC*, G-26, v. 19, Ch-349.

Hevia, James L. 1995. *Cherishing Men from Afar: Qing Guest Ritual and the Macartney Embassy of 1793*. Durham and London: Duke University Press.

Heyer, Virginia. 1953. "Relations Between Men and Women in Chinese Stories." In *The Study of Culture at a Distance*, ed. Margaret Mead and Rhoda Metraux, pp. 221–234. Chicago: University of Chicago Press.

Hirsch Jr., E.D. 1988. *Cultural Literacy: What Every American Needs to Know*. New York: First Vintage.

Hobsbawn, E.J. 1990. *Nations and Nationalism since 1780: Programme, Myth, Reality*. New York: Cambridge University Press.

Hofstadter, Richard. 1945. *Social Darwinism in American Thought, 1860–1915*. Philadelphia: University of Pennsylvania Press.

———. 1966. *Anti-Intellectualism in American Life*. New York: Knopf.

Howard, Jane. 1984. *Margaret Mead: A Life*. New York: Fawcett Crest.

Howard, Richard C. 1967. "Japan's Role in the Reform Program of K'ang Yu-wei." *K'ang Yu-wei: A Biography and a Symposium*, ed. Lo Jung-pang, pp. 280–312. Tucson: University of Arizona Press.

Hsia, C.T. 1971. *A History of Modern Chinese Fiction*, 2nd ed. New Haven, CT: Yale University Press.

Hsia Tsi-an. 1968. *The Gate of Darkness: Studies on the Leftist Literary Movement in China*. Seattle: University of Washington Press.

Hsiao Kung-chuan. 1975. *A Modern China and a New World: K'ang Yu-wei, Reformer and Utopian, 1858–1927*. Seattle: University of Washington Press.

Hsu, Francis L.K. 1981. *Americans and Chinese: Passage to Differences*. Honolulu: The University Press of Hawaii.

Hu Hsien-chin (Hu Xianjin) 1944. "The Chinese Concepts of 'Face.'" *American Anthropologist* 46, no. 1:45–64.

———. 1946. "The Foundation for a Secure Personality." *MMP-RCC*, G-21, v. 1, Ch-1.

———. 1947a. "Educational Methods." *MMC-RCC*, G-21, v. 1, Ch-13.

———. 1947b. "The Romance of the Three Kingdoms." MMP-RCC, G-21, v. 2, Ch-33.

———. 1949. "Remarks Concerning Husband and Wife in Chinese Culture." *MMP-RCC*, G-29, v. 31, Ch-667.

———. n.d.(a). "Differences between North and South Chinese." *MMP-RCC*, G-22, v. 3, Ch-38.

———. n.d.(b). "Siblings." *MMP-RCC*, G-22, v. 3, CH-54.

———. n.d.(c). " 'To Swallow An Enemy'—Orality." *MMP-RCC*, G-28, v. 28, Ch-632.

Hu Huanyong. 1928. "Yuehan Bailuna zhi rensheng dilixue" (Jean Brunhes' human geography). *DLZZ* 1, no. 1:5–15.

———. 1929. "Xiyang renwen dilixue wanjin zhi fazhan" (The recent developments of human geography in the West). *DLZZ* 2, no. 3:1–8.

Hu Lancheng. 1944. "Suibi liuzhe" (Six pieces of random writings). In *Zhang Ailing juan* (Materials on Zhang Ailing), ed. Tang Wenbiao, pp. 171–179. Taipei: Yuanjing Chuban Shiye Gongsi, 1982.

Hu Shi. 1985. "Xin Shenghuo" (The new life). In *Hu Shi wencun* (Hu Shi's collected essays), vol. 1, pp. 724–726. Taibei: Yuandong Tushu Gongsi.

———. 1985b. "Wode erzhi" (My son). In *Hu Shi wencun* (Hu Shi's collected essays), vol. 1, pp. 687–682.

———. 1920. "Guoyu de jinhua" (The evolution of our national language). *XQN* 7, no. 3:1–13.

———. 1923. "Du Liang Shuming xiansheng de dongxi wenhua ji qi zhexue" (Having read Liang Shuming's *Eastern and Western Cultures and Their Philosophies*). In *Hu Shi wencun*, vol. 2, pp. 158–179.

Hu Yilu. 1914. "Yuan luan" (minzu xinli guan) (The source of chaos [from the viewpoint of national psychology]). *Yongyan* 2, no. 5:1–5.

Hua Lu. 1922. "Minzu yi laole ma" (Is our race senile?). *DFZZ* 19, no. 23:1–2.

Huang Jie. 1905. "Huang shi" (Yellow history). *Guocui Xuebao* (The National Essence Journal), no. 1:4–10.

Huang, Philip C. 1972. *Liang Ch'i-ch'ao and Modern Chinese Liberalism*. Seattle: University of Washington Press.

Huntington, Ellsworth. 1915. *Civilization and Climate*. New Haven: Yale University Press.

———. 1924. *The Character of Races, As Influenced by Physical Environment, Natural Selection and Historical Development*. Reprint in 1977. New York and London: Scribner.

———. 1925. *West of the Pacific*. New York and London: Scribner.

Huntington, Samuel P. 1997. *The Clash of Civilizations and the Remaking of World Order*. New York: Touchstone Book.

Hurley, Kelly. 1990. "Hereditary Taint and Cultural Contagion: The Social Etiology of Fin-de-Siècle Degeneration Theory." *Nineteenth-Century Contexts* 14, no. 2: 193–214.

Ibsen, Henrik Johan. 1890. *Ghosts*, trans. Frances Lord. London: Griffith, Farran, Okeden, and Welsh.

Iggers, Georg G. 1997. *Historiography in the Twentieth Century: From Scientific Objectivity to the Postmodern Challenge*. Hanover, NH: Wesleyan University Press, published by University Press of New England.

Iikura, Akira. 1995. "The Precursors of the Yellow Peril Theories: Mikhail Bakunin and Charles Pearson." *RIAD Bulletin*, no. 3 (March):257–292.

Inge, William. 1958. *The Dark at the Top of the Stairs. A New Play*. New York: Random House.

Inkeles, Alex. 1997. *National Character: A Psycho-Social Perspective*. New Brunswick, NJ: Transaction.

Irokawa Daikichi. 1985. *The Culture of the Meiji Period*, trans. Marius B. Jansen. Princeton, NJ: Princeton University Press.

Jackson, Peter and Jan Penrose. 1993. "Introduction: Placing 'race' and nation." In *Constructions of Race, Place and Nation*, ed. Peter Jackson and Jan Penrose, pp. 1–23. London: University College London Press.

Jameson, Frederic. 1986. "Third-World Literature in the Era of Multinational Capitalism." *Social Text*, no. 15:65–88.

———. 1991. *Postmodernism, or, the Cultural Logic of Late Capitalism*. Durham, NC: Duke University Press.

Jansen, Marius B. 1970. *Japan and China: From War to Peace, 1894–1972*. Chicago: Rand McNally College Publishing.

———. 1980. "Konoe Atsumaro." In *The Chinese and the Japanese: Essays in Po-*

litical and Cultural Interactions, ed. Akira Iriye, pp. 107–123. Princeton, NJ: Princeton University Press.

Jay, Martin. 1973. *The Dialectical Imagination: A History of the Frankfurt School and the Institute of Social Research, 1923–1950*. Boston: Little, Brown.

JDSYJ. Abbreviation of *Jindai shi yanjiu* (Studies in modern history).

JHLSZX. Abbreviation of *Jinhua lun yu shanzhongxue* (Evolution and eugenics). Shanghai: Dongfang Zazhi She, 1923.

Jiang Yihua and Zhu Weizheng, eds. 1981. *Zhang Taiyan Xuanji Zhushi Ben* (Selected works of Zhang Taiyan, annotated). Shanghai: Renmin Chubanshe.

Jianmeng (Zhou Jianren). 1921. "Minzu zhi shuaitui" (Racial deterioration). *DFZZ* 18, no. 21:1–3.

———. 1922. "Meidu shi zhongzu shuaitui de yuanyin" (Syphilis is the cause of racial deterioration). *DFZZ* 19, no. 7:85–86.

———. 1923. "Peiou xuanze yu jibing" (The selection of spouse and diseases). *FNZZ* 9, no. 11:21–26.

Jianren. 1928. "Suiganlu yisanliu: rendao yu cansha" (Random thoughts 136: humanitarianism and cruel executions). *Yusi* (Word threads) 4, no. 22:41–44.

Jieshi (Zhang Jieshi). 1925. "Nanxingde dikang yu nuxingde dikang" (Masculine resistance and feminine resistance). *Xing shi* (The awakened lion), no. 38:1.

Jin Qisan. 1935. "Woguo nanbei zhi dili guandian" (Geographical views on the north-and-south of our country). *Fangzhi yuekan* (Topographical monthly) 8, nos. 7–8: 55–59

Jingwei. 1905. "Minzude guomin" (On the nation's citizenry). *Min bao* (People's journal), no. 1:1–33.

———. 1906. "Bo Xinmin Congbao zuijin zhi fei geiming lun" (Refuting New People's Magazine's most recent antirevolutionary statement). *Min bao* (People's journal), no. 4:1–43.

Jones, Greta. 1980. *Social Darwinism and English Thought: The Interaction between Biological and Social Theory*. Sussex, England: Harvester.

Ju Jiwu. 1987. *Zhongguo dilixue fazhanshi* (A history of the development of the Chinese study of geography). Jiangsu Jiaoyu Chubanshe.

Jung, C.G. 1959. *Aion*, in *The Collected Works of C.G. Jung*, vol. 9, Part II. New York: Pantheon Books.

———. 1919. "Instinct and the Unconscious." In *The Structure And Dynamics of the Psyche*, trans. R.F.C. Hull, as vol. 8 of *The Collected Works of C.G. Jung*, pp. 129–138. Princeton, NJ: Princeton University Press, 1975.

Kahn, Eugen. 1931. *Psychopathic Personalities*, trans. H. Flanders Dunbar. New Haven: Yale University Press.

Kaiming (Zhou Zuoren). 1924a. "Gou zhua ditan" (Dogs scratching carpets). *Yusi* (Word threads), no. 3:1–3.

———. 1924b. "Womende diren" (Our enemies). *Yusi* (Word threads), no. 6:7–8.

———. 1925a. "Gui de huose" (The Goblin's merchandise). *Yusi* (Word threads), no. 13:8.

———. 1925b. "Gui de jiaomai" (The goblin hawker). *Yusi* (Word threads), no. 10:1.

———. 1925c. "Shang xia shen" (Upper and lower sections of the body). *Yusi* (Word threads), no. 2:7–8.

———. 1925d. "Yongle de shengzhi" (The sacred edicts of Yongle). *Yusi* (Word threads), no. 11:8.

Kamachi Noriko. 1981. *Reform in China: Huang Tsun-hsien and the Japanese Model*. Cambridge, MA: Council on East Asian Studies, Harvard University.

Kang Baiqing. 1919. "Lun zhongguo zhi minzu qizhi" (On the national temperament of the Chinese). *Xin chao* (New tide) 1, no. 2:197–244.

Kang Youwei. 1895a. "Jingshi qiangxue hui xu" (Preface to the metropolitan Society for the Study of Strength). In Tang Zhijun 1981, vol. 1, pp. 165–166.

———. 1895b. "Shanghai qiangxue hui houxu" (Epilogue to the Shanghai Society for the Study of Strength). In Tang Zhijun 1981, vol. 1, pp. 171–172.

———. 1895c. "Shanghai qiangxue hui zhangcheng" (The constitution of the Shanghai Society for the Study of Strength). In Tang Zhijun 1981, vol. 1, pp. 173–179.

———. 1898. "Baoguo hui zhangcheng" (Constitution of the Society for the Preservation of the Country). In Tang Zhijun 1981, vol. 1, pp. 233–236.

———. 1956. *Datong shu* (The book of great harmony). Beijing: Guji Chubanshe.

———. 1975. *Kang Nanhai ziding nianpu* (Kang Nanhai's chronicle compiled by himself) Taiwan: Wenhai Chubanshe.

Karl, Frederick R. 1988. *Modern and Modernism: The Sovereignty of the Artist 1885–1925*. NY: Atheneum.

———. 1991. *Franz Kafka: Representative Man*. New York: Ticknor and Fields.

Karpf, Fay Berger. 1932. *American Social Psychology: Its Origins, Development, and European Background*. New York: McGraw-Hill.

Kaufmann, Walter. 1974. *Nietzsche: Philosopher, Psychologist, Antichrist*. Princeton, NJ: Princeton University Press.

Kawamura Nozomu. 1973. *Nihon shakaigaku-shi kenkyu* (A study in the history of Japanese sociology), vol. 1. Tokyo: Ningen no kagakusha.

Keenan, Barry C. 1969. *John Dewey in China: His Visit and the Reception of His Ideas, 1917–1927*. Ph.D. thesis, Claremont Graduate School and University Center. University Microfilms, Inc., Ann Arbor, MI.

Kelly, Alfred. 1981. *The Descent of Darwin: The Popularization of Darwinism in Germany, 1860–1914*. Chapel Hill: University of North Carolina Press.

Kelly, David. 1991. "The Highest Chinadom: Nietzsche and the Chinese Mind, 1907–1989." In *Nietzsche and Asian Thought*, ed. Graham Parkes, pp. 151–174. Chicago: University of Chicago Press.

Kequan. 1904. "Gailiang fengsu lun shang—benshe zhuangao" (On the reform of customs, part one—Editorial). *DFZZ*, no. 7:133–137.

Kern, Stephen. 1983. *The Culture of Time and Space, 1880–1918*. Cambridge, MA: Harvard University Press.

Kexuan. 1904. "Guochi pian" (Treatise on national shame). *DFZZ*, no. 10:221–231.

Keyes, Daniel. 1959. *Flowers for Algernon*. New York: Harcourt, Brace & World.

Kohn, Hans. 1944. *The Idea of Nationalism: A Study in Its Origins and Background*. New York: Macmillan.

———. 1960. *The Mind of Germany: The Education of a Nation*. New York: Harper and Row.

———. 1967. *Prelude to Nation-States: The French and German Experience, 1789–1815*. Princeton, NJ: Van Nostrand.

Kong Xiangji. 1988. *Kang Youwei bianfa zhouyi yanjiu* (Kang Youwei's memorials on reforms: a study). Shenyang: Liaoning Jiaoyu Chubanshe.

Kowallis, Jon E. 1986. Translation of Lu Xun's "Toward a Refutation of the Voices of Evil." *Renditions*, no. 26:108–119.

Kristeva, Julia. 1977. *About Chinese Women*, trans. Anita Barrows. New York: Boyars.

Kuang Bolin. 1982. "Tang Caichang cong heping gailiang dao fan qing geming de sixiang shuping" (A critical comment on Tang Caichang's intellectual evolution from peaceful reformism to anti-Qing revolution). *Xinhai geming shi congkan*

(Journal of the history of the 1911 revolution), no. 4:13–22. Beijing: Zhonghua Shuju.

Kuwabara Jitsuzo. 1930. "You lishi shang guancha de zhongguo nanbei wenhua" (Northern and southern Chinese cultures from a historical perspective), trans.Yang Yunru. *Guoli Wuhan daxue wenzhe jikan* (The literary and philosophical quarterly of the national Wuhan university) 1, no. 281–360.

La Barre, Weston. 1946. "Some Observations on Character Structure in the Orient, II. The Chinese, Part Two." *Psychiatry* 19, no. 4:375–395.

———. 1948. "Columbia University Research in Contemporary Cultures," *Scientific Monthly*, no. 67:239–240.

Lach, Donald F., and Edwin J. van Kley. 1993. *Asia in the Making of Europe*, vol. III, *A Century of Advance*, Book 4: *East Asia*. Chicago and London: University of Chicago Press.

Laitinen, Kauko. 1990. *Chinese Nationalism in the Late Qing Dynasty: Zhang Binglin as an anti-Manchu Propagandist*. London: Curzon.

Lamprecht, Karl. 1905. *What Is History?* trans. E.A. Andrews. New York: Macmillan.

Lao Mian. 1915. "Lun guojia yu guominxing de guanxi" (On the relationship between nation and national character). In *Jiayin* (Tiger) 1, no. 6:11–17.

Latourette, Kenneth Scott. 1942. *The Chinese: Their History and Culture*, 2nd ed. rev. First ed. 1934. New York: Macmillan.

LDZWJ. 1984. *Li Dazhao wenji* (The collected works of Li Dazhao) Beijing: Renmin Chubanshe.

Le Bon, Gustave. 1974. *The Psychology of Peoples*. Reprint of a 1924 translation. New York: Arno.

Leahey, Thomas Hardy and Grace Evans Leahey. 1983. *Psychology's Occult Doubles: Psychology and the Problem of Pseudoscience*. Chicago: Nelson-Hall.

Leary, Charles L. 1993. "Intellectual Orthodoxy, the Economy of Knowledge and the Debate Over Zhang Jingsheng's *Sex Histories.*" *Republican China* vol. 18, no. 2 (April):98–137.

Lee, Leo Ou-fan. 1987. *Voices from the Iron House: A Study of Lu Xun*. Bloomington and Indianapolis: Indiana University Press.

———. 1999. *Shanghai Modern: The Flowering of a New Urban Culture in China, 1930–1945*. Cambridge, MA: Harvard University Press.

Lei Haizong. 1940. *Zhongguo wenhua yu Zhongguo de bing* (Chinese culture and Chinese soldiers). Reprinted in 1968. Hong Kong: Longmen Shudian.

Leites, Nathan. 1953. *A Study of Bolshevism*. Glencoe, IL: Free Press.

Levenson, Joseph R. 1964. *Confucian China and Its Modern Fate: A Trilogy*, vol. 2. Berkeley: University of California Press.

Levin, Ira. 1953. *A Kiss Before Dying*. New York: Simon and Schuster.

Levy, Oscar. 1964. "The Nietzsche Movement in England." In *The Complete Works of Friedrich Nietzsche*, vol. 18, pp. ix-xxxvi. New York: Russell and Russell.

Li Changzhi. 1984. *Sima Qian zhi renge yu fengge* (Sima Qian's personality and style). Reprint of the 1946 edition. Hong Kong: Sanlian Shudian.

Li Chi. 1928. *The Formation of the Chinese People: An Anthropological Inquiry*. New York: Russell and Russell.

Li Dazhao. 1918. "Dongxi wenming gengben zhi yidian" (The basic difference between Eastern and Western civilizations). In *Li Dazhao wenji* (The collected works of Li Dazhao), 1984, vol. 1, pp. 557–571. Beijing: Renmin Chubanshe.

———. 1919. "Ying kao de yichuanxing" (The heredity of attending civil service examinations). *LDZWJ*, vol. 2, pp. 105.

Li Guojun, ed. 1986. *Liang Qichao zhushu xinian* (An annotated chronology of Liang Qichao's writings). Shanghai: Fudan Daxue Chubanshe.

Li Huang. 1924. "Xi guojiazhuyi" (On statism). *Xing shi* (The awakened lion), no. 1:1–15.

———. 1982. *Xuedunshi huiyilu* (Memoirs of the Learning-the-Hard-Way Studio), rev. ed., vol. 1. Hong Kong: Mingbao Yuekanshe.

Li Jianhua. 1925. "Zhongguo guominxing lun" (A discourse on the Chinese national character). *Xing shi* (The awakened lion), no. 61:1–2.

Li Kan. 1989. "Kang Liang sixiang tongyi lun" (On the similarities and differences between Kang's and Liang's thinking). *JDSYJ*, no. 50:92–117.

Li Ping, 1916. "Letter to Chen Duxiu" In the "Correspondence" section. *XQN* 2, no 3:6–7.

Li Yimin. 1916. "Oumei renzhong gailiang wenti" (The issue of race betterment in Europe and America). *XQN* 2, no. 4:1–4.

Li Yiming. 1997. "Yingmu huangyan: haolaiwu dianying zhong yaomohua de huaren xingxiang" (Silver-screen lies: the demonized Chinese images in Hollywood movies). *Dazhong dianying* (Popular movies), no. 529:16–19.

Li Yuanhong. 1913. Telegram. In *Zhengfu gongbao* (Government gazette), no. 585 (December 19), the "mingling" (order) section.

Li Zefen. 1978. *Yuanshi xintan* (A new study of the history of the Yuan dynasty), vol. 4. Taibei: Zhonghua Shuju.

Li Zongyi 1980. *Yuan Shikai zhuan* (A biography of Yuan Shikai). Beijing: Zhonghua Shuju.

Liang Ch'i-ch'ao (Liang Qichao). 1959. *Intellectual Trends in the Ch'ing Period*, trans. Immanuel C.Y. Hsu. Cambridge, MA: Harvard University Press.

Liang Qichao. 1896–1899. "Bianfa tongyi" (An overall view on reform). In *Heji*, vol. 1, "wenji," part 1, pp. 1–89

———. 1897a. "Chunqiu zhongguo yidi bian xu" (Preface to "The distinction between China and the barbarians in *The Spring and Autumn Annals*"). In *Heji*, vol. 1, "wenji," part 2, pp. 48–49.

———. 1897b. "Lun junzheng minzheng xiangshan zhi li" (The theory of monarchical rule yielding to people's rule). In *Heji*, vol. 1, "wenji," Part 2, pp. 7–10.

———. 1897c. "Lun zhongguo zhi jiang qiang" (China will eventually become strong). In *Heji*, vol. 1, "wenji," Part 2, pp. 11–16.

———. 1897d. "Yu Yan Youling xiansheng shu" (Letter to Mr. Yan Youling). In *Heji*, vol. 1, "wenji," part 1, pp. 106–111.

———. 1898. "Qingyi bao xuli" (The preface to *The Pure Opinion Journal*), *Heji*, vol. 1, "wenji," part 3, pp. 29–31.

———. 1899a. "Aiguo lun" (On patriotism). In *Heji*, vol. 1, "wenji," part 3, pp. 65–77.

———. 1899b. "Lun jinshi guomin jinzheng zhi dashi ji zhongguo qiantu" (On the general trend of modern national struggles and China's future). In *Heji*, vol. 1, "wenji," part 4, pp. 56–61.

———. 1899c. "Lun zhina duli zhi shili yu riben dongfang zhengce" (On China's power for independence and Japan's Eastern policy). In *Heji*, vol. 1, "wenji," part 4, pp. 67–71.

———. 1899d. "Lun zhina zongjiao gaige" (On the Chinese reformation). *Heji*, vol. 1, "wenji," part 3. pp. 54–61.

———. 1899e "Zizhu lun" (On self help). In *Heji*, vol. 6, "zhuanji," part 2, pp. 16–22.

————. 1899f. "Lun zhongguo renzhong zhi jianglai" (The future of the Chinese race). In *Heji*, vol. 1, "wenji," part 3, pp. 48–54.

————. 1899g. "Lun zhongguo yu ouzhou guoti yitong" (On the differences and similarities between the Chinese and European polities). In *Heji*, vol. 1, "wenji," part. 4, pp. 61–67.

————. 1899h. "Zhongguo hun anzai hu" (Where is China's soul?). In *Heji*, vol. 6, "zhuanji," part 2, pp. 37–39.

————. 1900a. "Ershi shiji taipingyang ge" (Song of the twentieth century on the Pacific Ocean). In *Heji*, vol. 5, "wenji," part 45(b), p. 17.

————. 1900b. "He pangguanzhe wen" (Diatribe against onlookers). In *Heji*, vol. 1, "wenji," part. 5, pp. 69–75.

————. 1900c. "Shaonian zhongguo shuo" (The young China thesis). In *Heji*, vol. 1, "wenji," part. 5, pp. 7–12.

————. 1901a. "Guodu shidai lun" (On the age of transition). In *Heji*, vol. 1, "wenji," part 6, pp. 27–32.

————. 1901b. "Guojia sixiang bianqian yitong lun" (On the vicissitudes of, and contrasts among, theories of the state). In *Heji*, vol. 1, "wenji," part 6, pp. 12–22.

————. 1901c. "Shizhong dexing xianfan xiancheng yi" (Five pairs of opposing yet complementary virtues). In *Heji*, vol. 1, "wenji," part 5, pp. 42–51.

————. 1901d. "Zhongguo jiruo suoyuan lun" (Tracing the origins of China's accumulated weakness). In *Heji*, vol. 1, "wenji," part 5, pp. 13–28.

————. 1902a. "Baojiao fei suoyi zunkong lun" (The preservation of teaching is not the reason to venerate Confucius). In *Heji*, vol. 1, "wenji," part 9, pp. 50–59.

————. 1902b. "Dili yu wenming zhi guanxi" (The relation between geography and civilization). In *Heji*, vol. 2, "wenji," part 10, pp. 106–116.

————. 1902c. "Du Lu Fangweng ji" (Having read Lu Fangweng's works). In *Heji*, vol. 5, "wenji," part 45(b), p. 4.

————. 1902d. "E huanggong zhong zhi rengui" (A living ghost in the Russian imperial palace). In *Heji*, vol. 11, "zhuangji," part 91, pp. 1–9.

————. 1902e. "Jiateng boshi tianze baihua" (Dr. Kato's *One Hundred Theses on Tensoku*). In *Heji*, vol. 6, "zhuanji," part 2, pp. 91–98.

————. 1902f. "Jinghua lun gemingzhe Jiede zhi xueshuo" (The theory of a revolutionary in evolutionism, Kidd). In *Heji*, vol. 2, "wenji," part 12, pp. 78–86.

————. 1902g. "Lun jiaoyu dangding zongzhi" (Education should be based on principles). In *Heji*, vol. 2, "wenji," part 10, pp. 52–61.

————. 1902h. "Nulixue" (Slaveology). In *Heji*, vol. 6, "zhuanji," part 2, p. 89.

————. 1902i. "Ouzhou dili dashi lun" (The general trends of European geography). In *Heji*, vol. 2, "wenji," part 10, pp. 101–106.

————. 1902j. "Sanshi zishu" (Autobiography at thirty). In *Heji*, vol. 2, "wenji," Part 11, pp. 15–21.

————. 1902k. "Sibada xiaozhi" (A short history of Sparta). In *Heji*, vol. 6, "zhuanji," part 15, pp. 1–19.

————. 1902L. "Xin shixue" (New history). In *Heji*, vol. 1, "wenji," part 9, pp. 1–32.

————. 1902m. "Xinmin shuo—diba jie: lun quanli sixiang" (On the new people—section 8: on the notion of rights). *XMCB*, no. 6:1–15.

————. 1902n. "Xinmin shuo—diliu jie: lun guojia sixiang" (On the new people—section 6: on national consciousness). *XMCB*, no. 4:1–21.

————. 1902o. "Xinmin shuo—disan jie: shi xinmin zhi yi" (On the new people—section 3: the definition of new people). *XMCB*, no. 1:8–10.

————. 1902p. "Xinmin shuo—dishiyi jie: lun jinbu" (On the new people—section 11: on progress). *XMCB*, no. 10:1–13.

————. 1902q. "Xinmin shuo—disi jie: jiu yousheng liebai zhi li yizheng xinmin zhi jieguo er lun ji qufa zhi suoyi" (On the new people—section 4: to use the principle of survival of the fittest to verify the result of renovating the people, and the suitable method to that effect). *XMCB*, no. 2:1–7.

————. 1902r. "Xinmin shuo—diwu jie: lun gongde" (On the new people—section 5: On public morality). *XMCB*, no. 3:1–7.

————. 1902s. *Xin Zhongguo Weilai Ji* (The future of new China). In *Heji*, vol. 11, "zhuangji," part 89, pp. 1–57.

————. 1902t. "Xiongjiali aiguozhe gesushi zhuan" (The biography of the Hungarian patriot Kossuth). In *Heji*, vol. 6, "zhuanji," part 10, pp. 1–27.

————. 1902u. "Zhongguo dili dashi lun" (The general trends of Chinese geography). In *Heji*, vol. 2, "wenji," part 10, pp. 77–101.

————. 1903a. "Ershi shiji zhi juling tuolasi" (The behemoth of the twentieth century—trust). In *Heji*, vol. 2, "wenji," part 14, pp. 33–61.

————. 1903b. "Huangdi yihou diyi wairen zhaowuling wang zhuan" (A biography of the first great man after the Yellow Emperor, King Wuling of Zhao). In *Heji*, vol. 6, "zhuanji," part 6, pp. 1–7.

————. 1903c. "Ji sibinsai lun riben xianfa yu" (Notes on Spencer's comments on the Japanese constitution). In *Heji*, vol. 6, "zhuanji," part 2, pp. 99–101.

————. 1903d. "Lun zhongguo guomin zhi pinge" (On Chinese people's quality and character). In *Heji*, vol. 2, "wenji," part 14, pp. 1–5.

————. 1903e. "Xinmin shuo—dishiqi jie: lun shangwu" (On the new people—section 17: on martial spirit). *XMCB*, no. 28:1–9.

————. 1903f. "Xinmin shuo—dishisan jie: lun hequn" (On the new people—section 13: on gregariousness). *XMCB*, no. 16:1–7.

————. 1903g. "Xinmin shuo—dishiba jie: lun side" (On the new people—section 18: on private morality). *XMCB*, nos. 38–39:1–18.

————. 1904a. "Mingji diyi zhongyao renwu Yuan Chonghuan zhuan" (The biography of the most important personage of late Ming, Yuan Chonghuan). In *Heji*, vol. 6, "zhuanji," part 7, pp. 1–24.

————. 1904b. *Xin dalu youji* (Travels of the new continent). In *XMCB*, special issue, February, pp. 1–228.

————. 1904c. "Xinmin shuo—dishiba jie: lun side (xu)" (On the new people—section 18: on private morality, continued). In *XMCB*, nos. 40–41, pp. 1–10; nos. 46–48, pp. 1–12.

————. 1904d. "Xinmin shuo—di shijiu jie: lun zhengzhi nengli" (On the new people—section 19: on political capabilities). In *XMCB*, no. 49, pp. 1–12.

————. 1904e. "Yuzhi sisheng guan" (My view of death and life). In *Heji*, vol. 2, "wenji," part 17, pp. 1–12.

————. 1904f. "Zhongguo de wushidao" (The Chinese bushido). In *Heji*, vol. 7, "zhuangji," part 24, pp. 1–57.

————. 1910a. "Guojia yunming lun" (On the fate of the country). In *Heji*, vol. 3, "wenji," part 22, pp. 94–103.

————. 1910b. "Shuo guofeng" (On national mores). In *Heji*, vol. 3, "wenji," section 25 (b), pp. 3–11.

————. 1911. "Zhongguo qiantu zhi xiwang yu guomin zeren" (China's prospects and the responsibility of the citizens). In *Heji*, vol. 3, "wenji," part 25 (b), pp. 1–40.

———. 1912a. "Guoxing pian" (Treatise on national character). In *Heji*, vol. 4, "wenji," part 29, pp. 82–86.

———. 1912b. "Zhongguo daode zhi dayuan" (The fountainhead of Chinese morality). In *Heji*, vol. 4, "wenji," part 28, pp. 12–20.

———. 1913a. "Geming xiangxu zhi yuanli jiqi eguo" (The principle of successive revolutions and its baneful effects). In *Heji*, vol. 4, "wenji," part 30, pp. 51–57.

———. 1913b. "Shuo youzhi" (On infantilism). In *Heji*, vol. 4, "wenji," part 30, pp. 45–51.

———. 1913c. "Yinian lai zhi zhengxiang yu guomin chengdu zhi yingshe" (The political phenomena of the past year and how they reflect on the level of the citizens). In *Heji*, vol. 4, "wenji," part 30, pp. 16–18.

———. 1919. *Ouyou xinyinglu jielu* (Excerpts of mental impressions of the European trip). In *Heji*, vol. 7, "zhuanji," part. 23, pp. 1–162.

———. 1920. *Qingdai xueshu gailun* (Intellectual trends in the Qing period). In *Heji*, vol. 8, "zhuanji," part 34, pp. 1–80.

———. 1922. *Zhongguo lishi yanjiu fa* (Research methods for Chinese history). In *Heji*, vol. 10, "zhuanji," part 73, pp. 1–128.

———. 1924. "Jindai xuefeng zhi dilide fenbu" (The geographical distribution of modern scholastic styles). In *Heji*, vol. 5, "wenji," part 41, pp. 48–80.

Liang Qixun. 1903. "Guomin xinlixue yu jiaoyu zhi guanxi" (The relationship between national psychology and education). *XMCB*, no. 25:1–9; no. 30:1–5.

Liang Shuming. 1985. *Dongxi wenhua ji qi zhexue* (Eastern and Western cultures and their philosophies). Reprint. Originally published in 1922. Taipei: Liren shuju.

Lin Yu-sheng. 1979. *The Crisis of Chinese Consciousness: Radical Antitraditionalism in the May Fourth Era*. Madison, WI: University of Wisconsin Press.

———. 1992. "Lu Xun gerenzhuyi de xingzhi yu hanyi—jian lun 'guominxing' wenti" (The nature and implications of Lu Xun's individualism—also on the 'national character' issue). *ESYSJ*, no. 12, pp. 83–91.

Lin Yutang. 1925a. "Gei xuantong de xin" (A letter to Qian Xuantong). *Yusi* (Word threads), 23:1–4.

———. 1925b. "Sa tianshi yulu" (Thus spoke the guru Zarathustra). In *Yusi* (Word threads), 55 and in Lin's *Dahuang ji* (The great wilderness collection). Shanghai: Shenghuo Shudian, 1934, vol. 2, pp. 158–170.

———. 1935. *My Country and My People*. New York: John Day.

Liu Chengyu. 1903. "Shixue guangyi neipian" (The study of history in a broad sense: the core treatise). *HBXSJ*, no. 1:1–12; no. 3:1–7.

Liu Guanghan. 1905. "Nanbei xuepai butong lun" (The differences between the southern and northern schools). *Guocui xuebao* (National essence journal) no 2:8–10; no. 6:1–8; no. 7:1–8; no. 9:9–12.

Liu Housheng. 1965. *Zhang Jian zhuanji* (A biography of Zhang Jian). Hong Kong: Longmen Shudian, 1965.

Liu, Lydia. 1995. *Translingual Practice: Literature, National Culture, and Translated Modernity—China, 1900–1937*. Stanford, CA: Stanford University Press.

Liu Yashu. 1916. "Ouzhou zhanzheng yu qingnian zhi juewu" (The European war and the youth's awakening). *XQN* 2, no. 2:1–8.

Lu Guancun. 1920. "Renlei jingbu zhi zhijing" (The limits of human progress). *DFZZ* 17, no. 3:59–63.

Lu Xun. 1903a. "Sibada zhi hun" (The soul of Sparta). In *LXQJ*, vol. 7, pp. 9–19.

———. 1903b. "Zhongguo dizhi lüelun" (A short discourse on Chinese geology). In *LXQJ*, vol. 8, pp. 1–21.

————. 1907. "Ren zhi lishi." Translation of Haeckel's "Man's History." In *LXQJ*, vol. 1, pp. 8–24.

————. 1908a. "Moluo shili shuo." (The power of satanic poetry). In *LXQJ*, vol. 1, pp. 63–115.

————. 1908b. "Po esheng lun." (A refutation of vile voices). In *LXQJ*, vol. 8, pp. 23–37.

————. 1908c. "Wenhua pianzhi lun" (The lopsided development of culture). In *LXQJ*, vol. 1, pp. 44–62.

————. 1918a. "Suiganlu sanshiba" (Random thoughts 38). In *LXQJ*, vol. 1, pp. 311–320.

————. 1918b. "Suiganlu sishijiu" (Random thoughts 49). In *LXQJ*, vol. 1, pp. 338–339.

————. 1918c. "Kuangren riji" (A madman's diary). In *LXQJ*, vol. 1, pp. 422–433.

————. 1918d. "Wozhi jielie guan" (My view of female chastity and martyrdom). In *LXQJ*, vol. 1, pp. 116–128.

————. 1919a. "Kong Yiji." In *LXQJ*, vol. 1, pp. 434–439.

————. 1919b. "Suiganlu liushiwu: baojun de chenmin" (Random thoughts 65: the subjects of tyrants). In *LXQJ*, vol. 1, pp. 366–367.

————. 1919c. "Suiganlu sishiyi" (Random thoughts 41). In *LXQJ*, vol. 1, pp. 324–326.

————. 1919d. "Women xianzai zenyang zuo fuqin" (How do we behave like a father now?). In *LXQJ*, vol. 1, pp. 129–143.

————. 1919e. "Yao" (Medicine). In *LXQJ*, vol. 1, pp. 440–449.

————. 1921–1922. "A Q zhengzhuan" (The true story of Ah Q). In *LXQJ*, vol. 1, pp. 487–532.

————. 1922a. "Bai guang" (White light). In *LXQJ*, vol. 1, pp. 542–548.

————. 1922b. "Nahan' zixu" (Preface to *Outcry*) In *LXQJ*, vol. 1, pp. 415–421.

————. 1992c. "Butian" (Repairing the heavens). *LXQJ*, vol. 2, pp. 345–356.

————. 1923. "Nola zouhou zenyang" (What will happen after Nora leaves home?). *LXQJ*, vol. 1, pp. 158–165.

————. 1924a. "Fuchou" (Revenge), *LXQJ*, vol. 2, pp. 172–173.

————. 1924b. "Fuchou (qi'er)" (Revenge 2), *LXQJ*, vol. 2, pp. 174–176.

————. 1924c. Letter to Li Bingzhong, dated September 24. In *LXQJ*, vol. 11, pp. 430–431.

————. 1924d. "Lun leifeng ta de daodiao" (On the collapse of the Leifeng Pagoda). In *LXQJ*, vol. 1, pp. 171–173.

————. 1924e. "Lun zhaoxiang zhi lei" (On photography and the like). In *LXQJ*, vol. 1, pp. 181–190.

————. 1924f. "Weiyou tiancai zhiqian" (Before there are geniuses). In *LXQJ*, vol. I, pp. 166–170.

————. 1924g. "Yingde gaobie" (Farewell of the shadow). In *LXQJ*, vol. 2, pp. 165–166.

————. 1925a. "Cong huxu shuodao yachi" (Rambling from moustache to teeth). In *LXQJ*, vol. 1, pp. 243–255.

————. 1925b. "Dengxia manbi" (Casual essay written under the lamp). In *LXQJ*, vol. 1, pp. 210–219.

————. 1925c. "Guafuzhuyi" (Widowism). In *LXQJ*, vol. 1, pp. 262–269.

————. 1925d. "Huran xiangdao, wu" (Sudden thoughts, 5). In *LXQJ*, vol. 3, pp. 14–20.

————. 1925e. "Lun 'tamade!' " (On "Your mother!"). In *LXQJ*, vol. 1, pp. 231–236.

————. 1925f. "Lun zhengle yan kan" (On opening one's eyes to see). In *LXQJ*, vol. 1, pp. 237–242.

————. 1925g. "The Misanthrope." In *The Complete Stories of Lu Xun*, trans. Yang Xianyi and Gladys Yang, pp. 232–252. Bloomington: Indiana University Press, published in association with Foreign Language Press, Beijing, 1981.

————. 1925h. "Nu xiaozhang de nannü de meng" (The female principal's dreams about male and female). In *LXQJ*, vol. 7, pp. 290–292.

————. 1925i. " 'Pengbi' zhi yu" (After "knocking against the wall"). In *LXQJ*, vol. 3, pp. 68–74.

————. 1925j. "Sihou" (After death). In *LXQJ*, vol. 2, pp. 209–215.

————. 1925k. "Tuibaixian de zhandong" (The tremor of the faltering line). In *LXQJ*, vol. 2, pp. 204–206.

————. 1925L. "Zailun leifengta de daodiao" (Again on the downfall of Leifeng Pagoda). *LXQJ*, vol. 1, pp. 191–196.

————. 1925m. "Zhayi" (Mixed memories). In *LXQJ*, vol. 1, pp. 220–230.

————. 1926a. "Congmingren he shazi he nucai" (The Wiseguy, the Fool, and the Lackey). In *LXQJ*, vol. 2, pp. 216–218.

————. 1926b. "Mashang zhiriji" (The sub-diary of Mashang). In *LXQJ*, vol. 3, pp. 321–348.

————. 1927a. "Da Youheng xiansheng" (Reply to Mr. Youheng). In *LXQJ*, vol 3, pp. 453–460.

————. 1927b. "Lüe lun zhongguoren de lian" (A brief comment on the Chinese face). In *LXQJ*, vol. 3, pp. 412–416.

————. 1927c. "You 'tianru' " (Worries about 'natural breasts'). In *LXQJ*, vol. 3, pp. 467–470.

————. 1928a. "Changong daguan" (The panorama of eradicating communists). *Yusi* (Word threads), 4, no. 18:38–40.

————. 1928b. Letter to Li Bingzhong, dated April 9th. In *LXQJ*, vol. 11, p. 619.

————. 1930. " 'Jinghua he tuihua' xiaoyin" (A brief introduction to *Evolution and Degeneration*). In *LXQJ*, vol. 4. pp. 250–252.

————. 1931. "Shanghai wenyi zhi yipie" (A glimpse of Shanghai literature). In *LXQJ*, vol. 4, pp. 291–307.

————. 1932a. " 'Liangdi shu' xuyan" (Preface to *Letters from Two Places*). In *LXQJ*, vol. 11, pp. 3–7.

————. 1932b. " 'Sanxianji' xuyan" (Preface to *Three Leisures Collection*). In *LXQJ*, vol. 4, pp. 3–10.

————. 1933. "Ye song" (A paean to night). In *LXQJ*, vol. 5, pp. 193–194.

————. 1976. "Waiting for a Genius." In *Lu Hsun: Writing for the Revolution*, pp. 85–88. San Francisco: Red Sun Publishers.

Lundberg, Ferdinand, and Marynia Farnham. 1947. *Modern Woman: The Lost Sex*. New York: Harper and Brothers.

Luo Jialun. 1937. "Minzu yu minzuxing" (Nation and national character). In *Luo Jialun xiansheng wencun* (Luo Jialun's collected essays), vol. 2, pp. 93–118. Taibei: Guomindang Zhongyang Weiyuanhui, Guoshiguan, 1976.

————. 1938. "Minzu yu dili huanjing" (Nation and geographical environment). In *Luo Jialun xiansheng wencun* (Luo Jialun's collected essays), vol. 2, pp. 139–155.

Luo Luo. 1919. "Minzu youlie zhi bijiao" (A comparison of racial superiority and inferiority). *DFZZ* 16:9:71–72.

LXQJ. 1982. *Lu Xun quanji* (The complete works of Lu Xun). Beijing: Renmin Wenxue Chubanshe.

Ma Lu. 1921. "Renlei tuihua shuo—aoguo shengwuxue jiaoshou de weiyan" (The theory of degeneration of the human species—words of warning from an Austrian professor). *DFZZ* 18, no. 16:67–69.

Ma Wenju. 1984. "Qingmo minchu xinlixue yizhu chuban zhong de ruogan wenti" (A few questions concerning the translation and writing of psychological works in the late Qing and early Republican period). In *Jiangxi shifan daxue xuebao (zhexue shehui kexue ban)* (Journal of the Jiangxi teachers' university (the philosophy and social sciences section)), no. 1, pp. 39–46.

Mancall, Mark. 1971. *Russia and China: Their Diplomatic Relations to 1728.* Cambridge, MA: Harvard University Press.

Manson, William C. 1986. "Abram Kardiner and the Neo-Freudian Alternative in Culture and Personality." In *Malinowski, Rivers, Benedict and Others: Essays on Culture and Personality*, ed. George W. Stocking Jr., pp. 72–94. Madison: University of Wisconsin Press.

———. 1988. *The Psychodynamics of Culture: Abram Kardiner and Neo-Freudian Anthropology.* New York: Greenwood Press.

Mao Dun. 1928. *Dongyao* (Vacillation). In *Mao Dun quanji* (The complete works of Mao Dun), vol. 1, pp. 101–258. Beijing: Renmin Wenxue Chubanshe.

———. 1984. *Hong* (Rainbow) In *Mao Dun quanji* (The complete works of Mao Dun), vol. 2, pp. 1–273.

Marcuse, Herbert. 1955. *Eros and Civilization.* Boston: Beacon Press.

Martin, Geoffrey J. 1973. *Ellsworth Huntington: His Life and Thought.* Hamden, CT: Archon Books.

Masson, Jeffrey Moussaieff. 1984. *The Assault on Truth: Freud's Suppression of the Seduction Theory.* New York: Farrar, Straus and Giroux.

Mayer, Ernst. 1982. *The Growth of Biological Thought, Diversity, Evolution, and Inheritance.* Cambridge, MA: The Belknap Press of Harvard University Press.

McDougall, William. 1920. *The Group Mind: A Sketch of the Principles of Collective Psychology with Some Attempt to Apply Them to the Interpretation of National Life and Character.* New York: Putnam.

McLaren, Angus. 1997. *The Trials of Masculinity: Policing Sexual Boundaries, 1870–1930.* Chicago and London: University of Chicago Press.

Mead, Margaret. 1951. "The Study of National Character." In *The Policy Sciences: Recent Developments in Scope and Method*, ed. Daniel Lerner and Harold D. Lasswell, pp. 70–85. Stanford, CA: Stanford University Press.

———. 1953. "National Character." In *Anthropology Today: An Encyclopedic Inventory*, ed. Arthur L. Kroeber, pp. 642–667. Chicago, IL: University of Chicago Press.

Mead, Margaret and Rhoda Metraux, eds. 1953. *The Study of Culture at a Distance.* Chicago: University of Chicago Press.

Metzger, Thomas A. 1977. *Escape from Predicament: Neo-Confucianism and China's Evolving Political Culture.* New York: Columbia University Press.

Milton, Colin. 1987. *Lawrence and Nietzsche: A Study of Influence.* Aberdeen, U.K.: The University Press.

Minutes. 1951a. Minutes of "Chinese Political Character" group meeting (Jan. 16, 1951). *MMP-RCC-CPC*, G-63.

Minutes. 1951b. Minutes of "Chinese Political Character" group meeting (Jan. 30, 1951). *MMP-RCC-CPC*, G-63.

MMP. Abbreviation of *Margaret Mead Papers*, in the Division of Special Collections, the Library of Congress.

Morris-Suzuki, Tessa. 1998. *Re-inventing Japan: Time, Space, Nation.* Armonk, NY: M.E. Sharpe.

Muensterberger, Warner. 1948. "Some Notes on Chinese Stories (in collaboration with Virginia Heyer)." *MMP-RCC*, G-23, v. 7, Ch-348.

———. 1951. "Orality and Dependence: Characteristics of Southern Chinese." In *Psychoanalysis and the Social Sciences*, vol. 3, pp. 37–69. New York: International University Press.

———. n.d. "Oral Fixation and Reaction Formation." *MMP-RCC*, G-23, v. 7, Ch-620.

Munguia Jr., E. trans. 1929. *The Under Dogs*. New York: Brentano's. A translation of Mariano Azuela's *Los De Abajo*.

Murata Yuujiro. 1993. "Kang Youwei de riben yanjiu ji qi tedian: 'riben bianzheng kao' 'riben *shumu zhi*' *guanjian*" (Kang Youwei's Japan studies and their characteristics: My humble opinion on *A Study of Institutional Changes in Japan and Annotated Bibliography of Japan*). *JDSYJ* no. 73:27–40.

Nagai Michio. 1954. "Herbert Spencer in Early Meiji Japan." *Far Eastern Quarterly* 14, no. 1:55–64.

Neige Guanbao (Gazette of the Cabinet). 1912. The twenty-sixth day of the twelfth month (the lunar calendar) of the third year of Emperor Xuantong.

Nietzsche, Friedrich. 1967. *On the Genealogy of Morals and the Origin of Tragedy*, trans. Walter Kaufmann. New York: Vintage Books.

———. 1968a. *Ecce Homo*. In *Basic Writings of Nietzsche*, trans. and ed. Walter Kaufmann. New York: The Modern Library.

———. 1968b. *The Will to Power*, trans. Walter Kaufmann and R.J. Hollingdale. New York: Vintage Books.

———. 1986. *Thus Spake Zarathustra*, trans. R.J. Hollingdale. New York: Viking Penguin.

Nordau, Max. 1968. *Degeneration*, translated from the 2nd ed. in German, translator unknown, first published in English in 1895. Reprint. New York: Howard Fertig.

Norton, Mary Beth. 1982. *A People and A Nation*, vol. 2. Boston: Houghton Mifflin.

Novick, Peter. 1988. *That Noble Dream: The "Objectivity Question" and the American Historical Profession*. New York: Cambridge University Press.

Nye, Robert A. 1975. *The Origins of Crowd Psychology: Gustave LeBon and the Crisis of Mass Democracy in the Third Republic*. London and Beverly Hills: Sage.

———. 1984. *Crime, Madness, and Politics in Modern France*. Princeton, NJ: Princeton University Press.

O'Brien, Mary. 1981. *The Politics of Reproduction*. Boston: Routledge and Kegan Paul.

Okamoto Shumpei. 1976. "Japanese Response to Chinese Nationalism: Naito (Ko'nan) Torajiro's Image of China in the 1920s." In *China in the 1920s: Nationalism and Revolution*, ed. F. Gilbert Chan and Thomas H. Etzold, pp. 160–175. New York: New Viewpoints.

Okakura Tenshin. 1894. "Shina nanboku no kubetsu" (The differences between north and south China). In *Okakura Tenshin shu* (Collected works of Okakura Tenshin), ed. Kamei Katsuichiro and Miyakawa Torao, pp. 309–311. Tokyo: Chikuma Shobo, 1968.

———. 1903. *Toyo no riso* (The ideals of the east). In *Okakura Tenshin Zenshu* (The complete works of Okakura Tenshin), ed. Kumamoto Kenjiro et. al, pp. 7–132. Tokyo: Heibonsha, 1980.

Osterwalder, F. 1994. "Pestalozzi and Education." In *The International Encyclopedia of Education*, 2nd ed., ed. Torsten Husén and T. Neville Postlethwaite, vol. 8, pp. 4415–4419. Oxford, U.K.: Pergamon.

Otani Kotaro. 1935. *Gendai shinajin seishin kozo no kenkyu* (A study of the spiritual structure of the modern Chinese). Shanghai: the Institute of Chinese Studies of the Toa Dobun Shoin.

Pan Guangdan. 1927a. "Wulin youlan yu renwen dilixue" (The Wulin tour and human geography). In his *Yousheng gailun* (A general introduction to eugenics), pp. 223–239. Shanghai and Chongqing: Shangwu Yinshuguan, 1946.

———. 1927b. "Zai lun zhongzu wei wenhua yuanyin zhi yi" (Again on race as a cause of culture). In *Pan Guangdan minzu yanjiu wenji* (Pan Guangdan's selected essays on the study of nation), pp. 1–6. Beijing: Minzu Chubanshe, 1995.

———. 1929a. "Renwen xuanze yu zhonghua minzu—liangge zhidu de taolun" (Man-made selection and the Chinese race—a discussion on two institutions). In *Xin yue* (Crescent moon) 3, no. 2:1–20.

———. 1929b. *Ziran taotai yu zhonghua minzuxing* (Natural selection and the Chinese national character). Shanghai: Xinyue Shudian.

———. 1981. *Youshengxue yuanli* (Principles of eugenics), reprint of a 1949 ed. Tianjin: Tianjin Renmin Chubanshe.

Pearson, Charles H. 1893. *National Life and Character: A Forecast*. London: Macmillan.

Pearson, Karl. 1901. *National Life from the Standpoint of Science*. London: Adam and Charles Black.

Peck, Joseph H. 1982. *The Myth of Masculinity*. Cambridge, MA: MIT Press.

———. 1987. "The Theory of Male Sex-Role Identity: Its Rise and Fall, 1936 to the Present." In *The Making of Masculinities: The New Men's Studies*, ed. Harry Brod, pp. 21–38. Boston: Allen and Unwin.

Perry, Helen Swick. 1974. "Introduction." In Harry Stack Sullivan, *Schizophrenia As A Human Process*, pp. xi–xxxi. New York: Norton.

Pick, Daniel. 1993. *Faces of Degeneration: A European Disorder, c.1848–c.1918*. New York: Cambridge University Press.

Pickens, Donald K. 1968. *Eugenics and the Progressives*. Nashville, TN: Vanderbilt University Press.

Pierrot, Jean. 1981. *The Decadent Imagination, 1880–1900,* trans. Derek Coltman. Chicago and London: University of Chicago Press.

Pipes, Richard. 1991. *The Russian Revolution*. New York: Vintage.

Pittau, Joseph. 1967. *Political Thought in Early Meiji Japan, 1868–1889*. Cambridge, MA: Harvard University Press.

Plaks, Andrew. 1977. *Chinese Narrative: Critical and Theoretical Essays*. Princeton, NJ: Princeton University Press.

Price, Don C. 1974. *Russia and the Roots of the Chinese Revolution, 1896–1911*. Cambridge, MA: Harvard University Press.

Pusey, James Reeve. 1983. *China and Charles Darwin*. Cambridge, MA: Harvard University Press.

———. 1998. *Lu Xun and Evolution*. Albany, NY: State University of New York Press.

Pye, Lucian. 1969. *The Spirit of Chinese Politics: A Psychocultural Study of the Authority Crisis in Political Development*. Cambridge, MA: M.I.T. Press.

Pyle, Kenneth B. 1969. *The New Generation in Meiji Japan: Problems of Cultural Identity, 1885–1895*. Stanford, CA: Stanford University Press.

Qian Zhixiu. 1916. "Duoxing zhi guomin" (A nation affected by inertia). *DFZZ* 13, no. 10:1–6.

Qianjin (Zhu Zhixin). 1914a. "Baomin zhengzhi zhe he" (What is mob rule?). *Minguo* (Republic) 1, no. 2 (June):1–15.

———. 1914b. "Geming yu xinli" (Revolution and psychology). *Minguo* (Republic) 1, no. 4:1–21.

Qiaofeng (Zhou Jiaren). 1923. "Feichang de genben wenti" (The basic problem of the abolition of prostitution). *FNZZ* 9, no. 3:6–8.

Qiming (Zhou Zuoren). 1928. "Suiganlu bashiba: fa zhi yi kaocha" (Random thoughts 88: A survey of the problem of hair). *Yusi* (Word threads) 4, no. 6: 37–41.

Qiu Zhuang. 1926. "Guojiazhuyi zhi zhexue jichu (yi)" (The philosophical foundation of statism, part one). *Xing shi* (The awakened lion), no. 98:2–4.

QNZZ. Abbreviation of *Qingnian Zazhi* (Youth magazine)

Quan Weitian. 1985. "Pan Guangdan zhuanluue" (A short biography of Pan Guangdan). In *Zhongguo xiandai shehuikexuejia zhuanluue* (Biographies of Chinese modern social scientists), 5th series, pp. 486–504. Taiyuan: Shanxi Renmin Chubanshe.

Rankin, Mary Backus. 1970. *Early Chinese Revolutionaries: Radical Intellectuals in Shanghai and Chekiang, 1902–1911.* Cambridge, MA: Harvard University Press.

RCC. Abbreviation of *Research in Contemporary Cultures*.

Redford, Donald. 1992. "The Criminal of Akhetaton." In *Makers of World History*, vol. 1, ed. J. Kelly Sowards, pp. 7–14. New York: St. Martin's Press.

Reinemer, V. 1955. "Is Fluoridation a Marxist Plot?" *Reporter* (June):28–30.

Reisner, Edward H. 1922. *Nationalism and Education Since 1789: A Social and Political History of Modern Education.* New York: Macmillan.

Reynolds, Douglas R. 1993. *China, 1898–1912: The Xinzheng Revolution and Japan.* Cambridge, MA: Harvard East Asian Monographs.

Rin Hsien. 1963. "Koro: A Consideration of Chinese Concepts of Illness and Case Illustrations." *Transcultural Psychiatric Research*, no. 15:23–30.

———. 1966. "Two Forms of Vital Deficiency Syndrome Among Chinese Male Mental Patients," *Transcultural Psychiatric Research*, no. 3:19–21.

Robinson, James Harvey. 1958. *The New History: Essays Illustrating the Modern Historical Outlook.* Springfield, MA: Walden, reprint of the 1912 edition.

Rocker, Rudolf. 1937. *Nationalism and Culture*, trans. Ray E. Chase. Los Angeles: Rocker Publications Committee.

Ru Song. 1931. "Ping youshengxue yu huanjinglun te lunzheng" (A comment on the debate between eugenics and environmentalism). *Ershi shiji* (The twentieth century) 1, no. 1:57–124

Ruddick, Sara. 1980. "Maternal Thinking." *Feminist Studies* 6, no. 2:342–367.

Russell, Bertrand. 1966. *The Problem of China.* Reprint, first published in 1922. London: Allen and Unwin.

Said, Edward. 1979. *Orientalism.* New York: Vintage.

Saneto Keishu, Tam Yue-him, Ogawa Hiroshi. 1980. *Zhongguo yi riben shu zonghe mulu* (The combined catalogue of Japanese books translated into Chinese). Hong Kong: Chinese University Press.

Saneto Keishu. 1983. *Zhongguoren liuxue riben shi* (A History of Chinese studying in Japan), trans. Tam Yue-him, Lin Qiyan. Beijing: Sanlian Shudian.

Sansom, George. 1963. *A History of Japan, 1615–1867.* Stanford, CA: Stanford University Press.

Sardar, Ziauddin. 1998. *Postmodernism and the Other: The New Imperialism of Western Culture.* London: Pluto.

Sass, Louis Arnorsson. 1992. *Madness and Modernity: Insanity in the Light of Modern Art, Literature, and Thought.* New York: Basic Books.

Sato Kazuki. 1997. " 'Same Language, Same Race'—The Dilemma of *Kanbun* in Modern Japan." In *The Construction of Racial Identities in China and Japan*, ed. Frank Dikötter, pp. 118–135.

Schafer, Roy. 1954. *Psychoanalytic Interpretation in Rorschach Testing: Theory and Application.* New York: Grune and Stratton.

Schama, Simon. 1989. *Citizens: A Chronicle of the French Revolution.* New York: Vintage.

Schiffrin, Harold Z. 1968. *Sun Yat-sen and the Origins of the Chinese Revolution.* Berkeley and Los Angeles: University of California Press.

Schneider, Laurence A. 1971. *Ku Chieh-kang and China's New History: Nationalism and the Quest for Alternative Traditions.* Berkeley: University of California Press.

———. 1976. "National Essence and the New Intelligentsia." In Furth 1976, pp. 57–89.

Schulz, Hans. 1942. *Deutsches Fremdworterbuch,* 2 Band. Berlin: W. de Gruyter.

Schwartz, Benjamin. 1964. *In Search of Wealth and Power: Yen Fu and the West.* Cambridge, MA: Harvard University Press.

Scott, Gini Graham. 1992. *Erotic Power: An Exploration of Dominance and Submission.* New York: Citadel.

Sebald, Hans. 1976. *Momism: The Silent Disease of America.* Chicago: Nelson Hall.

Semple, Ellen Churchill. 1911. *Influences of Geographic Environment, on the Basis of Ratzel's System of Anthropo-geography.* New York: Holt.

Shafer, Boyd C. 1955. *Nationalism: Myth and Reality.* New York: Harcourt, Brace.

Shan Zhi. 1914. "Pi nanbei pian" (A treatise refuting the north-south thesis). *Minguo* (Republic), no. 2:1–4.

Shanghai shi wenwu baoguan weiyuanhui. 1982. *Kang Youwei yu baohuang hui* (Kang Youwei and the Emperor Protection Society). Shanghai: Shanghai Renmin Chubanshe.

Shangxin Ren. 1900. "Shuo nuli" (Discourse on slave). *Qingyi Bao,* no. 69:4417–4424.

Shao Yuanchong. 1933. "Xinli jianshe yu minzu fuxing" (Psychological construction and the national revival). In *Xuanpu Yishu* (The works of Xuanpu published posthumously), pp. 361–370. Taibei: Zhengzhong shuju, 1954.

Shen Sung-chiao. 1997. "Wo yi woxue jian xuanyuan—huangdi shenhua yu wanqingde guozu jiangou" (The myth of Huang-ti [Yellow Emperor] and the construction of Chinese nationhood in Late Qing). *Taiwan shehui yanjiu* (Taiwan: A radical quarterly in social studies) 28:1–77.

Showalter, Elaine. 1986. "Syphilis, Sexuality, and the Fiction of the Fin de Siècle." In *Sex, Politics, and Science in the Nineteenth-Century Novel,* ed. Ruth Bernard Yeazell, pp. 88–115. Baltimore, MD: Johns Hopkins University Press.

Shulou. 1904. "Jiaocai zhi xuanze: jielu jinzhu 'zhongguo jiaoyu lun' " (The selection of teaching materials: excerpts from a recent work, *On Chinese Education*). *Jiangsu,* nos. 11–12:7–13.

Si (Lu Xun). 1918. "Suiganlu sanshisan" (Random thoughts, 33). *XQN* 5, no. 4 (Oct. 15): 405–409

Smith, Arthur H. 1894. *Chinese Characteristics.* New York: Revell.

Soja, Edward W. 1989. *The Reassertion of Space in Critical Social Theory.* London and New York: Verso.

Solomon, Richard H. 1971. *Mao's Revolution and the Chinese Political Culture.* Berkeley: University of California Press.

Sowards, J. Kelly, ed. 1992. *Makers of World History,* vol. 1. New York: St. Martin's.

Spackman, Barbara. 1989. *Decadent Geneologies. The Rhetoric of Sickness from Baudelaire to D'Annunzio.* Ithaca, NY: Cornell University Press.

Stalin, Joseph. 1954. *Marxism and the National Question.* Moscow: Foreign Languages Publishing House.

Stocking Jr., George W., ed. 1986. *Malinowski, Rivers, Benedict and Others: Essays on Culture and Personality.* Madison: University of Wisconsin Press.

————. 1987. *Victorian Anthropology*. New York: Free Press.

Strand, David. 1989. *Rickshaw Beijing: City People and Politics in the 1920s*. Berkeley: University of California Press.

Strickland, Charles and E. Andrew M. Ambrose. 1985. "The Baby Boom, Prosperity, and the Changing Worlds of Children, 1945–1963." In *American Childhood: A Research Guide and Historical Handbook*, ed. Joseph M. Hawes and N. Ray Hiner, pp. 533–585. Westport, CT: Greenwood.

Su Xiaokang and Wang Luxiang. 1988. *He Shang*. Hong Kong: Sanlian Shudian.

Sullivan, Harry Stack. 1974. *Schizophrenia As a Human Process*. New York: Norton.

Sun Chunzai. 1985. *Qingmo de gongyang sixiang* (The Gongyang thought in the late Qing period). Taibei: Taiwan Shangwu Yinshuguan.

Sun Lung-kee. 1986. "To Be or Not to Be Eaten." *Modern China* 12, no. 4:459–485.

————. 1991. "The Dialogue between Two Revolutions: 1789 and 1911." *Republican China* 17, 1:1–20.

————. 1993. "The *Fin de Siècle* Lu Xun." *Republican China* 18, no. 2:64–98.

————. 1994. "Historians' Warp: Problems in Textualizing the Intellectual History of Modern China." *Positions* 2, no. 2 (Fall):356–381.

————. 1995. "Shijimo sichao: qian wuqulu de lixiangzhuyi" (Fin-de-siecle thoughts: idealism without the prospect of a future). *ESYSJ*, no. 27:31–42.

————. 1996. "The Presence of the Fin-de-Siècle in the May Fourth Era." In *Remapping China: Fissures in Historical Terrain*, ed. Gail Hershatter et al., pp. 194–323. Stanford, CA: Stanford University Press.

Sun Zhongshan. 1924. "Minzuzhuyi" (Nationalism) In *Sun Zhongshan xuanji* (The selected works of Sun Zhongshan), pp. 615–691. Beijing: Renmin Chubanshe, 1981.

Sutton, H. Eldon. 1988. *An Introduction to Human Genetics*, 4th ed. San Diego: Harcourt Brace Jovanovich.

Tam Yue-him. 1980. "An Intellectual's response to Western intrusion: Naito Konan's view of Republican China." In *The Chinese and the Japanese: Essays in Political and Cultural Interactions*, ed. Akira Iriye, pp. 161–183. Princeton, NJ: Princeton University.

Tan Qixiang. 1987. "Zhongguo wenhua de shidai chayi yu diqu chayi" (The epochal and regional variations of Chinese culture). In *Zhongguo chuantong wenhua zai jiantao* (The re-examination of traditional culture), ed. History Department of Fudan University, vol. 1, pp. 27–55. Hong Kong: Shangwu Yinshuguan.

Tan Sitong. 1981. *Renxue* (A study of benevolence). In *Tan Sitong wenxuan zhu* (Selected works of Tan Sitong with commentaries), ed. Zhou Zhengfu, pp. 102–225. Beijing: Zhonghua Shuju.

Tanaka, Stefan. 1993. *Japan's Orient: Rendering Pasts into History*. Berkeley: University of California Press.

Tang Caichang. 1968. "Geguo zhonglei kao zixu" (Preface to a study of the racial classification of nations). In his *Juedianmin zai neiyan* (The inner treatise of the Juedianmin Studio), pp. 467–575. Taibei: Chengwen Chubanshe.

Tang Dahui. 1981. "Guanyu 'suluzhi yulu' " (About *Thus Spake Zarathustra*). In *Lu Xun yanjiu baiti* (One hundred topics in Lu Xun studies), ed. Zhu Zheng, pp. 173–180. Changsha: Hunan Renmin Chubanshe.

Tang Erhe. 1913. "Guangshuo youzhi pian" (A broader view on infantilism). *Yongyan* 1, no. 12:1–3.

Tang Junyi. 1982. *Zhongguo Wenhua zhi Jingsheng Jiazhi* (The spiritual value of Chinese culture), 4th rev. Taiwan ed. Taibei: Zhengzhong Shuju.

Tang Wenquan and Luo Fuhui. 1986. *Zhang Taiyan sixiang yanjiu* (A study of the thought of Zhang Taiyan). Wuchang: Huazhong Shifan Daxue Chubanshe.

Tang Xiaobing. 1996. *Global Space and the Nationalist Discourse of Modernity: The Historical Thinking of Liang Qichao.* Stanford, CA: Stanford University Press.

Tang Yizhong. 1981. " 'Jingpai' he 'haipai' zhi zheng" (The controversy between the "Beijing school" and the "Shanghai school"). In *Lu Xun yanjiu baiti* (One hundred topics in Lu Xun studies), ed. Zhu Zhengduo, pp. 448–455. Changsha: Hunan Renmin Chubanshe.

Tang Zhengchang. 1981. *Zhang Taiyan Wu Yu lunji* (Studies on Zhang Taiyan and Wu Yu). Chengdu: Sichuan Renmin Chubanshe.

Tang Zhijun, ed. 1977. *Zhang Taiyan zhenglun xuanji* (Selection of Zhang Taiyan's political essays), 2 vols. Beijing: Zhonghua Shuju.

———. ed. 1981. *Kang Youwei zhenglun ji,* 2 vols. Beijing: Zhonghua Shuju.

———. 1984a. "Lun nanxuehui" (On the Southern Academic Society). In *Kang Youwei yu wuxu zhengbian* (Kang Youwei and the hundred days reform), pp. 217–231. Beijing: Zhonghua Shuju.

———. 1984b. *Wuxu Bianfa Shi* (A history of the Hundred Days Reform). Beijing: Renmin Chubanshe.

———. 1984c. "Wuxu zhengbian yihou de Tang Caichang he zilijun" (The post-Hundred Days Tang Caichang and the Independent Army). In *Kang Youwei yu wuxu zhengbian,* pp. 271–284.

Tao Menghe (Tao Lügong). 1917. "Renlei wenhua zhi qiyuan (xu qian hao)" (The origin of human culture—cont'd. from the former issue). *XQN* 2, no. 6:1–7.

Tempest, Rone. 1993. "American TV: We Are The World." *TV Guide,* July 3–9 issue: 8–11.

Thompson, Laurence G. 1967. "Ta-t'ung Shu and the Communist Manifesto." In *K'ang Yu-wei: A Biography and a Symposium,* ed. Jung-pang Lo, pp. 344–354. Tucson, AZ: The University of Arizona Press.

Thompson, Richard Austin. 1978. *The Yellow Peril, 1890–1924.* New York: Arno.

Thornton, R.K.R. 1983. *The Decadent Dilemma.* London: Edward Arnold.

Thurer, Shari L. 1994. *The Myths of Motherhood: How Culture Reinvents the Good Mother.* Boston: Houghton Mifflin.

Toffler, Alvin. 1991. *Power Shift.* New York: Bantam Books.

Tokutomi Soho. 1986. *The Future Japan,* trans. and ed. Vinh Sinh, Matsuzawa Hiroaki, Nicholas Wickenden. Edmonton: University of Alberta Press.

Townsend, James. 1996. "Chinese Nationalism." In *Chinese Nationalism,* ed. Jonathan Unger, pp. 1–30. Armonk, NY: M.E. Sharpe.

Toynbee, Arnold J. 1934. *A Study of History,* vols. 1 and 2. London: Oxford University Press.

———. 1976. *Mankind and Mother Earth: A Narrative History of the World.* New York: Oxford University Press.

Tracy, Robert. 1990. "Loving You All Ways: Vamps, Vampires, Necrophiles and Necrofilles in Nineteenth-Century Fiction." In Regina Barreca, ed., *Sex and Death in Victorian Literature,* pp. 32–59. London: Macmillan.

Tu Wei-ming. 1991. "Cultural China: The Periphery as the Center." *Daedalus* 120, no. 2:1–32.

Vinh Sinh. 1989. *Tokutomi Soho (1863–1957): The Later Career.* Toronto: University of Toronto–York University Joint Centre on Modern East Asia.

Wan Jianing. 1987. "Woguo qingchao chuban de yixie xinlixue shuji" (Psychological works published in our country's Qing dynasty). *Acta Psychologica Sinica* 19, no. 1:109–112.

Wan Shengyang. 1903. "Zhongguo dangzhong guomin jiaoyu" (China should pay more attention to national education). *HBXSJ*, no. 2:9–18.

Wang, David Der-wei. 1997. *Fin-de-Siècle Splendor: Repressed Modernities of Late Qing Fiction, 1849–1911*. Stanford, CA: Stanford University Press.

Wang Fuzhi. 1992. *Huangshu* (The yellow treatise). In *Chuanshan quanshu* (The complete works of Wang Chuanshan), ed. Chuanshan quanshu bianji weiyuanhui, vol. 12, pp. 501–545. Changsha: Yuelu Shushe.

Wang Jiaping. 1995. "Huigui renshi de Lu Xun" (Returning Lu Xun to life size). *Duzhe* (Reader), no. 8:10–13.

Wang Runhua. 1994. "Shixi 'Luotuo Xiangzi' zhong de xing yi huo (A tentative analysis of *Camel Xiangzi's* sexual perplexity). In *ESYSJ*, no. 23, pp. 113–124.

Wang Shaolun. 1946. *Minzu zhexue dagang* (Outline of the philosophy of nation). 1st ed. in 1938. Shanghai: Zhengzhong Shuju.

Wang Tongling. 1913. "Lishi shang han minzu zhi texing" (The characteristics of the Han people in history). *Yongyan* (Justice) 1, no. 23:1–12; no. 24:1–12.

Wang, Y.C. 1966. *Chinese Intellectuals and the West, 1872–1949*. Chapel Hill: University of North Carolina Press.

Wang Zhaoshi. 1929. "Zhongguo shehui yuanlai ruci" (The true nature of Chinese society). *Xin Yue* (Crescent moon) 3, nos. 5–6:1–36.

Weakland, John H. 1950. "The Organization of Action in Chinese Culture." *Psychiatry*, no. 13:361–370.

———. 1951a. "Intrusion and Disruption of Organization." *MMP-RCC*, G-62, CPC-12.

———. 1951b. "On Depletion." *MMP-RCC*, G-62, CPC-11.

———. 1956. "Orality in Chinese Conceptions of Male Genital Sexuality." *Psychiatry*, no. 19:237–247.

Weininger, Otto. 1975. *Sex & Character*. Authorized translation from the sixth German edition. Reprint of the 1906 edition published by W. Heinemann. New York: AMS.

White, Hayden. 1973. *Metahistory*. Baltimore and London: Johns Hopkins University Press.

Wilbur, C. Martin. 1976. *Sun Yat-sen: Frustrated Patriot*. New York: Columbia University Press.

Wilhelm, Richard. 1928. *The Soul of China*, trans. John Holroyd Reece. New York: Harcourt, Brace.

Williams, Tennessee. 1976. *Suddenly Last Summer*. In *Tennessee Williams: Four Plays*. New York and Scarborough, Ontario: New American Library.

Wolfenstein, Martha, and Nathan Leites. 1950. *Movies: A Psychological Study*. Glencoe, IL: Free Press.

Wolff, Ernst. 1971. *Chou Tso-jen*. New York: Twayne.

Wong Young-tsu. 1989. *Search for Modern Nationalism: Zhang Binglin and Revolutionary China, 1869–1936*. Hong Kong: Oxford University Press.

———. 1992. "Revisionism Reconsidered: Kang Youwei and the Reform Movement of 1898." *Journal of Asian Studies* 51, no. 3: 513–544.

Wu Gou. (1914). "Jinhua yu tuihua" (Evolution and degeneration). *Yongyan* (Justice) 2, no. 5:1–5.

Wu Guanyin. 1913. "Shehui chongbai zhi renwu" (The personages whom society worship). *Yongyan* (Justice) 1, no. 18:1–7.

———. 1915. "Shuo guoxing" (On national character). *Da Zhonghua* (Great China) 1, no. 3:1–12.

Wundt, Wilhelm. 1916. *Elements of Folk Psychology: Outlines of a Psychological History of the Development of Mankind*, trans. Edward Leroy Schaub. New York: Macmillan.

Wusheng, trans. 1943. "Dongfang yu xifang" (East and west) by Richard Wilhelm. *Xueshujie* (Academic circles) 1, no. 3: 13–26.

Wylie, Philip. 1942. *Generation of Vipers*. New York: Rinehart.

Xia Dongyuan. 1979. "Zheng Guanying sixiang fazhan lun" (On the development of Zheng Guanying's thought). *Shehui kexue zhanxian* (The social science front), no. 2 of 1979:166–177.

Xia Liangcai. 1991. "Sun Zhongshan de guojia guan yu ouzhou 'zhuquan guojia' xuepai" (Sun Zhongshan's view of the state and the European 'state right' school). *JDSYJ*, no. 71:79–95.

XMCB. Abbreviation of *Xinmin congbao* (New people's magazine).

XQN. Abbreviation of *Xin qingnian* (New youth).

Xu Ben. 1998. " 'From Modernity to Chineseness': The Rise of Nativist Cultural Theory in Post–1989 China." *Positions* 6, no. 1, pp. 203–237.

Xu Guangping. 1961. *Lu Xun huiyi lu* (Reminiscences of Lu Xun). Beijing: Zuojia Chubanshe.

Xu Youchun, ed. 1991. "Zhou Jianren." In *Minguo renwu da cidian* (The great biographical dictionary of the republic). Shijiazhuang: Hebei Renmin Chubanshe.

Xu Youpeng, ed. 1914. *Yuan Dazhongtong shudu huibian* (Collected documents of President Yuan). Reprinted in 1928. Shanghai: Guangyi Shuju.

Xu Zhiying, ed. 1984. *Zhou Zuoren zaogi sanwen xuan* (A selection of Zhon Zuoren's early essays). Shanghai: Shanghai Wenyi Chubanshe.

Xuanjie (Zhu Zhixin). 1908. "Xinli de guojiazhuyi" (Psychological statism). *Min Bao* (People's journal), no. 21:1–24.

Xuanzhong (Shao Yuanchong). 1914. "Guominxing lun" (On the national character). *Minguo* (Republic) 1, no. 1, revised edition:1–7.

Xuanzhu (Mao Dun). 1929. *Zhongguo shenhua yanjiu ABC* (The ABC of the study of Chinese mythology). Shanghai: Shijie Shuju.

Xusheng. 1925. "Jinhua ne? tuihua ne?" (Evolution? or degeneration?). *Yusi* (Word threads), no. 10:5–6.

Yan Fu. 1895a. "Lun shibian zhi ji" (How rapidly the times change). *YFJ* vol. 1, pp. 1–5.

———. 1895b. "Yuan qiang" (The principle of strength). *YFJ* vol. 1, pp. 5–32.

———. 1898a. "Youru san bao" (As if there are three preservations). *YFJ* vol. 1, pp. 79–83.

———. 1898b. "Baojiao yuyi" (Further clarification on the preservation of teaching). *YFJ* vol. 1, pp. 83–85.

———. 1898c. "Baozhong yuyi" (Further clarification on racial preservation). *YFJ* vol. 1, pp. 85–87.

———. 1906. "Zhengzhi jiangyi" (Lectures on politics). *YFJ* vol. 5, pp. 1241–1316.

Yan Zhizhong. 1920. "Su yao duo, zhi yao hao" (Greater quantity, better quality). *XQN* 7, no. 4:1–5.

Yang Changji, trans. 1918. "Jiehun lun" (On marriage) by Edward Westermarck. *XQN* 5, no. 3, pp. 189–205.

Yang Dongping. 1994. *Chengshi jifeng: Beijing he Shanghai de wenhua jingshen* (Urban monsoon: the cultural spirits of Beijing and Shanghai). Beijing: Dongfang Chubanshe.

Yang Du. 1902. " 'Youxue yibian' xu" (Preface to *Translation Series of Overseas Students*). *YXYB*, no. 1:1–19.

Yang Hsien-yi and Gladys Yang, trans. 1972. *Selected Stories of Lu Hsun*. Peking: Foreign Languages Press.

Yang Tianshi. 1998. "Kang Youwei de lianman daoyuan jihua" (Kang Youwei's plan to ally with the Manchus in order to undermine Yuan Shikai). *Xinhua wenzhai* (New China digest), no. 2 of 1998:80–83.

Yans-McLaughlin, Virginia. 1986. "Science, Democracy, and Ethics: Mobilizing Culture and Personality for World War II." In *Malinowski, Rivers, Benedict and Others: Essays on Culture and Personality*, ed. George W. Stocking Jr., pp. 184–217. Madison: University of Wisconsin Press.

YFJ. 1986. Abbreviation of *Yan Fu ji* (Yan Fu's works), ed. Wang Shi. Beijing: Zhonghua Shuju, 1986.

Yi Baisha. 1916. "Kongzi pingyi shang" (A fair view of Confucius, part one). *XQN* 1, no. 6:1–6.

Yinbing (Liang Qichao). 1906a. "Da moubao disi hao duiyu benbao zhi bolun" (A retort to a refutation of our journal by a certain journal's fourth issue). *XMCB*, no. 79:1–95.

———. trans. 1906b. "Guojia yuan lun" (On the origin of the state) by J.K. Bluntschli. *XMCB*, no. 74:1–17.

You Xiong. 1921. "Renlei tuihua shuo" (The theory of degeneration of the human species). *FNZZ* 7, no. 8:77.

Young, Ernest P. 1983. "Politics in the aftermath of revolution: the era of Yuan Shih-k'ai, 1912–16." In *Cambridge History of China*, vol. 12, part I, ed. John K. Fairbank and Denis Twitchett, pp. 208–255. New York: Cambridge University Press.

Yu Zhen. 1913. "Guominxing yu jiaoyu" (National character and education). *Jiaoyu zazhi* (Journal of education) 5, no. 3 (June 10):38–46.

Yuan Shikai. 1913a. "Guohui kaihui songci" (A tribute to the inauguration of parliament). In *Collected Documents of President Yuan*, ed. Xu Youpeng 1914, pp. 12–13.

———. 1913b. "Dazhongtong liren xuanyanshu" (President Yuan's inauguration speech). In *Collected Documents of President Yuan*, ed. Xu Yonpeng 1914, pp. 5–9.

———. 1914a. "President's Order" dated November 3, 1914. *Zhengfu gongbao* (Government gazette), no. 898 (November 4, 1914), the "mingling" (order) section.

———. 1914b. "President's Order" dated November 20. *Zhengfu gongbao* (Government gazette), no. 915 (November 21), the "mingling" section.

———. 1914c. "President's Order" dated November 23. *Zhengfu gongbao* (Government gazette), no. 918 (November 24), the "mingling" section.

———. 1915. "President's Order" dated October 8. *Zhengfu gongbao*, no. 1229 (October 9), the "mingling" section.

Yuan Shunda. 1921. "Renlei shehui fan taotai zhi xianxiang ji qi jiujifa" (The phenomenon of negative selection in human society and its remedies). *DFZZ* 18, no. 24:34–43.

Yuyi. 1903. "Minzuzhuyi lun—xu diyi qi" (On nationalism—cont'd from issue number one). *Zhejiang chao* (The Zhejiang tide), no. 2:1–23.

YXYB. Abbreviation of *Youxue yibian* (Translation series of overseas students).

Zhang Dongsun. 1913. "Zhongguo zhi shehui wenti" (China's social problems). *Yongyan* (Justice), 1, no. 16:1–13.

Zhang Jinglu. 1954. *Zhongguo jindai chuban shiliao, erbian* (Historical materials of the modern Chinese publishing, the 2nd series). Shanghai: Qunlian Chubanshe.

Zhang Jingsheng. 1927. "Xingmei" (Sexual aesthetics). *Xin wenhua* (New culture) 1, no. 6:1–12.

Zhang Jingyuan. 1992. *Psychoanalysis in China: Literary Transformations 1919–1949*. Ithaca, NY: East Asian Program, Cornell University.

Zhang Jixu. 1903. "Jiaoyu guanxi guojia zhi chengli" (Education is related to nation-building). *HBXSJ* no. 1:1–7.

Zhang Junjun. 1935. *Zhongguo minzu zhi gaizao* (Reforming the Chinese race). Shang-hai: Zhonghua Shuju.

———. 1936. *Zhongguo minzu zhi gaizao (xubian)* (Reforming the Chinese race, a sequel). Shanghai: Zhonghua Shuju.

———. 1944. *Huazu suzhi zhi jiantao* (An examination of the racial qualities of the Chinese). Chongqing, Sichuan: Shangwu Yinshuguan.

Zhang Kaiyuan. 1990. "Lun guohun" (On the national soul). In his *Xinhai qianhou shishi luncong* (Studies of historical events before and after the 1911 revolution), pp. 132–139. Wuchang: Huazhong Shifan daxue Chubanshe.

Zhang Longxi. 1998. "Shenmo shi 'huairou yuanren'? zhengming, kaozheng yu hou-xiandaishi shixue" (What is "cherishing men from afar"? The rectification of names, textual evidence, and postmodern historiography). *ESYSJ*, no. 45:56–63.

Zhang Renquan. 1924. "Xishan de mao" (The cat of the West Hills). *FNZZ* 10, no. 10:1601–1607.

Zhang Taiyan. 1897a. "Du riben guo zhi" (Having read *A Brief History of Japan*). In Tang 1977, vol 1, pp. 47–49

———. 1897b. "Lun yazhou yi ziwei chunchi" (Asian countries should be interde-pendent). In Tang 1977, vol. 1, pp. 5–7.

———. 1897c. "Xingzhehui xu" (Manifesto of the Reviving Zhejiang Society). In Jiang and Zhu 1981, pp. 10–18.

———. 1899. "Kedi lun" (The guest emperor thesis). In Tang 1977, pp. 84–90.

———. 1900. "Kedi kuangmiu" (Correcting the erroneous guest emperor thesis). In Jiang and Zhu 1981, pp. 118–120.

———. 1902a. " 'Shehuixue' xu" (Preface to *Sociology*). In Jiang and Zhu 1981, pp. 145–148.

———. 1902b. "Zhongxia wangguo erbai sishier nian jinian hui shu" (Manifesto of the meeting to commemorate the 242nd anniversary of China's loss of nationhood). In *Zhang Taiyan quanji*, vol. 4, pp. 188–189. Shanghai: Renmin Chubanshe, 1985.

———. 1906. "Dongjing liuxuesheng huanyinghui yanshuoci" (Speech at the recep-tion party of Chinese students in Tokyo). In Tang 1977, vol. 1, pp. 269–280. Bei-jing: Zhonghua Shuju.

Zhang Xudong. 1998. "Nationalism, Mass Culture, and Intellectual Strategies in Post-Tiananmen China." *Social Text*, no. 55:109–140.

Zhang Yaoxiang. 1925. "Qingdai jingshi zhi dili de fenbu" (The geographical distri-bution of candidates attaining the highest imperial degree in the Qing period). *Xinli* (Psychology) 4, no. 1:330–346.

Zhang Zhidong. 1898. *Quanxue pian* (Exhortation to learning). Reprinted by Taiwan's Wenhai Chubanshe, no date.

Zheng Guanying. 1894. *Shengshi weiyan* (Alarming words in a reign of peace). In *Zheng Guanying ji* (Collected works of Zheng Guanying), ed. Xia Dongyuan, 2 vols. Shanghai Renmin Chubanshe, 1988.

Zheng Shiqu. 1992. "Wanqing guocuipai yu shehuixue" (Late Qing's National Essence school and sociology). *JDSYJ*, no. 71:43–61, 196.

———. 1994. "Cultural Outlook of the Late Qing *Guoci* School." *Social Sciences in China* 15, no. 3 (fall), trans. Huang Weiwei, pp. 180–190. Beijing: Social Science Publishing House of China.

Zheng Yi. 1996. *Scarlet Memorial: Tales of Cannibalism in Modern China*, trans. and ed. T.P. Sym. Boulder, CO: Westview Press.

Zheng Yunshan. 1992. "Xinhai qianhou de guominxing wenti tantao" (Discussions on the national characher issues around the time of the 1911 revolution). *JDSYJ*, no. 67:23–36.

Zheng Zhengduo. 1926. "Xiang guangming zouqu" (March toward the light). In *Zheng Zhengduo xuanji* (Selected works of Zheng Zhengduo), pp. 742–743. Fuzhou: Fujian Renmin Chubanshe, 1984.

Zhongguo shixue hui. 1957. *Wuxu bianfa*, 4 vols. Shanghai: Renmin Chubanshe.

Zhongguo zhi xinmin (Liang Qichao). 1903. "Zhengzhixue dajia bolunzhili zhi xueshuo" (The theory of the great political scientist, Bluntschli). *XMCB*, nos. 38–39:1–35.

Zhongmi (Zhou Zuoren). 1921. "Suiganlu yilingwu: yeman minzu de lifa" (Random thoughts 105: The rituals of barbaric tribes). *XQN* 8, no. 5:1–2.

———. 1923. "Ziji de yuandi, jiu: 'Chenlun' " (My own garden, 9: 'Sinking'). *Chenbao Fujian* (Supplement to the Beijing morning paper) (March 26):1.

Zhou Jianren. 1920a. "Shengcun jingzhen yu huzhu" (Struggle for survival and mutual aid). *XQN* 8, no. 2:1–7.

———. 1920b. "Shanzhongxue yu qi jianlizhe" (Eugenics and its founders). *JHLSZX*, pp. 49–62.

———. 1921a. "Daerwen yihou de jinghua sixiang" (Evolutionist thinking after Darwin). *JHLSZX*, pp. 33–48.

———. Trans. 1921b. "Jiequnxing yu nulixing" (Gregarious and slavish instincts) by Francis Galton. *XQN* 9, no. 5:1–8.

———. 1921c. "Manduier yu qi yichuan lü" (Mendel's law of heredity). *DFZZ* 18, no. 13:36–46.

———. 1921d. "Shanzhongxue de lilun yu shishi" (Theory and practice of eugenics). In *JHLSZX*, pp. 63–78.

———. 1922a. "Chan'er zhixian gaishuo" (A brief introduction to birth control). *DFZZ* 19, no. 7:7–19.

———. 1922b. "Duifolisi de zhoubian shuo" (De Vries' theory of mutation). *DFZZ* 19, no. 2:101–103.

———. 1922c. "Geti yu zhongzu de shuailao" (Individual and racial senility). *DFZZ* 19, no. 10:43–48.

———. 1923. "Yichuan yu huanjing" (Heredity and environment). *DFZZ* 20 no. 4: 81–84.

———. 1924. "Xin manduierzhuyi he xidexing yichuan shuo de fuxing" (New Mendelism and the revival of the theory of the transmittability of acquired traits). *DFZZ* 21, no. 5:97–102.

———. 1925a. "Da 'yifuduoqi de xin hufu' " (A reply to "a new excuse for polygamy"). *Mangyuan* (Wasteland), no. 4:5–13.

———. 1925b. "Zai da Chen Bonian xiansheng lun yifuduaoqi" (Another reply to Mr. Chen Bonian on polygamy). *Mangyuan* (Wasteland) no. 7:3–14.

———. 1979. "Guanyu Lu Xun de ruogan shishi" (Certain historical facts concerning Lu Xun). In *Wo xinzhong de Lu Xun* (The Lu Xun in my heart), ed. Zhou Jianren et al., pp. 7–14. Changsha: Hunan Renmin Chubanshe.

Zhou Zuoren. 1923a. "Chonglai" (Gengagere). In *Zhou Zuoren sanwen* (Zhou Zuoren's essays), ed. Zhang Minggao and Fan Qiao, vol. 1, pp. 189–190. Beijing: Zhongguo Guangbo Dianshi Chubanshe.

———. 1923b. "Ziji de yuandi, ba: Wenyi shang de yiwu" (My own garden, 8: The monsters in literature). In *ZJDYD-YTDS*, pp. 25–29.

———. 1923c. "Ziji de yuandi, shisan: Qingsi" (My own garden, 13: Love poems). In *ZJDYD-YTDS*, pp. 47–50.

———. 1923d. "Ziji de yuandi, si: wenyi yu daode" (My own garden, 4: Literature and morality). In *ZJDYD-YTDS*, pp. 78–80.

———. 1925a. "Chi lieshi" (The eating of martyrs). *Yusi* (Word threads), no. 38:3.

———. 1925b. "Jingguan" (A view on purity). *Yusi* (Word threads), no. 15:6–7

———. 1925c. "Heibeixin" (Sambenito). *Yusi* (Word threads), 31:11–13.

———. 1925d. "Yu youren lun guomin wenxue shu" (A letter to a friend discussing national literature). In *ZJDYD-YTDS*, pp. 308–310.

———. 1926. "Shanghai qi" (The Shanghai ethos). In *Zhou Zuoren zaoqi sanwen xuan* (A selection of Zhou Zuoren's early essays), ed. Xu Zhiying, pp. 159–160. Shanghai: Shanghai Wenyi Chubanshe, 1984.

———. 1970. *Zhitang huixianglu* (Zhitang's memoirs). Hong Kong: Sanyu Tushu Wenju Gongsi.

Zhu Junyi. 1925. "Xiandai zhongguo renwu zhi dili jiaoyu yu zhiye de fenbu" (The geographical, educational, and professional distributions of modern Chinese personages). *Xinli* (Psychology) 4, no. 1:319–330.

Zhu Qianzhi. 1980. "Shijieguan de zhuanbian—qishi zishu (er)" (The change of world-view—autobiography at seventy, part II). *Zhongguo zhexue* (Chinese philosophy), no. 4:473–497. Beijing: Zhongguo Zhexue Bianjibu.

Zhuang You. 1903. "Guomin xin linghun" (The new national souls). *Jiangsu*, no. 5: 1–9.

Zhuang Zexuan and Chen Xuexun. 1949. *Minzuxing yu Jiaoyu* (National character and education). n.p.: Shangwu Yinshuguan.

Zimmerman, Michael E. 1996. "Heidegger, Buddhism, and Deep Ecology." In *The Cambridge Companion to Heidegger*, ed. Charles Guignon, pp. 240–269.

ZJDYD-YTDS. 1988. Abbreviation of *Ziji de Yuandi—Yutian de Shu* (My own garden—writings on a rainy day). Beijing: Renmin Wenxue Chubanshe.

Zou Rong. 1958. *Geming jun* (Revolutionary army). Shanghai: Zhonghua Shuju.

Zuoren. 1924. "Nüku xinli zhi yanjiu" (The study of the psychology of woman's pants). *Yusi* (Word thread), no. 5:7–8.

Index

Lung-kee Sun was born in China but grew up in Hong Kong. He spent his college years in Taiwan and went on to advanced studies in the United States, first getting a masters degree in Russian history from the University of Minnesota and then his Ph.D. in East Asian history from Stanford University. Dr. Sun has taught at the University of Kansas, Washington University (St. Louis), the University of Alberta, and the University of Memphis. Among his numerous publications, the most influential one was *The "Deep Structure" of Chinese Culture,* excerpts of which have been translated into English; a complete German translation, *Des Ummauerte Ich: Die Tiefenstruktur der chinesischen Mentalitat,* was published in 1994.